THE UNIVERSITY

AN ILLUSTRATED HISTORY

This edition first published in hardcover in the US and UK in 2011 by
Overlook Duckworth
NEW YORK:
Overlook
141 Wooster Street
New York, NY 10012
www.overlookpress.com
For bulk and special sales, please contact sales@overlookny.com
LONDON:
Duckworth
90–93 Cowcross Street
London EC1M 6BF
info@duckworth-publishers.co.uk
www.ducknet.co.uk
Copyright © 2011 by Banco Santander / Turner

Cataloging-in-Publication Data is available from the Library of Congress
A catalogue record for this book is available from the British Library

Manufactured in Spain
ISBN 978-1-59020-644-7 (US)
ISBN 978-0-71564-083-8 (UK)
ISBN 978-84-7506-952-4 (TURNER)
2 4 6 8 10 9 7 5 3 1

THE UNIVERSITY

AN ILLUSTRATED HISTORY

EDITED BY FERNANDO TEJERINA

TURNER in association with OVERLOOK DUCKWORTH
New York and London

Edited by

Fernando Tejerina (University of Valladolid)

Coordinators

Josep M. Bricall (University of Barcelona)

Pablo Campos Calvo-Sotelo (University of Architecture San Pablo ceu)

César Chaparro (University of Extremadura)

Juan Ramón de la Fuente (International Association of Universities)

Mariano Peset (University of Valencia)

Manuel J. Tello (University of the Basque Country)

Contributors

Gian Paolo Brizzi (University of Bologna)

B.B. Bhattacharya (Jawaharlal Nehru University)

Manuel Burga (Major National University of San Marcos)

Lourdes Chehaibar Náder (National Autonomous University of Mexico)

Pablo Escalante Gonzalbo (National Autonomous University of Mexico)

Iván Escamilla (National Autonomous University of Mexico)

Enrique García Santo-Tomás (University of Michigan)

Elena Hernández Sandoica (Complutense University of Madrid)

Alma Herrera (National Autonomous University of Mexico)

Andreas Janousch (Autonomous University of Madrid)

Josef Jǎrab (University of Palacky)

Elisabeth Leedham-Green (University of Cambridge)

Gonzalo León (Polytechnic University of Madrid)

José Narro Robles (National Autonomous University of Mexico)

Antonio Malpica (University of Granada)

Alicia José Mayer (National Autonomous University of Mexico)

Adolpho José Melfi (University of São Paulo)

Goolam Mohamedbhai (Association of African Universities)

Shozo Motoyama (University of São Paulo)

Timothy O'Shea (University of Edinburgh)

José Luis Peset (Spanish National Research Council)

Luis E. Rodríguez-San Pedro Bezares (University of Salamanca)

Julio Samsò (University of Barcelona)

Francesc Santacana i Martorell (Knowledge and Development Foundation)

Steve Smith (University of Exeter)

Gustaf A. Söderlind (University of Lund)

Ignacio Sotelo (Free University of Berlin)

John R. Thelin (University of Kentucky)

Margarita Torremocha Hernández (University of Valladolid)

Luis Ugalde (Andrés Bello Catholic University)

Suely Vilela (University of São Paulo)

Nadia Villafuerte (National Autonomous University of Mexico)

Hans de Wit (University of Amsterdam)

Jie Yin (Shanghai Jiao Tong University)

Contents

V

THE UNIVERSITY IN THE AMERICAS

VI

THE MASS UNIVERSITY

VII

TOWARDS A KNOWLEDGE-INTENSIVE SOCIETY

VIII

THE UNIVERSITY AND ARCHITECTURE

Library of Alexandria Egypt (*c.* 2005)
In the third century BC the Ptolemaic dynasty founded the greatest library of the classical age. Within its walls were kept thousands of volumes on all branches of human knowledge. Sadly, the building and its contents were burnt down – who or what started the fire remains uncertain to this day. In the late twentieth century, UNESCO and the governments of Egypt and other countries revived this vast intellectual enterprise and built the New Library of Alexandria, which opened on 16 October 2002. The façade is blazoned with words in several languages professing the library's claim to universality.

I

SCIENCE IN ANTIQUITY

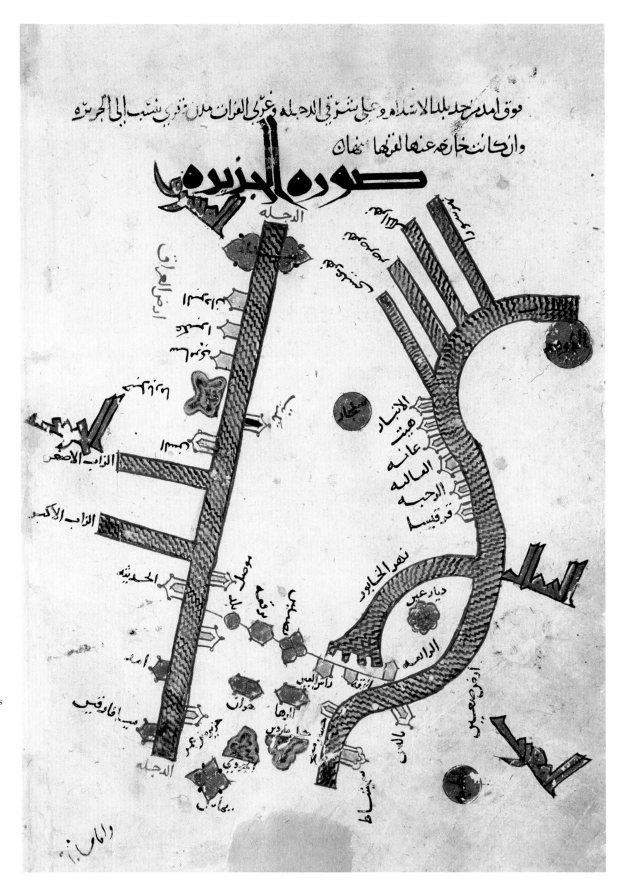

Al Istalhry, *Geographical Atlas* (10th to 11th centuries), depicting the Tigris and Euphrates rivers
This *Geographical Atlas* depicts Mesopotamia: the name is Greek for 'amid rivers'. This region – broadly coextensive with modern Iraq – saw the birth of the earliest urban cultures, to which later civilisations trace their roots. The Mesopotamians laid the foundations of future learning: they invented a type of writing, wrote the first codes of law, practised a germinal form of science and were skilled artists and architects.

Science in the Ancient World and its Transmission to the West

César Chaparro

Anyone hoping to learn about ancient science comes up against a number of intrinsic difficulties. The evidence that remains (written or otherwise) is scattered and fragmentary. Terms like 'science' or 'technique' were used then in a quite different sense from how they are used now. But, leaving all that aside, there is one fact that needs to be grasped at the outset: science as we know it today is a relatively recent feature of civilisation. Techniques, skills and instruments have nonetheless existed since the remote past. Known only to narrow classes of sages or skilled artisans, these things were in some sense scientific, though that scientific nature was subordinate to the constraints of the markedly religious and mythical philosophical tradition, or of artisanal lore. In fact, one could say that science has its historic roots in these two main sources. Master artisans honed their practical wisdom and passed it on from one generation to the next. Elsewhere, philosophers, sages and divines engaged in debate and lent increasingly complex form to human thought and aspiration. Much later on, once science had become a largely independent endeavour, its hybrid origins in both practical technique and philosophical theory meant that its implications were both technical and philosophical. Science thus came to have consequences for its own sources, and its effects were felt even in domains far removed from its beginnings.

This ongoing interaction between the ancient and the new, between historic significance and modern implications, lies at the core of what it means to be 'classical': we ascribe that term only to knowledge that has its roots in the past and that even then formed a self-consistent whole. To learn of the birth, development and transmission of the philosophical, scientific and technical knowledge of the ancient world is a difficult but enormously valuable proposition for the modern mind.

Rosetta Stone, The British Museum
Discovered by one of Napoleon's officers during the Egyptian campaign of 1799, the hieroglyphs of the Rosetta Stone were deciphered by Jean-François Champollion. He compared the figures to the demotic and Greek scripts also inscribed on the Rosetta, and so uncovered the secrets of the signs of ancient Egypt.

Science in Mesopotamia and Egypt

About a century before 3000 BC, the geographical areas surrounding the valleys of the Nile, the Tigris and the Euphrates witnessed the rise of the first urban civilisations. These early urban cultures developed a huge variety of techniques, instruments and scientific knowledge.

Mesopotamian science, created by the Sumerians and inherited and built upon by later Semitic peoples, was particularly deep. The priestly scribes primarily responsible for cultivating it displayed a strikingly scientific attitude. The earliest references to mathematical concepts appeared in the third millennium BC. Arithmetic was dominant, and some interest was shown in geometric measurement and calculation. The purpose was always practical: measuring supplies, or dividing a given number of things among a number of people. No mention was made of mathematical axioms or proofs. The number system was sexagesimal.

The Mesopotamian cultures later developed more sophisticated mathematics, exemplified in the thousands of cuneiform tablets that have come down to us. Some were number tables used to calculate the area of a field, say, or estimate the volume of an object. Others, posing geometrical problems and explanations, attest to knowledge of how to calculate surfaces and volumes.

To work out their horoscopes and prognostications (again, a practical purpose), the Mesopotamians acquired some knowledge of astronomy. Their techniques – involving number series and arithmetic and geometric progressions – were primitive tools by which to gain an understanding of empirical observations. Mesopotamian astronomers wrote up lists of stars, and partitioned the sky into three zones or 'ways' and into thirty-degree bands – these were the basis for dividing the year into four seasons, each comprising three months. All this demonstrated systematic study of the firmament: the Mesopotamians thought that the positions of the stars governed their own fate. Their astronomy was largely driven by the problems surrounding their calendar, one of the constituents of which was the lunar phase or synodic month.

Assyria and Babylon were theocracies, and their science of medicine was accordingly influenced by demonology and belief in magic. The art of diagnosis was taken to an advanced state of progress, however; the many compilations of Mesopotamian medical texts provided clinical descriptions of real value. The scrutiny of symptoms, prognosis and curative remedies – based on mineral, vegetable and animal ingredients – were all highly idiosyncratic. A Babylonian doctor was not a biologist; his interests lay not in constructing a theory of life, but in hitting on an effective cure through meticulous observation.

The Egyptians, too, were deservedly renowned for their scientific knowledge. The ruling classes – the priests in particular – were keen mathematicians. They used a peculiar numbering system, and geometrical knowledge gleaned from agricultural surveying, to perform the calculations needed to build their monumental works. Very old papyri have come down to us that show the Egyptians had a form of algebra by which to derive geometric formulae for surfaces and volumes. They studied and named the visible stars and the planets. Their physics was advanced enough for them successfully to develop a hydraulic system to channel and regulate the waters of the Nile. Later in their development, Egyptian chemists used secret formulas to make enamels, pigments and embalming substances.

Whereas Mesopotamia stood out in astronomy, Egypt developed sophisticated medicine. In the Egyptian tradition, medicine was bound up with magic. A complete cure was thought to require that the supernatural beings causing the disease be cast out with a spell. Medical knowledge was passed down the generations in medical families. A medic's training was rounded off in a special temple-based school called a 'house of life'. Egyptian medicine also contained empirical and rational elements derived from experiment and observation. Medical thinking revolved primarily around a single organ, the heart. There were two distinct forms of pharmacopoeia – the medical itself, and the magical. Medical drugs were used to palliate symptoms, while magic potions were intended

to induce such a powerful revulsion that the evil spir-it would be driven out of the body.

The priestly scribes of Mesopotamia and Egypt, then, knew and recorded those scientific disciplines that they had developed in the course of going about their duties. Mathematics served the purposes of accounting and of agricultural surveying; astronomy was needed to draw up calendars and astrological predictions; medicine was designed to cure disease and cast out evil spirits.

Bas relief depicting Egyptian scribes (*c.* 2494–2345 BC)
In ancient Egypt, a scribe enjoyed high prestige for his role as an amanuensis in what was largely an illiterate society. Required to become conversant with a wide range of subjects, the scribe was a cultivated man with a deep understanding of the ideas he was called on to transcribe, on topics such as astronomy and the deeds of the gods.

Raphael, *The School of*
Athens **(1510), Vatican Palace**
This fresco in the Vatican
recreates an imaginary scene
that brings together all the
leading sages of antiquity
– philosophers, astronomers
and mathematicians. The
gathering is presided over by
Plato and Aristotle, who
frame the vanishing point of
the composition. Likenesses
of Epicurus, Heraclitus,
Socrates, Pythagoras, Hypatia,
Euclid, Ptolemy and other
figures represent classical
learning as viewed in the reign
of Pope Julius II.

The Greeks saw a deep unity underlying all knowledge.
The notion of the 'sciences', in the plural, came later.
For the Greeks, there was only one science, one form
of knowledge. That form of knowledge was philosophy

The Birth of Science in Greece: Pythagoras

Greek science first emerged among the Ionians of Asia Minor. Their mathematics, geometry and astronomy drew on the knowledge of the Hittites, Phoenicians and Lydians, and ultimately on Egyptian and Babylonian sources. But the Greeks were different in one vital respect: they reflected on the nature of science and the things to be had from it; they ordered what they had learned into general and systematic theories; they constructed organised, rational schemes, and went beyond the purely practical aims of their forerunners.

In Greece, science slowly found a path through the fog of myth. Scorn for empirical knowledge gave way to the notion of science as knowledge founded on rational underpinnings (*episteme*), as opposed to mere opinion (*doxa*), and such knowledge was confined to the perceptible world. Artisanal knowledge, for its part, formed the basis of *techne*. In the Greek world, a thing was worth being thought about in scientific terms only if it was both 'universal' and 'necessary'. The status of science was never conferred on empirical or descriptive knowledge, which was treated as relating merely to individual facts.

Before Socrates (*c.* 470–399 BC), universality and necessity were conceived of in a physical way. Greek thinkers were looking for a physical principle (*arche*) common to all things. After Socrates, universality and necessity started to be thought of as formal properties of concepts, not as properties of the things that those concepts signified.

The Greeks saw a deep unity underlying all knowledge. The notion of the 'sciences', in the plural, came later. For the Greeks, there was only one science, one form of knowledge. That form of knowledge was philosophy. The speculative turn of Greek thought militated against drawing distinctions between sciences, and it was only very slowly that some branches of knowledge, while remaining within 'philosophy', began to acquire a distinct form. The exception, perhaps, were the three mathematical sciences – arithmetic, astronomy and geometry – which, being speculative, came to be regarded as a sort of required preparation for philosophy itself, as suggested by the inscription reputedly placed over the door of Plato's Academy: 'Let no one unversed in geometry enter here.' It is pointless to try to discern a boundary between positive science and philosophical speculation in ancient Greece. The Greeks themselves never thought of them as separate, and that is why a list of Greek philosophers and a list of Greek scientists turn up the same names.

The dominant feature of Greek positive science was the primacy of speculation over observation and experiment. One might describe another of its important features as 'rationalistic apriorism'. To an ancient Greek, it was not his reason that needed to be fitted round a closely observed world; rather, he saw the world as organised in conformity with the laws of reason. Hence the third distinctive characteristic of Greek science: it was primarily deductive, not inductive; it sought to deduce the laws of nature from a set of rational principles. Greek science was not concerned with finding those laws by painstaking scrutiny of the facts. It was modelled on the philosophical paradigm – in fact, on the most speculative and abstract branch of philosophy, metaphysics.

Greek science can be usefully divided into three distinct periods, each with its own specificities of time and place. The first period ran from the earliest glimmerings to the fifth century BC. In geographical terms one might call this the 'colonial' period, because science did not first emerge in the city-states on the Greek mainland, but in the belt of colonies scattered over the neighbouring seas. The second period encompasses most of the fifth and fourth centuries BC, and can be characterised geographically as 'Athenian', because it was coextensive with the political and cultural pre-eminence of Athens. The third period – geographically, 'Alexandrian' – can be viewed as running through the third and second centuries BC. The Greeks, whether consciously or not, now gave up their abstract approach to scientific questions and allowed higher credence to observation and experiment. Even at this later stage, however, science continued to be largely speculative. After all – and this point is vital to the development of Western thought –

Greek science only existed at all because it had emerged and taken shape in the realm of a philosophical mindset, and in the causational rationalism which that mindset brought forth.

The first period – also known as Pre-Socratic – saw the rise of 'natural philosophers', who hoped to derive the material principles underlying the diversity of beings in the world from a rational understanding of causes. They were not interested in gaining mastery over nature; they were guided by intellectual curiosity alone. They realized that natural phenomena are due not to supernatural causes but to relations that are amenable to human understanding, and it was against the background of this insight that there arose the earliest theories about the essence or foundation of nature. Theories were constructed to account for the origin of the universe: water (according to Thales of Miletus, *c.* 625–546 BC) intelligent fluid, or *nous* (Anaxagoras, 500–428 BC) or air (Anaximenes, 585–524 BC). The doctrine of the four elements, namely earth, water, fire and air, was also developed (by Empedocles, *c.* 495–435 BC) and the propositions of atomism and of the mathematical structure of nature were advanced by Pythagoras (*c.* 582–507 BC). Debate arose as to whether Being was immutable or permanent (Parmenides, *c.* 530–470 BC) or, according to Heraclitus (*c.* 535–484 BC), subject to change and transformation ('Being and Becoming'). A dispute flared up about whether knowledge is to be obtained from reason or from the senses.

The best-known exponent of science in this early period is Pythagoras. He founded a brotherhood of disciples who, living under an ascetic code in worship of Apollo, were initiated into cultic knowledge and enjoined to keep it secret. For the Pythagoreans, the unifying rational principle of knowledge was quantitative relation. The study of quantitative relations led to the science of number and geometry, the constituents of mathematics. The philosophy of the Pythagoreans – indistinguishable from Pythagoras' own contribution, as he seems not to have written anything down – was accordingly a 'mathematicism': they saw everything as a reflection of that unifying rational nature of quantitative relations. The essence of all things was number, and all things obeyed a numerical regularity. One of the bulwarks of this creed was the discovery

that sound and music – which the Pythagoreans saw as a mode of purification and catharsis – are intelligible as numerical magnitudes. They must also have drawn inferences from the realisation that number plays a role in other phenomena of nature: the year, the seasons, the months, days, and so on.

However, the Pythagoreans did not, in the end, regard number as the ultimate origin. Number itself derived from antecedent elements – one was an indeterminate or unlimited principle, the other a determinant or limiting principle. Number sprang, then, 'from the fitting together of limiting and unlimited elements'. This led to a subsequent fundamental precept: if number is order – the 'concord of unlimited and limiting elements' – and all things are determined by number, then all things *are* order. In Greek, the word for 'order' is *kosmos*; so the Pythagoreans gave the name *kosmos*, that is to say 'order', to the universe. Ancient sources have it that 'Pythagoras was the first to call the set of all things by the name cosmos, for the order that runs through all things'. Pythagorean science was cultivated as a means to an end; it was the practice of a way of life that enabled one to purify one's soul and free it from the body.

Science was seen as a form of purification. This way of life was known as 'the contemplative life' (*bios theoretikos*), a life dedicated to the search for truth and for 'the good' through knowledge, which was the highest form of purification or communion with the divine.

Science in Classical Greece: The Academy and the Lyceum

The second period is congruent with the cultural and political hegemony of Athens. The developments begun in the early period continued, but there was a major shift in perspective: a theory was no longer seen as something finished or perfect; it could always be further improved upon, or refuted. Socrates and the sophists introduced the inductive method. Philosophical and scientific thought – medical science in particular – began to focus on the human, on humans as specific individuals and social beings.

Astronomy was given a strong forward push by Anaxagoras (500–428 BC). The influence of the Pythagorean school fostered mathematical progress in the Platonic Academy; a particularly important figure here was Eudoxus of Cnidus (*c.* 390–337 BC), whose early astronomical theory, which saw the universe as a sphere, became the predominant model of the classical age. Greek speculative physics attained to maturity with the work of the atomists (Democritus, *c.* 460–370 BC), Empedocles' theory of the elements, and the hylomorphic doctrine expounded at length by Aristotle. As against the modern idea of physics as an account of material reality, which human technique seeks to act upon and harness to its purposes, the Greeks viewed physics purely as an explanation of nature. Their tendency to rationalise – sometimes, over-rationalise – often led them to examine nature without observing it first; they treated it as a mere reflection of the principles of reason.

Medical science, too, came into its own, notably in the work of the great fifth-century physician Hippocrates (*c.* 460–377 BC). Making use of the knowledge amassed by earlier generations of healers, Hippocrates placed medicine on a scientific footing – he turned it into a body of knowledge constructed by a specific method. The origins of Greek medicine, of course, lay in Egypt, but it is equally true that, if the early Greek 'natural philosophers' had not encouraged a scientific cast of mind, and if the Greek sophists had not developed their special skills of argumentation, medical knowledge would never have crystallised into science.

The circle of Hippocrates and his disciples produced the *Corpus Hippocraticum*, a set of over fifty treatises embodying the most impressive legacy of scientific medical literature to have come down to us from antiquity. The *Corpus* vindicates the medical method as anti-dogmatic and independent from philosophy; it requires that medical art be pursued to the standard of accuracy warranted by a systematic and orderly description of diseases; it takes an interest not in any 'essence' of man, but in humans as specific physical beings, seen in relation to their specific life regimens. The core features of Hippocratic medicine were the doctrine of the four humours, a disease being a particular imbalance among them; an interest in preventive medicine through accurate determination of the most suitable diet; the rapid development of surgery; and the codification of prognosis as a synthesis of the patient's past, present and future.

The age of Athenian hegemony witnessed the rise of Plato's Academy and Aristotle's Lyceum. Plato founded his school shortly after 388 BC. The event was momentous, insofar as Greece had not seen an institution of this sort before. Plato may have presented the Academy as a community dedicated to the worship of the Muses and Apollo and committed to the search for truth; the acquisition of knowledge and its ordering into a system would form new men able to revitalise the State. Plato drew in people of diverse training and interests, including mathematicians, astronomers and even physicians, all of whom enriched debate in the school. Under its second head, Speusippus (*c.* 393–339 BC), who rejected the theory of Forms and denied the existence of ideal numbers, the Academy swiftly declined. By the first century BC, the school – itself and its founder's thought now both unrecognizable – had virtually died out.

Aristotle founded his school, the Lyceum, in 334 BC, in a grove on the outskirts of Athens dedicated to Apollo *Lykeios* and the Muses. He and his tutees would take a morning walk through the woods, discussing scientific and philosophical issues; in the evenings, a simplified form of these topics was laid before a larger audience. Members of the school were

***Hippocrates with a mythical beast*, persian miniature (18th century)**
The foundations of medical science evolved from the legacy of Hippocrates, who in the fifth century BC compiled and gave systematic form to Greek knowledge and technique relating to the human body. His medical theory was preserved and passed on by the scholars of Islam, and remained a living force in the West until very late in the Middle Ages. In the nineteenth century there was a revival of the Hippocratic oath, a statement of principle that safeguards the ethics of medical practice.

accordingly called 'Peripatetics'. The years at the Lyceum were a quiet and highly productive period of Aristotle's life. It was at this time that he composed his main works, drawing on a huge library – a forerunner of the libraries of Alexandria and Pergamon. The school of the Lyceum was concerned chiefly with the particular sciences, and the empirical aspect of philosophy predominated. Unlike Plato, Aristotle saw science as being directed to perceptible reality; not to things taken individually, but things classified into genera and species. The importance of Aristotle's work turns on his attempt to organise the knowledge of his day into a consistent and systematic whole, an integrated system of nature, so as to lend an abstract and congruent expression to a wide range of unmediated perceptions of the observable world – observations that were prior to his articulating them into verbal, logical and rational form. Besides his ideas about the structure of matter and his cosmology – a universe of two spheres – Aristotle wrote important biological works ranging over a mass of different species and making real contributions to biological science. He recognised that whales were not fish, but mammals; he described the four parts of the stomach in ruminant species; he studied embryology; he distinguished between primary and secondary sexual characteristics; and he introduced comparative methods in the study of anatomy.

The Platonic Academy and the Aristotelian Lyceum were 'novel' institutions in Greek education at a time when the individual – as a free, responsible citizen of a city-state – came to the fore. Techniques and forms of knowledge emerged that made humans more aware of their own selves, and of their achievements and potential. This development owes a great deal to the sophists, who, in tune with the times, introduced a new element into the scheme of Greek education. A child was educated first in the family household, and was then sent to school – generally a public institution provided by the State – under the tutelage of a grammarian or schoolmaster who taught reading, writing and arithmetic. The culminating stage of education took place in the gymnasium, chiefly in the form of military training and musical instruction. And Socrates and his heirs taught Athenian citizens the techniques of debate and persuasion through the

theory and practice of the arts of rhetoric and dialectic, which were seen as necessary to the healthy carrying on of a political life imprinted with the precepts of a personal and civic ethic. The Academy and the Lyceum accordingly became open and fruitful forums for dialogue, discussion and the framing of a wide variety of philosophical, political, social and scientific propositions.

Physician examining a patient (n.d.)
Dedicated to Amphiaraus, a mythical king revered as a healer, this bas relief shows a medic treating a young man's shoulder. In the background, the same young man is being treated with a snake. This may be a specific reference to the cult of Asclepius, the god of healing.

Hellenistic Science: The Museum and Library of Alexandria

Hellenistic civilisation, with its Greek core, spread throughout the Near East in the wake of the military conquests of Alexander the Great (356–323 BC). It overthrew older forms of civilisation, such as Egypt's, imposed a common language, or *koine*, and engendered a uniform culture that was centred on large cities, Alexandria particularly. It was in the cities that science and literature flourished, under the patronage, but also the control, of the Hellenistic monarchs, who drew in the talent of scientists and scholars by founding richly endowed schools.

Increasingly free of religious prejudice and philosophical dogma, Alexandrian science was distinctive for its emerging specialisation. Knowledge was divided into different branches, and an attempt was made to demarcate the scope of each branch as an independent domain. But this did not signify an absolute break with the past. It was in fact the Peripatetic philosophers Demetrius of Phaleron (350–282 BC) and Strato of Lampsacus (c. 340–268 BC) who designed a school for Alexandria on the model of the Aristotelian Lyceum. And Hellenistic science, despite shifting its attention from the whole to the parts, in large measure retained the contemplative and theoretical approach of the older philosophy, whereby the visible was a mere imitation through which one might reach the invisible; the applied, technical aspect of science in its modern sense was dismissed as trivial. Even Archimedes of Syracuse (c. 287–212 BC) thought of his discoveries in the field of mechanics as a recreational sideline to his central concern, mathematics; and, centuries later, Galen (c. 130–216) held that a true physician must first be a philosopher.

Greek science came to its height mostly in the third and second centuries BC, under the patronage of the Ptolemaic dynasty in a cosmopolitan and multicultural Alexandria. The Hellenistic period of Greek science is closely tied to the founding in Alexandria in the early third century BC by Ptolemy II Philadelphus (308–246 BC) of the Museum, an institution

Library of Alexandria Egypt (c. 2005)
The building for the New Library of Alexandria was designed by a Norwegian architectural partnership, Snohetta. It symbolises the light of the Egyptian sun illuminating civilisation. Housing over eight million books, fifty thousand maps, a hundred thousand manuscripts and fifty thousand audiovisual records, the New Library emulates its classical namesake by specialising in certain fields.

dedicated to the Muses, the spirits credited with protecting intellectual activity, and the Library. Both the Museum and the Library were modelled on the Athenian Academy and Lyceum, and the driving force behind them was Demetrius of Phaleron. The founders hoped to bring together in a large institution all the books and scientific instruments required for undertaking inquiries in medicine, biology and astronomy, so the Museum was equipped with an astronomical observatory, a zoological garden and a botanical garden.

The Museum and the Library were probably built on adjacent sites. The Library housed the full complement of classical literary output, while the Museum became the workplace of mathematicians, astronomers, physicians and geographers. Notable among them were Aristarchus of Samos (310–230 BC), who departed from the geocentric vision of Greek astronomy to put forth a heliocentric theory; Archimedes of Syracuse, who uncovered the physical laws of hydrostatics and used them in support of both a theoretical account and of practical purposes; Euclid (c. 330–265 BC), who constructed a rational spatial system on the basis of definitions, axioms and postulates from which all theorems are logically deducible; Eratosthenes (276–194 BC), renowned for his astronomical erudition and his ability to determine the size of the Earth; and many other scientists and thinkers. The available sources on the Museum and its Library are scant and fragmentary, but it can be said nonetheless that the design of the Museum brought together the Greek tradition of the cult of the Muses and the model of the Aristotelian Lyceum with the Eastern tradition of schools attached to temples – the Mesopotamian 'house of knowledge' or the Egyptian 'house of life'. And this Hellenistic institution displayed, in incipient form, some of the features of the later university: the interaction of literary and scientific knowledge; the necessary material resources; a staff of professional scholars paid by the State to undertake research; and an express concern with the transmission of knowledge.

In the first half of the third century BC, the Library of Alexandria amassed a collection of around five hundred thousand rolls of papyrus (the exact figure fluctuated over time). The librarians' job was to search out texts – whether Greek, Jewish, Egyptian or Assyrian – and buy them or have them copied out in the Library's scriptoria, sort and classify the vast collection (as in the *Catalogue* compiled by Callimachus, 310–240 BC), settle on a definitive text for a given ancient author (inserting marginal notes known as *scholia*, compiling glossaries, and so forth) and produce critical editions, thus creating the discipline of philology. The Library was headed by scientists and philologists, including Zenodotus of Ephesus (c. 340–265 BC), Eratosthenes, and Apollodorus of Athens (c. 180–119 BC). The name of Didymus Chalcenterus (second half of the first century AD) marks the end of the period, but not of Alexandrian scholarship, which continued through-out the age of the Roman Empire. It was at this later time, in fact, amid a host of mere followers of tradition and lesser scholars, that there emerged two of the greatest ancient scientists, whose legacy lived on into the modern age: Ptolemy in astronomy, and Galen in medicine.

Ptolemy (87–170), whose major work was a mathematical treatise best known by its Arabic name *Almagest*, believed that the highest form of science was theoretical, particularly the field of mathematics devoted to the immutable realm of the celestial and 'divine'. He claimed that the universe – the sky – is spherical, like the Earth; the Earth lies at the centre of the universe, and, in comparison to the sphere of the fixed stars, is no more than a point. The Earth is wholly immobile. This geocentric conception of the cosmos was to endure until the Copernican revolution. Ptolemy's ingenious calculations and elegant way of combining the geometric rationalism of his cosmic theory with his doctrine on the influence of the stars on human fate earned even wider acceptance in the latter stages of Greek learning, because the old belief in a Fate that governs all things could now find support in mathematical reasoning.

Galen, who also lived in the second century AD, produced a huge literary and scientific output. He accused the physicians of his time of corruption and infighting, and claimed that they lacked any methodical knowledge of the human body – they were unable to distinguish between the genera and species of diseases, and had no clear notion of logic, without which no sound diagnosis could be made. Galen, for his

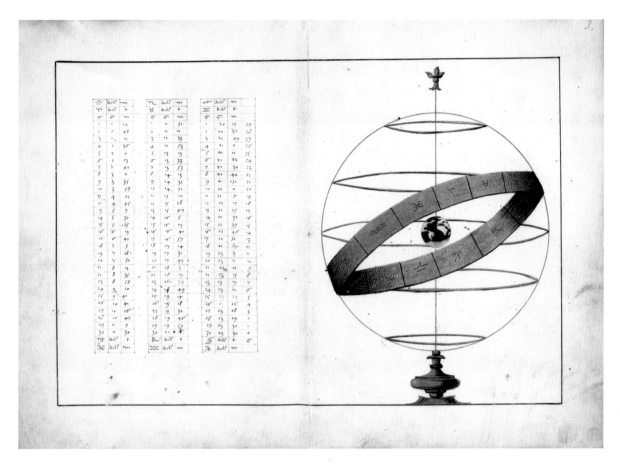

Armillary sphere and numerical table (n.d.)
Claudius Ptolemaeus, or Ptolemy, was born in Alexandria in AD 87 and died there in 170. He was the most distinguished astronomer of the classical world, and his inquiries also extended to optics, scientific instruments, music and astrology. He advanced the idea that the Earth is at the centre of the universe and the Sun, the stars and the planets – represented in this armillary sphere in the form of a horoscope – revolve around it. Ptolemy used observational tables like the one shown to predict planetary movements.

part, regarded logic and experiment as equally necessary to his method. The imposing scientific edifice of Galen was built from materials of his own – such as the doctrine of the natural 'faculties' – and from earlier scholarship. This prior science included the anatomical knowledge of the physicians of the Alexandrian Museum, elements of Aristotelian zoology and biology, the doctrines of the elements, qualities and humours first mooted by the Hippocratic school, and the doctrines of vital heat and *pneuma*. Galen's teleological conception chiefly derived from the Platonic and Aristotelian tradition that 'nature does nothing except for a reason'. A considerable degree of systematisation of medical knowledge and of its underlying disciplines, a clear theoretical scheme and its elevated religious and moral sense won huge success for Galen's thought in the Middle Ages and the Renaissance.

University Education in Imperial China

From its early beginnings in 124 BC, the Imperial Academy of China and, by extension, the entire official education system, did duty as a state agency for the recruitment of civil servants. The Academy was only one of the avenues by which one might enter imperial service, but its historical role and development were closely tied to the other modes of recruitment – recommendation and preferment, privilege, rising through the ranks from subordinate positions and, later on, a system of competitive examinations.

The Early Phase (123 BC–AD 220): The Han Dynasty

The history of higher education in China began in 124 BC, when the sixth ruler of the Han dynasty (209 BC–AD 220), the Emperor Wu, founded the Imperial Academy (Chinese *taixue*, literally, 'greatest studies'). Over its long history, the Academy was attached to the Ministry of Ceremonies, one of the nine ministries of the Han dynasty. The subjects taught were brought together compendiously in five texts, the repositories of the five main classical traditions: the *Book of Changes*, the *Book of Odes*, the *Book of Documents*, the *Rites*, and the *Annals of the Springs and Autumns* – also known as the Confucian classics. There were originally established five professorial chairs, one for each of the five texts; but with the emergence of different interpretative traditions, chiefly during the Han dynasty, the number of these 'Erudites' increased, until there were fourteen. Each Erudite would teach a text in accordance with his own interpretative tradition.

The Erudites were not academics in the modern sense but state functionaries who had won distinction by their scholastic achievement. Required to be at least fifty years of age, and already holding a position in one of the nine ministries of the imperial government, they were appointed to academic office by recommendation or by direct preferment from the Emperor. An Academy appointment was a stepping-stone on the way to a higher position elsewhere in the bureaucracy. So there was no exclusively academic career with a specifically academic profile; it was simply the case

Scribes copying the *Tao Te Ching* and presenting it to the Emperor, Bibliothèque nationale de France (n.d.)
The teachings of Taoism spring from the book by Lao Tse, *The Book of the Way and Virtue* (*c*. third century BC). The Taoist canon was the most widely copied and disseminated work in the Chinese tradition, only surpassed at a later date by the writings of Confucius.

that functionaries were expected to have attained to a general standard of erudition in the classic texts.

When the Academy was founded, an official quota was laid down of fifty students, ten for each professor. A student would enrol at the Academy for one year and specialise in the study of one of the five classics. After passing an examination, a graduate would get a position in the imperial civil service at a junior or middling grade. The quota of Academy students was gradually driven up by each Emperor, and stood at 3,000 students by 33 BC. Later, the official quota was abolished entirely, and by the mid-second century AD the Imperial Academy had up to 300,000 students enrolled. To accommodate such a large student body, 240 buildings were built, equipped with 1,850 lecture rooms. This huge complex was erected by 112,000 convicts within the space of a single year.

To be admitted to the Imperial Academy, one had to be over eighteen years of age, conform to 'good manners', and display 'correct conduct'. The prerequisites were further specified as follows: a candidate had to have shown in his place of origin a predilection for literary education, respect for his social superiors and elders, and serious-minded support for government policy and 'harmonious relations' in the locality. These virtues had to be demonstrated consistently in one's every deed and word, whether publicly or within the confines of one's own household. A candidate would be nominated by the functionaries of his native town and sent, at government expense, to the capital, where he would undergo a final scrutiny of his moral worth.

The Imperial Academy was decisive in the process of 'Confucianisation' of the new local elite of landowners emerging during the Han dynasty. The number of students rose spectacularly, but only a few would ever get a job in the civil service. The prestige of the Academy, however, was not its only attraction: students also poured in for the sake of the social advantages that enrolment entailed. First, the Academy enabled one to meet and make oneself known to members of the bureaucracy. Presence in the capital afforded a rich seam of opportunities to weave networks of support for one's own career and for the fortunes of one's family. Secondly, the fact of being enrolled meant one had transcended local limits to join a national elite. The Imperial Academy attached elite status to one's knowledge of a canon of Confucian classic texts and to 'exemplary' behaviour as defined by that canon.

The Academy played a central role in the definition and advocacy of an orthodoxy. Towards the end of the Han dynasty, from AD 175 to 183, in an effort to thwart any textual emendation in support of deviant opinions, the approved texts of the Confucian classics were engraved on large steles of stone and put up within the Academy grounds.

Attributed to Yen Li-Pen,
Scholars Compiling Classical Texts
(7th century), detail
Yen Li-Pen (d. AD 673) was the most representative artist of the early Tang dynasty. His paintings on silk explored the themes of Taoist doctrine and portray the leading figures and events of the age. He had a vital influence on the taste of the imperial court.

The long and chequered history of China's Imperial University was split into three phases. The first phase ran parallel to the formation of the Empire under the Han dynasty (209 BC–AD 220). The second phase saw the reemergence in the medieval Empire, during the Sui (581–618) and Tang (618–906) dynasties. The third phase was the so-called 'Late Period' (960–1911)

The Second Phase (581-906): The Sui and Tang Dynasties

After the fall of the Han dynasty in AD 220, there followed a long period of political turmoil. The Empire was finally drawn back together in 589. During these centuries of war, internal strife and short-lived dynasties, no educational institution survived for very long. It was in the seventh and early eighth centuries, under the Tang dynasty, that institutions of higher learning re-emerged. A new state body, the 'Board of the State Academy' (sometimes anachronistically called by its old name, 'the Imperial Academy') acquired powers to form the most elaborate system of higher education institutions in the history of China.

The new structure reflected the social changes that had been brought about and now underpinned Chinese medieval society, with its cultivated aristocracy and finely graded social and political stratification. The first three of the six schools that constituted the 'Board' were all devoted to the transmission and teaching of the Confucian classics, but each school took in students from different social groups. The School of Sons of the State, the Great School and School of the Four Gates, with student bodies of three hundred, five hundred and 1,300 students respectively, taught the sons and grandsons of state officials stratified in accordance with their various echelons. The School of the Sons of the State was the institution for the scions of the highest-ranking functionaries; the Great School accepted the children of middling civil servants; and the School of the Four Gates trained students from the lower bureaucratic echelons and commoners holding no official rank. Each School had its own precinct within the Board, and its own teaching body: five Erudites and five assistant instructors at the School of the Sons of the State, and six Erudites and six assistant instructors in the case of the other two Schools. The main role of the schools was to prepare students for the various competitive examinations held annually in the capital. The curriculum was circumscribed to the canon of Confucian classics and commentaries on it; students' progress was monitored by internal examination. However, the Schools did not prepare students for the main subjects of the most prestigious competitive examinations, the *jinshi*, in which candidates were required to compose poetry and write dissertations on political subjects. This may partly explain the fairly meagre reputation of university education at this time. Critics frequently complained that students were unruly, and more interested in the worldly goal of passing their examinations than in genuine study. Corruption and bribery were frequent in a setting in which only about two or three out of every hundred students had any real chance of examination success. Despite these drawbacks, the student body did not shrink significantly during the Tang dynasty owing to the perquisites of enrolment: study at government expense and residence in the capital. Many students preferred not to attend lectures at all and instead prepare for competitive examinations independently.

The other three schools of the Board of the State Academy, the School of Laws, the School of Calligraphy (sometimes translated as 'Orthography') and the School of Mathematics taught special disciplines. The students here, mostly the sons of lesser civil servants and commoners, aspired to a career in government in more specialised – and therefore less prestigious – roles, as clerks or scribes, or in the astronomy departments in charge of drawing up the calendar that the emperor was to announce at the beginning of each year.

THE THIRD PHASE (960–1911): THE LATE EMPIRE

This long period saw the development of an extensive national system of state schools in all prefectures and, from the fourteenth century onwards, in all districts of the Empire. The Imperial Academy in the capital stood at the summit of this system, accepting students who had won special preferment.

In the two phases preceding the Late Empire, entry to the civil service had been dependent on recommendation and preferment, as in the Han dynasty, or on privileges inherent to kinship relations, such as in the Tang dynasty. Attendance at the Academy was a rite of passage of both these recruitment systems. However, during the Late Empire period, getting a job in the bureaucracy was dependent on examination success alone. After the failure of the reforms of the eleventh century, in which competitive examinations were replaced as the basis for recruitment by graduation from official schools, local schools in general and the Academy in particular began a long period of decline. During the last two dynasties, Ming and Ching (fourteenth to nineteenth centuries), the schools and the Academy actually imparted very little teaching at all. Students were enrolled only nominally, because most examination candidates preferred to study independently. From the twelfth century onwards, private academies, located in remote mountains or forests to escape government influence, offered more rigorous training and a richer intellectual environment than anything available at the schools and the Imperial Academy. The decline of the educational system and of the Academy was reflected in the proliferation of these private institutions, especially from the sixteenth century onwards. However, the vast symbolic importance of the Imperial Academy survived, on the strength of its long history and its connection to the Han dynasty. Moreover, it lay at the centre of the ritual and religious system as a place of official worship of Confucius and later sources of legitimacy of the Confucian ideology. It was only with the reforms of 1898 that the Imperial Academy finally came to an end. It was replaced by the Imperial Capital University, later renamed the University of Peking, a modern institution in the image of Western centres of learning.

Andreas Janousch

Mandarin students (*c.* 1890–1923)
In the nineteenth century, the Imperial University was stunted by a forced change in its purposes. University study had so far led to jobs in the imperial civil service, but from then onwards positions were to be won by competitive examination only. This irreversibly sundered the university from society.

The Imperial University came
to an end in the late
nineteenth century, when it
was replaced by the 'Imperial
University of the Capital'.
This was the forerunner of
Peking University, a modern
institution organised along
Western lines

The Scientific and Cultural Legacy of Rome

Much like Sparta, the least intellectual of the Greek city-states, Rome was originally a community of farmers and warriors. The Romans lacked the quantitative awareness of the merchant or the spatial sensitivity of the traveller, and were accordingly unskilled in mathematics. 'Greek mathematics lead the field in pure geometry, while we limit ourselves to reckoning and measuring,' admitted Cicero (106–43 BC).

The Roman people did not take on board Greek science in its entirety. As we have seen, mathematics left them unmoved; they produced no mathematician or astronomer of distinction. There was one important Roman geographer, Pomponius Mela (first half of the first century AD), but he was interested only in the qualitative aspects of Eratosthenes' geography, eschewing the mathematics and measurements it involved. The Romans did, however, engage more fruitfully with medicine, perhaps for practical reasons. Celsus (*c.* 25 BC–AD 50), a follower of Asclepiades of Bithynia (*c.* 129–40 BC), wrote a major work in about AD 30, *On Medicine*, a good compilation of Greek sources.

And yet the Romans failed to attain even the inadequate unity that the Greeks had established between scientific theory and experiment. They left out the method of Greek science, and adopted only the content – and not whole-heartedly, nor from the outset. Their works were either philosophical, such as *On the Nature of Things* by Lucretius (*c.* 99–55 BC), the philosophical tenor of which was that knowledge of nature enables one to know oneself and master the passions; or they were largely empirical, like the *Natural History* of Pliny the Elder (23–79), an uncritical miscellany that concentrated on how useful a particular thing was, on the principle that nature exists in order to satisfy human needs.

It can be safely said that the Romans made no great contribution to science. Their concerns lay elsewhere, such as in gaining mastery of organisation – the creation of a public medical service, the construction of roads and aqueducts, the introduction of the Julian calendar, and, presiding over it all, the edifice of Roman law. But although for a number of economic, social and cultural reasons the Romans were no scientists, they did make more of an effort in the technical domain, and in fact the Western world came under the influence of Roman, rather than Greek, technical expertise and technical language. Technical mastery is not science, but 'art' (*ars*), and its function is accordingly determined by utility alone. Technical knowledge was regarded as a necessity, so the books dealing with it were usually didactic in some form or another. Latin technical texts, unlike those of our own day, formed just one of many literary genres, insofar as they obeyed rhetorical rules and commonplaces that varied only with regard to the intended readership.

Latin technical literature – prose, for the most part – came in two well-defined forms. The manual was the typical form for teaching purposes, and faithfully reflected the applied, practical approach of Latin technical letters. A manual could be a mere repertory of facts (such as the first-century books by Scribonius Largus and 'Apicius') or a work of reference, like the epitomes produced by Pomponius Mela and Vegetius (fourth century AD). The other form was the encyclopaedia. A source of general knowledge, an encyclopaedia evinced a theoretical unity of intention; it was an organic whole that was greater than the sum of its parts. The encyclopaedia would become the leading didactic form of the liberal learning that flourished in the Empire and in the Middle Ages.

Quite a number of classical scholars have perpetuated the commonplace put about in earlier centuries according to which Roman culture was little more than a crude imitation of Greek achievement; only Rome's contributions to social, political and technical organisation are regarded as original. But it is truer to say that the Romans had a multifarious and decisive influence on Western culture.

The major Roman intellectuals and writers of the first century BC (Cicero, Horace, Virgil, etc) manifested the Hellenisation of Rome and the recognition of the Greek legacy as the classical norm. The adoption of that Hellenic legacy by the Roman national spirit brought about a cultural fertilisation and vigour that was later to prove essential to the development of

Wounded Aeneas with his son Ascanius, and Venus, **Casa di Sirico, Pompeii. Museo Archeologico Nazionale, Naples (n.d.)** The significance of Roman culture lies in its having consolidated Greek and Eastern learning and extended it throughout the West. This achievement depended on the unifying role of Latin across a continent harbouring myriad languages. Thanks to the spread of Latin, classical learning suffused the fundamental domains of law, science and the humanities.

Western learning. Of the many peoples with whom Greece came into contact, none drew so deep an inspiration as the Romans, or underwent such far-reaching social and cultural change as a result. That was the original and essential genius of Rome – to allow itself to be captivated by Greek culture, a universal tradition grounded in nature, expressed in philosophical thought and beautifully embodied in Greek poetry and art.

It was Cicero who coined the ideal of the Roman intellectual by construing the term 'philosophy' in its etymological sense of 'love of wisdom', and honouring it as 'the mother of all the arts'. Cicero regarded philosophy as an exercise in the study of words (*uerba*) and things (*res*). The orator and the philosopher were two complementary and inseparable aspects of one and the same figure, just as philosophy brought together the twofold dimensions of eloquence and learning. The subject matter of philosophical knowledge was circumscribed to the human world, excluding the world of nature (which had been the concern of the Ionian philosophers), and was closely bound up with words. The technical hub of this method – the *ratio nova*, in Cicero's terminology – was rhetoric or the art of words, applicable to all fields of human endeavour. This was the ideal that was later to be passed on in the form of the *studia humanitatis* or *humaniora*, a term encompassing all the disciplines traditionally known as the 'liberal arts', the arts that it behoved a free man to know.

The Romans cultivated this art of language in a fairly standard form; at different times and under the influence of different fashions, it varied only in its secondary aspects. The system in which a typical Roman was educated, and the social and cultural setting in which he lived his life, made him intimately acquainted with a whole literary tradition, whose major sources were the works of poets and orators: the exponents of eloquence in verse and prose. Historians and critics generally agree that the crowning moment of the formal elaboration – the 'Romanisation' – of Roman literature was the time of Cicero, Horace and Virgil. It was in this period that the Roman historic experience, with its chronological schemata and literary documents, became integrated with the critical methodology learned from the Greeks and cultivated in the schools of grammar and rhetoric.

One of the greatest contributions of Roman culture, of course, was the vehicle by which it was transmitted: the Latin language, which survived for centuries. In the transition from the classical age to the medieval period, and in the Upper Middle Ages, Latin lived on as the language of learning. It was the language of law, of diplomacy, of philosophy and science, and, crucially, of the Church. Until the tenth century it was almost the only vehicle for intellectual life and written communication, albeit in a form as crude and formulaic as that exhibited in early medieval diplomas and chronicles. Latin also fulfilled the social functions of a language of culture: it was the language of school, of historiography, of the liturgy and of the public ceremonies of the myriad courts of Europe, from that of the Holy Roman Emperor to those of the feudal barons.

After the humanistic Renaissance of the fifteenth and sixteenth centuries, a time in which the classical Greek and Latin writers were studied, assimilated and imitated, Latin continued to be used as a language of writing, learning, theology, science and government. Spinoza, Leibniz, Locke, Newton, Descartes, and many others wrote much of their work in Latin. For the West, Latin was the natural and historic 'home' of the technical language of the various disciplines that were later to form modern learning.

MAXIMIANVS

Justinian and his entourage, Basilica of San Vitale of Ravenna (AD 547)
This mosaic portrays the Byzantine emperor surrounded by his court – government functionaries, soldiers and Church dignitaries. His followers are shown bearing Christian signs such as the chrismon, the cross and the paten. Justinian sponsored the compilation of the *Corpus Iuris Civilis*, which was to become the seminal compendium of Roman law. The juristic science of Rome attained to a high state of development and its principles still lie at the base of Western law.

It was Cicero who coined the ideal of the Roman intellectual by construing the term 'philosophy' in its etymological sense of 'love of wisdom', and honouring it as 'the mother of all the arts'

The Transmission of Ancient Science:
From the Monasteries to the Schools of Translators

In the closing centuries of Antiquity, the Roman Empire became a landscape of physical ruin and religious crisis. It was in this setting that Christianity fought a social and political war against its pagan enemies on the outside, and, on the inside, a religious and cultural battle of its own. Were Christians to accept a pagan learning, the origins of which predated their creed by more than a millennium? This was the culture that had undergirded the ideology and religion of the greatest empire the world had ever known – Rome. The argument was eventually won by those advocating that the classical pagan legacy be preserved, but not in its entirety: only those parts were to be carried on that would prove useful in elevating Christian belief and its biblical tradition. This notion wholly permeated the learning of the medieval Europe that was to come, and, specifically, the tradition that was to take root in the Western monasteries as a vehicle for the knowledge and spread of Christian texts.

For a Christian, there existed two essential 'books'. One was the Bible; the other was the 'book of nature' – or, rather, of Creation. Both books had been 'written' by God. To read, understand, comment on and divulge the Bible, one had to have mastery of the arts of language, which were systematised into the *trivium* of grammar, rhetoric and dialectic. To read, understand and teach the 'virtual' book of Creation, a miraculous work that instantiated a perfect proportion of *numerus, pondus* and *mensura* (*Sap.* 11, 21), one had to have recourse to the arts of number, the *quadrivium* of arithmetic, geometry, astronomy and music. And the foundations of all these arts were all to be found in the pagan classical tradition. That is why it had to be preserved, even if selectively.

It is here that one might blame the Christian religion for holding back science in the early Middle Ages, however unwittingly. Science as a whole can be thought of as an effort to know nature and its forces, and to harness those forces to human ends. The Christian, however, was not interested in the things of this world in themselves, but only as signs or vestiges of God. The best use one could make of nature,

in this view, was to treat it as 'a journey of the mind towards God'. This is a truth of theology, perhaps also of metaphysics. But if one's stance towards nature is thus circumscribed, the outcome is liable to be that seen in the early Middle Ages: a manifest neglect of the cultivation of positive knowledge.

To this Christian attitude to the sciences of the pagan classical tradition were added further obstacles, such as the continuing influence of Rome's lack of interest in science and, more decisively, pervasive insecurity and the difficulty even of bare survival. Teaching resources fell far short. There were few books; those able and willing to transcribe them were hard put to find them; there were few teachers. And the earliest medieval masters in the field of science were the same, in fact, as in philosophy and theology: Isidore of Seville (*c.* 560–636), the Venerable Bede (*c.* 672–735) and so forth. All they could do was to present a summary of what they knew of classical science, the elements of the disciplines in the *trivium* and the *quadrivium*.

The labour of passing on the legacy of the ancient world – and its scientific texts – came under two main influences. First, the role of the transmitters themselves, whom we shall discuss presently. Secondly, the role of the monasteries. Once cities lost their ability to keep their dwellers safe, monastic institutions moved to the countryside, and here they became precincts within which intellectual life found shelter in hard times. The monasteries were primarily responsible for the safekeeping, selection and transmission of the classical legacy; it is largely the institution of the monastery, therefore, that one has to thank for the benefits that those efforts have had for Western culture.

Leaving aside natural causes and other hindrances, such as inevitable shifts in literary fashion or the switch from papyrus to parchment, the image of the scriptorium, with 'workers of God' intent on copying codices of classical works with which to nourish the monasterys rich library, though idealised, has an undoubted basis in reality. But it chiefly reflects the time of the Carolingian *renovatio* in the eighth and

occurrentur aque adnuolunta eosdns
Inmediis fluctib. Reuerea suna aque et
operuerunt cursus et equites cuncat exercis
pharaonis quisequati est Ingressi fuerunt
mare. Neunusquidam superfuit ex eis.

moyses	aharoht

Filii autem isrl per exiccuna pmedium sicci maris
et aque eis erant quasi pro muro ad dextris
et sinistris. Liuerauiruq dns Indie illo isrl

*Moses closing the Red Sea
over the Egyptians,
Mozarabic Bible*
(10th century)
In the early Middle Ages,
thought and learning took
shelter in the rural
monasteries. The intellectual
labour of the age was to
study Christian scripture and
the Bible, of which copies
and transcriptions were
made continuously. To aid
understanding, manuscripts
contained illustrations and
marginal notes, often in
several languages at once.

ninth centuries, once the Church had seen off its
pagan rivals and, from a position of political, social
and cultural supremacy, could turn to pagan classical
texts unburdened by the misgivings of three or four
centuries before. The classical works retrieved in that
period of revival were preserved and transmitted in
some of the monasteries (such as Montecassino and
Bobbio) where knowledge, much endangered in that
time, had found refuge.

But the story of the transmission of classical texts
must be understood with reference to a fact that casts
a not entirely flattering sidelight on the contribution
of the monasteries. The difficulty of finding the material wherewithal for the task of transcription is
undeniable. But, in addition, the classical tradition
thus preserved is largely the tradition as the Church
chose to have it, insofar as the Church subjected the
texts to a meticulous process of selection and filtering, to such an extent that it is a wonder that some
works escaped that test, and we are lucky to be able to
read them today. 'Everything we have of the profane
literature of antiquity was passed on through the
medieval monastery', in the words of Louis Holtz (in
a collection of papers edited by Oronzo Pecere).

Scriptorium of the St Michel monastery, France (n.d.)
Scriptoria lay at the heart of monastic life. A *scriptorium* would be attached to the monastery's library, and here monks spent long days transcribing and meticulously 'illuminating' codices. The *scriptoria* were crucial to the transmission of knowledge: the original aim of understanding holy scripture led scholars to copy and disseminate classical texts that might otherwise have been lost.

Despite the role of the monasteries in the transmission of knowledge, and the support they drew for this work from the framers of the monastic rules – notably St Benedict (480–547), the father of Western monasticism – these efforts might not have succeeded had it not been for the involvement of a number of specific people who bridged the gap between ancient civilisation and medieval learning. Cassiodorus (*c.* 485–580) and later Isidore of Seville, the Venerable Bede, Alcuin of York (730/735–804) and others took stock of the pervasive decline in scholarship, the gradual loss of sources of knowledge, and the scattering of the tools of study. Classical learning was in danger of fading away. In the conviction that they were personally called upon to fight these ills, they read the demands of the present as requiring that the past be connected to the future. By preserving the old, they created new models for religion and scholarship.

In the sixth century Cassiodorus founded the monastery of Vivarium, an institution intended not only as a centre of religious life but as an active school, the seat and fount of learning. Special heed was paid to the philological aspects, such as textual emendation and grammatical and rhetorical expertise. The school's characteristic concerns were the reading, scrutiny and copying out of texts. Cassiodorus' overarching plan is laid out in his *Institutions*. The central idea is that an accurate understanding of the Bible, in which God reveals his scheme for the salvation of Man, requires familiarity with the profane arts and disciplines, including medicine and cosmography. He gave his monks this advice:

> If you do not know Greek, you have, in the first place, the herbal of Dioscorides, who described and drew the plants with admirable fidelity. Also read Hippocrates and Galen... and other treatises on the medical art, all of which I have left in readiness for you on the shelves of our library. (*Institutions* I, 31)

The scholarly project of Isidore of Seville, in keeping with his episcopal office, was designed to light a spiritual path. In all his work one finds his concern to draw from every text, whether Christian or pagan in origin, a lesson towards a Christian truth. *Sunt hic plura sacra, sunt hic mundalia plura* ('here are many holy works, here the worldly works are many'): this inscription over the door of his library suggested a 'peaceful coexistence' of the sacred and the pagan, and a desire to find a synthesis of both. And that aim was manifest in Isidore's major work, the *Etymologies*, the most comprehensive and complex bringing together of two kinds of learning, the old (classical, pagan) and the new (Christian).

The scholarly movements of Cassiodorus in Italy, Isidore in Spain and the monasteries in Ireland and England all converged in France, giving rise to a vigorous revival under the auspices of Charlemagne and the guidance of Alcuin of York. The Carolingian renaissance was a cultural revival with Christian roots that drew on classical prototypes. At its core was the transmission of ancient texts, transcribed in Carolingian minuscule – a more legible script that became a widespread standard – and the reorganisation of schools. The period saw the foundation of monastic schools (divided into *schola interior* for the monks themselves, and *schola exterior* for the lay clergy), cathedral or 'capitular' schools, and palatine schools. It was in this multifarious setting of the schools that medieval thinkers did their work, and so got the name 'scholastics'. Later, some of the schools were to become 'minor schools', providing elementary education,

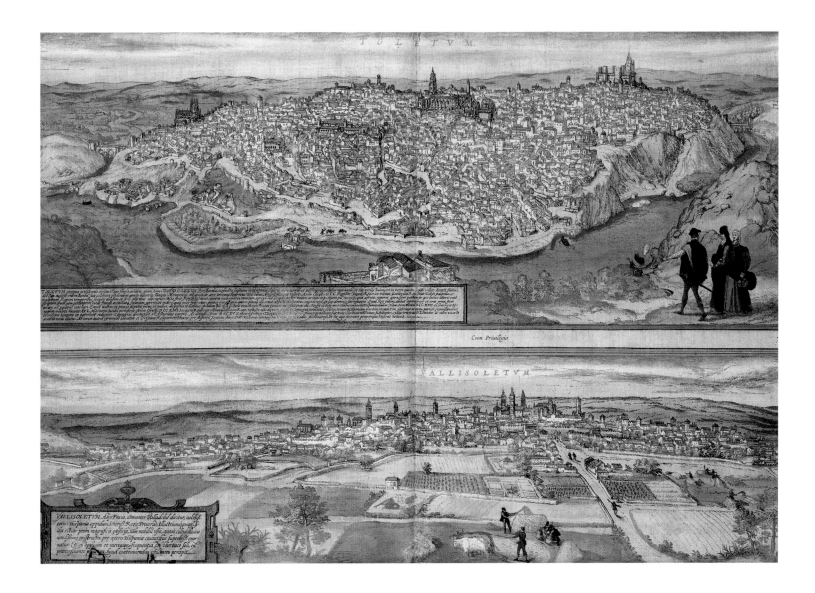

while others rose to be *studia generalia*, the seats of university training.

The transmission of ancient learning before the advent of print can be divided into two periods. Up to the sixth century, books were copied to individual commission by specialist bookmen, each with a scriptorium of his own. Private scriptoria existed, too, which would transcribe books for their patron. In either event, the actual work was done by a skilled slave. In the second period, after the fall of the Western Roman Empire, most of the scriptoria moved to the monasteries, which zealously carried on the tradition. The materials of the two phases were little different; the distinction was that the role of transmission shifted from one dominant social group to another.

In the early years of the spread of Christianity, the task of copying out the scriptures fell to the communities themselves, whose members would have included highly literate individuals such as government officials and *antiquarii*. Leaving aside the financial straits that the early Christians had to face, bookmaking workshops were initially reluctant to produce scripture, insofar as it would stand in defiance of the imperial persecution of Christianity – one policy being the confiscation of Christian books. But, from the fourth century onwards, the social climate changed. Codices of scripture then began to be produced in properly equipped copying establishments, and, by this 'emancipation', developed several varieties. Some transcription workshops also transcribed

Georg Braun and Franz Hogenberg, *Views of Toledo and Valladolid,* **in** *Civitates Orbis Terrarum* **(c. 1572)**
Created as a supplement to the work of Abraham Ortelius, *Theatrum Orbis Terrarum*, this collection of views of the leading cities of Europe includes a number of Spanish locations, such as Toledo and Valladolid. The figures in the foreground are meant to typify the local people. Each view of a city came with a brief account of its history and main economic pursuits.

en las calas z uuear algunas mane
ras te uregos con que huum plazer z
se conorten z no esten lulbios.

Por enta nos ton
Alffonso por la gra
cia te dios rey te
Castiella. te Tole
to te Leon te Bal
uzia te Seuilla i
te Cordoua te Avur

mas verdaderas. son estas.
Segunt cuenta en las ystorias
antiguas en India la mayor ouo
un rey que amana mucho los
sabios z tenielos siempre consigo. z fa
zieles mucho amenudo razonar sobre
los fechos que nascen telas colas. E te

Alfonso X 'the Wise', *Libro de los Juegos* **[Book of Games] (13th century)**
The medieval city of Toledo saw a confluence of the three religions of the book: Judaism, Christianity and Islam. The coexistence – or *convivencia* – of the three communities gave rise to a fluid exchange of knowledge. It was this climate that propitiated the founding of the School of Translators, of which Alfonso X of Castile was a keen patron. The School's translations of the three cultures' classic texts enabled Toledo to thrive as Europe's leading intellectual hothouse. Today, the School lives on, fostering cultural ties between Europe and the countries of the Mediterranean basin.

It was the Arab copyists, in fact, who translated and transcribed a plethora of philosophical and scientific Greek texts. This Arabic corpus was one of the greatest and most fruitful processes of assimilation of classical learning

profane literature, but others were founded specially to satisfy religious demand.

The codex – the Christian codex particularly – had broken out of the narrow circle of regular users of books, and the old workshops were no longer able to meet new demand from churches, religious institutions and a public of both old and new readers. This was the time when the Christian scriptoria emerged. Early testimony has come down to us from the Greek-speaking Eastern Empire, which suggests that the main establishments were those attached to certain episcopal libraries. They produced books chiefly for internal purposes, and only exceptionally sent books elsewhere – to fulfil imperial commissions or Church requirements. These places, then, can be suitably termed 'scriptoria', and a medieval atmosphere was starting to take hold.

The scriptorium procedure was adopted both by the imperial library of Constantinople and by the Arab public and semi-public libraries, which, at least in the time of the Abbasid dynasty, employed staffs of copyists. It was the Arab copyists, in fact, who translated and transcribed a plethora of philosophical and scientific Greek texts. This Arabic corpus was one of the greatest and most fruitful processes of assimilation of classical learning. The philosophers, mathematicians and physicians of Islam – mostly in Spain – thus became the heirs and bequeathers of a Greek cultural legacy, which they developed and enriched with ideas of their own. Their work was later to exert a highly positive influence on the cultivation of the sciences and arts in the medieval universities.

The monasteries and the episcopal libraries, with their attached scriptoria, were not the only places where ancient learning was passed on. The medieval schools of translators interpreted and transmitted classical texts from Arabic or Hebrew into Latin, using vernacular languages as a staging-post. This impressive effort of translation flourished in Amalfi in Italy, and Ripoll and Toledo in Spain, with the latter playing an especially large role. Toledo, a city where Christians, Muslims and Jews coexisted peaceably, saw the beginnings of a translation tradition in the eleventh century under the patronage of Raymond de Sauvetât (Archbishop of Toledo from 1125 to 1152). Advised by Dominicus Gundissalinus and Juan Hispano – a Jew who had converted to Christianity – Sauvetât promoted a number of translation efforts in response to requests from a number of Christian European courts.

The chain of translators had its last and most distinguished link in the School of Translators of Toledo founded in the reign of Alfonso X 'the Wise' (1221–1284). The translation tradition made it possible for Arab learning and, through the Arabs, a large part of classical learning to be preserved and reach the heart of medieval European schools and universities.

ISLAM

Science and Learning in the Muslim Age

The spread of Islam in the seventh and eighth centuries brought the Muslims into contact with the great civilisations of antiquity – Greece, India and Persia – and involved a long process of 'appropriation' of their various branches of knowledge. From the eighth to tenth centuries, practically all the available scientific and philosophical Greek texts were translated into Arabic under the patronage of the newly formed affluent classes. These translations met a societal demand: those in power needed astrologers to predict the future and physicians to tend to the health of the ruling class; and the imperial administration required competent functionaries conversant with literature and science. By the end of the tenth century, science had flourished, and a number of works had been produced that surpassed the Greek legacy from which they had sprung.

During the reign of the caliph al-Ma'mūn (813–833) two distinct astronomical traditions were adopted, the Indo-Iranian and the Ptolemaic Greek. Observatories were founded at Baghdad and Damascus to reconcile the resulting differences. These institutions turned out to be short-lived, but their observations served to rectify a number of Ptolemaic dogmas.

From the ninth to the eleventh centuries, the work of Galen was subjected to the criticism of al-Rāzī, and that of Ptolemy came under the scrutiny of Ibn al-Hayṯam. Arab science had by now matured, rising to the status of an active and critical continuation of classical science. The Arabs invented a new decimal arithmetic, algebra – which had been unknown to the Greeks – and a geometry that further developed the ideas of Euclid, Archimedes and Apollonius, and created forerunners of infinitesimal calculus. In the eleventh century, Umar Jayyām introduced algebraic geometry in a form comparable to that later used by Descartes (1596–1650) and Fermat (1601–1665). Geometrical optics advanced spectacularly under the auspices of Ibn al-Hayṯam (c. 965–1040); his eighth-century predecessor, Ibn Sahl, had framed an early version of the second law of refraction, later known as Snell's Law (c. 1621). Trigonometry, too, made progress; as against the 'chord' function of the Greeks, the Arabs introduced sines, cosines, tangents, cotangents, secants and cosecants. Ptolemy had known only one trigonometric theorem, Menelaus' theorem, which relates six elements (sides or angles) of two spherical triangles; it was in the tenth and eleventh centuries that there were developed all the theorems in use today, providing

Madrassa at Khiva, Uzbekistan (n.d.)
This city of Central Asia was a waypoint on the Silk Road, the trade route that served as a channel for cultural exchange between East and West.

the solution for any spherical triangle. This was the only trigonometry known to Copernicus and Kepler.

In al-Andalus (Islamic Spain), important progress was made from the tenth century onwards in astronomical calculation instruments and theory. And it was in tenth-century Cordoba that scholars first determined the real size of the Mediterranean. Arab science took the postulates of Greek science to their final consequences, thus helping to usher in the crisis of the Renaissance. Ptolemy's system had drawn credence from its predictive power: he had constructed geometric models on the basis of which astronomical tables could be calculated that predicted planetary positions in accordance with observation. Tables remained accurate for about forty years, after which they became obsolete. Arab astronomers made fresh observations, corrected the models and modified the numerical parameters. These new data were used to create new tables, but even these held good only for a time. It was realised that there was a need to leave behind the Ptolemaic model and create a new one: this was the work eventually done by Kepler. The observatory is an Islamic invention. After some early attempts (Baghdad and Damascus, 828–829), many similar institutions were founded, two of which survived to become long-lived facilities equipped with large instruments: Marāga (1259–c. 1316) and Samarkand (1420–c. 1500). The Marāga observatory's instruments were identical to those later used by Tycho Brahe (1546–1601) at Uraniborg – his pre-telescopic observations allowed for the formulation of Kepler's laws.

Marāga was also a centre of theoretical inquiry whose astronomers designed non-Ptolemaic planetary models. Ptolemy's assumptions were hard to fulfil: he wanted to account for the irregular movement of a planet by a combination of circular and uniform movements. The model was impossible to apply rigorously; Ptolemy took a number of liberties that attracted the disapproval of cosmologists, whose aim was to uncover the real structure of the universe. A number of failed attempts were made from the eleventh century onwards, until the Marāga school used a range of geocentric models that avoided the contradictions of Ptolemy's scheme but were just as accurately predictive. The Marāga school survived until the seventeenth century; in 1957 scholars unearthed evidence that some of these thirteenth- and fourteenth-century schemes were the same as those appearing in *De Revolutionibus Orbium Celestium* (1543) by Copernicus, whose genius consisted in combining the heliocentric assumption of Aristarchus of Samos with the non-Ptolemaic models of Marāga. A second instance of 'obscure transmission' is that of the discovery of pulmonary circulation by Ibn al-Nafis (Damascus and Cairo, thirteenth century). In his description, which closely resembled later accounts by Servet (1553), Valverde (1554) and Colombo (1559), the pulmonary artery transfers the venous blood from the right ventricle to the lungs, where it is mixed with air. The oxygenated blood then passes into the pulmonary vein, from where it is pumped to the left ventricle.

Julio Samsò

Arab science came to Europe and entered the medieval universities by way of the translations made in Spain in the twelfth and thirteenth centuries. The influence of Arab learning on the Renaissance and the scientific revolution was to have a direct effect on Western science

Taqi al-din al Rasid with other astronomers in the Galata Observatory, Istanbul (16th century)
Founded in 1557, the Galata Observatory enabled astronomers to update their tables to predict the positions and movements of the stars and planets, the Sun and the Moon. It had two main rooms: a large space used as a library and workplace, and a smaller room housing observational instruments.

The Madrassa

The term *madrassa*, in its modern sense, refers to a centre of Islamic learning, a school of 'higher education' as opposed to the traditional elementary school (*kuttāb*). In the Middle Ages, however, the term referred mainly to a law school, where the other Islamic sciences, such as literary and philosophical disciplines, were merely auxiliary. A madrassa, then, is an institution of Islamic learning, particularly of Islamic law, a 'university of stud', according to Pedro de Alcalá in the sixteenth century.

The system of Islamic education went through three stages before it arrived at the institution of the madrassa. First, before the emergence of Islam itself, educational institutions consisted of informal schools for children. With the rise of Islam, education was centralised in mosques. Because many students in search of higher learning came from beyond the local community, a special building had to be provided to accommodate them, the *jān*. Finally, the madrassas combined the functions of mosque and student accommodation within one and the same architectural unit. The madrassa's role of mosque continued as a major element in Islamic society and in the transmission of knowledge.

The madrassa first emerged in the eleventh century in the East. It is attributed to Niẓām al-Mulk, a Seljuk vizier. After he conferred official status on the madrassa, this form of institution swiftly spread. He erected the earliest madrassa in 1067, and by 1184 there were thirty in eastern Baghdad alone. This rapid proliferation is explained by the need to frame a programme of the Sunna – orthodox Islam – to counteract its persistent enemy, which came in the guise of *Shiʻa* or heterodox Islam.

The madrassa came somewhat later to the Islamic West, with the shift towards orthodoxy which that region of Islam underwent after the Almohads (with a number of doubtful precedents). The new Marinid rulers, feeling a lack of dynastic legitimacy, sought to control religion in a fairly direct way by training their adherents in Islamic religion and law. Madrassas were called on to play a vital role.

In 1271, the Marinid sultan Abū Yūsuf built the al-Ṣaffārīn in Fez, the oldest madrassa still standing in North Africa.

The policy of instituting new madrassas across the Maghreb continued apace. A typical early exemplar would be architecturally simple, designed as a hall of residence attached to an oratory, an ablutions area and sometimes a minaret. Later, the buildings became more complex. Some rooms gave onto a courtyard, in the manner of the *iwans*.

In the fourteenth century, urban madrassas came under tight control by the authorities, the Marinid *majzan*, who needed to

With the rise of Islam, education was centralised in the mosques, which became vital links in the transmission of Muslim learning. The large influx of students required that lodgings be built to accommodate them, and this was the origin of the madrassa

create a new class of educated and skilful administrators. In al-Andalus, the madrassa movement came later still than to North Africa. Other than a privately founded Sufi institution in Malaga, the only madrassa on the Iberian peninsula was created in Granada byYœsuf I and his prime minister Ri¢wãn. The influence of the Marinid kingdom is evident both in this and in other aspects of the Nasrid emirate. Begun in 1340, the madrassa was completed in 1349, according to its foundational stone plaque.

It was built on a site that has been ascribed first to the eleventh-century Zirid dynasty, and later to authorities wielding delegated power in Granada. Recent excavations have discovered that the place was in public use up until it was turned into a madrassa. It is thought that it was architecturally similar to a well-known Marinid precedent, the al-'Aṭṭārīn in Fez. The front entrance gave way to a hall and a courtyard graced by a pool and walkways on all four sides; there was an oratory at the south-eastern end which opened onto a *mihrab*. A side room to the right may have been used for lectures; and there were two pavilions separated by a garden. The students lived in rooms on the first floor.

The location, plan and historic development of the madrassa all suggest that it was a close concern of the ruling class: they hoped to shape a new town plan that would return to Granada's great mosque the centrality that it had lost.

Antonio Malpica

Madrassa of al-'Aṭṭārīn, Fez, Morocco (14th century)
Madrassas were public or private religious foundations. Study involved the rote learning and recitation of set texts – chiefly Islamic scripture. Students who failed to keep up with the memorisation regimen were promptly expelled.

Henricus de Alemannia lecturing his students, *Liber Ethicorum des Henricus de Alemannia* **(c. 1350)**
After the breakup of the Roman Empire, classical learning was preserved largely by the Muslims. Aristotle's *Ethics*, for instance, was translated and disseminated by Arab intellectuals. This is why depictions of lessons in Aristotelian philosophy portray the lecturer wearing a turban – it was an allusion to the route by which the classical writers had become known in the Western schools.

II

THE BIRTH OF AN INSTITUTION

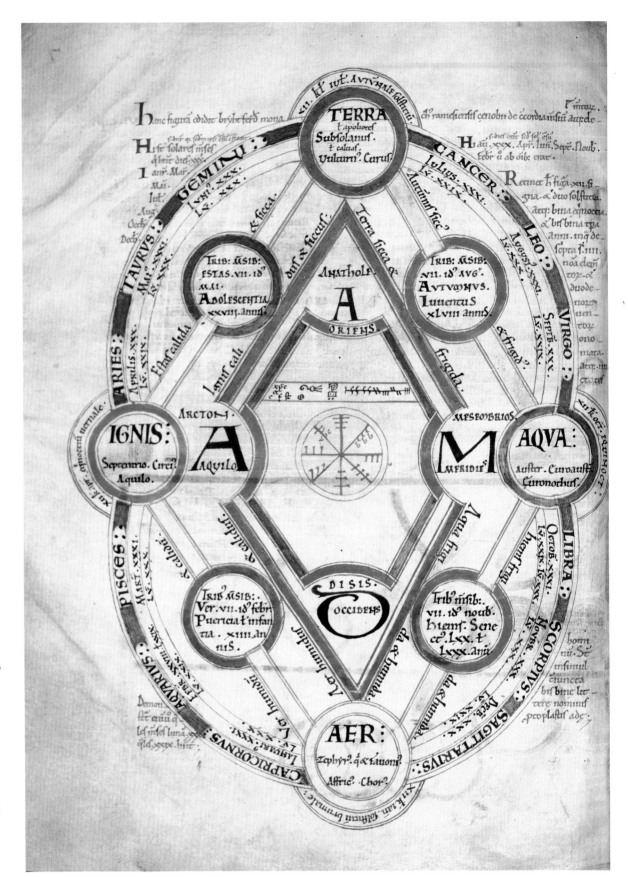

Computus at Thorney Abbey, Cambridgeshire, England (c. 1102–10)
In the Middle Ages these diagrams were used to fix the exact date of Easter and other milestones of the liturgical calendar. A *computus* was a compendium of medieval scientific knowledge about the structure of time. The one shown here is divided into the twelve months, corresponding to the signs of the zodiac, the four seasons and the four elements of which the world was made: water, earth, air and fire.

Europe and the Universities

Mariano Peset

Every age had its schools in which masters passed on their learning to disciples. Classical Greece and Rome were no different: the *Code* of Justinian, the sixth-century Byzantine emperor, tells of the law schools of Constantinople and Beirut. In the Middle Ages there were schools attached to monasteries and bishoprics, and even parishes. The Emperor Charlemagne, crowned in AD 800 by Pope Leo III, encouraged the study of the liberal arts. His court became a gathering-place for sages who formed a 'Palatine School', as it was termed by Alcuin, the foremost among them. The liberal arts were divided into two sets, the *trivium* and the *quadrivium*. As part of the *trivium*, grammar made one conversant with Latin prose and verse. Rhetoric was the art of persuasion and argument; its masters were Tertullian and Cicero. Rhetoric also embraced *ars dictaminis*, the art of writing letters, and was required knowledge for the notaries and jurists who were to draft the laws. The third element, dialectic or logic, was the foundation of reasoning, based on classical texts retrieved by logicians such as Scotus Erigena and Gerbert of Reims. The *quadrivium* brought together arithmetic, geometry, astronomy and music. Medicine sometimes qualified as a liberal art, but was otherwise regarded as mechanical. All the arts were the path towards understanding the divine art, theology.

Universities did not emerge until the twelfth century. Europe had seen the formation of cities or boroughs: settlements of merchants who won privileges and freedoms from monarchs and feudal lords for their dealings and travels, and were entitled to elect their city authorities. Feudal society grew more complex. The three estates of the Upper Middle Ages – nobility, clergy and peasantry – were joined

by burghers or city-dwellers, who enjoyed a wider freedom. In his *Libro de los estados* the *Infante* Juan Manuel describes the first estate – the aristocracy – but his account of the third estate contains the beginnings of a distinction between peasants and townsmen. All the same, under the feudal kings and lords the hierarchical structure was to survive for centuries yet. At the cusp of Christendom stood the Emperor and the Pope, its two heads, the Sun and the Moon.

Scholarship shifted from the monasteries – the ecclesiastical fiefdoms – to the cathedrals in the cities. There arose the mendicant orders of Dominican and Franciscan friars, who directed their labours to the new bourgeois. The cathedral schools gave instruction in the new disciplines. In Castile, the inventories of monastery and cathedral libraries reveal differences in taste: urban schools preferred more recent authors and gave shelf-space to law books. Both canon law and Roman civil law were strongly present, in response to the interest of the

Rabanus Maurus,
***De Rerum Naturis* (AD 840)**
Ever since the *Etymologies* of Isidore of Seville, there was felt to be an abiding need to compile and systematise all of human learning in a single work. In the twenty-two volumes of the *De Rerum Naturis,* Rabanus Maurus, a disciple of Alcuin of York, discussed the nature of 'all things' in an attempt to embrace the entirety of the scientific, humanistic and theological learning of his age with an encyclopaedic vision.

Alfonso X 'the Wise',
Las Siete Partidas (1252–84)
Alfonso of Castile personally
oversaw the composition of
a juristic code that shaped the
history of Spanish law. The
significance of the *Partidas*
goes beyond its legislative
character; the work was of a
piece with Alfonso's ambitious
project to foster and spread
knowledge in all its realms.

schools' clerical staff. The cathedral schools lived on into later centuries and sent their best scholars to the *studia generalia*, or universities.

So far, Arab science had predominated over Christian. The Arabs had translated the Greek and Roman legacy, and their physicians, mathematicians and scholars commanded high prestige for their knowledge. In the mid-twelfth century in Salerno, contact with Greek and Arab science in Sicily and southern Italy gave rise to a medical school. It was chartered by Frederick II Hohenstaufen, who, when he founded a *studium generale* in Naples in 1224, left the medical faculty at Salerno, even though by then it was but a shadow of what it had once been, falling behind Bologna or Montpellier. Salerno had nothing like a university organisation; the royal court gave its physicians licence to practice, but no degrees.

In the Iberian peninsula, another point of contact with Islam (like Byzantium, the capital of the Eastern Roman Empire), Arab science made powerful inroads, and from there spread to the rest of Europe. When Alfonso VI captured Toledo in 1085, he appointed as archbishop one Bernard, a monk of Cluny, the French abbey of black-clad friars. His successor Raymond, also a Cluniac, was the patron of a school of Jewish, Christian and Mozarab translators, the greatest of whom was Dominicus Gundissalinus, the author of several works inspired by Arab science that became renowned throughout Europe. Avicenna and Avicebron were two of the Arab authors translated. Gerard of Cremona was a tireless translator of Arab and Greek texts, including Aristotle, Ptolemy and Euclid.

The Arabs had translated the Greek and Roman legacy, and their physicians, mathematicians and scholars commanded high prestige for their knowledge

Avicenna (Ibn Sina), *The Canon of Medicine* (980–1037) The fourteen volumes of Ibn Sina's *Canon*, which bore the imprint of Aristotelian and Neo-Platonist thought, are the highest exemplars of medieval medical knowledge. Ibn Sina's influence was decisive in science; it exhibits the superiority of the Muslim learning of the Middle Ages over the Christian.

Cathedral of Nôtre Dame, Paris (12th–13th century) Intellectual pursuits moved from rural monasteries to the cathedrals, which had risen up with the cities. It was in this context that in the twelfth century there was founded the cathedral school of Nôtre Dame, one of Europe's leading centres of learning, which later evolved into one of the first universities. Its large student body and high academic standard made the Parisian school famous throughout Europe.

The Origins of University Corporations: Universities of Paris, Bologna and Oxford

The earliest universities then came into being. One sprang from the cathedral school of Nôtre Dame in Paris; it was similar in form to the schools in the cathedrals of Chartres, Laon, Tours and Reims. Nôtre Dame attracted a great many scholars; other academic sites in Paris were the collegiate church of Sainte Genevieve and the church of canons regular of St Victor on the banks of the Seine. The principal was a 'Scholastic' or *magister scholarum* appointed by the bishop, with authority over both masters and students. The Third Lateran Council of 1179 ordained that the masters should examine candidates and give licences to teach, endorsed by a chancellor. In 1218, at the Fourth Lateran Council, each cathedral had to appoint a *magister scholarum* to instruct students and theologians to teach Scripture. In the time of Abelard, a brilliant scholar whose logic lectures at Paris drew crowds, no corporation yet existed. In his *Historia Calamitatum* Abelard reported that he had attended several schools before coming to Paris. His master, William of Champeaux, took a dislike to the young genius for disputing his philosophical tenets. After a protracted illness, Abelard returned to Paris to the same master, who had become a regular cleric in hopes of winning a bishopric. Abelard succeeded Champeaux as a master, but the intense persecution remained until he was hounded out of the school. He then met Heloise, niece of the canon Fulbert, to whom he taught lessons in exchange for room and board. Then came the love affair, her pregnancy and their secret wedding, which did not save Abelard from castration.

In thirteenth-century Paris a corporation of arts graduates came into being. The cathedral school's chancellor had abused his power by refusing to award degrees unless candidates swore to obey him. Masters and graduates mounted a defence by forming a corporation – a university – headed by a rector. A papal bull issued in 1212 by Innocent III upheld the corporation's case. Robert of Courson, sent by the Pope to resolve the conflict, drew up the first statutes (1215), later endorsed by the masters. The statutes prescribed that the chancellor was to award a degree when the masters accepted it, and could not charge a fee. The university could now adopt its own rules and withhold obedience if the courts failed to award redress for death or mutilation; it could also set various fees and the price of lodgings. But disputes continued to rage, because the bishop and chancellor were unwilling to accept statutes passed without their consent. Pope Honorius III backed the corporation: the chancellor's role would be simply to assure that graduates were indeed suitable, and formally to award degrees. This 'university' of masters was much like a guild, in the mould of artisans' and merchants' guilds.

By 1245 there had emerged a university in fully fledged form, with a rector and procurators, each heading a 'nation' of masters and bachelors brought together by regional origin. The rector was elected by the procurators of the four 'nations' of arts: the French nation – meaning natives of the Île de France – the Norman nation, the Picard nation and the English nation, which included members from central and northern Europe. The core was the assembly of the faculty of arts, which decided on the main issues; the so-called 'major' faculties voted separately. The faculty of laws had been suppressed in 1219. Masters and graduates, even those without teaching duties, owed allegiance to the university and rector.

From its beginnings the university enjoyed the protection of the French kings. Philip Augustus removed

Seal of the University of Paris (13th century)
For a university to have its own seal was of high significance: it marked the recognition of its legal personality. The seal was used to authenticate documents issued by the university. Emerging academic institutions were invariably eager to win the grant of a seal.

the provost or judge sitting in Paris for 'outrages' to a scholar; thereafter, the provosts had to swear an oath of observance of university privileges and thus became royal 'conservators'. Innocent IV instituted papal conservators. In 1225, a struggle erupted with the chancellor over the right to bear the university seal, which entailed recognition of the university's legal personality. The dispute required the intervention of the papal legate, Cardinal Sant Angelo, who ended up smashing the seal. Even the king's troops were involved. A new seal was granted only in 1246, and in 1270 seals were granted to the faculties of canon law and theology. 1228 was a year of unrest against the authorities in the student quarter. Both the bishop and the Queen Regent, Blanca of Castile, mother of Louis IX, intervened. The masters called off lectures, threatening to suppress the university and accept the English king's invitation to Oxford or Cambridge. Gregory IX and Cardinal Sant Angelo managed to settle the dispute, and lectures resumed. University privileges were confirmed by papal bulls in 1231 and 1245: the power to set lodging fees and to pass statutes. The chancellor was to remain impartial and had to consult masters for the award of the degrees; the pope reduced his jurisdiction. Judicial authority lay with the archbishop and the royal conservators, while the papal conservators judged the appeals to Rome. The Parisian rector had no jurisdiction of his own; he and his procurators decided only on issues of discipline and accommodation, appeals being available to the plenary session of the assembly.

In Bologna, new universities arose spontaneously. In the early twelfth century the city was under the rule of Countess Matilda, a confirmed Ghibelline, or partisan of the Holy Roman Emperor. A scholar in her service, Irnerius, lectured on Roman law. Even before this, a Bologna scholar named Pepo, in criminal proceedings being heard before Emperor Henry IV, had invoked the 'Emperor's law' – Roman law – to challenge the lawfulness of *Wergeld*, redress for a person killed quantified by the victim's rank, on the basis that all men are equal. Around 1140, a monk called Gratian started to write the *Corpus Iuris Canonici*, the law of the Church, with the *Decretum*, a compilation of the canon law issuing from the Church councils. At first, masters and scholars formed private *societates* or partnerships: a group of students would engage a master, whom they paid by a subscription collected by a 'beadle'. Certain doctors were authorised to award degrees. The Bologna Commune, the city's governing body, wanted to draw in an inflow of students and their concomitant wealth, but a foreign student had little in the way of legal protection. In the mid-twelfth century, when Frederick I Barbarossa was in Italy on one of the raids he was wont to undertake, the Bolognese masters and scholars complained to him about the city's treatment of them. The Emperor then promulgated a constitution, the 'Authentic *Habita*', to protect students living far from their country of origin, assure their freedom of movement, and outlaw the claims of moneylenders who would force them to stand surety for fellow students even in the absence of a bond. The *Habita* placed students under the jurisdiction of their masters or of the bishop – much like Justinian's solution for the law school at Beirut.

By the end of the twelfth century there was in place a *universitas scholarium*, and later records reflect two universities of law and other schools of medicine and the arts. Unlike Paris, the universities were congregations of law scholars alone, while doctors came together in colleges remaining outside the university. One such body grouped together so-called Cisalpine students – those native to the Italian peninsula – while another comprised Transalpine students originating outside Italy. In 1265, the Transalpine University included Germans, Normans, Burgundians, Picards, Englishmen, Frenchmen, Provençals, Spaniards, Catalans, Poles and men of Tours and of Maine, each distinguished by his region of provenance; a Catalan nation also had a presence in Perugia. Records still survive of the Germanic nation, which embraced natives of central and northern Europe.

The scholars of Bologna would annually elect from among their number two jurist rectors, one for each university. Doctors and graduates would then give them an oath of obedience *in licitis et honestis*. Matriculation and the oath were required for entry to the corporation. The rector presided over the university guild, supervised enrolment and the trade in books, and had a hand in appointing professors and overseeing the fulfilment of their duties. His broad

jurisdiction encompassed powers to sit in judgment on scholars and university officials in civil matters and as to minor offences; killings and serious injuries were referred to the judges of the Commune. The rector was aided in his task by 'councillors', representatives of the 'nations'. The nations appointed their own procurators, also annually, by a vote cast by delegates representing individual regions within each nation. The procurators performed administrative duties, handled the nation's cash and managed members' funds. According to Odofred, a Bolognese professor, there were over a thousand students in times of Azzo (1180–1230), most of whom hailed from beyond Italy. Pope Honorius III gave the archdeacon of the cathedral – as chancellor of the university – the power to award universally valid degrees after examinations adjudged by the appropriate college of doctors.

The Commune and nobility of Bologna sometimes clashed with the scholars, who would threaten to leave the city and go elsewhere, as they in fact did several times. The universities aligned themselves with the pro-papal Guelph faction against the emperor and the Ghibelline nobility. Frederick II, Emperor and King of Sicily, upon founding a new *studium generale* in Naples, forbade his subjects to go to Bologna (though he lifted the ban soon after). Later, Bologna was besieged by Enzo, a son of the Emperor and King of Sicily; but the Commune overpowered him and gaoled him for twenty-three years. The students' collaboration eventually eased matters with the Commune,

Vincent of Beauvais, Frederick II Crowned by Pope Honorius III, in *Speculum Maius* (13th century)
Medieval universities were closely tied to the Church. The popes wielded great power over the academic hierarchy and the workings of a university. Royal patrons, too, wanted a share of university power for themselves, so disputes between popes and kings blazed constantly.

the assembly would appoint thirty electors, one half of whom were Italian and the other half non-Italian, who elected the professors. The Commune funded professorial chairs, because it was in its interests that the business of teaching be kept up; some professors, like Accursius, are said to have collected the city salaries and then demanded the students' subscription money, too. From the fourteenth century on, the Commune appointed *reformatores* to oversee studies and regulate the functioning of the university and the subjects taught. Professors or 'doctors' formed one college of laws and another of canon law. The colleges of medicine and of arts only came later. Vacancies at the law colleges were filled by co-optation. All doctors were also members of the college of theology. The professors heard examinations, while the papal representative, the chancellor, formally conferred degrees.

These first, spontaneously emerging universities were organised according to two distinct patterns. Those adopting the pattern of Bologna were universities of students. Paris, however, was a body of lecturers and masters, men who already held degrees and came together in a corporation much like a guild to advocate their interests, separate from the cathedral school.

Yet a third model was that of the English universities, which borrowed some of the features of Paris. An early migration of Parisian masters may have been the origin of Oxford. Later, the execution upon royal instructions of a handful of Oxford scholars set off an exodus to a second university, Cambridge. Oxford had no rector, but was headed by a chancellor appointed by the Bishop of Lincoln, whose jurisdiction was both ecclesiastical and civil, the latter by a grant from the king. The first chancellors were appointed with the universities' acquiescence, and later by the university directly for a term of two years, which became lifelong from the fifteenth century onwards. Since the chancellor was usually an absentee, his executive functions rested with a vice-chancellor assisted by two 'proctors' appointed by the assembly of the faculty of arts. This assembly, the Black Congregation – as at Paris, the essential core of the university – conducted debate on the university's statutes, which were later endorsed by the body of doctors and 'regents', who voted by faculty in the

who gave them citizenship and exemption from certain taxes; and, whereas the slayer of a student would hitherto have gone unpunished because his victim would have had no relations to prosecute him, the Commune now decreed a penalty of exile. The struggles between Guelphs and Ghibellines filled the history of Italy over the course of development of the university. From 1274 onwards the Commune returned to the students the property they had lost during the war, gave them lodgings, allowed them to stay in Ghibelline houses even if they were Guelphs, and ordered that rent should be fixed by a joint board of residents and scholars, subject to the endorsement of the rector. The professors – doctors, *legentes* or *regentes* – were elected at the beginning by the scholars themselves and paid by subscription. Later, every year,

Great Congregation. Educational and financial matters were the preserve of a body of faculty regents which gradually gained wider powers.

Student halls and colleges took on considerable importance. In the halls, the principal was named by the chancellor, while colleges, endowed by a bishop or nobleman, were largely independent. The oldest was Merton. The principal – known as the 'master' or 'warden' – was appointed by the college fellows, or, in some colleges, by the king or another patron. Life-long fellows lived in the same quarters as students: both scholars, who had won bursaries, and paying commoners. Tutors appointed by the principal guided students through their studies. Teaching largely took place in the colleges, while the university retained the power to award degrees.

Toulouse was the first *studium generale* created by a pope. It lay in the French Midi, which had seen the rise of the Albigensian heresy, finally destroyed by Pope Innocent III and Philip Augustus of France at the Battle of Muret (1213); King Pedro II of Aragon, defending the heretics, died in battle. The Inquisition, run by the Dominican order, was created to stamp out any vestige of heresy. Honorius III, in a bull of 1217, encouraged the Paris masters to teach religion in that 'deserted land full of brambles and nettles, a haven to dragons and benighted by shadows, concupiscence and oblivion of justice, so that the Lord might return...' Popes Gregory IX and Innocent IV confirmed the *studium generale* and the corporation and gave them the privileges of Paris, though more closely tied to ecclesiastical authority. A *studium generale* was established in the environs of the papacy itself. And the *Partidas* of medieval Spain accorded the status of *studium generale* to any academic establishment where 'there are masters of arts, masters of grammar and masters of logic and arithmetic and geometry and astrology, and also where there are masters of decrees and of laws. And this study must be established by a mandate of the Pope or of the Emperor or of the King'.

Many scholars came to these and other *studia generalia*, though no significant records have come down to us from before the fourteenth century, when the popes of Avignon claimed the right to grant a wide range of prebends. The universities – like kings, princes, bishops and lords – would apply to the popes for graces and benefices for their scholars, using rolls (*rotuli*) or lists of petitions, in which there appear strings of names of clerical scholars and their respective dioceses – a good source by which to trace their number and their travels. The first *rotuli* were granted to Paris and Oxford, although before this graduates were already on the move from one institution to another. A student would frequent several universities to hear famous professors and see new lands: this form of pilgrimage was known as the *peregrinatio academica*. At first, travel was a necessity because universities were few and far between. Later, the prevalence of Latin and similarity of academic content meant scholars could travel large regions of Europe. Most were clergymen, collecting their stipends as absentees. They went to the more prestigious centres – Paris, Bologna, Orleans or Montpellier – in a bid to climb the ladder of an ecclesiastical career. Laymen, too, saw a degree as a means to win position and employment. And the errant life of the student let you meet people, see places, enjoy yourself and lead a life of excitement, as Chaucer suggests in his *Canterbury Tales* or German Goliards sing in the *Carmina Burana*, later set to modern music by Karl Orff. François Villon, a scholar, poet and rogue, speaks of that life in his ballads: whether you trafficked in false indulgences or forged coins, or lived off dice-gambling, robbery, adultery or ill-got gold, 'all is frittered away on taverns and women'.

For theology, Spanish scholars went to Paris, almost the only place for the study of divinity until the late-fourteenth century. Others went to Bologna for its jurists, and to other Italian universities, such as Padua or Naples. Still others travelled to the south of France: Montpellier, Toulouse, or Avignon, the seat of the papacy in the fourteenth century. The popes were exiled to that city, and there later arose the schism that divided Christendom. The Iberian kingdoms sided with the Avignon Popes, Clement VII and Benedict XIII, an Aragonese originally named Pedro de Luna, who never gave up his pontifical ambition and in his final years took refuge in Peñíscola.

STVDIO PVBLICO IN BOLOG

College de Boulogne.

La meta della facciata.
La moitié de la façade.

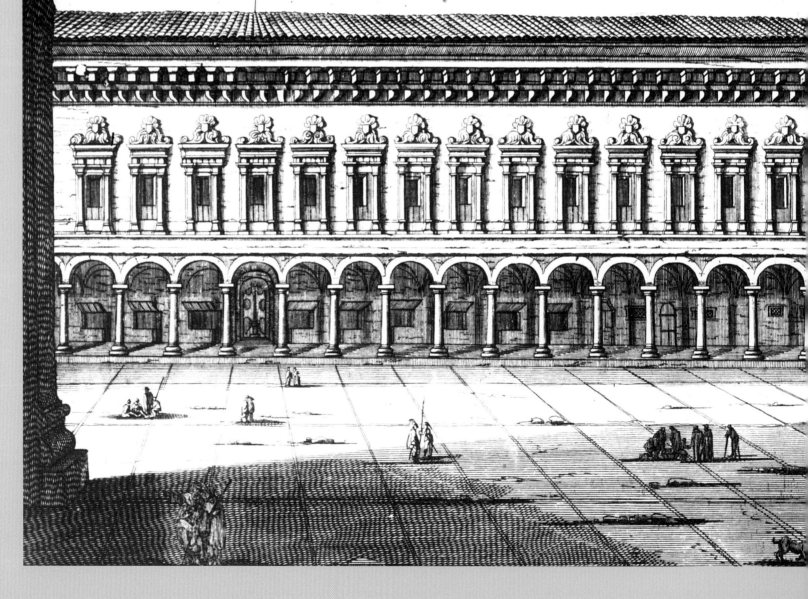

THE COLLEGES OF BOLOGNA

At Bologna, the university and colleges made a close partnership. From the outset, in the complex arrangement of the *studium generale* the colleges were just one element, each of which functioned independently from the rest (university, student 'nations', doctoral colleges).

The founding of the colleges was a momentous advance in the history of the Bologna schools. Bologna saw the creation of seven student colleges in the Middle Ages, and a further thirteen were formed in the sixteenth and seventeenth centuries. In quantitative terms, Bologna is hardly comparable to the contemporary scheme at Paris, where college members were generally young clerics enrolled at the faculty of arts; the Bolognese scholars were matriculated at the 'major' faculties: law, medicine and theology.

The aim pursued by the typical college founder, as set out in detail in his will or in college statutes, was primarily to put impoverished young men from a specific region or diocese through a course of higher learning that they would not otherwise be able to afford. But historians have perceived other, unspoken intentions. The presence of colleges has been used as a sort of barometer gauging the incursion of the Church at the universities. This view looks to the many ways in which the Church endeavoured to control the colleges and their lodgers and thus exert influence over the university as a whole. This also applies to the *studium generale* at Bologna, although here the role of the Church authorities was less pervasive than it may have been elsewhere: suffice it to say, for example, that the chancellor of the *studium* was not the bishop but the archdeacon. The College of Avignon (1257) was founded by a bishop, and the founder of the College of Brescia (1326) was also a churchman; the Urbanian (1364) and Gregorian (1370) colleges were owed to their two eponymous popes, and the Spanish college – which is active even today - was founded by Cardinal Gil de Albornoz. It was Albornoz, in fact, who, after the overlordships of Taddeo Pepoli, Giovanni Visconti and Giovanni da Oleggio, placed Bologna once again under papal rule. This was a good time to demonstrate the benefits that the *studium* could get from the city's obedience to the pope: over a period of nine years (1362–70) there were founded a further five colleges.

At first, ecclesiastical control focused on the internal organisation of the colleges and the lives of their residents. The drafting of college statutes was

Studio Publico, Bologna (c. 1790)
The history of the University of Bologna is indissolubly linked to the university colleges. Originally founded for the benefit of poor students, they eventually became lodging-houses for the scions of the ruling classes.

often commended to Church jurists, and their adoption as enforceable rules was usually subject to the bishop's endorsement. Student admissions lay within the purview of the bishop of a candidate's diocese of origin, and the archbishop of Bologna himself exercised a right to visit college residents, thus extending his authority well beyond merely administrative matters.

The care with which founders and administrators watched over scholars' progress, rewarding special dedication to study and individual merit, fostered the perception that a college was the ideal environment for the determined student. This was one of the reasons why the institution flourished – and in the modern age it was to prosper all the more. The colleges attracted students from beyond Italy – chiefly Spaniards and Germans, but also Frenchmen, Flemings, Hungarians, Bohemians and Englishmen. All this, wedded to the high standard of scholarship at the Bolognese schools, helped preserve the international flavour of the Bolognese *studium* up until the seventeenth century.

In the modern age, patronage was dispensed mostly by laymen, professionals, merchants and university professors. The typical pattern was for a foundation to grant a modest number of study bursaries and guide their beneficiaries' efforts towards the so-called 'lucrative sciences', law and medicine. Admission criteria tended to exclude *pauperes scholares* (poor scholars): instead, bursaries mainly went to the progeny of the middle classes, the professions and the lesser nobility, thus wholly modifying the original aims of the colleges. This change at Bologna in the modern age was paralleled elsewhere, such as in France, as recorded by Harvey Chisick, or at the colleges of Oxford and Cambridge. The halls and hostels once intended for poor scholars turned into expensive lodgings for moneyed students. The charitable role of the medieval colleges fell into decay, and the modern colleges paved the way for the functions ascribed to each social stratum of the *ancien régime* to harden into an enduring norm: the successful culmination of this purpose made the colleges a veritable nursery of the ruling class.

Gian Paolo Brizzi

Cardinal Albornoz (1310-1367)
In the fourteenth century Don Egidio Álvarez de Albornoz y Luna (known as Don Gil de Albornoz), Archbishop of Toledo and Primate Cardinal of Spain, ordered the founding of the Royal College of Spain at Bologna.

College founders had originally hoped to support impoverished students. The Church found ways to exert control over the colleges and their members and thus influence the university world

Royal College of Spain, University of Bologna (14th century)
The construction of the Royal College of St Clement of the Spaniards was begun within the lifetime of Cardinal Albornoz, in 1364. Under the royal patronage of the Emperor Charles V in the sixteenth century there were added the present cloister and portico, following the Renaissance style.

The First Universities of the Kingdoms of Spain: Salamanca, Valladolid, Coimbra and Lérida

Aided by the Church, the Iberian monarchs founded schools and *studia generalia* to save their subjects the discomfort and risk of travel and of life in a foreign city. The charter which Alfonso V of Aragon granted to Catania, Sicily, in 1434 suggests that another motive was to restrict the export of coin. Paris and Bologna had not sought papal confirmation, nor had Frederick II for his university at Naples. But the Spanish king asked the popes for protection, income, and universal validity of the degrees, *ubique docendi*.

The first Spanish university was created in the cathedral of Palencia in the early thirteenth century by Bishop Tello and Alfonso VIII of Castile. In 1220, at the behest of Tello and King Ferdinand the Saint, Pope Honorius III granted tithes to pay salaries, and some time afterwards he issued a bull dispensing his protection. Subsequent papal bulls mentioned 'the university', or the 'corporation': no further trace remains. Palencia faded away after a few decades, perhaps running out of funds.

But Salamanca, founded a little later by Alfonso IX of León, survived over the centuries. The Salamanca University of scholars originated in the cathedral school – as at Paris and elsewhere – with royal backing. It may have been a reply to Palencia: each king wanted his own *studium generale*, and León and Castile were separate kingdoms. The kings of Portugal and Aragon, too, soon established their own universities.

The chancellor or *maestrescuela* of Salamanca cathedral, appointed by the chapter, was also chancellor and 'judge' of the university: he conferred degrees under papal authority and heard civil and criminal proceedings concerning the *studium*. A rector elected annually chaired the assembly of scholars, doctors and masters; wider in scope than those of Paris or Bologna, its plenary sessions brought together all members of the *studium generale*. The rectors alternated among natives of León and of Castile, the two original 'nations', a home nation and a foreign nation, by analogy to the Cisalpines and Transalpines of

Candida Höfer, *Biblioteca Geral da Universidade de Coimbra IV* **(2006)**
The University of Coimbra was founded in 1308, when the city became the new home for the *studium generale* of Lisbon founded by King Dinis. Broadly following the pattern of the University of Bologna, Coimbra was a single corporation of scholars and rectors.

Bologna, but both forming a single university. The *lectores*, originally appointed by the cathedral, came later to be elected by students.

In 1254 Alfonso X 'the Wise', in response to a petition from the scholars of Salamanca, confirmed privileges and appointed conservators to administer an endowment for professorial salaries – although these were commonly funded by church tithes. But he did not grant the university its own seal, which would have recognised its independent legal personality, as the university would have liked, to resist the encroachment of the bishop. The king, the bishop and canons applied to Pope Alexander IV for protection and confirmation of the university; their pleas were heard in the bull issued on 6 April 1255. But the university of rectors, masters and students then asked the pope for their own seal and greater protection against the episcopal judges. Alexander IV granted a common seal, much like the one garnered earlier by Paris; he laid down that no papal legate or official could, without a special mandate, excommunicate or interdict any master, scholar or rector, *pro facto vel occasione universitatis*: i.e. on the occasion of the congregation of the university assembly, by two bulls of 15 July. Perhaps the pope misread the university's intentions, or was reluctant to satisfy them. The scholars now sought to escape episcopal power with the help of the chancellor. Assembly meetings, they claimed, were rife with brawls; it was common for a scholar to be excommunicated for injuring a cleric, according to the privilege of the canon – *Si quis suadente* under the second Lateran Council. The pope allowed that, except in serious cases, excommunication could be dispensed by the chancellor, but the ultimate decisions were reserved for the Holy See, so that those incurring the penalty should not die in mortal sin. He accepted in his bull of 22 September that a scholar who had passed his examinations need not be examined again, except by Paris and Bologna. Those two powerful universities could not be forced to admit degrees awarded elsewhere; though later even this restriction disappeared.

Valladolid, too, was an early seat of learning funded by the royal purse and by the Church, in the collegiate church of Santa Maria la Mayor. In 1293, Sancho IV founded a similar institution in Alcalá de Henares,

'a study of general schools', and his father, Alfonso X, established yet another in Seville, for Arabic and Latin studies, but neither flourished. Valladolid became a *studium generale* under a bull of 1346 issued by Clement VI. This university could award universally valid degrees, and grant tithes and privileges to lecturers and scholars. The chancellor was the abbot of the collegiate church. He would award degrees in the chapel of San Lorenzo; the actual job was usually carried out by a vice-chancellor, because the abbot – commonly a scion of the high nobility – was usually an absentee. The rector was a scholar, elected by the assembly on a yearly basis on St Martin's Day, the eleventh of November. He had civil and criminal jurisdiction over all members of the corporation, unlike his counterpart at Salamanca. Given this function, the rector was generally a graduate or a man of high prestige.

In the late thirteenth century, King Dinis, at the behest of the clergy, founded a *studium generale* at Lisbon. In 1290, it was chartered by Pope Nicholas IV, with income to pay salaries and confirm privileges: lodging fees and a residential dispensation of the prebends granted to clerical professors and students, collectable even *in absentia*. Scholars were subject to the royal courts for serious crimes, and otherwise to ecclesiastical courts. The chancellorship and powers to confer degrees rested with the bishop of Lisbon. In 1308, the university moved to Coimbra because the students were too rowdy and the presence of the royal court was putting pressure on the availability of accommodation in Lisbon. Thirty years later, the university returned to its original seat, and thereafter made three more moves before finally settling in Coimbra. Structured along the lines of Bologna, the corporation comprised scholars and their rectors. As in Bologna, there were two rectors; but, whereas in Bologna and in Padua there were two distinct universities of jurists, the Portuguese version was a single body. The method of electing rectors is not known until a much later date, when the rectors were chosen from among the faculties of law and of canon law, and appointed in the assembly of scholars of both; there is no trace of 'nations'. Rectors had disciplinary powers under the jurisdiction of royal conservators.

University of Salamanca
Founded in 1213 by King Alfonso IX of León, like other universities of the age Salamanca had its origins in a cathedral school. Alfonso X then raised the *studium generale* to the status of a university – one of Europe's earliest. Salamanca was granted a papal seal only later, in the reign of Pope Alexander IV. The antiquity and prestige of Salamanca have enabled its distinguished tradition to survive to our own day.

Aided by the Church, the Iberian monarchs founded schools and studia generalia *to save their subjects the discomfort and risk of travel and of life in a foreign city*

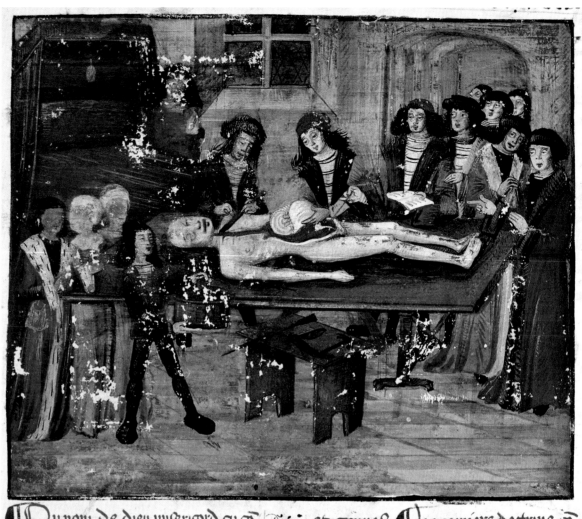

Du nom de dieu misericord cy co ... et compost La premiere doctrine co

Guy de Chauliac,
The Anatomy Lesson **(1363)**
Medical science sprang from
Arab and Greek learning, and
many of its most distinguished
professors were Jews and
Muslims. Students were
expected to learn the canonical
texts, and experimental
methods played only a
secondary role. In the late
Middle Ages, however, interest
in empirical observation rose,
and the first anatomy lessons
were performed using
human corpses.

King Dinis, inspired by the 'Authentic *Habita*' –
as collected in the *Partidas* – conceded that clergymen be judged by the bishop or his vicar, or by the
chancellor, but did not deprive the masters of their
jurisdiction; he inhibited his own royal judges, except for especially serious crimes. In 1310, the monarch established two conservators – as in Salamanca
or Valladolid – to look out for his interests, make sure
that professors fulfilled their duties and were paid
their salaries, and prevent violence to students.
Later, the conservators were empowered to hear civil
cases involving scholars and strangers. The early
role of the university in the appointment of lecturers
remains unclear. It seems that the king retained considerable traction, because he funded salaries; they
also collected money raised by subscription. At the

Lisbon parliament of 1378, the procurators peti-
tioned King Fernando to reform the university and
install good professors, lest students go elsewhere.
The king duly made a promise, urging students to
profit from their studies.

Aragon founded its first university at Lérida in 1300.
This lateness – leaving aside an abortive attempt in
1245 in Valencia – may have been due to the proximity of Toulouse and Montpellier. On 1 April 1297,
Pope Boniface VIII, at the behest of Jaime II, authorised the creation of a *studium generale* in some city
or signal place of his land, which was to enjoy the
privileges, indulgences, and immunities of Toulouse.
The king of Aragon decided to site his university
at Lérida, in agreement with the Saragossa parliament, but he organised it at his own whim, in close

resemblance to Bologna. As he lacked the means to sustain the university, he commended its government and regulation to the consuls or *paers* – the municipal authorities – while reserving to himself any privileges that he might wish to grant and the 'conventions or any other ordinances that might be made for the good of the university by himself or his successors'. In its early days, the university was shut down owing to disputes among the scholars, the bishop and his cathedral chapter, and the municipal authorities. A measure of peace was attained soon thereafter; the university assembly began its proceedings, assisted by a higher organ that was to decide on matters of professorial appointments and finance; this body was composed of six *clavarii* – two municipal representatives, two cathedral representatives and two university appointees.

The king could appoint the chancellor and authorised the university to elect a rector every year to preside over the university and *studium generale*. With the councillors – representing the university's 'nations' – the rector heard disputes and endorsed university rules in the assembly. He was to be elected by foreign students of laws and canon law, clerical and lay, who were not citizens of Lérida, for these already had the protection of the city laws. The university was therefore constituted by foreign law scholars. The students of other faculties – physicians and scholars of arts excluded from elections, i.e., from the *universitas* – were nonetheless members of the *studium generale* and hence governed the rector, as were the doctors and masters. The rector and councillors were law students, and had powers analogous to those of their counterparts in Bologna and other *studia generalia*. Why did the king of Aragon set such store by the model of Bologna? Probably for the prestige of its law teaching, which drew so many students; Toulouse, however, was under the thumb of the pope and its local bishop. Jaime II, who had had his differences with the papacy two years earlier, wanted a university that was loyal to the crown.

Besides the royal rules, a notary of Lérida wrote up a large book entitled *Liber Constitutionum, et Statutorum*. The *Liber,* influenced by Bologna, *legum nutricem,* mother of the laws, was endorsed at the first meeting of the scholars' assembly. It called for the election of a rector. On first February, the eve of the feast of the Purification of the Virgin Mary, the rector gathered the university of law students in the church of the Blessed Martin. After a solemn Mass, each 'nation' appointed its elector, unanimously or by a majority. Electors were sworn in and promised to pay no heed to 'hatred, favour, price, fear or love'. They voted in secret in the presence of the outgoing rector, his notary and three councillors. If the tally should show any scholar to have won two-thirds of the vote, he was proclaimed rector; if none got this support, voting continued, or was submitted to three or more arbitrators, appointed by and among the electors. The rector had to be a member of each of the twelve university nations in succession. The drafters of the *Liber Constitutionum* were optimistic about the future. Only Catalan and Aragonese rectors alternated up until the fifteenth century, when the rector Alfonso de Borja, the future Pope Calixtus III, a native of Valencia, established a turn for the Valencian nation. Lérida imitated the universal vocation of Bologna and the first universities, which attracted students from all over Europe and congregated different 'nations'.

Jaime II stipulated the rules governing jurisdiction in detail: in civil cases, and criminal cases not involving death or severance of a limb, masters and scholars had a choice of the bishop's court, the rector's court or the municipal judges of the city. But not for damages or 'banns': scholarly tumult involving weapons or musical instruments, whether within university grounds or elsewhere, were to be redressed with money. Crimes attracting bodily punishment, however, lay outside the scheme; by agreement with the city government, they were judged by the *curia*, a city judge, with the help of two city magnates or *paers* and ten city appointees. The fourteenth century saw the creation in Aragon of two more universities, Perpignan and Huesca, north and south of the Pyrenees.

After the demise of the Hohenstaufen dynasty the struggles between the papacy and emperors gave way to peace. But then Philip IV of France challenged the authority of Boniface VIII, and won. The following pope, the Frenchman Clement V, moved the Holy See to Avignon. After years of exile, a schism ensued. Now the popes became particularly concerned with universities. Clement granted privileges to Bologna and gave tithes to Salamanca, which Eugene IV was later to make perpetual, thus shoring up the university's endowment. A steward of the institution's income was appointed; the conservators were restricted to maintaining order.

The fifteenth century witnessed far-reaching change and civil war: student uprisings at Salamanca drove popes and kings to intervene in an attempt to settle the waters. Benedict XIII – the last schismatic pope – made some reforms, but it was Martin V who restructured the university in depth. He hoped to prevent the scholars' assembly from meeting at the rector's bidding, because this was an excuse to loiter among seedy venues, neglect studies and fall short of the upstanding behaviour expected of a student. And, worse still, Martin said, once unmoored from iron discipline, many, in their youthful foolhardiness, were ready to leave their studies; some actually did, as we can see from experience, Life's teacher. To set this right, for the good of the university and with the help of God, a handful of wise men, representing the student body as a whole, must decide on all business. They are better qualified than the mob, who bring only confusion, discord and strife.

The new rector and councillors were to be selected by their outgoing counterparts. These officials represented eight 'nations', encompassing the Iberian peninsula and lands beyond the Pyrenees: the rector's *claustrum*. Scholars swore allegiance to the rector in the cathedral. The original student-dominated assembly almost died out. It no longer met to elect the rector, and matters formerly coming before it were now referred to a body of *diputados*, ten professors and ten assembly delegates, along with the rector and chancellor. This body then appointed the *maestrescuela* – chancellor and 'judge of studies'. There existed yet a third body of doctors, chaired by a *primicerius*. In the sixteenth century, the gathering of these three bodies formed a plenary session of the university's governing powers: the *claustrum plenum*. The rector and councillors were still schoolmen, and held onto their right to elect professors for over two centuries yet.

Universities continued to multiply. Early on, Bologna had its offshoots, like Padua, and shorter-lived experiments at Siena, Verzelli and Arezzo. City authorities supported the upstarts and set them up as rivals to Bologna. In the fourteenth century Henry VII of Luxembourg and Ludwig of Bavaria's Italian raids sowed discontent: Padua was shut down and Treviso was founded, but soon disappeared. Naples was in a state of decay, according to Cino da Pistoia. There were fresh migrations from Bologna to Padua and Siena, to Florence, Perugia and Pisa. In Rome, Boniface VIII created the Sapienza by his bull *In Suprema Preeminentia* (1303), building on the foundations of the former *studium generale* of the Curia. The Sforza and Visconti families sponsored the university at Pavia, the house of Savoy patronised the university at Turin, and Alfonso V founded Catania. Since its conquest in 1405 by Venice, Padua had come under the patronage of the doge; the appointment of its professors lay with the Senate.

The earliest universities in the Holy Roman Empire were Prague and Vienna, founded in the fourteenth century by Emperor Charles IV of Luxembourg to attract students and masters from all Europe. In his forays into Italy, Charles attempted to found further universities at Arezzo, Perugia, Pavia, Florence and Lucca; but these went no further than plans on paper. The popes, too, aided the proliferation of *studia generalia*. The universities became more regional: Cologne and Erfurt, Uppsala and Copenhagen in the north, and Krakow in Poland to the east. Louvain, founded in 1425 by the Duke of Brabant, was funded by the city. Basel was chartered during the Council and suppressed when it ended. Years later, Pius II, a secretary to that Council, persuaded the city burghers to reopen the institution.

Montpellier had from early on a famous school of medicine, chartered in 1220 by the papal legate Cardinal Conrad of Urach; later, a school of laws, which also won renown, and was given statutes in 1339; the Bolognese jurist Placentinus had taught here in the twelfth century. Paris gave rise to new universities at Orleans, which inherited the Parisian faculty of law, and Tours, Poitiers, and Avignon, created by Boniface VIII and lent grandeur by the popes during their exile and schism. In the fifteenth century, universities arose at Poitiers and Bordeaux, created by the English after the Hundred Years War. Aix-en-Provence was founded by Louis II of Sicily, Count of Provence.

Academic Subjects and Degrees

Academic disciplines and degrees were common to all *studia generalia*. The differences were superficial, being limited to the incidents of local custom and rites. A common tradition ran through the medieval period: a single language, Latin, the same texts, method and degrees.

Medieval universities generally had five faculties. A minor faculty, of arts or philosophy, prepared admission to the major faculties: theology, medicine, laws and canon law, the last two sometimes the same. Many universities had only one or two. Paris suppressed its law faculty; Orleans taught only law. Bologna had two law universities and a medicine university, as did Montpellier. Some of these features were reproduced at Lérida, where the university is only formed by foreign law students, though everyone, including masters, swore obedience to the rector.

The faculty of arts taught grammar, supplemented by rhetoric and an Aristotelian philosophy channelled by Averroes. Aristotelianism had accordingly incurred condemnation as heresy until Thomas Aquinas, using a better translation by Moerbecke – archbishop of Corinth – got it accepted by the Church. Then there were the liberal arts of the *quadrivium*, mathematics and astronomy, where Euclid, Ptolemy, Boethius and John of Holywood were rounded out by Arab scholarship. The astronomical tables of Alfonso the Wise remained in use for centuries.

Theology was the preserve of the Sorbonne, Oxford and Cambridge until the fourteenth century, when it was taught elsewhere, too. The pre-eminence of the Parisian faculty was vast: its masters' opinions were revered by clergy and even popes and kings. Professors used the *Sentences* of Peter Lombard, who in the twelfth century had taught at Paris the great themes of the Trinity, the Creation, Christ the Saviour and the Sacraments. Based on this work, the regular orders, Dominicans and Franciscans, developed their own scholastic interpretations, one following the Thomist school, the other a Scotist school. They addressed themselves to disputatious issues, enlisting arguments and authorities, as seen in the *Summa Theologica* and in the commentaries to Lombard by

Thomas Aquinas. In late medieval Paris, at the college of Montaigu, there erupted the 'nominalist' philosophy of William of Occam, which later spread to Alcalá, Valencia and Salamanca, whose proponent, John of Oria, was condemned by the Inquisition for Lutheranism. Nominalism sought to develop a complicated logic which the humanist Vives later criticised as 'pseudo-dialectic'. Disputes blazed continuously, serving as a spur to theologians, whose mastery of divine letters brought them the highest regard in faculty bodies and at university ceremonies. They were marked out by their attire, black robes at Paris and Oxford, white robes at Salamanca and Coimbra.

The Arab legacy and Greek medicine formed the core of medical knowledge. Medicine was learned halfway between university and the Jewish quarter. The great Jewish and Muslim doctors cast a long

Theologians of the Sorbonne come before Charles V of France, *Grandes Chroniques de France* (1375)
Theology, the divine or spiritual art, was thought of as the ultimate form of knowledge. The acquisition of the liberal arts – the *trivium* and *quadrivium* – was a preliminary to the proper understanding of theology. Of all Europe's schools of divinity, the most famous was the Sorbonne in Paris, which became the locus for a leading current of religious thought. Paris rose to such high prestige that popes and kings alike looked to it for spiritual guidance.

Justus van Gent,
Thomas Aquinas (c. 1475)
The work of St Thomas
Aquinas exerted a seminal
influence on medieval thought.
His works – the *Summa
Theologica* especially –
succeeded in adapting
Aristotelian thought to the
pious scholastic spirit.

Jean Andre, *University
Lecture* **(14th century)**
Although each university had
its own rules, a number of
features were common
to medieval university life
everywhere. Professors gave
lectures; the standard teaching
method was the disputation;
a bachelor or graduate would
write down the conclusions
he had drawn from a particular
lesson; and there would ensue
an elaborately structured
debate among the students
about whether the statement
was accurate.

shadow. In fifteenth-century Bologna, the study of medicine followed the aphorisms of Hippocrates and the *Ars Parva* of Galen – the second-century Hellenistic physician – and also readings from the Canon of Avicenna, from Averroes and from the *De Regimine Sanitatis* by the Jewish physician Maimonides. Surgery was also based on Galen and Avicenna. Some Spaniards taught at the faculty of medicine of Bologna, while Arnau de Vilanova, a clergyman and physician conversant with Arab medicine, taught at another great medical centre, Montpellier. Academic medical training was discursive, based more on authorities and texts than practical experience. The twentieth-century Spanish medical scholar Laín Entralgo has posited three steps in medical learning: hearing, seeing, and doing. The Middle Ages was the apotheosis of hearing, although towards the end of the period anatomy classes were taught using human corpses.

The law faculties taught the *Corpus Iuris Civilis*, a sixth-century compilation sponsored by the Byzantine emperor Justinian. Although some of these texts were already known, early medieval kingdoms had abided by crude forms of law, custom and a vulgarised

Roman law, assimilated only partly by the new peoples of Europe. Justinian's *Corpus* suffered a chequered history; it was not until the Renaissance that the Florentine version, the oldest codex of the *Digest*, owned by the Medici, won widespread currency. Instead, the most widespread version was the Vulgate, a defective and corrupt text. Professorial chairs bore the names of the books they taught: *Old Digest* or *New Digest*, *Infortiatum*, *Code* or *Volume*, according to the division of the *Corpus Iuris* in the Vulgate. Chairs of canon law bore the name of *Decree* and *Decretals*, the collection of pontifical rules made by Gregory IX in 1234 and transmitted to Bologna and Paris, along with other books: the *Liber Sextus*, the *Clementine Constitutions* and the *Extravagants*. Professors did not teach the full texts, but only those parts the rector instructed them to read. Over time, teachings were set down in constitutional statutes which stipulated the subjects to be studied over a period of four years. Students heard a different exposition of the same texts according to which year they happened to be in. Students were not expected to memorise the texts of the *Corpus* or of canon law or acquaint themselves with the material in its entirety. Rather, they had to learn the essentials, and, above all, find their way around the concepts and construct arguments.

Books, which had to be copied out by hand, were expensive at Bologna and Salamanca. Oral teaching and note-taking were accordingly essential to the academic experience. The professor read a text from the *Code* or a fragment of the *Digest*, and explicated it to resolve any difficulties. Odofred gave precise instructions: first, make a summary of the title and determine the cases that the laws are to deal with; then read the text afresh to correct it; and then continue with the maxims, distinctions and disputatious issues, bringing up arguments – *pro, et contra; sic, et non* – authorities and other texts so as to arrive at a solution.

Almost all legal doctrine came ultimately from Bologna. That university heard the teachings of the great jurists: the four disciples of Irnerius – Jacob, Hugo, Bulgar and Martin – followed by the generation of Accursius, the collector of the so-called *Glossa Magna* (marginal interpretative notes), and of Azzo, author of the leading *Summa* of the *Code*. In the fourteenth and fifteenth centuries, other notable professors wrote

On est no
uum. Sic
incipit gli
sup pica
cuius glo
principio
i fini resi
stes satia
plura no
na fint p
mu/q̃ per
alphabetum ad minus dupli ponderati
reglas p̃sequar/i no co ordine quo sut sẽp
tc/sic in glo.resi sta monet.q̃ hec lectura
nonelle no i scolis legenda e sz surdenda.si
lu aut ordine studio magis hic expedie pr

dubias iminanit/q̃ de mltis utalibz quas
p matias sup descripsi/idem in sia scribendis si
turu fore p̃suo/nec hec me retlit alabore.sz
ci p io scariopus usui/i sic es lautë minui/tam
si tal fructus decimnatois creabit/et ñe siie
otctor/Na nalde desctat q̃ p̃ dcio opus actuu
ut puto no simpl p̃utissimu ipsius mca
rius sic coi eccc monarchiaz gubnat i regit.
sics parei aibuias q̃ pacifice suam ostonum
sina sices i montas decui sices i firma suscipuit.
q̃ q̃ a dullas scdentias utilie i prudet in gilat.
Ss q̃ monarchia ipsi iardudu no mul
migint/nec labozauit ad sui uisotibz dccte
da legistas exuiglio q̃bz optie agniet opus
ullo/hec ico dixiquia meas cees no potcas.per
me alibi nolocatas hic in seta/ide potius ali
quas reficelaboabo/Alioru/iq no siit plus
actu legetes nec habiles ad legendu hic mt
tas sb reglis q̃bz uenuet collocabo/illas scip̃

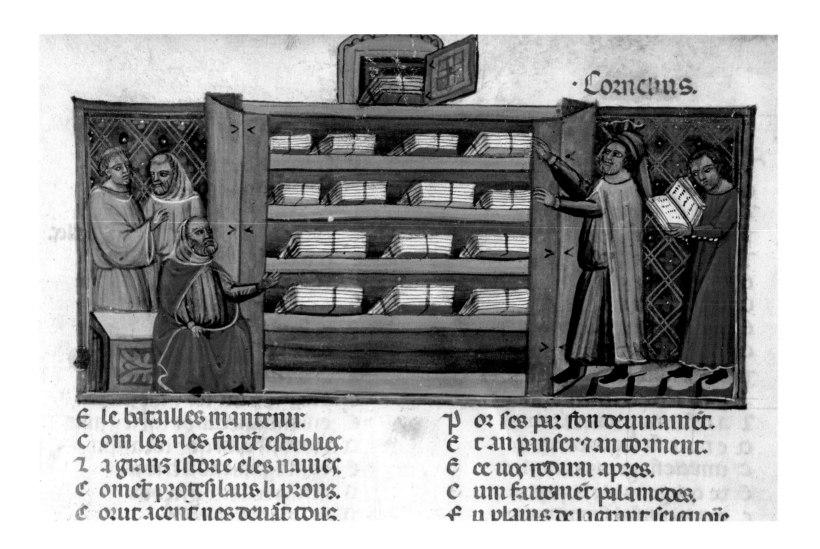

·Cornelius·

E le batailles mantenir.
C om les nes furet establies.
Z a grans istorie eles navies.
E omet protesilaus li prous.
E orut acent nes devat tous.

P or ses par son demainet.
E t an panser ian torment.
E ce nos redurn apres.
C um fautemet palamedes.
F u plains de la grant seignoie

Benoit de Sainte-More,
***Roman de Troie* (15th century), Bibliothèque nationale de France**
Libraries were of course a central element of university life, but books were so valuable and costly that they were made available only to masters and a narrow circle of students. The library was under the oversight of the stationer, who played a key role in the sale and transcription of manuscript codices.

Students read law at a faculty for about five years. There were no examinations from year to year, only 'finals' for the degree itself. A student first graduated as a bachelor, and was henceforth no longer required to attend lectures

lengthy commentaries on the laws and fragments of Justinian's *Digest*: Bartolus of Saxoferrato, Baldus de Ubaldis, Cino da Pistoia. One Bolognese author, Vaccaro, taught at Oxford early on, although England did not receive the *Corpus* into its tradition, because lawyers trained in the courts of the national 'common law' – hence the difference that even today sets English law apart from the Romanist tradition.

Students read law at a faculty for about five years. There were no examinations from year to year, only 'finals' for the degree itself. A student first graduated as a bachelor, and was henceforth no longer required to attend lectures. He spent another five years teaching 'extraordinary' lessons, intended as a supplement to the 'ordinary' lectures delivered by the doctors. Disputes were another vehicle of academic training: a bachelor of law would advocate a set of conclusions; these were then fixed by the beadle over the door of the lecture hall, and scholars argued for and against the propositions. After the lesser degree of bachelor, a scholar went on to attain a 'major' degree, master of arts and theology or doctor of law or canon law. The 'major' degrees – 'licentiate' and 'doctor' or 'master' – were acquired, first, by a preliminary examination spoken privately before two masters, in two separate sessions: this attempt was known as a *tentamen*. If the examiners disagreed, a third was brought in to decide. If the candidate had passed, he went before a panel of examiners – in Bologna, this was the college of doctors of theology or of laws and canon law. Twenty hours before the examination itself, the candidate would turn up with some of the examiners and make three cuts in the faculty's fundamental book, the *Sentences* of Peter Lombard or the *Digest*, or one of its parts. Of those three marks he had made, he had to pick one, thus selecting the subject of his examination. He then secluded himself with books and writing materials and prepared a lesson in Latin, which he delivered orally the following day before the tribunal. The examiners took turns to present objections or suggest other lines of argument for a set period of time. Then they put the examination to the vote, using beans to signify their opinions: a verdict of *nemine discrepante* meant the vote had been unanimous; *ex communi consensu* meant the scholar had passed, but by a majority only; or he might be reproved or failed. If he passed, in a solemn ceremony he would receive his degree from the chancellor, who would embrace him and hand over the cardinal book of his faculty, the gloves and the ring, which were the symbols of his admittance into the college or *numerus* of doctors.

As another way of graduating, a candidate sat a 'sufficiency examination', with no requirement of evidencing attendance at lectures – the examination itself, however, was harder. Begun at Bologna, this tradition lived on at European law faculties for centuries.

Manuscript books were expensive, and accessible only to masters and select students. In 1411, Benedict XIII commanded that the rector and doctors of Salamanca buy a number of books using the money left over from the income of the university: the *Novels*, the Bible with the ordinary gloss, the works of Baldus, Cino da Pistoia, Thomas Aquinas, Nicholas of Lyra, Arnold of Vilanova, Avicenna and others. The idea was to provide good copies of these works to the 'stationer', a university beadle. The office of stationer was essential for the sale and copying of manuscripts. Alfonso X stipulated the following rule for Salamanca: 'And I do also command and it pleases me that there be a stationer, and that I shall give him a hundred *maravedis* every year, and he shall have all exemplars in good and correct state'. In the *Partidas*, the function of the stationer was explained as follows: 'It is necessary that there be a stationer at every *studium generale* for it to fulfil its purpose, and he must have at his stations good books, legible and accurate in text and gloss, and these must be lent to scholars so that they make of them new books or use them to emend those already written'. In Lérida, the stationer's workshop, adjoining the church of Santa Maria, held an exclusive licence to sell books and correct copies; any profit it made came under the supervision of four scholars. The stationer's office lent out copies of books, for a fee, for further copying or for the correction of other codices, and took commissions to make copies from its own collection. At Bologna and Paris books were copied in fascicles – that part which was of interest at a given time to the student, who could complete the entire book by increments. All this changed with Gutenberg's invention of the printing press, ushering in the Renaissance.

OXFORD AND CAMBRIDGE:
THE FOUNDATION OF THE COLLEGES

Like most of the medieval universities of Europe, Oxford and Cambridge had no formal instrument of foundation. (A notable exception is the University of Salamanca founded in 1213, and refounded in 1243.) The very term 'university' did not originally denote a corporate body, but merely indicated an informal collective of masters and scholars. The official term emerged as *studium generale*, which came to mean a place where students from outside its region came to study under teachers sufficiently distinguished to attract them, or, according to another theory, a place where teachers in at least two of the senior faculties, theology, law and medicine, were to be found.

From time to time schools of theology and law, and especially in Italy, of medicine, sprung up, usually in cathedral towns, flourished for a few years and then faded away. (The Italian medical schools of Salerno and Padua were unusually enduring.) It seems that the formal recognition of *studia generalia* was a product of competition between emperors and popes, Bologna representing the imperial model and Paris the papal. Students commonly sought their teachers at more than one place of learning.

To come to the English universities: at Oxford, although there had certainly been distinguished teachers, at least from the time of Theobald d'Etampes (*c.* 1100) and Robert Pullen (*c.* 1133), there is no evidence of continuous teaching until later in the twelfth century. The banishment of foreign students from Paris in 1167 very probably caused an influx of students to Oxford, while Thomas Becket's flight to France in 1164 had prompted King Henry II to forbid clerics to travel abroad without the permission of the crown. Nonetheless, it appears that it is not until the 1180s that we find a continuous presence of teaching masters.

At Cambridge also there are records of teaching from the late twelfth century, but its beginnings as a continuous institution have at least a possible date in 1209 when the hanging of two Oxford students, whose housemate had killed a woman and fled, led to a mass migration from the university, which virtually ceased to exist until 1214. (England being under papal interdict at the time, there was no protection of the clergy.) One of

University of Oxford
Teaching is known to have gone on at Oxford as early as the twelfth century, though there was as yet no formally constituted university. Modern Oxford retains the pattern of medieval halls and colleges clustering together to form a university corporation.

the groups leaving Oxford was led by one John Grim, who had been Master of the Schools, and he doubtless chose Cambridge because it was his home town.

In order to function as corporations the universities needed, in theory, recognition from church (the pope) and state (the king), although such recognition effectively arrived some time after they had in fact so functioned, in the first decades of the thirteenth century.

At both universities all members, except friars and the occasional monk, lived in rented accommodation in the town. Sometimes a master would rent a house and then sublet rooms to students. From this arrangement there evolved hostels or halls; 123 are known in Oxford by 1313. They varied greatly in size and longevity. A few had halls, chapels and libraries, but unlike the colleges that started to grow up beside them in the thirteenth century (Merton and Balliol Colleges in Oxford, and Peterhouse in Cambridge) the hostels had no charters, statutes or, most importantly, endowments.

The concept of a college in the English context was probably taken directly from Paris, but the colleges of Oxford and Cambridge were, and are, unusual in that they were not specific to nations, like the celebrated Spanish college of Bologna (although many developed non-exclusive regional affiliations when, for example, endowments of land were conditional on preference being given to students born in or near those lands). Moreover, they gradually began to acquire prominence both in the teaching and the administration of the universities. Even today they are responsible for the admission of undergraduate students, and the cycle of proctors is still constructed on a collegiate basis. Heads of houses (i.e., colleges) by the late sixteenth century were solely eligible as vice-chancellors, the office of chancellor having, since the time of John Fisher at Cambridge, become a post rather for a representative of the university at court than for one directly dealing with the internal administration of the university.

Although the colleges, unlike the universities, were founded by formal instruments, their precise dates of foundation are not always easy to define, a situation that still leads to debates as to the relative antiquity of the earliest Oxford colleges. This is because there could be a lapse of several years between the granting of a licence to found a college and its actual achievement, with the acquisition of a site, the initial endowment and the granting of a charter and statutes.

Elizabeth Leedham-Green

The concept of a college in the English context was probably taken directly from Paris, but the colleges of Oxford and Cambridge were, and are, unusual in that they were not specific to nations

Bridge of Sighs, St John's College, University of Cambridge (*c.* 1900)
Colleges lie at the heart of the 'Oxbridge' academic model, playing a decisive role in academic concerns and governance alike. At Cambridge today, the university's 31 colleges have broad powers to oversee all aspects of student admissions and teaching.

Copernican planisphere (n.d.)
The astronomer Nicolaus Copernicus (1473–1543) set off a scientific revolution when he ousted the hitherto undisputed geocentric model with the heliocentric system. In his view, the Sun lay at the centre of the Universe, orbited by the planets. Only the Moon orbited the Earth. Beyond Saturn, the outermost planet then known, was the sphere of the fixed stars, which, just as in the times of Ptolemy, was thought to remain immobile.

COPERNICANVM
Systema
TIVS CREATI
THESI
CANA IN
EXHIBITVM.

III

HUMANISM AND REFORM
IN THE UNIVERSITY

Antonio de Nebrija,
Introductiones Latinae
(16th century)
Lecturer, historian, astronomer
and poet, Antonio de Nebrija
(1444–1522) was one of the
great humanists of the Spanish
Renaissance. His crowning
work was to create the first
grammar of Castilian Spanish
and two dictionaries of the
Spanish and Latin languages.
His achievement was that a
vernacular or 'vulgar' language
should for the first time have
a theoretical underpinning
and fixed rules. Philologists
elsewhere in Europe looked
to his work as a model for
distilling the grammatical rules
of their own languages.

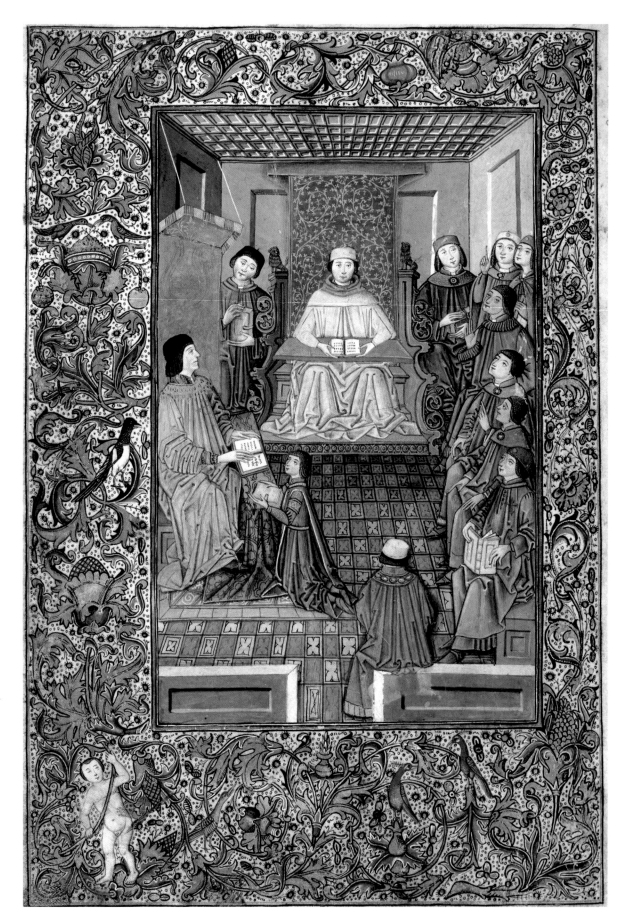

Universities in the Age of the Habsburgs

Mariano Peset

The European Renaissance

Renaissance humanism emerged in Italy in the fourteenth century from Petrarch onwards. There ensued a revival in the arts. In the Middle Ages the classics, with the Bible and Patristic writings, had been seen as founts of knowledge: Antiquity was a lost golden age presided over by Aristotle and Cicero. But Renaissance humanists thought differently. They were the equals and heirs of the classics: they affirmed the present and fixed their gaze on future horizons. The humanistic 'grammarians' scorned medieval scholasticism for its uncouth Latin and defective readings of classical texts. Lorenzo Valla, an imitator of elegant Ciceronian prose, denounced the donation of Constantine – which purported to grant Rome to the popes – as a crude eighth-century fake to shore up papal power. Angelo Poliziano cultivated Greek and read the old codices. Marsilio Ficino, of the Florentine Academy, combined Platonism with cabbala and esoteric arcana. A new spirit of dialogue with the classics flourished, a revival shared and sponsored by kings, princes and republics alike.

Humanism appealed to princes and noblemen: the Medici in Florence, Alfonso V of Aragon at the court of Naples and the Renaissance Popes, Nicholas V, Pius II (the humanist Enea Silvio Piccolomini), Alexander VI Borgia, Julius II de la Rovere, Leo X Medici and Paul III Farnese. The palace of the Vatican was erected, Raphael adorned its halls, Michelangelo painted the frescoes of the Sistine Chapel and sculpted

the funeral vault of the Medici in Florence. A new way of life flourished. Machiavelli exalted courage – *virtù*. This was the quality he attributed in *The Prince* to Cesare Borgia and to Castruccio Castracani, a fourteenth century Ghibelline enemy of Florence. Castiglione's *The Courtier* proposed new forms of politeness. Humanism was not just a revival of learning: it demanded political and social change.

The humanistic grammarians knew this was no easy venture. Antonio de Nebrija, dedicating *Lexicon Juris* to his patron Juan de Zúñiga, master of the military order of Alcantara, set out his project to apply a grammatical perspective to other disciplines. He sought Zúñiga's protection, because he feared imitators, detractors and envious rivals, that odious class of men who, affecting deep learning, advised, judged

Giovanni da San Giovanni, *Lorenzo of Medici Surrounded by Artists Admiring Michelangelo's Faun* **(17th century)** Lorenzo the Magnificent (1449–1492) was of the House of Medici, a dynasty of merchants, statesmen and popes who earned distinction for their patronage of the great artists of the Italian Renaissance. Foremost among their protégés was Michelangelo, who designed and made the sculptures for the Medici Chapel in the Florentine basilica of San Lorenzo, where his patron was buried.

and issued commands and would hate the idea of being lectured to by a man of lower profession: 'But I have found a way to allay their envy: I shall say I am to discuss the words of the civil law not as a jurist but as a grammarian.' He planned a vocabulary of medicine, a glossary clarifying the knotty points of the Bible and five books of Christian 'antiquities', to prove that the literature about the past two thousand five hundred years after the Flood was full of falsehoods and silences about Spain. Finally, he appealed for his patron's support for this Herculean task to which he had so long applied himself. Nebrija's fears turned out to be warranted. His theological writings prompted the Inquisitor General Diego de Deza to threaten him with trial and confiscate his papers; Nebrija had recourse to the civil powers to get them back. The application of philological technique to Scripture was fraught with risk. A few years later, philology was to lie at the root of Martin Luther's Reformation.

The universities taught the pure classical sources – the *litterae humaniores* – and attracted the most distinguished scholars of the age. Pietro Pomponazzi lectured at Padua and Bologna; Lorenzo Valla taught grammar at Pavia, then moved to the court of Naples and finally entered the service of Nicholas V at Rome. Galileo lectured at the universities of Padua and Pisa, then joined the court of Cosimo of Medici. Padua was also graced by Andrea Vesalius, who taught anatomy there until he was appointed court physician to the Emperor Charles V.

The acknowledged centre of legal learning continued to be Bologna, but Andrea Alciato and Jacques Cujas drew crowds of jurists to Bourges. Pantagruel, Rabelais's character, when speaking of his peregrination from one university to another mentions his profitable studies at the law faculty of Bourges; however, at Orleans – another great legal university – the lumpish scholars welcomed him and taught him to play ball.

Theologians flocked to Paris. Juan Martín Cordero tells of his month-long pilgrimage on the back of a mule from Valencia to Barcelona, crossing over the Pyrenees to Lyon; he and his companions rested their mounts there for a few days, and arrived in Paris on 24 September 1550: '... all our countrymen there came to welcome us.' He heard lectures, including Ramus – Pierre de la Ramée – reading Plato's *Republic* in Greek. Two years later, amid rumours of war, Cordero was advised to move to Louvain. On the way, he was seized and thrown into gaol. He made his escape, saw Louvain, travelled to England with a diplomatic mission and witnessed the wedding of the Infante Philip to Mary Tudor. Back on the continent, Cordero lived at Antwerp writing translations for his friend the printer Christopher Plantin. He returned to Valencia only in 1563 – after an absence of thirteen years – took holy orders and was given a parish to take care of, the first step in a successful career.

To study the Greek and Latin classics, students from across Europe crowded the lecture halls of Italy: Bologna and Padua, Siena, Florence, Pisa, Ferrara and Pavia. At some universities, Transalpine students outnumbered Italians. This *peregrinatio* (pilgrimage) reached its height in the early sixteenth century. Salamanca, however, only attracted students from within the Iberian peninsula, including many Portuguese. The other two main Spanish universities – Valladolid and Alcalá – held still less appeal for foreigners. With the Reformation the patterns of scholarly movement changed. Humanism spread northward. Johannes Reuchlin taught Greek and Hebrew at Basel, Ingolstadt and Tübingen. In France, Francis I took the advice of Guillaume Budé and founded the Collège de France (1530), a humanistic centre which spread its doctrine to the other Parisian colleges. Oxford and Cambridge were endowed with chairs of Hebrew, Greek, theology, civil law and medicine. Education towards the bachelor of arts degree embraced philosophy, logic and the classics, and took place in the colleges, which administered examinations; the award of degrees rested with the university itself. It was under the auspices of the university that one progressed to bachelor's and master's degrees in theology, medicine and law.

Louvain was the hub of a revival fostered by Erasmus of Rotterdam, who helped form a college founded there by Cardinal Busleyden for the study of Latin, Greek and Hebrew. Salamanca and Alcalá were to adopt this trilingual pattern later on. Erasmus rose to fame in 1516 on the strength of his Greek edition of the New Testament, in the preface of which he urged students to read Scripture and the word

Anatomical theatre at the University of Padua (1594–95)
The University of Padua was graced by one of the earliest medical buildings still standing today. A hall standing on an oval plan, its six storeys are enclosed by wooden balustrades. Students could listen to their lecturers' explanations and watch him perform a dissection on a table on the ground floor.

of Christ first-hand, not filtered through scholastic writings. Erasmus had already published several influential books: the *Enchiridion Militis Christiani* (1501), the *Adages* (1508) and *In Praise of Folly* (1511). Erasmus satirised the aspects of the Christian religion that he regarded as outdated; he espoused a new form in spirituality, the 'philosophy of Christ', preferring meditation on the Bible to dogma and ceremony. He declined invitations from princes, bishops and other universities. Cardinal Cisneros asked him to Alcalá to assist in editing a huge multilingual Bible. But Erasmus was wary of Spain; he complained in a letter to Thomas More that it was 'full of Jews'.

Neither did he join the court of the young Charles of Habsburg, to whom he had earlier dedicated *Institutio Principis Christiani* (1516). He stayed at Louvain for a period, but got on badly with his scholastic colleagues – Dominicans and friars of other orders who labelled him a Lutheran.

Lucas Cranach the Younger,
The Resurrection of Lazarus
(1558), detail
The core of the Protestant
Reformers are portrayed in
this painting made by Cranach
the Younger for the epitaph of
Michael Meyenburg. The
artist depicts the atmosphere
of Reformist Germany by
constructing a religious
iconography in alignment with
the new state of Christianity.
The figure in the foreground
on the left is Martin Luther; to
his right, Johannes Bugenhagen,
Erasmus of Rotterdam,
Justus Jonas, Caspar Cruciger
and Philip Melanchthon.

*The new philology was recruited in aid of a better
understanding of the Bible, which Luther translated
into German. But the Catholic Church held fast to
the Vulgate Latin version and banned translations
into vernacular languages*

Humanism and Reform

Martin Luther taught theology at the academy of Wittenberg and drew a growing crowd of listeners. Founded by Augustine friars with the aid of Maurice of Saxony, Wittenberg became the first Reformed university. In 1517, Luther nailed to the door of the church his 95 theses: Faith and Grace came from God through Christ, not from indulgences or papal bulls. Luther was condemned by the University of Louvain in November 1519. Erasmus disagreed with Luther, but hoped to prevent a sundering of Christendom. He wrote to Leo X, who, regardless, promulgated a bull in condemnation, *Exsurge Domine* (1520), ordering that Luther and certain books of canon law be burned together at the stake. In Louvain, the theologians attacked Erasmus and demanded that he condemn Luther. Joan Lluís Vives soon decided his position. Erasmus kept in touch with advisers to Charles V and to Maurice of Saxony in a continued bid for reconciliation. He proposed that the points in dispute be submitted to a commission of wise men appointed by the emperor and the kings of England and Hungary. But in his letters he admitted that he had finally lost heart. Luther was heard by Charles V at the Diet of Worms. He was condemned and imprisoned in the castle of Watzburg in Saxony. At the Diet of Augsburg (1530), the Emperor tried to reach agreement with Philip Melanchthon, professor of Greek at Wittenberg, representing Luther. Melanchthon presented to the Emperor the Lutheran credo; again no agreement succeeded, and violence and war ensued. In the end, Charles V was forced to concede the Peace of Augsburg (1555), whereby each German Elector was free to decide which religion he was to impose on his subjects.

As a Reformer, Luther rejected the filtering of theology through a scholastic interpretation of Aristotle. Instead, he advocated that the Bible be studied afresh and on its own merits. The new philology was recruited in aid of a better understanding of the Bible, which Luther translated into German. But the Catholic Church held fast to the Vulgate Latin version and banned translations into vernacular languages. At first Luther mistrusted the universities, viewing them as strongholds of the papacy; he hoped to suppress the doctoral degree in theology altogether. But Melanchthon persuaded him that schools of theology were useful for the spread of doctrine. He got Luther to see that the humanities were an effective support for interpreting Scripture, attaining salvation and performing public office. With the support of German princes, the Reformers disseminated humanism and Reformation, *sapiens et eloquens pietas*. In 1536, Wittenberg was endowed with ten chairs in the arts, but the other faculties were less generously treated – Luther hated jurists and thought of them as bad Christians. The University of Marburg was founded with imperial privileges in 1541 and adopted a similar curriculum. Several universities across the Holy Roman Empire adhered to the Reformation – Tübingen, Frankfurt an der Oder, Rostock, Basel and Leipzig – and attracted a great many foreign scholars. New universities sprung up at Konigsberg, Helmstedt Giessen and Jena. Greifswald, which had been closed for a number of years, reopened in 1539, whereas Copenhagen threw out its Catholic professors and ceased teaching until that same year. A similar process went on at Uppsala until about 1595, when the Swedish ecclesial assembly chose Lutheranism.

Lutheranism spread also to the 'gymnasia' or high schools, which, lacking the rank of universities, could not award degrees. Papally approved degrees were of course now unavailable, but the new universities gained imperial endorsement. Princes gave some of the high schools the power to award degrees. Of special note was the gymnasium of Strasbourg, founded by Johannes Sturm, flourishing with its religious and scientific teachings. It was soon conferring bachelor's and master's degrees in philosophy, and later rose to the status of a university. Other high schools did not get as far; their role was restricted to training the nobility and the upper classes to an intermediate level of learning, much as the Jesuit schools did in the Catholic ambit.

High schools were founded at Zurich, Berne and Lausanne by the Presbyterians on the initiative of Zwingli. The first Presbyterian university was the

academy at Geneva (1559), where, with city patronage, power was wielded by Calvin and his clerics. Lacking imperial endorsement, Geneva did not award degrees but issued certificates of life and doctrine, and these documents gained acceptance in some places. Geneva was organised on a pattern of its own; it had faculties of arts and theology; law and medicine were dealt with by single professorial chairs. The Scots centres of learning also arranged themselves around a faculty of arts under the protection of the city authorities and a council of elders. High schools spread throughout France, such as the academies at Saumur, Sédan and Montauban. After the Massacre of St Bartholomew's Day, Henry IV issued his Edict of Nantes (1598), allowing a limited form of religious freedom. A number of high schools were permitted to award degrees under the Edict. But a century later Louis XIV ended this period of tolerance. Huguenot scholars then emigrated, mainly to the Dutch universities.

The Calvinist universities of Heidelberg and Leiden preserved their traditional features, and theology was less dominant. Leiden was founded in 1575 purportedly in the name of Philip II, who immediately disowned it; the new university adopted the statutes of Louvain as its own. Patronised by the nobility and rich burghers, it attained high prestige, and its tolerance drew many foreign scholars, including Huguenots and Jews. Leiden's degrees were not recognised in Germany or France until much later, however. In

Scotland, the medieval universities of Aberdeen, Glasgow and St Andrews all took up Calvinism, but were later outstripped in prestige by the University of Edinburgh, founded in 1582 by King James VI as an institution dependent upon parliament, which drew up the university's statutes.

In England, the Act of Supremacy of 1534 made Henry VIII head of the Church of England. He assumed power over Oxford and Cambridge, suppressed the ecclesiastical courts, the regular orders and the monasteries, and confiscated their property; he came close to confiscating college property, too. Under Edward VI, the Act of Uniformity introduced the *Book of Common Prayer*. After a short-lived Catholic restoration under Mary, Elizabeth I firmly entrenched the Anglican Church.

Catholic orthodoxy, allied with the emperor and the pope, was upheld by universities old and new. The Counter Reformation was spearheaded by the universities of Rome and Paris, followed by those within Habsburg domains: Alcalá, Cologne, Vienna, Salamanca, Louvain and Coimbra. For their part, Bologna, Padua, Siena, Orleans and Montpellier took up a more tolerant stance. The religious orders suppressed in Protestant countries played a great role in the Counter Reformation. The Benedictines founded Irache and Salzburg. The Dominicans, Franciscans and Augustine friars taught at faculties of arts and theology, as did the Fathers of the Company of Jesus recently created by Ignatius of Loyola. The orders founded

universities of their own, in Spain and the Americas particularly, while the Jesuits also spread across Europe. They attained great influence over those in power, becoming the confessors of kings and princes and opening a vast number of schools in which they trained the children of the nobility and the upper classes. Jesuit teaching methods and set textbooks were governed by the *Ratio Studiorum* (1599), a statute which had its counterpart in Melanchthon's academic laws for Wittenberg and Calvin's rules for Geneva.

In 1537, the main Portuguese university was finally settled at Coimbra. John III tried to endow the university with prestigious lecturers, but many Portuguese students continued to travel to Salamanca and Paris. The Jesuits dominated the Colégio das Artes, the newly founded faculty that acted as a gateway to the major schools. At Evora, the university conferred degrees in the arts and canon law, and several colleges opened their doors.

The Jesuits controlled many schools in France. Some, such as Clermont, Louis le Grand and La Flèche, catered to an aristocratic elite. La Flèche tried to become a university in 1603, in which year Jesuit teachings received the support of the Edict of Rouen enacted by Henry IV. The Jesuits were given a university of their own in Pont-à-Mousson, Lorraine. Elsewhere they controlled professorial chairs or whole faculties. Their expansion was notable in Italy, too; at Messina, the Jesuits controlled the faculties of arts and theology, whereas law remained within the power of the city authority. Later, the city drove out the Jesuits and took over all faculties. The Jesuits were later authorised to award degrees at Milan, Palermo and Mantua. Their college at Rome became the Gregorian University in 1556, and the student body grew larger than that of La Sapienza. The Dominican University of St Thomas was not to be founded until 1727. La Sapienza, the papal university, revived by Leo X, closed down after the sack of Rome in 1527. It was restored by Paul III and entrusted to a congregation of cardinals.

The Jesuits gained influence in the Holy Roman and Austrian Empires. Dominant at the old universities of Cologne, Mainz, Ingolstadt and Freiburg, they founded new ones at Dillingen, Osnabrück, Graz, Paderborn, Innsbruck, Linz and Lemberg. At most of these, the Jesuits directly taught only theology and the arts, but had a general privilege to award degrees granted by Pius IV, and this faculty was later extended to the Americas. In 1611, the Jesuits were given the seminary at Bamberg and turned it into a university. The old University of Prague merged in 1654 with the Jesuit college, whereas the University of Krakow resisted Jesuit influence.

Barriers were thrown up between the competing creeds of Christianity; united Christendom was a thing of the past. Places of learning were divided up by the Reformation and Counter Reformation. Papal power faded, and the Holy Roman Emperor lost ground to local princes and electors, who took on the tutelage of

Willem Boonen, *Parade at Louvain*, in *History of Louvain* (1594), Museum of Louvain, Belgium
Since its founding in the fifteenth century it has been a tradition of the Catholic University of Louvain to mount a procession through the streets of the city at the opening of the academic year. The university's academic authorities would don ceremonial attire and process from the university seat to the church, where a Mass was spoken. Today, the ritual survives, complete with medieval costumes.

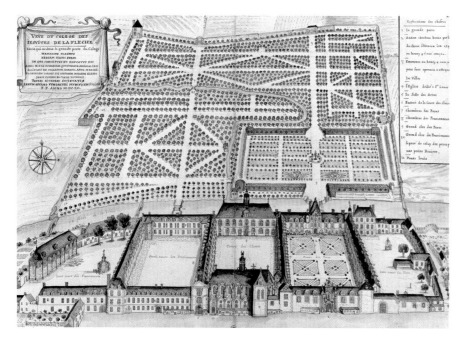

lectures, because all doctors were allowed to give them; unlike in the Middle Ages, Bologna had no eminent professors. Padua became subordinate to a permanent invigilating committee of three Venetian senators. The independence and power of scholars waned and the local Jesuit college competed fiercely until the end of the century, when it was restricted to training Jesuit novices alone. In Catania, the power of the scholars' rector declined. In 1687, his jurisdiction was reassigned to the bishop and chancellor. Later, in Pisa, the rector was replaced by a vice-rector chosen from among professors by the Duke of Tuscany.

In the Holy Roman Empire, electors, princes and bishops founded universities, granting them statutes and privileges. In Protestant regions, this trend found support in the process set in motion by Luther; in Catholic areas potentates patronised Jesuits and Dominicans in the faculties of theology and arts; faculties of law and medicine retained wider independence. City authorities, too, upheld their local universities: the religiously tolerant Basel, and Louvain, created in the Middle Ages by the Duke of Brabant, were dependent on their cities. Leiden was an exemplar of combined sources of power: the rector, with legal jurisdiction, was appointed by the stadholder William of Orange, and was advised by four officials chosen by the faculties and four curators appointed by the city and the province of Holland. All three strata of power were present.

The Spanish universities were not the most distinguished, but Salamanca and Alcalá shone in the Catholic ambit. Enrolment in the Iberian peninsula was high, and the doctrine imparted was fit for its intended purposes: the defence of the faith and the training of the upper echelons of Crown and Church. The Jesuit model of educational organisation spread across the Catholic globe. Eminent Spanish scholars included the Dominican theologian Francisco de Vitoria and the Jesuit Francisco Suárez, and the jurists Diego de Covarrubias and Vázquez de Menchaca. Or should consideration be given only to the founders of modern science, such as Vesalius or Galileo? My concern here is different. An overview of the universities of Europe does not allow for much detail; I have decided to focus on the universities of Spain, which lie closer to my own research.

academic learning and gave it a regional character. Students came from a narrower milieu, cleaving to the local court and its ecclesiastical establishment. City authorities, too, increasingly had a hand in university patronage.

In France, the Church was an appendage of the throne of the 'Most Christian' monarch; this Gallicanism was set up in defiance of Rome. The French kings defended the Catholic faith against the Huguenots (leaving aside the Edict of Nantes). The parliaments of Paris and Toulouse framed university statutes and decision-making and had powers of inspection. The University of Paris claimed to be subject to pope and king alone, but Charles VII subjected its litigations to the French parliament.

Italian universities, too, became subject to princely or republican power. Bologna, dependent on the popes since 1506, now came under the influence of the *riformatori* and the cardinal sent by the pope as the university's protector. Towards the mid-sixteenth century, a higher decision-making body, the *Assunteria di studio*, was established, formed by four senators. The rectorate was suppressed in 1607, and its functions went to the prior of each university 'nation' by turns. The colleges of doctors managed academic affairs. The decline in the standard of Bologna's lectures and degrees was visible: too many

From Ferdinand and Isabella to Philip II

The fifteenth and sixteenth centuries saw the rise of the powerful Spanish dynasty of the Habsburgs. Aragon and Castile, united by the marriage of Kings Ferdinand and Isabella, grew with the conquests of Granada and Naples and later gained an empire in the New World. When Isabella died, Castile came under the rule of her daughter Joan, married to the short-lived Philip of Habsburg. Ferdinand, who had retired to his Aragonese estates, came back as regent and conquered Navarre, exploiting the papal excommunication of its reigning couple, Catherine of Foix and John of Albret. Charles, the Catholic monarchs' grandson, inherited all these kingdoms, as well as his paternal legacy: the Austrian Empire of Maximilian of Habsburg and, through Maximilian's wife Mary, Burgundy. In 1520, Charles was crowned Holy Roman Emperor at Aachen. At his death, he left Austria to his brother Ferdinand – elected Holy Roman Emperor – and the rest of his possessions, including Flanders and Milan, to his son Philip II, who later annexed Portugal and won the Philippines.

Ferdinand and Isabella enjoyed a privilege of Church patronage granted by Alexander VI and other pontiffs, which, in 'the Indies', was universal, these being lands Spain had won for Christendom. So the Catholic monarchs could appoint bishops, give prebends, and play a role in university governance. As early as March 1475, they had sent to Salamanca a *corregidor* to demand that the university swear allegiance. The Crown asked Salamanca for a loan of 100,000 *maravedis*, which would have been hard to pay back. The institution no longer functioned as a corporation of doctors and scholars. Pope Martin V had created 'deputies', seeking a balance between professors and students. The assembly no longer met, not even to elect deputies. Instead, they were appointed by outgoing deputies, as in the election of rector and councillors. As there was usually a lack of agreement, under the university's constitution the decision fell to the rector and the *maestrescuela*. To resolve disputes, the governing bodies would meet, the rector and councillors on the one hand and the deputies on the other; the college of doctors was sometimes convened. But the assembly ceased to be convoked at all. Students only ever congregated in the cathedral to swear allegiance to the new rector or for special events. On 15 June 1479, after a Mass for the Holy Ghost, with the sermon *Nolite sapere plus quam oportet*, the canon law books of Pedro de Osma, condemned by the archbishop of Toledo, were burned in front of the 'major schools'.

The Catholic monarchs asked Sixtus IV to appoint as chancellor Gutierre Álvarez de Toledo, the sixteen-year-old son of the Duke of Alba, overriding the candidate chosen by the university deputies. Thereafter, the royally appointed *maestrescuela* or chancellor was typically a churchman from a great noble house – sometimes illegitimate – who delegated his duties to a vice-chancellor. Under the law known as the *Concordia de Santa Fe* of 1492, the Catholic monarchs widened the chancellor's jurisdiction.

In the autumn of 1479 plague drove the rector and several professors away from Salamanca. Replacement lecturers fell to be appointed; if none were found, lectures were to be given by students. On the day, two rectoral candidates took an oath in the cathedral. But Ferdinand and Isabella ordered that both be struck out and sent Tello de Buendía to resolve the resulting 'schism' of rectors. At a meeting of university doctors he decided that the chancellor, the *primicer* and the two longest-serving professors appoint new councillors. Absent the *primicer*, his place was filled by Buendía himself. The newly elected councillors in turn chose the new rector, invested in the cathedral before the gathering of scholars. Even on this occasion the assembly was not convened. In 1512, Ferdinand, on the pretext of some trivial breach, sent another inspector, Diego Ramírez de Villaescusa, who wanted rector and deputies to be appointed by royal officials, and to limit professorial tenure to a finite term. He suggested that judicial decisions of the *maestrescuela* be subject to appeal to the bishop. If these rules had been adopted, the old university's independence would have perished.

The Catholic monarchs were behind the creation of the Spanish Inquisition, endorsed by a bull of Pope

Sixtus IV in 1478. The Inquisition was directed against witchcraft and superstition, 'dishonest conduct' and converted Jews suspected of practising their old creed in secret after the expulsions of 1492; it oversaw the universities, too. The Jewish physician Abraham Zacut exiled himself to Portugal, where he was protected by John II and wrote *Almanach Perpetuum*. The Portuguese explorer Vasco da Gama used Zacut's tables and his own adapted astrolabe. The governing bodies of the Spanish universities made some attempts to apply the statute of *limpieza de sangre* against the descendants of Moors and Jews, but Philip II stymied this initiative. The statute did prevail in colleges, in the military, in the regular orders and in the cathedrals, but, other than at Osuna, not at the universities.

The Valencian humanist Joan Lluís Vives, a 'new Christian', left at a young age for Paris and Louvain. In exile he learned of the destruction of his family: his father burned at the stake; his dead mother's body exhumed and burned. Years later the University of Alcalá offered him *cathedra*, which he declined. At the Valencia medical faculty the surgeon Lluís Alcanys was tried along with other *conversos* and sentenced to burn. The professor of surgery Jaume Torres was luckier: he simply had his property confiscated, and his daughter had to sell his library at public auction.

In 1529, Charles V sent to Salamanca two inspectors who deposed and banished the rector, Pedro García Lagasca (later viceroy of Peru). In his place they appointed Hernán Pérez de Oliva; they looked for an order to exclude college members, canons, cathedral stipendiaries, clergymen in general and professors from office as rector or councillor. But the university's ecclesiastical oligarchy successfully held out. Reform was not achieved until the statutes of 1538, which did exclude them from power. The new statutes regulated the full congregation or *claustro pleno*, a supreme power that consolidated the three existing bodies, councillors and deputies with professors, doctors, graduates and bachelors, presided over by the rector and the chancellor. Doctors and professors enjoyed a majority to decide upon the largest issues, such as relations with the king or adoption of new statutes. The emperor enacted statutes for the *studium generale* at Valladolid. This university,

being subject to royal patronage, was inspected by Valtodano (1567) and Contreras (1612). In the late sixteenth century, when the diocese was created, the chancellor became the bishop; the rector had jurisdiction over masters, scholars and officials; behind his authority lay papal and royal power. A master, doctor or licentiate, he had to be unmarried, a layman and aged twenty-five or over, and was appointed yearly by lot among three men nominated by the outgoing rector, chancellor and deputies. After Valtodano's reform, the College of Santa Cruz tried to restrict the drawing of lots to only two candidates, one being named by the College. Contreras entrusted the election of rector to the Council of Castile, which chose among six candidates designated by chancellor, college and assembly – each authority could nominate two men. The rector's term was extended to two years.

The governing bodies of Valladolid resembled those of Salamanca. The council of rector and councillors endowed chairs and handled academic matters, but the appointment of a new rector and councilmen – up to seven – lay, respectively, with the College of Santa Cruz and the deputies, of whom there were twelve, six being professors and six being elected by the general assembly. A claustrum of professors managed and allocated university tithes, divided into twenty-three portions or *millares*. Eighteen and a half portions went on the varying pay of the twelve perpetual professors, while the rest – 4.5 *millares* – was set aside to pay for temporary chairs, official expenses and other costs.

Philip II, a consummate bureaucrat, continued to send inspectors to Salamanca. Upon welcoming one of them, the rector wryly said, 'This shows that Your Majesty had not forgotten us, for you do us a signal honour in keeping us in remembrance by sending for us to be visited.' Noteworthy visitors were Diego Covarrubias in 1561 and Juan de Zúñiga in 1594. The resulting statutes enshrined the claustrum model, which, with few changes, endured for centuries. The original assembly of doctors and students was replaced by the general congregation.

College of San Gregorio, Valladolid

The College of San Gregorio was founded and built in the late fifteenth century. Architecturally, the building typifies the era of Ferdinand and Isabella, in which the medieval style coexisted with an incipient Renaissance. In the nineteenth century, the building was abandoned as a result of the expropriation of ecclesiastical lands. In 1933, the college became the National Museum of Sculpture, and to this day houses major exemplars of Spanish processional sculpture.

There were many colleges in Spain, 'major' and 'minor'. Bishops and higher clergy laid out big sums to found houses for the benefit of poorer students. The first colegio mayor, *San Bartolomé, was built in 1401 by Diego de Anaya, bishop of Salamanca*

CERVANTES AND THE UNIVERSITY IN SPAIN'S GOLDEN AGE

Cervantes was born not in Salamanca but in the university city of Alcalá de Henares in 1547. But he did have ties to the city on the River Tormes: his paternal grandfather Juan studied there in the closing decade of the fifteenth century and graduated as a 'licentiate of law'. Cervantes's father, Rodrigo, a well-known but down-at-heel petty nobleman or *hidalgo*, was also a native of Alcalá, born there in 1509, soon after Cardinal Cisneros's university was founded. He practised as a rudimentarily trained surgeon. The Cervantes family left Alcalá in 1551, when Miguel was barely four years old. And the future writer was to invoke his university and student-inspired sentimental 'homeland' of early childhood, not by the name of his native Alcalá, but as the legendary Salamanca. He may have imagined his grandfather Juan de Cervantes' Salamanca, haloed by the inherited lore of a family that had seen better times.

The Cervantes household wandered across Spain. In 1564, when Miguel was eighteen, they settled in Seville. This fact, combined with certain references in *The Dialogue of the Dogs*, has suggested to some that Cervantes went to the city's Jesuit school. This quiet period lasted only two years. From 1566 to 1569, the Cervantes family lived in Madrid. It appears that here Miguel attended the *Estudio de la Villa*, a sort of municipal school were he would have been a pupil of the grammarian Juan López de Hoyos, who had been influenced by Erasmus. Not much to talk about there, then. In late 1569, after some imbroglio involving a duel, Cervantes skipped town. His patchy education had come to an end.

So he did not, as has sometimes been assumed, undergo formal academic training. Cervantes, unlike the Golden Age writers Góngora, Calderón or Quevedo, does not seem to have gone to university at Salamanca or Alcalá; he must be regarded as an autodidact, albeit with a humanistic bent and a love of books. All the same, Salamanca was a literary talisman and an object of intellectual fascination for Cervantes throughout his oeuvre.

Salamanca is mentioned in several chapters of *Don Quixote*, more often in the second part than in the first. In chapter 12 of the first part, the shepherd Chrysostom turns out to have been a student at Salamanca. In chapter 39, the Tale of the Captive, another Salamanca scholar makes an appearance.

Manuscript room, library of the University of Salamanca (16th century)
The library of the University of Salamanca holds over 3,000 manuscripts. Most of these documents are the outcome of the university's acquisitions policy; many are private gifts and bequests, and others are the legacy of other institutions, such as the *colegios mayores*.

In part II, chapter 1, the complex gradations of the University of Osuna make a ridiculous counterpoint to those of Salamanca. In chapter 2, the bachelor Samson Carrasco, recently arrived from the city on the Tormes, enters the story. In chapter 7, Carrasco silences the housekeeper with 'Don't set yourself to argue with me, for you know I am a bachelor of Salamanca, and one can't be more of a bachelor than that'. This same boast is repeated in chapter 10. In chapter 16, the son of the Knight of the Green Riding-Coat is said to have studied six years' worth of Latin and Greek at Salamanca. Later, in chapter 18, Salamanca is claimed to be the equal of Paris and Bologna. In chapter 19, Sancho apologises for not having trained at Salamanca, and a character appears who turns out to be a Salmantine licentiate of canon law. In chapter 33, the claim is advanced that a bachelor of Salamanca cannot tell a lie. And, in chapter 66, the heightened chances of Salamanca scholars gaining lay and ecclesiastical preferment is made much of. All this is contained in the second part of *Don Quixote*, published in 1615. But Salamanca students are everywhere in Cervantes's oeuvre. The most famous is of course the bachelor Samson Carrasco in *Don Quixote* itself; there are many others, though. For instance, Tomás Rodaja, the hero of *The Lawyer of Glass*, and, in *The Illustrious Kitchen-Maid*, Tomás de Avendaño, who had schooled in the classics at Salamanca for three years as a boy. Then, with his fellow student Diego de Carriazo, he carries on his studies until his plans go awry and he takes up adventuring instead. And then, of course, there is the famous theatrical sketch *The Cave of Salamanca*, with its prototypical student, on this occasion an initiate in the magical arts.

Cervantes apparently viewed study as a form of social climbing and attainment of position. Don Quixote asserts that 'letters… founded more great houses than arms' (*Don Quixote*, II, chapter 24). The reference to 'letters' really meant the study of law. It was jurisprudence that could elevate a student to 'govern the world', despite the travails and uncertainties of the road ahead. This idea underlies the contest of 'arms and letters' in chapters 37 and 38 of part I of *Don Quixote*.

Several unnamed students cross paths with Don Alonso Quijano. They appear as companions of the 'dead body' in chapter 19 and among the forced galley slaves in chapter 22 of the first part of *Don Quixote*. Having their sons take degrees and rise in the world turns out to be the aspiration of many social classes, ranging from gentlemen like the Knight of the Green Riding-Coat to common ploughmen. Throughout his works Cervantes often evokes the 'glory and quietude' of academic life. This was a life he most likely never lived; he imagined it by dint of aspiration only, and from what he may have heard of his grandfather, Juan de Cervantes, a master of law of the University of Salamanca, that institution which is 'always praised, but never as much as it should be'.

Luis E. Rodríguez-San Pedro Bezares

Juan de Jáuregui y Aguilar, *Portrait of Miguel de Cervantes* **(1600)**
Cervantes' literary career started in 1567 when he published a sonnet. The fame of his novel *Don Quixote* aided the spread of the Spanish language itself, also known as 'the language of Cervantes'.

Unlike Góngora, Calderón or Quevedo, Cervantes does not seem to have gone to university; he must have been an autodidact. But Salamanca was a literary touchstone and object of intellectual fascination throughout his oeuvre

EL INGENIOSO
HIDALGO DON QVI-
XOTE DE LA MANCHA,

Compuesto por Miguel de Cervantes
Saauedra.

DIRIGIDO AL DVQVE DE BEIAR,
Marques de Gibraleon, Conde de Benalcaçar, y Baña-
res, Vizconde de la Puebla de Alcozer, Señor de
las villas de Capilla, Curiel, y
Burguillos.

Año, 1605.

CON PRIVILEGIO,
EN MADRID, Por Iuan de la Cuesta.

Vendese en casa de Francisco de Robles, librero del Rey nro señor.

First edition of *The Ingenious Gentleman Don Quixote of La Mancha*, Madrid (1605)
Don Quixote was first printed at the workshop of Juan de la Cuesta on 16 January 1605, and sold in the form of separate fascicles at the bookshop of Francisco Fernando de Robles. Ten years later, the second part of the novel was published, proving one of the most influential in modern literature.

Newly Founded Universities

Spain's population had grown, but university lecture halls were open only to a few. The high aristocracy swore off university – their avocation was war. Juan de Valdés, in his *Diálogo de la lengua*, encourages a nobleman to read: 'Have you not heard that letters do not blunt the spear?' It was not aristocratic practice to go to university. The Count-Duke of Olivares, upon the death of his brother, inherited his family's estates and left his studies. At Salamanca, the scholars' roll listed noblemen, collegers and commoners separately: those classed as 'noblemen' were in fact younger sons and petty gentry seeking jobs in the service of the crown and the Church. At the other end of the social arch, study was not a thing to interest labourers and artisans, or even scriveners and notaries, who learned their trade by practice – although Bologna did teach a notaries' course and Valencia endowed a short-lived chair at the city's notarial college.

Universities were aimed chiefly at clergymen, who filled the faculties of theology and canon law, aspiring to office in the Church and the royal bureaucracy, and also drew budding lawmen and physicians, the bulk of medical practice then resting with mere barbers and medical trainees. Degrees were a promising route for petty gentlemen and professionals' and rich burghers' sons after a placement in royal service, whether in Spain, Italy or the Americas.

The king needed graduates to man the scaffolding of power – the network of councils that did the business of government for his remote possessions. The Council of State drew together leading noblemen, soldiers and bishops; other councils were dominated by lawmen, canon lawyers and theologians. The king employed advocates and notaries, barristers and procurators in his chancelleries and courts. His viceroys and military *corregidores* also needed jurists; the high nobility wanted trained lawmen to administer their estates. So many graduates found jobs, but most were mere bachelors of law who vainly boasted of licentiate standing. Physicians, too, were in demand, under the supervision of the *Protomedicato,* of the king's physicians. Surgeons were indispensable in the army.

Theologians were called on to preserve the faith, keeping the monarch within orthodoxy and doing his bidding at ecclesiastical councils, bishoprics, cathedrals and parishes.

In the mid-fifteenth century there were only half a dozen *studia generalia*, but by the seventeenth century a further thirty universities existed on the Spanish mainland. The king could not afford to found, build and maintain new Salamancas. Royal income was sucked dry by the army and the bureaucracy, court expenses, interest on borrowings and *juros* (bonds). Few centres of learning were funded by the crown. Charles V convened a council of notables in Granada and granted surplus tithe income to build a foster home for *morisco* children and a college and university to train clergymen to shepherd the Muslims forced to convert some years before. Endorsed by Clement VII in 1531, the university was entrusted to the archbishop, but the pressure of the academic assemblies and royal inspectors restored some balance. A similar plan underlay the universities of Mexico and Lima, chartered in 1551 by the future Philip II. The founding statutes pointed to Salamanca as their model, but they were organised differently, having no equivalent of Salamanca's powerful *maestrescuela*. The archbishop was chancellor, while legal jurisdiction – granted later – rested with the rectors. Only exceptionally was the rector a student; mostly he was a doctor or judicial *oidor*. In the following centuries, the Habsburgs and then the Bourbons founded a further thirty universities across the Spanish Americas.

The crown of Aragon could create *studia generalia* at no cost to itself by following the old model of the University of Lérida, where city dignitaries provided most of the funds. The formula was used at Huesca in the fourteenth century and later at Gerona and Barcelona, though both institutions were slow to open their doors. In the sixteenth century, centres of learning opened in Valencia and Vic. This city-funded formula did not find favour in Castile: aristocratically dominated city authorities were unimpressed by universities.

The *consell general* and *jurados* ('juries') of Valencia founded a university in 1499, endorsed by the bull *Inter Ceteras Felicitates* (1501) of Alexander VI Borgia, former bishop of Valencia. The next year, the university was chartered by King Ferdinand. The city funded the institution and became its trustee; it exercised governance and annually appointed the rector, professors and examiners. The archbishop of Valencia was the chancellor and awarded degrees. Professors and masters played no real role in governance, and students even less so. In 1585, Sixtus V made reforms favouring ecclesiastical power: the rector was to be a cathedral canon named by the city for a three-year term. A new *claustro mayor* adopted and implemented the university's rules or constitutions. Members included the *jurados* and other city officials, and the chancellor, rector and two canons regular.

Universities also increased in number by the founding of colleges. The college was an institution that had proliferated at Oxford, Cambridge and Paris; it served as a lodging-house for professors and students and took on a major share of teaching. In some German universities, colleges were set aside to accommodate professors alone, such as at the Collegium Carolinum in Prague, the Ducale in Vienna, and the three colleges at Krakow in Poland, *Maius, Minus* and *Juridicum*. In 1364, Cardinal Gil de Albornoz founded the College of St Clement of the Spaniards at Bologna. Having no teaching functions, it was intended to harbour impoverished Spanish students.

Giorgio Vasari, Clement VII Conversing with Charles V (1560) Relations between the emperor and the pope went through a succession of alliances and clashes in their struggle for European hegemony. Charles V and Clement VII engaged in protracted negotiations, such as the talks in 1530 at Bologna on the occasion of the Emperor's coronation by the Pope.

Colleges were rare in Italy, but there were some: seven at Pavia, eight at Bologna and twelve at Padua, for example.

There were many colleges in Spain, 'major' and 'minor'. Bishops and higher clergy laid out big sums to found houses for the benefit of poorer students. In the fourteenth century, Santa Maria opened in Lérida and Pan y Carbón at Salamanca. The first *colegio mayor*, San Bartolomé, was built in 1401 by Diego de Anaya, bishop of Salamanca. Anaya, a former tutor to the children of John II, had discharged various duties for his monarch: he had presided over the council of Castile, brokered the surrender of the Antipope Benedict XIII and attended the Council of Constance which ended the schism. Later there were founded three 'major colleges' at Salamanca – Cuenca, Oviedo and Fonseca – and the colleges of Santa Cruz in Valladolid and of San Ildefonso in Alcalá. Only this last played any role in teaching. At Salamanca, some colleges gave lessons, or even purported to award degrees; the university successfully resisted these pretensions. Thereafter, colleges were confined to hosting ceremonies and reviews and became privileged halls of residence, a nursery for academics and senior bureaucrats. They forgot their charitable role and catered to the scions of the nobility and former graduates. The convents provided board and a place to study for monks and friars, who reigned over the faculties of theology and philosophy; the residents of the *colegios mayores* were more inclined to law and canon law. The rest of the students – known as *manteístas*, 'commoners' – lodged on pupillage terms with 'companies', or in private homes, under the eye of the rector and chancellor.

The minor colleges obeyed a simple pattern. Pan y Carbón at Salamanca, under its first statutes, was home to six paupers, students of canon law hailing from the diocese of Oviedo or, failing this, Palencia or Toledo. The college rector was chosen by the rector of the university and the *Decretals* professor of canon law. Absent agreement, the decision fell to the bishop. The college rector handled the institution's property, paying out a quarterly allowance to each lodger, and using the rest to defray collective expenses. The scholars of the minor college of Oviedo or of the archbishop of Toledo, Alonso Carrillo, eight

canon law students and four theology students, elected a rector and two councillors every year. Carrillo was described by Fernando del Pulgar as a warm and generous man who nonetheless was 'belligerent, and accordingly it pleased him to go about with men-at-arms and get embroiled in wars and battles.' Carrillo was reputedly a keen treasure-hunter and sponsored alchemical experiments in search of riches.

The statutes of the college of San Bartolomé made for a more complex form of organisation. A rich college with a large membership and high ambitions, its fifteen scholars – jurists and theologians native to Castile – already held bachelor's degrees. After completing their 'licentiatures' and their doctorates they hoped to win a chair, and thence climb to high positions in royal or ecclesiastical service. The collegers wore a brown habit and a scholar's ribbon. They elected the college rector and three councillors, and employed a large staff: chaplains, familiars, a quartermaster, a procurator, a treasurer, a cook. Like other *colegios mayores*, San Bartolomé was subject to the statute of 'cleanliness of blood'.

More interesting were the colleges that became universities in cities where formerly there were none. Having begun to teach, they would apply to the pope for a power to confer degrees. The first such university college was Sigüenza, founded by the archdeacon Juan López de Medina at the College of San Antonio de Portacoeli under a bull of Innocent VIII in 1489. Under papal and royal protection, the founder himself was the college patron. Upon his death, patronage passed to two holders, one appointed by the cathedral and the other by the Hieronymite prior. They saw to it that the statutes and scholarly order were abided by, and could appoint three professors, each with a canonship attached. Administrative duties were entrusted to the college rector and two councillors, elected by and among the college's thirteen scholars. These academics ran competitive examinations for professorial chairs and handled other administrative matters. But not all university colleges followed such a hierarchical scheme.

Most notable of all was the Colegio Mayor de San Ildefonso, the seat and soul of the University of Alcalá. It was built by Francisco Ximénez de Cisneros, Cardinal of Toledo, and in 1499 Alexander VI licensed it to teach and award degrees. Its statutes were drawn in 1510, well after the university had opened, endorsed by Julius II and confirmed by Queen Joan of Castile.

Cisneros tried to keep the college independent, but failed. His statutes called on the king's protection on the grounds that a 'prince' must succour his people, and all the more 'those whose love of wisdom drives them to poverty and calamities, all for the sake of salvation'. The other protectors were the archbishop of Toledo and the Duke of Infantado: if time or mismanagement should diminish the college's wealth, or if it should come under violent attack, it was to resort first to these lesser patrons and only in the last instance to the king. The chancellor was the abbot of the church of St Justo and St Pastor; a canon of this church was to inspect the college annually. In 1555, Charles V, on learning that the statutes had been breached, sent the bishop of Segovia, Gaspar de Zúñiga, and from then on the college received royal inspectors regularly, Juan de Ovando in 1565 and García Medrano a century later.

Alcalá aped Paris as a university of several colleges, all ultimately subject to the rector, members and income of the College of San Ildefonso. This *colegio mayor* accommodated thirty-three members – in honour of the age of Christ – who annually elected a rector and three councillors from among their number on the Eve of St Luke. The rector had jurisdiction over college and university members in civil and criminal matters, holding both ordinary and papal mandates – under the *Concordia de Santa Fe*. This vast responsibility generally devolved upon a young man in his twenties. College members themselves ran admissions to the institution. One had to be at least twenty, a pauper, a student of arts or theology, not a native of Alcalá, unmarried, and not a monk or friar. Admissions officers first scrutinized a candidate's way of life and general aptness. Later, under the statute of 'cleanliness of blood', they would make detailed genealogical inquiries. Chaplains and orderlies were appointed, while rector and councillors took in *porcionistas*, paying commoners, and retained a notary and a *receptor*, who managed the college's cash and kept its accounts, accountable to the rector and collegers.

Professors and doctors of Alcalá were fairly powerless. The statutes prescribed that the University appoint three councillors who, with the two other collegial councillors, would manage teaching and endow chairs, subject to a student vote. After the Zúñiga reform, there came into being the full congregation of professors and doctors. San Ildefonso led a cluster of minor colleges that lodged scholars upon the sufferance of the rector: the colleges of Madre de Dios for theology students, San Pedro y San Pablo for Franciscan friars, Santa Catalina for philosophers, Santa Balbina for logicians, and San Eugenio and San Isidoro for grammarians and students of Greek.

Cisneros's collegial model spread throughout Castile, but not to Aragon or the Americas. A bull issued by Julius II in 1505 authorised the canon Rodrigo Fernández de Santaella to build the college of Santa María de Jesús in Seville. In Santiago de Compostela, archbishop Fonseca established a college backed by the Count of Monterrey. Royal intervention on behalf of the college's lecturers gave the institution its own governing body. The college of Toledo, founded by the cathedral's *maestrescuela*, won sanction to award degrees in 1520. A university also flowered at Osuna from 1548 onwards, founded by Don Juan Téllez de Girón, fourth Count of Ureña, who retained decision-making power. Similar institutions were set up at Baeza, Oñate, Burgo de Osma and Oviedo. Philip III, upon chartering the Oviedo college in 1604, said there were too many places of learning; but they continued to multiply in the Americas, where convents and religious schools gained university status.

Members of religious orders commonly took their degrees at Salamanca or Alcalá, gained professorial tenure in the arts and theology, and taught in the tradition of the scholastic schools: Thomist, Scotist, nominalist, Jesuit, etc. They also sought to found universities of their own. A college-based university, even a much smaller affair than Alcalá, required a big outlay. It was easier to adapt an existing monastery or a convent, which already had the buildings and taught philosophy and theology. Degrees from these universities were more readily awarded and less costly, attracting a large number of students. At the Jesuit University of Gandía, two or three degrees could be had in a couple of days. This academic

Ceremony at the University of Alcalá (19th century)
From their beginnings, the universities have cultivated ceremony to reinforce their institutional prestige. Fixtures such as the start of the academic year, the appointment of new doctoral graduates and other events of academic life have been clothed in rites and formulas that purport to sustain a university spirit. Many of these traditions still survive, and it is not unusual to see an academic ceremony decked in the paraphernalia of a bygone age.

Most notable of all university colleges was the Colegio Mayor de San Ildefonso, the seat and soul of the University of Alcalá. It was built by Francisco Ximénez de Cisneros, Cardinal of Toledo. Its statutes were drawn 1510

'fugue' was far removed from the tradition of scholarly peregrinations. Orleans and Bourges, too, got into the business of 'selling' cheap degrees. High schools with no power to award degrees further encouraged this trend.

Religious orders began to found academic institutions early on. Around 1517, the archbishop of Seville, the Dominican Diego de Deza, got papal blessing to award degrees at the convent of Santo Tomás for the benefit of Dominican and other friars. In 1539, Paul III allowed the institution to give degrees even to secular clergy and laymen; this was later restricted again to Dominican scholars only. In 1534 did the Benedictines of Sahagun get powers from Clement VI to teach and award degrees at their monastery. The faculty moved to the monastery of Santa María la Real at Irache in Navarre. The Dominicans won bulls to confer degrees at Almagro (1550), Tortosa (1551), Orihuela (1552), Ávila (1576), Solsona (1614) and Pamplona (1621). Teaching took place at the convent itself or an adjacent building under the supervision of the prior; philosophy and theology teachers were friars. Most universities were of this kind in the Spanish Americas and the Philippines.

At Almagro, the Dominicans made an unusual alliance with the military order of Calatrava. Founded by Fernando de Córdoba, a knight of the order and head of its council, the college was chartered by Julius III in 1550 and by Charles V in 1553, but took another fifty years to open its doors. The order of Calatrava exercised an outward power in the name of the king, the honorary master of the order, adopting statutes and sending inspectors. Adjoining the convent there was established a college which granted scholarships to Dominican friars and priests of Calatrava. The prior was the chancellor and rector of the university and college; he had disciplinary powers, but his jurisdiction was narrower than that of his counterparts at Salamanca or Valladolid. He was assisted by two councillors, a Dominican friar and a layman. College members were powerless; professors appointed by the Dominican provincial taught unpaid. The priest-dominated assembly of masters fulfilled certain functions of governance.

Orihuela followed a more complex pattern. It was founded by the archbishop of Valencia, Fernando de Loaces, a lawyer and theologian who after study at Paris and Pavia took a doctorate. After its endorsement by Julius III in 1553, construction was begun of the costly college and university buildings. The institution opened fifty years later, and its royal charter was delayed until 1646 by disputes between the city and the cathedral and the opposition of the nearby university of Valencia. Abutting the Dominican convent there was built a college for twenty Dominican scholars on full board under the authority of the general of the order and of the provincial for Aragon. The college rector and chancellor – a single officer – and his councillors were elected for two-year terms by the lecturers. The university's own rector was a cathedral canon appointed by the assembly of doctors. The chairs of theology, arts and grammar, held by Dominicans, lay at the discretion of college rector and councillors. Other chairs, funded by the city, were appointed by the assembly of doctors, with some intervention by city officials, the two rectors and a college representative.

On the Iberian mainland, the Jesuits had two universities, Evora and Gandía. On Majorca there was a municipal university under a fifteenth-century grant, but it was closed to students for long periods. In the seventeenth century, the Jesuits were allowed to grant degrees until the old town-funded university should reopen. Gandía was promoted by Francisco de Borja, who entrusted to the Jesuits the college of San Sebastian for neophyte *morisco* children. He gave away land and a pension levied on the barony of Corvera, added by his wife with other contributions. Later, the Jesuits amassed vast wealth on the strength of legacies, gifts and transactions. Given the tithes of Denia, granted by the pope for *morisco* children, the money was later released from that purpose because the intended beneficiaries were 'vile, fruitless people'. The college, endorsed by Paul III in 1547 and by Charles V in 1550, was hierarchical: a rector, appointed by the general of the order, managed administrative and disciplinary matters and appointed and removed professors, but not the collegiate church canons, who taught for their probends. He awarded degrees, also being chancellor, and amended the statutes, assisted by two councillors chosen by himself, subject to inspection by the Jesuit provincial.

Isolation and Closure in Europe

The European academic world was split among the various creeds, and many universities denied enrolment or graduation to anyone who fell short of religious requirements. Geneva demanded that entrants sign a profession of faith, but from 1576 onwards this was required only of lecturers. In Germany and Scandinavia, it was mandatory to adhere to the Augsburg Confession. Much the same was true in England: Oxford barred from matriculation anyone who refused to accept Anglican doctrine, and Cambridge applied this rule to graduands. Charles II tried to remove this stricture, and James II, the last Stuart, opened the universities to Catholics: the measure was short-lived. The Presbyterian Scottish universities did not admit 'papists', but were willing to take in foreign Protestants who accepted the Westminster Confession of Faith, a Calvinist credo embraced by Scottish Presbyterianism in 1647.

After the breakup of time-honoured Christian unity, the popes had no role to play at Protestant universities, and even in the Catholic institutions, owing to the growing power of the monarchs, their importance was on the wane. The emperor lost ground to the German electors and princes. A dispute between the emperor Charles V and Pope Clement VII culminated with the sack of Rome. Alfonso de Valdés, an adviser to Charles V, in *Diálogo de Mercurio y Carón*, said this was 'done more by the just judgment of God than by the strength or will of men'. He blamed the pope, who, in alliance with the king of France, 'resolved to disturb Christendom'. Vives wrote to Erasmus: 'Christ has given to our time the most beautiful opportunity for salvation by the most brilliant victories of the emperor and thanks to the captivity of the pope.' Months earlier he had predicted the loss of the Holy City.

In 1545, backed by the emperor and the monarchs of Catholic Europe, Paul III gathered a huge council at Trent. Over a series of sessions up to 1563, the Council of Trent reformed the Church, defined beliefs and dogmas, restored discipline. Besides its direct impact on theology, its effect on universities was seen in the graduation oath and the drawing up of indices of banned books.

The bull *In Sacrosancta* (1564) issued by Pius IV introduced the oath of orthodoxy – the Credo – to exclude Protestants from graduation. At a late Valencian ceremonial book graduands had to swear that they believed in a single God, the Creator of Heaven and Earth and of all things visible and invisible, that they believed in Jesus Christ, His only Son, the Virgin Mary, the Church, and the Gospels. Louvain required an oath upon matriculation. At Valencia, as at Paris, lecturers and graduates swore to teach and defend the mystery of the Immaculate Conception of Mary.

Bologna, Padua and other Italian universities were more tolerant, and continued to attract many foreign students, from Germany and other countries. Bologna gave them privileges and Padua won from the Venetian doge an immunity that prevented the Inquisition from prosecuting its students; this was the rule that Galileo relied on to fend off the early charges against him. Venice was later to set up a special examination tribunal which required no oath. Enrolment nonetheless declined. Lectures went unattended and students prepared for degrees with private tutors. The Jews, formerly barred from taking degrees, got papal dispensations and graduated at Padua and Siena. The Dutch universities – Leiden, Groningen, Franeker, and Utrecht – were also very open.

In 1558, the Spanish Inquisitor General Fernando de Valdés presided over a trial of followers of Erasmus and Luther in Seville and Valladolid. From his retirement at the monastery of Yuste, Charles V called for an exemplary punishment, and many of those convicted were burned at the stake. The archbishop of Toledo, Bartolomé de Carranza, underwent a long trial that ended only at Rome. There was a panic that the Church would be infiltrated by heresy. Valdés, in a letter to the pope, said his predecessors had had no real experience of 'Lutheran error'. Trials were common, but punishment abated: Juan de Vergara, a disciple of Erasmus and a professor at Alcalá, was made publicly to forswear in Toledo's plaza de Zocodover; he then paid a fine and was sent to a monastery. In 1559, Philip II banned Castilians from studying abroad. His reasoning was that his kingdoms already contained many famous universities where all the arts and sciences were taught. Foreign study was risky and drove coin out of the country. A Castilian was restricted to study at Coimbra, the kingdoms of Aragon, Catalonia and Valencia, and the Spanish college at Bologna, at Rome and Naples. Later, study was allowed at some of the other Italian universities, such as Pisa, requiring an oath of orthodoxy and of fidelity to the Duke of Tuscany. Louvain was off bounds because an Inquisition report detected some suspect Spanish scholars there. Similar rules designed to close down foreign study were passed in Portugal, Poland, Brandenburg and France, by the ordinances of Henry II of Orleans (1561) and Blois (1579). Looser rules were introduced in Austria, Bavaria and Sweden. Isolation became the norm, with each country preserving its universities to secure the orthodoxy of the national clergy and the king's subjects.

Academic study was impaired by the indices of prohibited books drawn up at the Council of Trent. The first indices were issued in 1557 and 1559 by Paul IV. The index of Pius V, begun at the 18th session of Trent, was unfinished. Session 25 of the Council resolved that the list be commended to the pope, who sanctioned it in his bull *Dominici Gregis* (1564). The long series of papal indices continued right up until only fifty years ago. The practice may have been discontinued only because prohibiting an author augmented his fame. André Gide and Jean Paul Sartre were among the last authors indexed (both won the Nobel Prize; Sartre refused to pick it up).

Even before the papal index other European rulers had issued literary bans. Charles V commissioned an index from the University of Louvain (1546) that inspired the first Spanish indices from 1551 onwards. The inquisitor Valdés made a catalogue of prohibited editions of the Bible (1554) to combat the versions put out by the Protestants or translated into vernacular languages. The Dominican Bonifacio Ferrer had translated the Bible into Valencian or Catalan in the fourteenth century; printed a century later, only the odd page has survived. A luckier fate awaited the Spanish translations of Friar Ambrosio Montesinos.

Gaspar de Quiroga, Valdés's successor as Inquisitor General, promulgated indices of banned and expurgated books in 1583 and 1584. Some books could neither be read nor possessed, others were allowed minus certain passages. The indices, directed against the Protestant Reformation, stood in the way of science. Machiavelli's *The Prince* was banned because its political realism ran counter to the vision of the Christian prince with which the monarchy was customarily flattered. The index banned some of Bodin's texts, although his fundamental work, *De la République*, was merely expurgated in 1594. Some jurists, too, were banned, such as Charles Dumoulin; also brutally expurgated was Budé's *De Asse*. Prohibited physicians included Servet, a 'great heretic', and expurgation extended to Paracelsus, Arnau de Vilanova, Amato Lusitano and Huarte de San Juan, together with scientists such as Scaliger, Girolamo Cardano and Conrad Gessner, a lecturer at Tübingen and son-in-law of Zwingli. At Rome, Clement VIII published a very restrictive index in 1593, but this was soon withdrawn and replaced by the index of 1597. This index attended opinions from the Jesuit Antonio Possevino in his *Bibliotheca Selecta* (1593), written in reply to Gessner's vast *Bibliotheca Universalis* (1545), published in the wake of the destruction by the Turks of the collection of Matthias Corvinus, king of Hungary.

The abrupt break with emerging science came about with Rome's condemnation of Copernicus in 1616 and the trial against Galileo. Neither scholar was included on any Spanish index, but the prohibition prevailed throughout the Catholic world. In 1632, Galileo published his *Dialogues* in defence of the Copernican system; he incurred a ban, and was forced to recant and sentenced to life imprisonment, later softened to permanent house arrest at his villa at Arcetri. The Church resisted the heliocentric world view that contradicted Scripture. Religion sought to impose itself upon science. On the Protestant side, Kepler was convicted by the Tübingen theologians, and Calvin sentenced Servet to burn; Servet was also meant to be tried in Saragossa, to where the inquisitors wanted to lure him. Erasmus had warned in his *In Praise of Folly* that theologians were an irascible brood who cried heretic against anyone who disagreed with them.

96

The Years of Decline

The Reformation and Counter Reformation divided Europe and set off persecution, exile, and wars of religion. The absolutist monarchies crossed swords in a play of shifting alliances. The Turks invaded Europe and reached the gates of Vienna (Constantinople having fallen in 1453). The discovery and conquest of the Americas enlarged the known world but destroyed civilisations, albeit bringing riches to Europe. Disease and famine scourged the continent.

The seventeenth century was an age of decay. The balance struck by the Peace of Augsburg (1555) was torn asunder by the Thirty Years War of the Habsburgs and Bourbons, abetted by Gustavus Adolphus of Sweden. The Peace of Westphalia (1648) extended religious freedom to Lutherans and followers of Calvin and Zwingli. The imperial court of law, hitherto composed of graduates of imperial faculties only, was split equally between Catholic and Protestant judges. France won European hegemony, confirmed at the Peace of the Pyrenees (1659) with Spain.

Did the universities decline, too? Enrolment dropped sharply. Over the Middle Ages there had been an ever-growing number of universities and student enrolment advanced at a faster rate than the general population. The rise was particularly swift in the sixteenth century, as found in Oxford and Cambridge by Lawrence Stone, who dubbed this movement 'the educational revolution'. Other scholars have confirmed similar trends elsewhere. But from the mid-seventeenth century on, the number of students fell away. The economic slump must have played some role, but cannot explain the reversal entirely: clergymen enjoyed church stipends and noblemen could afford to pay their own way. Perhaps religious barriers played a part. Stone explains the decline on the basis that the nobility left university lecture halls for other forms of education, while clerics lost heart when they saw how ecclesiastical office routinely went to the offspring of Anglican vicars. In Spain, the rise of an absolutist monarchy and of the Church had lured many into the universities. They, too, soon saw that highest office was reserved for the privileged, collegers, powerful families and the religious

Candida Höfer,
Trinity College Library Dublin I **(2004)**
Built in 1592, Trinity College Library was given the privilege of 'legal deposit' in 1801; it must accordingly receive a copy of every publication publishedt in Ireland or the United Kingdom. Today, it houses over five million books. The collection includes manuscripts and bibliographical treasures such as the ninth-century *Book of Kells*, now permanently on display in the Library's exhibition room.

orders; even in the lower reaches of the bureaucracy influence and patronage was rife. The members of the six *colegios mayores* were no longer paupers but, giving the lie to the foundational statutes, noblemen and sons of high officials – they acquired the chairs of laws and canon law, went on to win jobs on governing councils and in the courts, or were made canons or bishops. A board of colleges coordinated strategy. Italian postings were left to members of San Clemente, whereas a smaller number of 'major collegers' went to the Indies. The colleges' power over the universities peaked in 1641, when the student vote on the election of professors was suppressed. Competitive examinations, it was claimed, bred disorder and bribery. The colleges stood to benefit from the change: the tribunals were now to send a triad of nominees to the Council of Castile, dominated by men of their same kind. College old-boy networks became the norm and nepotism reigned, as in other European universities of the time, with few exceptions: Halle, Göttingen or Edinburgh. At Mexico and Lima, the student vote was also suppressed, and governance placed in the hands of boards of notables. In the Salamanca of the early eighteenth century, enrolment was right down, the university was awash with college members and churchmen, commoners were on the wane. By 1719, a report to the Council of Castile acknowledged that things were in a poor state and urged the closing of minor universities, among other measures, such as reforming legal studies, or introducing

botany and raising the frequency of anatomical dissections.

Newly issued indices further deepened Spain's isolation and its break from emerging science. In 1612, the inquisitor Bernardo de Roxas y Sandoval published a huge index of prohibited and expurgated titles; books were 'mute masters' able to spawn heresy. In 1632, an index by Antonio Zapata added over 2,500 authors. He commissioned the work of expurgation from 'persons of erudition, doctrine and zeal, residents in this court and others from the most qualified universities of these realms'. There followed the indices of Antonio de Sotomayor and multiple edicts of condemnation. The censors got stricter about scientific writings, turning their attention to L'Ecluse, Kepler and Tycho Brahe and the geographers Mercator and Münster. An extensive expurgation was undertaken of Andrés Laguna's edition of Dioscorides and the *Sacra Philosophia* of the physician Francisco de Valles; far-reaching 'corrections' were made of Paracelsus and his disciples and of Arnau de Vilanova (but his medical books survived scrutiny).

The European universities changed in structure and came under civil authority. Governed by academic oligarchies, they kept up an embattled intellectual tradition, resisting science. Many universities held on to their original corporations, but were increasingly subject to the doctors and civil authority. In Paris, the rector was still a master elected by the four nations of the faculty of arts; the electoral body at Orleans was made up of law students. In 1619, Louis XIII suppressed university assemblies and corporations throughout his kingdom. The corporations survived at Salamanca and Louvain, the Scottish universities, Padua and Bologna, Vienna and Leipzig, and Prague, but in diluted form. The nations lived on in the tradition of peregrinations, but subject to the constraints of the various religious splits. Clashes between scholars of differing origin were frequent. Foreign students – Germans in particular – formed brotherhoods to protect themselves, sometimes recognised by the host university, such as in Padua; elsewhere, they were tolerated, such as at Leiden, Groningen or Salamanca, with its nations of Biscay and Portugal. The German universities saw the creation of fraternities called *Burschenschaften*, which fought each other

Hic Genio locus hicq. duces Morumq Magistri
Accumbunt epulis ædiotiore loco. Inde sedent reliqui positis, ex ordine menfis
Sumendum quoties denotat hora cibum.

and wore their scars as blazons of honour; they survived into the twentieth century – Soma Morgenstern, in his biography of Joseph Roth, remembers encountering them at the University of Vienna on the eve of the First World War. Politicised by the German nationalists, they were already hotbeds of anti-Semitic sentiment. Later, in the mid 1930s, 'Professors and students alike agitated under the sign of the swastika, but still not loudly enough even to ruin one's day.'

Bologna declined further, though Cardinal Paleotti tried to make improvements. The archdeacon Antonio Felice Marsili, in a draft reform, upbraided the colleges of doctors for bad practice and a surfeit of lecturers: the list of 150 should be cut down to about twelve. But the universities of Italy saw no real reform until the eighteenth century; neither did the Spanish universities or Portuguese Coimbra.

Oxford and Cambridge kept up their old tradition, with a number of changes. At Oxford, the chancellor, elected by the dons and sitting in the House of Lords, was the university's protector and assured its loyalty. Each university also had two members of parliament in the Commons. The vice-chancellor was generally a college warden appointed by the chancellor. To deal with administrative affairs he convened the proctors and college principals for weekly sessions of the Hebdomadal Board. The proctors presided over degree ceremonies and university assemblies and saw to it that discipline was upheld. The body known as 'Convocation', comprising all doctors and masters, made the most important decisions, while 'Congregation' was formed only by college regents and principals. Within colleges, fellows – unmarried clergymen – taught and tutored the scholars. Fellows lived in college for life, and sometimes earned ecclesiastical stipends that let them marry and form a family; they would elect a college warden to chair their assemblies. A scholar in receipt of a bursary paid no lodging fees, unlike commoners. In 1592, Trinity

University Banquet at Tübingen, Germany (1600)
This German university founded in 1477, also known as 'Eberhard Karls' in honour of its leading patrons, stood out for its theology faculty – one of its most promising students was in fact Philip Melanchthon. Other distinguished alumni were Kepler, the astrophysicist, and Hegel, the philosopher. Since the nineteenth century, Tübingen has been a distinguished scientific university, with many of its former students winning the Nobel Prize.

College was created in Dublin; it was an Anglican divinity school for the conversion of Catholics, who heard lessons but could not earn degrees until 1793.

The German Empire had been ravaged by war. After the Peace of Westphalia, the German princes and electors reopened and improved the universities. In the Palatinate, Prince Karl Ludwig tolerantly restored Giessen, which held the Lutheran primacy, and Heidelberg, the heart of Calvinism. But the armies of Louis XIV were still to wreck Freiburg, Cologne, Mainz, Trier and Strasbourg. Maximilian I of Bavaria, too, restored the University of Ingolstadt, passing new statutes in 1642. Louvain, the centre of Jansenism, fell into decay, despite the protection of Albert of Habsburg and Isabella Clara Eugenia.

In Sweden, Uppsala was protected by the royal court, which, looking to the training of the nobility and clergy, gave it fresh endowments. Gustavus Adolphus II wanted Uppsala to be the country's only university, supported in the bishoprics by gymnasia or high schools – some, with schools of medicine and law, rose to the status of academies or universities, such as Dorpat (1632) and Abo (1640) in Finland, and, after Sweden took over Denmark, Lund (1668), which annexed the German University of Greifswald. The statutes of 1665 of Charles X for Uppsala were extended to other institutions. Copenhagen, however, educated the Danish nobility at the academy of Soro (1643), which resembled the Collegium Illustre (1596) of Tübingen, founded by Frederick of Wurttemberg. The curriculum included history, politics, modern languages and exercises found suitable for gentlemen.

The European nobility had a long military tradition. Charles V sometimes called his noblemen to war with their hosts and urban militias. In Renaissance Italy, there were schools of condottieri mercenaries. The monarchies created the modern army equipped with firearms and artillery, manned by mercenaries and commanded by noblemen. In Paris, the cadet school admitted commoners for 'good conduct'. In Spain, the military schools of the eighteenth century continued to demand 'cleanliness of blood'.

To train his cannoneers, Charles V created schools in Milan, Barcelona and Burgos. An artillery academy was established at Douai in France. Holland, Denmark and England formed naval schools; in France, Louis set up schools at Toulon, Rochefort and Brest. Earlier than this, Spain had endowed a chair of cosmography and navigational art at the Casa de Contratación and the College of San Telmo in Seville.

Some aristocrats – younger sons and gentry – went to university to attain degrees and get jobs at court or in the Church. There were gentlemen's riding and fencing schools attached to universities or run privately at Bologna, Palermo, Padua – the Delia academy – and Naples, and also at Ingolstadt, Wittenberg and Leiden, Orleans and Paris.

In the late sixteenth century the nobility secluded itself in private establishments. The projects of Sir Humphrey Gilbert and François de la Noue called for specific forms of education. This took shape at the academy for noblemen or Ritterakademie at Tübingen, which spread to Kassel, and, after the Treaty of Westphalia, to Wolfenbuttel and Berlin. In the Catholic world, class segregation was achieved at Jesuit seminaries for nobleman at Cologne and Vienna, Parma and Bologna, or the Imperial College of Madrid. On a lesser scale, similar institutions were set in motion by other orders, the Oratorians, Benedictines and Barnabites. Their curricula focused on the arts and philosophy, politics and mathematics, riding and fencing. The aristocratic trend was perceptible within the Church: the Jesuit Collegium Germanicum et Hungaricum (1533) became a seminary for highborn central European priests.

There was interest in sustaining ecclesiastical training. The Council of Trent had entrusted to the bishops the creation of seminaries to school future priests, and these centres sprang up in Rome, Eichstatt, Milan and Munster, and, later on, in Spain and France.

Faculties and Academies

In the sixteenth and seventeenth centuries, Europe underwent a scientific revolution. How did the universities contribute? Baron Francis Bacon attacked the schools for running counter to the progress of science. University study, he claimed, was in the grip of authors from whom no dissent was allowed.

The new astronomy and philosophy did not originate at the university; it was not a congenial setting nor were its curricula conducive to renewal. But elsewhere universities continued to play a role: theology was reformed by professors like Erasmus and Luther; law came under the transforming influence of Alciato and Cujas, Grotius and Pufendorf; medicine advanced by the influence of Vesalius, Harvey and Baglivi. Classical languages, grammar and philology were assiduously cultivated at the faculties. Many of the creators of the new science were university graduates and lecturers. Some new ideas found acceptance within university cloisters, while others were stubbornly rejected, particularly if they went against religious dogma: Galileo was forced to recant, and Giordano Bruno and Miguel Servet were burned at the stake.

In Italy, there emerged academies and informal circles of litterateurs and scientists. The earliest sprang up in Florence, sponsored by Lorenzo de' Medici (1459). Later, the Accademia della Crusca compiled a dictionary of the Tuscan dialect, which became modern Italian. A later institution, the Accademia del Cimento, backed by Cardinal Leopoldo de' Medici, sponsored experiments directed by Torricelli and Viviani, a disciple and the earliest biographer of Galileo. In Naples, the physician Giovanni Battista della Porta headed another academy and published an encyclopaedia of physical and technical knowledge. In Rome, the Accademia dei Lincei (1603), paid for by Federico Cesi, Prince of Aquasparta, of which Galileo was a member, sought to form a network of academies across Europe, but Galileo's conviction brought the plan to ruin. Later, the physics and mathematics academy of Cardinal Ciampini sought to revive the teachings of Galileo and publish his works, but his attempt failed when the inquisitorial proceedings began against the atheists of Naples.

But in England this new flowering put forth roots. The universities were unwilling to accommodate new learning, so an academy was needed. Gatherings and informal clubs of scientists met at London's Gresham College and at colleges in Oxford and Cambridge. In 1662, there was formed the Royal Society, endorsed the following year by Charles II 'for the glory of God and the benefit of mankind'. In 1666, the Académie des sciences was founded at Paris. These were the institutions that would guide science in the eighteenth century.

Looking at the contributions of the various disciplines, grammar transformed to become philology or textual criticism, the first renovated subject in academia, taught at Pavia by Valla, who became a symbol of this new branch of intellectual endeavour: at Valencia, the chair of Latin was named after him. The old primers of scholastic Latin gave way to the modern grammars of Antonio de Nebrija, Sánchez de las Brozas and Johannes Despaterius. Logic and dialectic broke with tradition in the work of Ramus. Philology, vital for biblical study, emerged at Louvain and developed at Leiden in the works of Joseph Justus Scaliger, Johann Friedrich Gronovius and Gerhard Johann Vossius. Justus Lipsius taught history with a political and moral slant inspired by Tacitus. The earliest chairs of history – Marburg in 1529 – were chronology-bound and concentrated on antiquity. Critical rigour only came with Mabillon, although the history of Roman law was precocious, with Cujas.

The mathematical sciences and astronomy – the old *quadrivium* – had played a peripheral role in the old faculties of arts; now they gained the centre. In *De Revolutionibus Orbium Coelestium* (1543), Copernicus destroyed Ptolemy's astronomical system, which had placed the sun at the centre of the universe. Having studied at Krakow, Padua and Bologna, where he graduated in law, Copernicus was a canon and an administrator of the diocese of Ermland in Poland. The Dane Tycho Brahe modified Copernicus' theory: the Sun and Moon and the sphere of the fixed stars all revolved around an immobile Earth, while the planets orbited the Sun. Called on by the

University of Copenhagen, he preferred to work privately on the Isle of Hven, funded by the king and compiling a mass of observations using instruments he had built himself. He later went to Prague in the service of the Emperor Rudolph II. The earliest university telescopes came late in the day, at Leiden, Copenhagen and Altdorf and some Jesuit schools. In the eighteenth century, Uppsala and Glasgow also had their own telescopes.

Prague was a port of call for Johannes Kepler – an errant sage dogged by misfortune – who came in search of Brahe's data and laid down the first two laws of the new astronomy in the *Astronomia Nova* (1609) and the third law in the *Harmonices Mundi* (1619). Galileo, even after his conviction for advocating Copernicus' ideas, published his *Discourses* (1638) on the analysis of movement, which he sent to Holland in secret. Isaac Newton's *Philosophiae Naturalis Principia Mathematica* (1687) reorganised the new knowledge with the discovery of gravity. Newton framed the modern corpuscular theory of light; Christian Huygens, a Dutch physicist who formulated the law of the pendulum, had conceived of light as a wave.

Modern science was built up by hypothesis, observation and the mathematical expression of results. Meanwhile, the universities continued to teach the physics of Aristotle as an addendum to his metaphysics, both being tied to late scholastic theology. Bologna saw the introduction of the natural philosophy of the English practitioners of calculus, and opponents of Aristotelianism became common. Plato aroused less interest, but his thought was present at the academy of Marsilio Ficino and in some English colleges, and taught at Pisa, Ferrara, Rome and Pavia. Modern philosophy emerged in contact with mathematics and physics; it broke with tradition and created new systems deduced rationally from evidence. Thinkers wrote outside university walls: Descartes and Gassend, the Oratorian Malebranche, Spinoza, Pascal and Leibniz. Pierre Gassend lectured at Aix-en-Provence, but none of the rest ever taught at university. Baruch Spinoza was invited to Heidelberg with a promise that he could philosophise freely within the bounds of religion; he decided to stay in Holland. Gottfried Wilhelm Leibniz, having won a law doctorate at Leipzig, made a career as a politician

and diplomat, a philosopher, and a noted mathematician. Descartes studied with the Jesuits at La Flèche, and settled in Holland; late in life he went to Sweden at the bidding of Queen Christina. In his *Discourse on the Method* (1637) he affirmed the figure of the thinking man and relied on 'innate' ideas to deduce the existence of God and the world; animals were soulless machines. Mathematics and physics owe much to the rationalist philosophers. Descartes created the analytical geometry, Leibniz and Newton invented infinitesimal calculus and applied it to mechanics. Pascal and Torricelli – who taught at Florence – found the weight of the atmosphere.

The philosophical and scientific advances of the age sprang from a narrow circle of brilliant minds working in different places and linked to one another by personal relations and their published books; some minor figures followed and assisted them. What they shared was a sort of 'invisible college'; D'Alembert called Descartes a 'ringleader'. There abounded encyclopaedias and panoramic visions aiming to encompass all branches of knowledge. Giovanni Battista della Porta accommodated the new sciences. Other notable compendia included Bacon's *De Dignitate, et Augmentis Scientiarum* (1623) and the *Encyclopaedia* (1630) of Johann Heinrich Alsted, a lecturer at the Calvinist high school of Herborn. Other encyclopaedic visions were provided by the Jesuits Giambattista Riccioli and Athanasius Kircher, a teacher at Paderborn.

Medicine continued the Arab-influenced tradition of Galen. Miguel Jerónimo de Ledesma, a professor at Valencia, edited part of Avicenna's *Canon*, taught at Padua even in the early seventeenth century. Wider knowledge of Greek allowed for better acquaintance with Galen and a rediscovery of the *Corpus Hippocraticum*, attributed to Hippocrates, the physician of the fifth century BC. The humanistic direction was encouraged by Niccolò Leoniceno at Ferrara, Girolamo Cardano at Pavia and Bologna, and Giovanni Argentario at Pisa, Naples and Mondovi, who moved later to Turin. The two chairs of Alcalá alternated Galen and Avicenna. The professor and humanist Francisco Valles, in his old age, commented on Hippocrates in the light of his own medical experience: his work was praised by Hermann Boerhaave, the founder of modern clinical science.

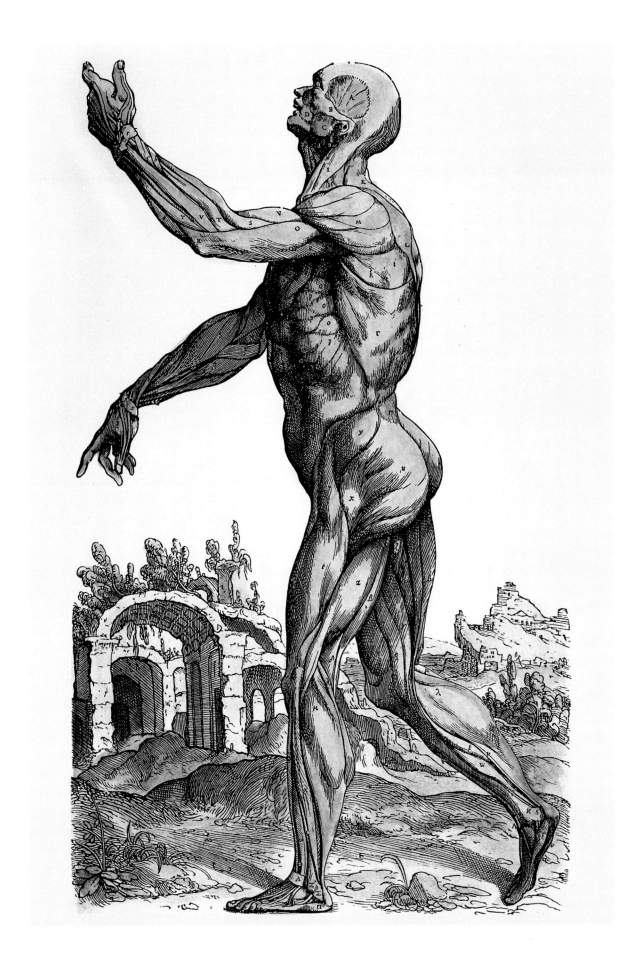

Vesalius, *De Humani Corporis Fabrica* (1543)
The dissection of human corpses led to a better understanding of the body; progress was made at a rate unknown since Galen. Vesalius, a professor at the University of Padua, offered wholly new knowledge about mankind which swiftly spread to all faculties of medicine.
His work, illustrated with detailed plates, revolutionised the practice of anatomy and enriched artists' representations of the human body.

The Royal Colledge of Phisitians London

Robert Morden, *The Royal College of Physicians*, London (*c.* 1700)
In 1660 the gatherings of British scientists that had been taking place for a number of years were given official sanction. The aim of these extramural meetings was to create a forum for discussion. Scientific rigour was preserved by a ban on topics outside science, such as politics or religion.

Padua heard the lessons of Vesalius, who transformed anatomy with his *De Humani Corporis Fabrica* (1543). Dissection of corpses led to a knowledge of the human body unparalleled by Galen, who had dissected only animals. Vesalius' lectures drew many scholars, including Pedro Jimeno and Luis Collado, future professors at Valencia. Jacobus Sylvius attacked Vesalius from the faculty of Paris, as did Realdo Colombo, who had trained at Padua with him. Colombo taught Juan Valverde de Amusco, author of *Historia de la composición del cuerpo humano* (1556), which was read widely, although it derived many of its plates from the *Fabrica* and only amended minor errors. Anatomical theatres for dissection were built at Padua and Leiden, and later at Paris, Oxford, Copenhagen and Uppsala. At some universities existing premises were adapted: at Salamanca, the church of San Narciso from 1555 onwards; at Saragossa, a 'house of anatomy' was opened in 1586.

Andreas Vesalius' anatomy became the touchstone for university training, supplemented by Bartolomeo Eustachi in Rome, Felix Platter in Basel, Gabriele

Falloppio in Padua. Falloppio began to regard the fibre as the true element of the animal body. In the late eighteenth century, the Vesalian cycle came to an end, with contributions from Felix Vicq-d'Azyr, at the Jardin du Roi, and Samuel Thomas von Sömmerring, who taught at Kassel, Mainz, Frankfurt and Jena.

The University of Basel briefly heard the teaching of Paracelsus, an eccentric physician who used his books of Galen and Avicenna to make a bonfire. Sceptical of local anatomy, 'the study of quartered men', he pursued an 'essential' anatomy reflecting the effects of sulphur, mercury and salt, which he believed caused disease, as did the atmosphere and the stars, which mapped onto the human body in subtle ways. For Paracelsus, the world was a pharmacy: he introduced alchemical and mineral medicines by the rule 'contraries cure contraries', hoping to destroy the seed of disease even before the fact. He widened Galenic pharmacology, which used animal and vegetable products alone. Of his many followers the most prominent was the Belgian aristocrat Jan Baptista van

104

Helmont, an erudite and mystical cultivator of medicine and chemistry.

William Harvey's discovery of the circulation of the blood inaugurated modern physiology and buried the Galenic theory of the humours – Servet had independently discovered pulmonary circulation. After study at Cambridge and Padua, Harvey taught at the London College of Physicians. His work dazzled the medical world, and found support in later discoveries by Jean Pecquet, Thomas Bartholin and others. In Spain, it was accommodated by Gaspar Bravo de Sobremonte, a professor at Valladolid, purportedly within the Galenic tradition, whereas at Valencia Matías García stubbornly resisted it, using his own data from dissections and animal experiments.

In seventeenth century Italy, the influence of Galileo – experiment, weight and measure – Descartes and Gassend drove medicine to a mechanistic vision, first advanced by Giovanni Alfonso Borelli, Galileo's disciple, and carried on by Marcello Malpighi and Giorgio Baglivi, who had the aid of the microscope, and continued further by the Englishmen William Cole and George Cheyne, and the Scotsman Archibald Pitcairne, a professor at Leiden: but none yet saw the 'anatomo-pathological lesion' discovered in dissections as a cause of disease.

At the faculty of Leiden, Silvio (Franz de la Boë), a great clinician and laboratory man, continued the iatro-chemical tradition of Paracelsus and van Helmont. He tried to explain digestion and glandular activity with the idea of fermentation or 'acrimony'. The question exercised Thomas Willis at Oxford, who also paid attention to mental illness or 'disorders of the rational soul', as distinguished from neurological disease or 'disorders of the sensitive soul'. His disciples, like Robert Boyle, described the chemistry of respiratory processes.

Thomas Sydenham, a Fellow of All Souls College at Oxford, was a distinguished practitioner and an observer and classifier of diseases. He described and catalogued species of disease, with their constant and particular symptoms, distinguishing between chronic and acute and attributing the latter to atmospheric influences. These mechanistic, chemical and clinical currents came together in Hermann Boerhaave, the great professor at Leiden.

Botany was indispensable to medicine. In earlier centuries, Theophrastus, Pliny and Dioscorides, together with the Arab authors, had predominated; now carefully edited humanistic books were being printed. Andrés Laguna translated Dioscorides into Spanish, professorial chairs were created of 'simples' or 'herbs': in Rome (a short-lived chair), Padua, Pisa, Bologna, Ferrara, later at Naples and Messina, and in conjunction with anatomy at Montpellier. In 1561, at Bologna, botany was called 'the ordinary reading of natural philosophy on the fossils, plants and animals'. Botany attained wider independence with Leonhart Fuchs, a professor at Tübingen, Rembert Dodoens at Leiden and Charles de l'Ecluse (Clusius), but was tied to Aristotelian taxonomy – herb, shrub and tree. Conrad Gessner was more modern, but his work was not published for another two centuries. Botany came to encompass American flora with data compiled by Sahagun and Acosta, the physicians Nicolas Monardes and Francisco Hernández, some of whose plates were lost in a fire at El Escorial. European naturalists travelled the world amassing fresh data. At Valencia, 'herbs' was taught in 1567 by Juan Plaza, a noted physician who corresponded with L'Ecluse and sent him specimens and news. Plaza had a botanical garden which he tended with his students. Around 1542 the first botanical garden was created at Pisa by Cosimo de' Medici, who restored the city's wartorn university. He brought Luca Ghini from Bologna, who wanted the garden urgently as he had collected some plant specimens and feared they would dry out. There was little difference between a garden of 'simples' and a botanical garden. The real step forward came when plants ceased to be grown for medicinal purposes only. Botany was to attain maturity with Linnaeus.

At the law faculties the medieval tradition survived. Some humanists deplored the corrupt Vulgate version of Justinian's *Corpus Iuris Civilis* and the forced and arbitrary interpretations of the glossators and the commentators. Antonio de Nebrija, in his *Lexicon Iuris*, addressed Accursius thus: 'O miserable state of our time, in which we hear and suffer these things! Who heard such folly other than from thoughtless women working their distaffs?' The humanists trusted in a version of the *Digest* culled from an ancient codex – contemporary with Justinian – that was in the library of the Medici. Access to the fresh discovery was restricted. One who saw the book and recorded his impressions was Poliziano. A Dutchman, Haloander, published careful editions of the *Corpus* in Nuremberg, but without reference to the Florentine manuscript. Antonio Agustín saw it and collected passages in Greek that had been adulterated in the Vulgate. At last, in 1553, the Florentine version was published by Lelio Torelli, secretary to Cosimo I Medici; thirty years later, an edition was brought out by Denis Godefroy, who held chairs at Strasbourg, Heidelberg and Altdorf.

Around 1530, Andrea Alciato lectured at Bourges on the three last books of the *Code*, on vanished Roman public institutions. Reviving the genuine Roman law, free from the distortions of Accursius and Bartolus. Alciato was erudite in the classics and had an acute sense of history; he corrected older versions and reconstructed text using old codices and the Haloander edition, which he squared with the Florentine *Pandects*. But, knowing that history cannot resolve the issues of the present, in his commentaries on the first nine books of the *Code* and the *Digest* he abided by tradition. He debated city charters, the primacy of the pope and other questions of the day. Alciato taught at Milan and Bologna, where he drew crowds of students.

Other Bourges men were Jacques Cujas and François Hotman. The new humanism in law was termed the *Mos Gallicus*, as contrasted with the old doctrine, *Mos Italicus*, which lived on at Bologna and Salamanca. With Cujas, the study of Roman law resembled legal history. He improved and emended versions of the *Corpus*, clarified the meanings of words, settled on sound interpretations. He edited the *Pauli Sententiae* and the *Codex Theodosianus*, the Byzantine *Basilicos*, and analysed the texts of classical and post-classical jurists. Hugues Doneau, an exiled Huguenot with a chair at Heidelberg, also helped systematise Roman law.

But for their legal practice lawyers needed a form of Roman law that cleaved to the present – a distorted form. Most continued to teach the old method of the commentators or post-glossators, in consonance with law as practised. They adorned their lectures with historic and philological accretions, but their reasoning was traditional. The Dutch at Leiden, Utrecht and Groningen cultivated humanism while paying attention to the present and to Batavian law: Arnold Vinnen, Johannes Voet and Cornelius van Bynkershoek. German jurists concentrated on private Roman law, in connection with imperial and regional law. As theoretical and practical humanists, the lawmen of the *usus modernus Pandectarum* applied greater rigour and erudition than had Bartolus and the commentators.

This period saw the beginnings of modern natural law and international law. The scholastics had propounded a natural law sown in the human mind by God. Grotius, in *De Iure Belli ac Pacis*, used classical and doctrinal sources to found natural law upon self-evident rational principles, addressing war and peace, property, and marriage. The axioms were to be implemented by reason and attain universal force, 'even if we were to say that there is no God, which would be a serious crime, or that He cares not for human things'. Grotius' work was continued by Samuel von Pufendorf at Heidelberg and Lund, and by Christian Thomasius at Leipzig and Halle.

Luther shifted the focus of theology to Scripture, advocating an unconstrained interpretation inspired by God. Exposition of the Bible alone being thought insufficient, it was supplemented by Melanchthon's *Loci Communes* and Calvin's *Institutio Christianae Religionis*. There later appeared textbooks for teaching purposes specifically. Theology remained the central discipline, but the variety of competing beliefs engendered a rationalist natural theology – the theodicy of Grotius, Leibniz and Kant.

In the Catholic world, Peter Lombard's *Sentences* gave way to the *Summa Theologica* of St Thomas. The Dominican Francisco de Vitoria had studied at Paris, where all three theological traditions – Thomist, Scotist and nominalist – were taught. Vitoria, the leading professor at Salamanca, opted for the Thomist *Summa*, on which he published lengthy commentaries. Robert Bellarmine introduced it to Louvain and Rome. Pius V gave it his backing, elevating St Thomas to the status of 'Doctor of the Church'. Nominalism was watered down in the version of Durand, a Dominican teaching in Paris in the early fourteenth century. There now also emerged an independent Jesuit current led by Francisco Suárez, who lectured at Coimbra and Rome, and by Luis de Molina, professor at Evora. Disputes among the various faiths raged on, and among different currents of opinion within each creed. The religious orders competed for professorial chairs in the arts and theology, until separate chairs were founded for each school of thought at Salamanca and other leading universities. At Valencia, a minor university, a distinction was drawn only between Thomist and anti-Thomist chairs.

Recently attention has been paid to the late scholastic school of Vitoria and Suárez. This movement restored Thomist theology, predominant almost up to the present day. They argued that the conquest of the New World and the subjection of its natives was a 'just war', while rejecting old titles granted by popes and the emperor. The issue particularly exercised Bartolomé de las Casas, who promoted theological debate. Theologians were seen as experts in serious political, legal and economic issues. St Thomas's *Summa* contained a major section on the foundations and problems of law, and theologically inspired treatises were produced: *De Iustitia, et Iure* by Domingo de Soto, or the writings of the Jesuit Luis de Molina. Suárez followed this tradition with his *De Legibus ac Deo Legislatore* (1612).

During the crisis of the seventeenth century, theologians and jurists sought economic solutions; Blai Navarro and Miquel Bertomeu Salón of Valencia scrutinised the fairness of taxes. The theology faculties' chairs of biblical studies taught the Old and New Testaments in their Vulgate version, such as at Salamanca since the time of Pope Martin V. At Alcalá, Cisneros promoted a monumental polyglot Bible, surpassed years later by the Antwerp Bible edited by Arias Montano, chaplain to Philip II. A Salamanca professor, León de Castro, accused Montano of heresy, but the king came to his aid. Castro also persecuted followers of the Parisian Petrus Ramus, and, allied with the Dominican Bartolomé de Medina, attacked the Salamanca Hebrew scholars Gaspar de Grajal and Martín Martínez de Cantalapiedra, Alonso Gudiel, a professor at Osuna, and Friar Luis de León for his translation of the *Song of Songs*. Being

Complutensian Polyglot Bible (1514–17)
In 1514, the printing press of Arnao Guillén de Brocar finished the first run of an edition in Greek and Latin of the New Testament. In 1517, the firm printed a Greek Old Testament, or Septuagint Bible. The result was a work in six volumes, including texts in Hebrew and Aramaic, that marked a milestone in the development of philology. The mind behind this project was the humanist and Cardinal Francisco Ximénez de Cisneros, founder of the University of Alcalá de Henares, from which the Bible took its name.

'new Christians', they were ripe for trial: Cantalapiedra lost his professorship, Grajal and Gudiel died in prison. Friar Luis, after recanting, was reinstated in a lesser tenure.

The universities partly revived in the eighteenth century. Their governing bodies were transformed, the new sciences were absorbed and expanded upon. Monarchs saw it as their duty to support higher learning; they gave the universities new laws and endowed them with funds to improve lecturers' pay. The Enlightenment began.

STUDENTS: WELL-SCHOOLED ROGUES

The most attractive figure of the traditional university is the student. Young, ambitious and perhaps brilliant, when contrasted with the grey, mediocre foil of the institution itself he arouses sympathy. This was the image forged by some of those who trod the lecture hall before rising to fame as professors or men of letters. Quevedo and Torres Villarroel, in particular, gave the student the air of a witty and resourceful rogue.

The Swindler tells the adventures of an apprentice, while Villarroel's *Life* portrays a professor of mathematics who, bored of his job, toys with sorcery, and, as an afterthought, science. Both are bold, cunning and lustful for life. They reject the tedium of study, in a manner that Pérez Lugín was later to make part of the Spanish literary canon in *The House of the Troya*.

But at the most illustrious faculties – theology and canon law – many students, whether by inclination or compulsion, conformed to the rules: clergymen who studied the Bible and the classics, spoke Latin, aspired to a canonship or even a bishop's mitre, and jockeyed for professorial tenure or a job in the ecclesiastical courts. Jurists, on the other hand, were typically hard-working laymen, aiming at careers in the civil courts, in academia, or in legal practice. A handful of them dominated the colleges, forming veritable pressure groups which, with the religious orders, kept the university under their thumb. Torres Villarroel, with mingled horror and annoyance, describes a harsh routine of antiquated Latin treatises that used syllogisms to recreate tired doctrines and obsolete disputes: the embers of a dead learning that nonetheless retained its hold on the curriculum.

This stereotype did not apply to medical students. The faculty of medicine ranked as a 'major school' but carried less prestige than its peers, law and theology. It was poorer, its professors were less important, and it was less influential. Its students, too, were said to be paupers who just wanted to marry and practise their chosen profession as soon as they could. But it was physicians who began to gain prominence for their scientific curiosity and their role in the intellectual revolution of the modern age. Medicine, with its up-to-date textbooks and practices, was the handmaiden of educational reform. The faculty of philosophy, the 'minor school', was lower in rank, a mere preparation for the major schools. Its students were more numerous, younger, and broad-ranging in their

'Universitas Studii Salamantini'
This phrase comes from the old ritual – still performed today – of investiture of a doctor *honoris causa* at the University of Salamanca. After an exhaustive protocol of oaths, speeches, medals and the university anthem (*Gaudeamus igitur*), the rector ends the ceremony with the cry '*Universitas Studii Salmantini*', to a chorus of cheers by all those present and the sound of calumet pipes.

interests – their behaviour was accordingly worse, but even here there would be many a budding clergyman who aspired to high ecclesiastical office.

Students of grammar, who had to learn the Latin required for further study, were at the lowest rung of a university degree. They were the most numerous and the youngest; many who never went on to study philosophy or to the major schools have remained anonymous to history. It is only for the higher reaches of academia – professors particularly – that the records can tell us about individual careers. Books of matriculations and degrees, reports on competitive examinations and minutes of assembly proceedings enable us to follow their progress. But the mass of those who hoped to make a place for themselves at university and failed have fallen into oblivion. Theirs might not have been an academic failure: they ran out of money to pay the high costs of board and lodging, and graduation itself, or they were thrown out if anyone in their family did anything disreputable or they were accused of defective lineage. Physicians, in particular, were suspected of impure ancestry, because of the former prominence of Jews and Arabs in the medical tradition. Even the illustrious Lluis Alcanys was burned on suspicion of covertly upholding the Jewish faith.

It was not unusual in one's university life to come up against the justice system – whether in the royal courts or, more commonly, in the courts operated by the university itself by virtue of its privileges. The records of university chancellor's courts are a wonderful source for following student lives that would otherwise have been unknown to us, since their academic prospects were so often destroyed. This was the case at the University of Alcalá of a student of grammar called Julián Rodríguez, as penniless as he was dazzled and led astray by Baroque luxury: he acquired a taste for wearing silver buckles and buttons, took to gambling, then turned to thievery to fund his new-found pursuits. After several run-ins with the courts, he was sentenced to the galleys. A life ruined by a yearning for glamour, leisure, and perhaps love.

José Luis Peset
Elena Hernández Sandoica

Students of grammar, who had to learn the Latin required for further study, were at the lowest rung of a university degree. They were the most numerous and the youngest; many who never went on to study philosophy or to the major schools have remained anonymous to history

German school of the 17th century,
Young Man in a Studio
Students often came from well-to-do families who would fund several years of education. The purpose of this outlay was for the young man to attain the academic qualification required for him to get a job in the upper reaches of the bureaucracy. But it was not unusual for affluent students to dawdle over their studies, putting off graduation for as long as their funds held out.

Façade of Humboldt University, Berlin
Wilhelm von Humboldt (1767–1835) founded the University of Berlin in 1810. It was created as the first wholly modern university. Education was based on teaching and research combined, and the humanities provided an overarching context. It has carried his name since 1949.

IV

UNIVERSITY, ENLIGHTENMENT
AND LIBERALISM

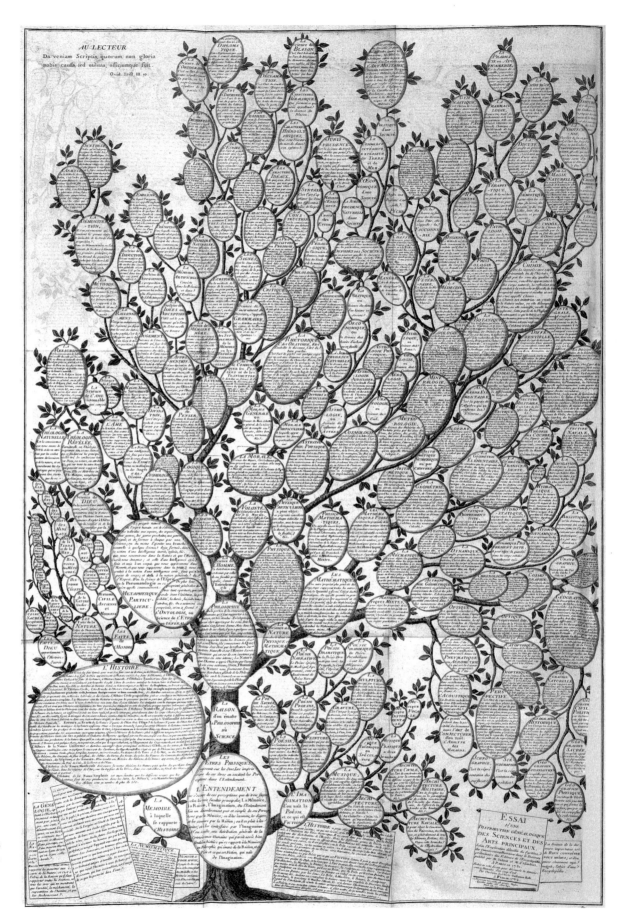

Denis Diderot and Jean d'Alembert, *Tree of Knowledge* **(1751–65)**
This plate is the frontispiece of the first of fourteen volumes making up *Encyclopaedia, or a systematic dictionary of the sciences, arts and crafts.*
The *Tree of Knowledge* encodes the entire structure of learning, divided into three sections – memory, reason and imagination – encompassing the various disciplines.

From the Enlightenment to Liberalism

Mariano Peset

The Enlightenment

The Enlightenment signified freedom of thought: in the words of Kant, *sapere aude*, dare to know. The famous Königsberg professor thus epitomised the optimism of that century of rapid intellectual progress, though he limned its boundaries in *Der Streit der Fakultäten* [The Conflict of the Faculties]. Universities were autonomous, for only the wise could judge the wise, and yet subject to the government – power could not teach, but regulated the faculties' workings, while lecturers undertook their roles under contract.

Outside universities, independent intellectuals gathered in academies and pursued learning free from official stricture. Graduate professionals and civil servants were also on the outside – churchmen, officials and physicians, they were knowledge technicians, instruments of government, unable freely to address the public and censored by university and State. Within the university, only the philosophy faculty could discuss and seek the truth freely. The rest – theology, medicine and law – came under princely control, yet could reach truth through engagement and struggle with the philosophy faculty, which would voice and advocate truth so that both State and faculties would be cognisant of what was beneficent and what harmful. Kant hoped to reconcile truth with power: he was well aware of the reality. Absolute monarchs – Enlightened despots – and a cultivated aristocratic minority had universities under their control, while universities aspired to free thought, the handmaiden of knowledge.

The Enlightenment broadened the experimental sciences, physics and medicine, fostered mathematics and rationalism (Descartes, Leibniz, Newton), cemented natural and international law and engendered new political visions. The period witnessed a rise in Neoclassicism in art, strict Jansenism and deism in religion.

In Germany, Enlightenment thought took root at the newer universities. The University of Halle, founded in 1693 by Frederick Wilhelm I of Prussia, equalled the Saxon schools of Wittenberg and Leipzig by the strength of its teaching and size of its student body. The monarch appointed chancellors, built

Immanuel Kant (c. 1750)
The German philosopher (1724–1804) held a professorship of logic and metaphysics at the University of Königsberg. His works, such as *Metaphysical Foundations of Natural Science, Prolegomena to Any Future Metaphysics, Religion Within the Limits of Reason Alone* and *Critique of Judgement*, laid the foundations of the future development of thought.

modern buildings, and introduced strict examinations and requirements. Unlike the old corporations, study was under the tutelage of the king and his advisers, through the rector and the corporation, both dependent on royal favour. Leipzig produced Halle's great jurists Christian Thomasius, Christian Wolff and Nicolas Gundling. All three claimed the protection of Frederick; Wolff was thrown out for atheism, while Thomasius – the then chancellor – kept his counsel. On the accession of Frederick II, Wolff returned from Marburg. Georg Ernst Stahl and Friedrich Hoffmann shone in the medical realm.

Göttingen was founded in Hanover under an imperial charter in 1733; three years later, it was endorsed by the Hanoverian Elector, George II of England, whose absence allowed room for manoeuvre to the secret council and the local estates. Promoted by the ministers Münchhausen and Gruber, alumni of Halle, from which Göttingen drew off students, the new centre was subject to the State, which regulated and funded it, and its law faculty especially attracted highborn scholars. Though Lutheran, Göttingen admitted Catholics and retained non-partisan lecturers, accusations of heresy being banned. Professors were allowed academic freedom and encouraged to publish books and papers. The philologist Johann Matthias Gesner, who founded the university library, introduced the seminar method, which had had its forerunners and now became the norm. Lessons were rounded out with the exposition and critique of a research paper by lecturer and students together. Seminars were soon adopted at Halle and elsewhere: research became integrated with teaching. The centre of gravity shifted from theology to political science and law with Putter and to medicine with Albrecht von Haller, who edited the *Göttingische Gelehrte Anzeigen* (1739), Germany's first academic journal. Göttingen created an attached science research academy. The Enlightenment spread to other German universities which cultivated science, philology, history, law and medicine.

The claim that the Enlightenment went further at Protestant centres of learning may be disputed, but seems accurate upon comparing the revival at Halle to the decline of French and Italian universities. In France – during the century of Louis XIV –

the decline was offset by the academies, while Italy slowly caught up. In Germany and Austria, Enlightened princes and electors renovated the Catholic universities. The bishop of Mainz, the Enlightened Friedrich Karl von Schönborn, introduced expermental physics and chemistry and ecclesiastical and legal history. Though retaining the Tridentine oath, Schönborn admitted Protestant scholars; he recruited the surgeon Heister, while the physician Wolter introduced the teachings of Boerhaave. At Ingolstadt, Schönborn appointed the legal rationalist Johann Adam von Ickstatt, a disciple of Wolff, both being made imperial barons. The Jesuit university at Bamberg was given law and medicine faculties. Elsewhere, reform came later, after the expulsion of the Jesuits that left education in some disarray. Empress Maria Theresa created an educational committee. The physician Gerhard van Swieten reformed Vienna, under the control of a government representative, and a gift was made of the Jesuit library. Joseph II continued the changes, giving new statutes to Louvain. The orthodoxy of Cologne prompted the founding of new centres at nearby Bonn and Münster.

As a result of its war with Russia, some of Sweden's universities were forced to move their seat. The Royal Academy of Science, founded at Uppsala in 1739 by Linnaeus and other academics, fostered renewal in botany and chemistry, medicine and jurisprudence, and embraced the antiquarianism favoured by Gustav III. Copenhagen was rebuilt after the fire of 1728 and preserved its traditional focus on training clergymen in theology and law – the nobility went to school at the Soro academy. The new learning soon flourished at Geneva. Of the Presbyterian universities, Leiden was foremost during this period. In a country of religious diversity it remained tolerant, but the ecclesiastical authorities forced some expulsions. Pierre Bayle, author of *Dictionnaire historique et critique* (1695–97), a foundational work of the early Enlightenment, was expelled from the Rotterdam gymnasium for opposing the House of Orange. The Scots universities were stricter still: as late as 1697 a student was executed for denying the divinity of Christ. English became the language of lectures, and physics and mathematics were taught.

Oxford and Cambridge suffered the political upheavals of the seventeenth century. The Civil War and Cromwell's Puritan revolution upset academic life; the Lord Protector appointed his own creatures. The Puritan John Hall accused the universities of failing to teach mechanistic chemistry or to conduct experiments and dissections. A physics chair had been created at Oxford in the sixteenth century, and another scientific professorship was endowed in the early seventeenth century. Cambridge was slower. Newton's mathematics chair was founded in 1663, and those of chemistry, anatomy and astronomy followed in the eighteenth century.

Charles II restored the Anglican church and left the faculties largely untouched. The universities accepted him, despite his authoritarian style: at one point he shut down Parliament. His brother James II, who succeeded him, was more troublesome: a Catholic, he enacted the Declaration of Indulgence in 1687, and imposed Catholic professors at the universities – including a 'papist' rector at Magdalen College, Oxford. The following year he imprisoned several Anglican bishops. In 1688 William of Orange landed with his army in Devon and James II went into exile in France. Some professors held that William could only be regent, because a king could not be deposed; others said James had vacated the throne. A majority swore allegiance to William, and only a few resigned. A Calvinist, William hoped to open up education. The Act of Toleration of 1689 allowed private non-Anglican schools, which multiplied. At Oxford, which was more conservatively Anglican, the Tories resisted this development, which found greater support among the Cambridge Whigs. The Whigs predominated throughout the reign of Queen Anne and the early Hanovers. In 1760, George III imposed tolerance by repealing the requirement of adhering to the Thirty-Nine Articles of Anglican doctrine.

The universities of France, Italy, Portugal and Spain were Catholic. Louis XIV, with his minister Jean-Baptiste Colbert, stamped out the last traces of autonomy at the French universities. To the chairs of Roman law Louis added chairs of French law to teach ancient Gallic customs and royal ordinances. He regulated the duration of degrees, enrolment and

Carolina Rediviva Library at the University of Uppsala, Sweden (1841)
The main library building was completed in 1841, although this Swedish university, founded in 1477, is the oldest in Scandinavia. The library holds an important collection of incunables, manuscripts, maps and paintings.

Library of the University of Leiden (1610)
William of Orange built the first university of the Netherlands in 1575 as a gift to the citizens of Leiden for having withstood a siege by the Spanish *tercios*. From its beginnings, Leiden was known for religious tolerance, as stressed by its motto *Praesidium Libertatis*, 'bastion of freedom'.

attendance requirements, professorships – creating auxiliary *docteurs agregés* – and the medical and legal professions, and assured orthodoxy by revoking in 1685 the Edict of Nantes and condemning Jansenism. Except at Paris, Toulouse and Montpellier, universities declined; lecturers and students alike neglected their duties of attendance, reading and graduation. Theology remained scholastic, law barely moved – although Robert Joseph Pothier taught at Orleans – and only medicine attained to a high standard in Paris and Montpellier. Newtonian mechanics arrived only in the second half of the century. The *Encyclopédistes* complained about the state of education.

French science was pushed forward in the academies and special schools were founded for the Crown's purposes: military academies at La Flèche, Sorèze and Mézières, admitting aristocratic students; civil engineering and mining schools (1747 and 1783); and centres of surgical training at Paris and elsewhere.

The Italian universities underwent less severe decay. Their controlling potentates sought to revive them by endowing new chairs and engaging leading intellectuals from other Italian principalities or overseas. At Bologna in 1709, General Luigi Ferdinando Marsigli laid before the Assunteria di Studio a proposal for academic renewal and offered his own collection of instruments, only to be rebuffed. The Vatican sponsored an academy of science in 1714 which taught and experimented at the Poggi palace. In 1715, Scipione Maffei proposed reforms for Turin and Padua. The first was overseen by Victor Amadeus II of Savoy through a *magistrato della riforma*. He stripped noblemen and clergymen of their privileges, subdued the college corporations, assumed a power to grant professional licences, retained foreign lecturers – royalist professors of law and theology and *novatores* in the sciences – installed a physics laboratory, and endowed a chair of botany. Victor Amadeus III introduced new statutes and created the academy. The Savoy dynasty also reformed the universities of Sassari and Cagliari on Sardinia. Change was slow at Padua – only in 1760 did Simone Filippo Stratico, professor of physics and mathematics, set change in motion and increased the number of chairs. The ancient 'nations' were now each represented by a lecturer.

Under the Peace of Vienna (1725), Lombardy became a part of the Habsburg Austro-Hungarian Empire. Empress Maria Theresa created a board of studies in 1765 for Milan and Pavia, displacing the university assemblies and city senate from power. Joseph II expelled the Jesuits and ended the privileges of the professional bodies of architects and physicians. He brought the eminent professors Lazzaro Spallanzani, Alessandro Volta, Johann Peter Frank and Samuel Auguste Tissot to Pavia, rebuilt premises, raised pay, funded physics and anatomy laboratories and a clinic, founded a natural history museum and a botanical garden. The number of students at Parma and Modena similarly made progress, subject to a magistrature composed by councillors and deans of the faculties. Leopold of Tuscany, of the house of Habsburg-Lorraine, made education at Florence and Pisa subject to a superintendent general. Rome's La Sapienza was restructured in 1748 by Benedict XIV, a great canon lawyer who scaled down the law faculty and opened the door to the emerging sciences.

Reform in Portugal was imposed at Coimbra by the draconian rule of the Marquis of Pombal, minister to Joseph I. The Jesuit expulsion of 1759 ended the university at Evora and transferred the Lisbon seminary of noblemen to the Oratorians. Pombal created a

Sant'Ivo alla Sapienza, Rome
The Roman university's church is dedicated to St Ivo, patron saint of jurists. Its Baroque design is one of the most spectacular works of Francesco Borromini (1599–1667).

directorate general of studies headed by Thomaz de Almeida, appointed a reformist rector, Francisco de Lemos, and formed committees to draft new statutes and to justify the change with a fierce attack on the Jesuits. The curriculum was turned around and funding increased. In 1777 the king was succeeded by his daughter Mary I, who removed Pombal and Lemos. Reform continued regardless, and Lemos was reinstated in 1799.

Henri Testelin, *Jean-Baptiste Colbert Presenting the Members of the Royal Academy of Science to Louis XIV* (c. 1667) Palace of Versailles, Paris
The academies, inspired by and named after the school founded by Plato, were created in the sixteenth and seventeenth centuries as a complement to university education. The Académie des sciences was formed in 1666 under the sponsorship of Jean-Baptiste Colbert, minister to Louis XIV. With royal blessing, the academy had its quarters in the Louvre.

In France, Academicians were classified as honorary, pensioners, associates, correspondents and trainees or students. Honorary academicians were royally appointed noblemen, bishops and senior functionaries

The Academies of Science

The decline of the universities was made up for by the rise of the academies. Numerous and early in Italy – since Galileo's time – they were repeatedly crushed by orthodoxy. In 1714 a science academy was formed at Rome by Cardinal Gualtieri and the monk Celestino Cesi, who promoted science and reissued the works of Galileo with some success, until the Inquisition accused them of promulgating Newton and Locke and brought the venture to ruin.

The Royal Society in England, however, flourished, and took the lead in European science. Aiming for progress in the natural sciences, arts, manufacturing techniques, inventions and discoveries, it avoided religious clashes by shying away from theology, metaphysics, moral and political philosophy, grammar, rhetoric and logic. It won the support of the aristocracy, and many of its members were highborn. Presided over by Newton, the Royal Society was the model and arbiter of Enlightened science; its *Philosophical Transactions* were read and respected across Europe. Newton had taught eight hours a year of mathematics at Cambridge while writing his *Principia*. He was made head of the Royal Mint and chaired the Royal Society for years.

In France, too, extramural intellectuals promulgated the new science and the exchange of knowledge, such as the Oratorian Marin Mersenne, a friend to Galileo, and the academies of Thévenot and Le Pailleur. Monarchs created academies of sages to benefit from the glow of their prestige and keep them under control. Cardinal Richelieu founded the Académie française (1635), concerned with language, and Mazarin the Académie de peinture et de sculpture. Under Louis XIV in 1666, Colbert promoted the Académie des sciences, and academies of inscriptions, architecture and navigation. In 1671 Paris gained an observatory five years before Greenwich. Louis XVI formed the Société de médecine (1778) to oversee the profession and the health of the realm.

Under its regulations of 1699 the Academy of Sciences was a technical body of the Crown, able to license discoveries and inventions and run mathematics, physics, chemistry and hydraulics competitions.

The Academy was equipped with a good library and laboratories for research. Academicians were classified as honorary, pensioners, associates, correspondents and trainees or students. Honorary academicians were royally appointed noblemen, bishops and senior functionaries who integrated the Academy with the Bourbon bureaucracy. Pensioners drew a salary and were famous scientists who did research and committee work, divided by discipline: mathematics, astronomy, chemistry and botany. They were aided by young trainees, while associates and correspondents were a network of French and foreign scholars exchanging ideas. The Academy issued *Mémoires*, scientific papers, and *Histoires*, recording its proceedings. Research was the concern of the Academy, while teaching rested with universities. The model was adopted on a smaller scale in Orleans, Toulouse, Montpellier and even non-university cities.

Monarchy and Academy encouraged voyages of discovery, cartography and scientific experiment. The European powers equipped ships to roam the seas: Cook and La Pérouse sailed the Pacific. In 1735 the French Academy mounted expeditions to the Arctic Circle and Peru to measure the meridian. As Newton had foreseen, it was found that the Earth is not a perfect sphere but compressed at the poles. The Peruvian expedition led by La Condamine included the naval officers and scientists Jorge Juan and Antonio de Ulloa, who published their results. In 1790, the French Academy defined the metre as a ten-millionth of the quadrant of the terrestrial meridian.

The Spanish monarchy, too, sponsored expeditions. In 1789, the Italian nobleman Alessandro Malaspina, a captain in the Spanish navy, took two sloops, with scientists aboard, to the western coasts of the Americas to make better maps, conduct research and enhance political prestige. The five-year expedition sailed from Cape Horn to Alaska, and landed in Australia and the Philippines. Malaspina presented his results and earned promotion and fame. But the envious royal favourite, Godoy, had him dismissed and imprisoned, a sentence commuted to banishment to his family estates. The materials collected at Madrid's

Alexander von Humboldt and Aimé Bonpland, *Géographie des Plantes Equinoxiales. Tableau physique des Andes et pays voisins* **(1810–15)**
Humboldt's expeditions in South America produced a mass of data on the geography, wildlife and, most particularly, botany of the continent.

Eduard Ender, *Humboldt and Bonpland on the Orinoco* **(c. 1850)**
In 1799 and 1800, these two naturalists explored the jungle of Venezuela following the course of the Orinoco. They discovered the Casiquiare canal, which connects the Orinoco to the Amazon, and made contact with several indigenous tribes.

Hydrographic Deposit were scattered. Years later, Charles IV licensed the voyage to the Americas of Alexander von Humboldt, who from 1799 to 1804 visited those lands and gathered a mass of observations, later published. He returned to Germany, continued his work and won high prestige; he taught several lessons at Berlin.

The French model was to be imitated throughout Europe; only Holland and the United States followed the English pattern. In 1657, Germany saw the creation of an academy at Schweinfurt, with no fixed seat; endorsed by the Emperor, it was named 'Leopoldine'. In Berlin, Frederick I, heeding Leibniz, founded the Akademie der Wissenschaften (1711), which Frederick II expanded. Maupertuis said its members were free men, unfettered by university or government. In Russia, the Tsar Peter I started the Academy of Sciences of St Petersburg, confirmed by Catherine I in 1725, aiming to encourage sciences and create universities. It attracted scientists both Russian – Lomonosov, the Russian Lavoisier – and foreign, such as Leonhard Euler and Nicolas and Daniel Bernoulli. The University of Moscow (1755) trained professionals and functionaries; Diderot drew up an

Enlightened curriculum for Catherine II. The Swedish Academy was founded in 1739 and the Danish in 1742. There followed Munich in 1759 and Bonn in 1777. In Naples, Celestino Galiani, head chaplain and director of studies, founded one in 1733, and proposed a curriculum rejected by Vienna. At Turin, Victor Amadeus III of Savoy erected the Accademia delle Scienze in 1783.

No academy of sciences was founded in Spain. Under Ferdinand VI, the Marquis of the Ensenada tried, sending Ulloa, member of the Royal Society, throughout Europe to put flesh on the idea. But Ensenada lost royal favour; some foreign traveller recorded that, though he was present daily at the royal luncheon, the king never spoke to him. Years later, the Count of Floridablanca revived the project and commissioned the building now housing the Prado. The intended foundation came to fruition only in 1847. Yet some local academies were formed: in Seville, the Royal Society of Medicine and Sciences, in Madrid, the Royal Academy of Medicine, in Barcelona the Royal Academy of Medical Practice and the Royal Academy of Natural Sciences and Arts, and in Valladolid a Medicine and Surgery Academy. A luckier Portugal opened the science academy in 1779.

The Bourbon Dynasty: Philip V and Ferdinand VI

The Habsburg dynasty died out with Charles II of Spain; he was succeeded by Philip of Anjou, grandson of Louis XIV. But the Emperor Leopold I advocated the Archduke Charles of Austria. Bourbons and Habsburgs were sucked into a war in which France and Spain battled Austria, England and Holland. Peace was signed at Utrecht (1714) and Vienna (1725).

Philip V reorganised the royal bureaucracy, shifting power away from the old councils to secretaries of state and ministers. Some councils disappeared through the loss of Italy and Flanders. The Council of Aragon perished, giving way to Castilian administration. With the founding of the Royal Spanish Academy and the Royal Academy of History, noblemen and intellectuals were charged with 'clarifying, fixing and lending splendour' to the Spanish language and giving shape to the history of Spain. The aristocracy aspired to the distinction promised by letters, frequenting the French academies and even the Royal Society, which, looking for their support, admitted noblemen of dubious scientific merit.

In 1713, Melchor de Macanaz, secretary of state, laid before the king a memorial proposing chairs of royal law at the faculties of law and canons, as in France. Hitherto, Roman and canon law had been taught with reference to the *Partidas* and the *Recopilación* and the authors relied on in practice. Macanaz was fighting the college establishment of the Council of Castile, which he weakened by reform. Finally, he was tried by the Inquisition, and exiled himself to Paris in defeat.

In response to royal prompting, Salamanca expressed willingness but did nothing. Valladolid claimed proudly that its graduates were lawyers who 'have a solid training in the courts were experienced and practical advocates for the defence of their cases; doctors cin schools to discuss questions that exercise the wits of their disciples, so cultivating glorious minds, and masters in the teaching of rules and practical principles for the framing of firm discourse and sound understanding'. Alcalá, too, was offended, in so far as

Assembly hall of the University of Barcelona
Alfonso the Magnanimous granted the charter of the University of Barcelona in 1450 as a *studium generale*. The university developed and grew over time, and, in 1863, construction work began on its present building, designed by Elies Rogent and declared national heritage in 1970.

Plan and elevation of the University of Cervera (1720)
The building was erected at the instigation of Philip V to bring together all the universities of Catalonia in Barcelona. The façade obeys a strict symmetry, with the axis running through the doorway, crowned by the Immaculate Conception.

the royal order accused its lecturers of ignorance of the law of the realm, whereas the latest reform prescribed that attention be given to 'all those laws of the kingdom which, whether in agreement or in contradiction, have a bearing on the matter in hand'. And law professors aspired to the councils and courts, more than to their wage of three or four hundred *reales*, and were thus under a duty to know the regal laws. The chairs founded by Cisneros were addressed to other subjects; if the king wants a royal law chair, he must fund it. Mediocrity was their safe haven; tenure was the stairway to preferment.

The king gave way and upheld the colleges' and religious orders' claims. At Salamanca he introduced a new collegial rotation, whereby, out of every five chairs falling vacant, four were set aside for the *colegios mayores* and only the fifth was open to competition from commoners. In theology, the king sanctioned the *alternativa* system: the orders were to occupy various chairs segregated by doctrine – Thomist, Suarist, or the new Scotist chairs.

However, Philip V did reform the universities of Aragon. After the defeat of Archduke Charles of Austria at the Battle of Almansa (25 April 1707) Philip restructured the kingdoms of Aragon and Valencia

and suspended municipal power over the universities. In Catalonia, the change was greater still. The king amalgamated at Cervera the seven former universities: old Lérida, the municipal *studia* of Barcelona, Girona and Vic, the Dominican schools of Tortosa and Solsona and the pontifical seminary of Tarragona. Barcelona had held out until 1714, when the Archduke Charles left to take up the imperial throne; war nonetheless continued until the Peace of Vienna. Charles was followed by several professors and noblemen. When Barcelona fell, the Duke of Berwick closed down the university and moved it to Cervera to prevent clashes between students and troops. After consultations, it was decided there were too many universities competing for too few students and too little income, and they should thus be consolidated. The draft proposal made provision for a chair of physics, but the king's confessor, the Jesuit Daubenton, thought a philosophy chair sufficed, and barred the creation of a Cartesian chair for its dangers to the Faith. The chancellorship devolved upon the chancellor of Lérida, Francesc Queralt; the congregation of doctors and masters chose a rector, but his office was abolished when he clashed with Queralt. Building and maintaining the university's beautiful seat burdened the royal coffers, and required the endorsement of a recalcitrant pope who, pressured by an approaching imperial army, had recognised the Habsburg Pretender's claim to the Spanish throne. The bull expressing Clement XII's approval, the *Imperscrutabiles Divinorum* (1730), took some time; it lifted a possible excommunication from the university's founders.

These difficulties may have discouraged Philip V from reforming Valencia. The city had maintained teaching using interim vice-rectors and lecturers. In 1720, Valencia sought restoration of the former municipal patronage, and the captain general, the duke of San Pedro, hinted this would be granted if the teaching of grammar was handed over to the Jesuits. Valencia gave way, though the lawsuits continued for twenty years. In 1721, an inspection of Huesca was only cursory, while in 1722 the king confirmed the old statutes of the University of Saragossa.

Under city patronage, Saragossa had a doctors' congregation, and students voted to elect professors.

Casimiro Gómez Ortega, cover of *Curso elemental de botánica dispuesto para la enseñanza del Real Jardín de Madrid* (1785), detail
The first site of the botanical garden founded by Ferdinand VI was at Huerta de Migas Calientes, adjoining what is now Madrid's residential district of Puerta de Hierro. Charles III moved the garden to its present location and commissioned the design from the architects Sabatini and Juan de Villanueva.

The year's rector was the previous vice-rector, appointed by lot among bachelors, excluding professors and clergymen. He was aided by councillors elected from among professors and doctors. But the cathedral canons, as at Valencia, coveted the rector's seat, and the king humoured them in 1728. Student election of professors engendered conflict, so appointments later rested with the Council of Castile, based on a report by five city officials and five faculty masters designated by lot. These changes were reflected in the 1753 statutes.

The reign of Ferdinand VI saw little change. Improvement was advocated by some; the Benedictine Benito Jerónimo Feijoo advertised European progress and other advanced ideas, attracting both attacks and royal protection. The monarch needed surgeons for the army and formed a school at Cadiz (1748) of a more modern and practical sort, the language of teaching being Spanish; further such schools opened in Barcelona, Madrid, Burgos and Santiago. Ferdinand founded an astronomical observatory at Cadiz and the botanical garden in Madrid.

The Reforms of Charles III

In 1759, Charles III returned to Spain from his Kingdom of the Two Sicilies, his by virtue of the Peace of Vienna (1735) ending the War of the Polish Succession; he had earlier governed Parma and Piacenza. With the minister Tanucci, Charles had built the palaces of Caserta and Capodimonte and the academy of Portici. He supported chaplain-major Celestino Galiani's plan for the University of Naples, continued by his son Ferdinand IV.

One of Charles's ministers was the Marquis of Squillace, soon brought down by the uprising set off by his abolition of fixed grain prices, which drove up the cost of bread. Other Enlightenment ministers sought to improve government: the Count of Aranda presided over the Council of Castile, seconded by the Counts of Campomanes and Floridablanca, Manuel de la Roda being secretary of state of 'grace and justice'. They hoped to destroy resistance to change.

In 1767, the King decreed the expulsion of the Jesuits, imitating Portugal and France. A secret report by Campomanes accused them of instigating the wheat scarcity unrest and manoeuvring to detach their Paraguayan missions from the Crown. The issue went beyond universities: Jesuit power as a whole was ripe for destruction. The royal confessors of the first Bourbons had been Jesuits, who schooled the ruling classes and wielded influence in the Church and the bureaucracy. After expulsion, Jesuit property was auctioned off for the Crown, which paid the banished fathers life pensions. Clement XIV suppressed the 'company of Jesus' in his bull *Dominus ac Redemptor* (1773).

Suarist professorships were extinguished, and Latin grammar, hitherto under Jesuit control, was returned to universities. Chairs of theology were no longer distributed among the various currents of opinion. Some of the Jesuits' books and paintings went to the universities, and their buildings put to use at Salamanca, Valladolid, Seville, Alcalá, Palma de Mallorca, Granada and Santiago. The Valencia seminary of noblemen was reassigned to the lay clergy and the Imperial College of Madrid became the Royal Studies of San Isidro. The Jesuit Gandía disappeared, as did other universities in the Americas; an attempt to continue under a new curriculum failed for lack of income and of canons willing to teach.

The next power to be crushed were the *colegios mayores*. Collegians ran a network in which old placement helped fresh graduates gain position, and dominated the universities, the Crown and the Church. Francisco Pérez Bayer sent the king a long memorial titled 'For the Liberty of Spanish Letters' (1771). Professor of Hebrew at Valencia and Salamanca and tutor of princes, Bayer had excellent court connections; he complained the 'major colleges' were in breach of their duty to help paupers and in league to keep professorships and jobs for themselves. He exposed their vices, mediocrity and meagre literary output. Charles III had all six colleges inspected. The collegians were taken by surprise; their bid to parley was ignored by the king and fobbed off by Aranda, who replied to their pleadings with a curt report of royal displeasure. In 1777, new decrees prescribed a ceiling on the income of candidates for collegial admission, banned the expensive inquiries into 'clean' lineage and barred the practice of lodging graduates while they awaited getting the right job. College wealth later suffered the depredations of a penurious Charles IV, and colleges were suppressed entirely by the liberals.

The universities were thus disarmed and readied for reform. In 1769 members of the Council of Castile had been appointed as university directors to ascertain the state of affairs and collate university statutes and documents. Thesis censors were appointed in response to an anti-royalist screed defended at Valladolid, and to combat arguments attributed to the Jesuit Father Mariana in favour of regicide and tyrannicide.

Education came under a storm of royal charters, provisions and orders of varying levels of generality, and each university had to print all rules governing it. By 1786, at the end of this process, the mass of provisions were consolidated in a single royal charter sent to all centres of learning, but their diversity made it hard to apply in practice. The spate of royal provisions faced by university assemblies was so heavy that I shall address three aspects only: organisational matters, selection of lecturers and curricula.

Structure and number of professorial chairs remained the same: only names and syllabuses changed. At Salamanca, the student rector became a doctor or licentiate reigning for two years, to strengthen his power against the *maestrescuela*. At Alcalá, reform went further: the wealth of San Ildefonso was transferred to the university, which paid the college a fixed annuity. The King appointed an interim rector, and the office subsequently lay in the discretion of the doctors' congregation, bringing Alcalá closer to the Salamanca model. Municipal universities – which were few, after the suppression of the Catalan *studia* – were untouched. Doctors infighting at Valencia attracted royal intervention. Absent the Jesuit professors, the question was whether anti-Thomists had to teach Thomism. The king suspended the municipal patronage and gave the rectorship to Vicente Blasco, a philosophy professor, a friar of the order of Montesa, and tutor to princes, who, sponsored by Floridablanca, wrote a new curriculum. He had patronage restored, but was re-elected rector several times until his death. His curriculum had the city and the archbishop both endow the university with fixed amounts to be managed by the rector and professors; candidates for tenure were examined by the university prior to appointment by the city.

Pleased with his plan, Blasco showed it to the Edinburgh physician and clergyman Joseph Townsend, who thought it good, but backward in the medical sphere. Humboldt praised the amalgamation of medicine and surgery, but was otherwise critical – and yet the counter-proposal shown to him by Blasco seemed to him to hark back to the sixteenth century. Humboldt was on his 'Grand Tour', in fashion among aristocratic and affluent northern European intellectuals, the medieval scholarly peregrinations having disappeared. After Paris, he visited the university and the college of Santa Cruz at Valladolid, and met Cavanilles and others in Madrid. Humboldt's interests were history, philology, and centres of learning. His robust conclusion was: 'It can be said with certainty that all Spanish universities and centres of education are, without exception, inadequate, and of no use whatever'.

Charles III's reformers were suspicious of the small convent universities that awarded cheap and easy degrees to scholars from elsewhere. Under threat of suppression, the Dominican Ávila and Almagro were forced to improve standards. Campomanes wanted to turn Orihuela into a language school with arts and theology faculties. University and city both refused, and a deal was made in 1783, dissolving the medical school. Enlightenment ministers wanted few, well-endowed universities that would suffice for the elite; the mass of the people was to devote itself to manual trades. Pablo de Olavide wrote: 'A nation would be in a poor state if the pursuit of literature should lure young lads away from their fathers' ploughs and workshops and transport them to a school'.

The second issue was professorial appointments. Merit was of little consequence – influence was decisive. At Valencia, selection rested with city officials, whom the physician Andrés Piquer described as 'barbaric and ignorant'. At Salamanca, the college system of rotation rendered competitive examinations meaningless. Pérez Bayer claimed exercises were purely formulaic: a collegian gave a three-quarter-hour lesson – the timekeeping officer would put the clock forward by fifteen minutes – and sometimes did not bother to address the subject assigned to him by lot. No discussion or classification of merit ensued. Candidates read under their breath to remain unheard, and some might spend over half an hour on the preliminary invocation of saints, or offer a prayer for the college founder, thus prompting all collegians to stand piously. Examinations were sometimes waived altogether on pretext of illness.

First, the reformers abolished rotatory professorships. Then they regulated tribunal membership: the rector and three doctors elected by the congregation. The reading was to take one hour; candidates were heard in groups – *trincas* – who would engage in debate among themselves. No *aegrotat* waiver was allowed. The tribunal's report went to the council, which, with the advice of an advocate-general, would elect a *terna* of three, the final selection resting with the king. The aim was to choose 'among persons stepping up and reciting, those ablest, fittest and most deserving, with no regard whatever to rotation or length of service or connection with other chairs, but only to merit, aptitude and virtues adorning them'. The universities of the religious orders did not use these proceedings.

Did teaching and professorial quality improve? Examinations, at least, were more open, competitive and rigorous.

The third branch of reform were the curricula endorsed by the Council of Castile. Roda commissioned Mayans y Siscar to draw up uniform rules for all, but existing diversity stood in the way. Specific plans were adopted instead. Seville led the way, where Pablo de Olavide, leader of the city government, aided by professors, wrote a curriculum for the Collegial University of Santa María de Jesús. The Council approved the plan in 1769 and sought reports from Salamanca, Valladolid and Alcalá to improve their teaching and adapt subjects to the new four-year bachelor's degree now in place. The Council's intervening advocates-general modified the reports as they pleased and introduced sundry curricula; others followed for Oviedo (1774) and Granada (1776). The assembly of Cervera considered the Salamanca model but modified only its medical faculty in 1784. Valencia was reformed in 1786. Juan Sempere y Guarinos judged that only the Council officials' amendments saved the curricula from displaying ignorance. A couple of lines from the Salamanca report suffice: Newton's ideas 'prepare the learner as a perfect mathematician but do nothing for him as a logician and metaphysician; those of Gassend and Descartes symbolise not revealed truth but the ideas of Aristotle'.

At that time, Masson de Morvilliers, in his *Encyclopédie méthodique* (1782), asked the famous question: all European nations, even Poland, have contributed to the sciences and arts, '*Mais que doit-on à l'Espagne?*' What is owed to Spain over the centuries? This continued the Black Legend against Spain, originating with the expulsion of the Jews, the Inquisition, and injustices done in the colonisation of the Americas, as denounced by Las Casas. The Black Legend became a tool in the clash between Christian creeds and in the war propaganda of France and other powers. Feijoo noted that Spain had had

great theologians and jurists, while acknowledging that the country's scientific contribution was small. Spain's universities made no reply to Masson. Tacit agreement, or contempt? Replies came from the Enlightened abbot Carlo Denina (expelled from his chair at Turin for his ideas), from Cavanilles, head of Madrid's botanical gardens, and from the learned judge Juan Pablo Forner, and newspapers such as *El Censor* commented on the matter.

Under Charles IV, reform stalled for fear of revolution. In 1799, medical teaching was consolidated in the Royal Colleges of Surgery, renamed 'of Medicine and Surgery' – but this lasted only a year. In 1802, the legal disciplines were reformed. In 1807, in a vast plan devised by the Marquis of Caballero and several academics of Salamanca, the Crown suppressed collegial and convent universities, leaving only ten. Juan Antonio Llorente, chancellor of Toledo, deplored the move:

> It pains me to record the savagery, worthy of the tenth century, with which swift destruction came to the universities of Toledo, Ávila, Sigüenza, Orihuela, Osuna, Gandía and others. Is it even conceivable that at the dawn of the nineteenth century the number of houses of public instruction in Spain should be decreased? Is this not proof of a desire to level Spaniards with Hottentots and so enslave them?

Two Models of University: France and Germany

In 1789, the French National Assembly proclaimed the sovereignty of the people and the rights of man and of the citizen. The Constitution of 1791 enshrined the separation of powers. A new age began, the old political structures of monarchy, nobility and Church lost their privileges and wealth. England had completed its revolution in 1688 without attacking the Anglican Church or the aristocracy. It now opposed France, adopting the position explained in Edmund Burke's *Reflections on the Revolution in France*.

The Assembly passed no law on universities; it considered the draft laws of Talleyrand and Condorcet, which did not pass. The universities suffered the abolition of tithes, confiscation of Church property and freedom of profession: no qualification was now required for the practice of medicine or law. The Convention, in its Law of 7 Ventose III (27 February 1794), abolished colleges and corporations and established special schools. Universities were regarded as part of the *Ancien Régime*; the Revolution created the École Polytechnique to train engineers and the École Normale for teachers, and schools of jurisprudence and medicine.

The Consulate, presided over by Napoleon, again regulated education, based on a project drawn up by Fourcroy, director-general of public instruction, which distributed education into three levels – primary, lyceums and special schools, which were simply a range of higher departments attached to a lyceum. The lyceums were the core: boarding schools under military discipline where schoolboys learned sciences and letters. Eleven of them included a higher school of law, with two chairs – one of private law, the other of criminal law. Others came later: public law, government, and Roman law. There were three schools of medicine and others concerned with sciences and letters.

Napoleon used this structure to create the Imperial University, named in the singular, because all centres were identical and subordinate to a single hierarchy. Introduced under the Law of 10 May 1806 and implemented by a string of regulations, it was crowned by a *grand-maître* advised by a board. The first was the politician and poet Louis de Fontane, who appointed university district rectors. Twenty-four former universities were suppressed, somewhat more than the cull under Caballero's Spanish plan of 1807. The Sorbonne ruled the rest, whose functions were limited. The Polytechnique and École Normale stayed untouched, as did the Collège de France and the Jardin du roi, renamed Jardin des plantes and attached to the Muséum d'Histoire naturelle. Academies were integrated within the Institut de France.

The faculties were five. Theology, law and medicine survived, while philosophy was divided into sciences and letters, a solution later adopted elsewhere, as in Russia from 1884. Arts remained one, however, in the Germanic and Baltic areas, though containing separate departments, except in Bavaria and Denmark. The special or technical schools remained separate and enjoyed high prestige. The Imperial University was reformed by later ministers who encouraged research. The Third Republic decentralised, raised funding and staff numbers and allowed also private universities.

The early nineteenth century, with its wars and economic slump, saw many European universities close. Of the original 143, only 83 remained by the Peace of Vienna (1815), when Napoleon was confined to St Helena; but these sufficed for the minority they catered to. The clergy, the erstwhile majority of the student body, retired to the seminaries, while special schools absorbed another high number. New universities opened at a steady rate: growing from about twenty in the eighteenth century to fifty in the nineteenth. There were about two hundred by the eve of the Second World War.

There were hardly any openings in Spain, Portugal, Italy and France, except Douai's move to Lille at century's end. Germany also languished: Bonn revived, Ingolstadt moved to Munich. In 1810, Frederick Wilhelm III of Prussia founded the University of Berlin following a proposal by Humboldt. In his handwriting, published in 1896, he exposed his learning drafts, following the vision of Kant. The purpose of a university was knowledge, requiring freedom and solitude. But knowledge calls for union and voluntary cooperation within the group, and this the State must provide unconditionally, remaining aloof, unlike its role in secondary or technical schools. It was to appoint lecturers through curators, unlike academies, which elected members themselves. The German tradition shows that research need not be left to the academies. The university teaches through seminars: a lecturer addresses his students, who are 'thinking heads' who help dissect the matter in hand and so make it their own. This arouses a thirst for knowledge for its own sake, free of extraneous motivations. German intellectual yearning is readily awakened. Knowledge is not a settled issue but a continuing inquiry. Private lecturers – *Privatdozenten* – taught at Berlin, awaiting the call of universities. Berlin drew the best, and crowned academic careers. Hegel taught philosophy there, while Roman law had Friedrich Karl von Savigny, who trained Rudolf von Jhering and Bernhard Windscheid; both disciples competed for professorships and Windscheid won Berlin itself.

Humboldt's merit is shared by the theologian Friedrich Ernst Daniel Schleiermacher, who guided the University of Berlin as principal. Liberty encountered difficulties: Prince Metternich, minister to the Emperor Franz Josef I, decided at Carlsbad (1819) to exercise censorship and ban scholarly associations. Lecturers were thrown out, and Schleiermacher was dismissed, but he was not expelled.

Modern Europe thus witnessed two models: the teaching-based and bureaucratic French, and the research-inspired German scheme. Oxford and Cambridge continued their traditions. Other countries formed new universities. Switzerland raised the status of former high schools: Zürich, Lausanne, Berne, and the Catholic school at Freiburg. The Baltic countries did similarly, as did Norway with Oslo; the Finnish school of Abo moved to Helsinki. In the Netherlands, French occupation had left only Leiden, Utrecht and Groningen. William I of Orange-Nassau concentrated teaching staff at Leiden and re-established other centres; in the south, he restored Louvain, Ghent and Liège. After Belgian independence, Leopold I of Saxe-Coburg chartered two private institutions: the Free University of Brussels and the Catholic Malinas, which moved to Louvain. Holland recognised private universities in its constitution of 1848, the Free University of Amsterdam being a late arrival.

The United Kingdom retained Oxford, Cambridge and the Scots universities, and made new creations based on existing schools: Durham, London, Leeds, Manchester, Birmingham and Cardiff, and Belfast and Dublin in Ireland. The Industrial Revolution was the occasion of a strategy to advance in the sciences and train technical specialists. The Austro-Hungarian Empire preserved Austria's six universities and created numerous special schools, while universities were founded in other territories of the Empire: Iasi, Bucharest, Kolosvar, Zagreb, Ljubljana, Czernowitz and Warsaw in Poland, which closed for thirty years owing to nationalist unrest. Athens opened in 1837. Russian universities multiplied: Kazan, Kharkov, Kiev, Odessa, Olomouc, St Petersburg and Tomsk in Siberia. At the end of the century the old madrassa in Istanbul was the basis for the city's new university.

The liberal state exerted strict control over its universities. Providing funds and topping up its shortfalls, it kept them on a short reign. Parliaments legislated and governments executed. Prussia saw the first ministry of culture, education and health in 1817, followed elsewhere: in Spain, the ministry of public instruction and fine arts in 1900. University was hierarchical in France. Napoleon III allowed academic freedom, but used inspectors, and full liberty arrived only with the Third Republic. Intervention was gentler in Britain; Parliament legislated, the monarch assented and the Church supervised. Oxford and Cambridge were regulated late.

Unlike France and Spain, at several central European universities the persistence of a vestigial corporation meant that the assembly or senate continued to elect rectors. Technical schools were less free, and in Germany acquired the ability to elect authorities and award degrees only in 1899. Assemblies were powerless: their role was to take orders, write reports and disclose requested information; they made requests from higher authorities and dealt with teaching methods. Humboldt said that lecturers were to cooperate for both the outward and the internal

organization of the discipline but within their subjects were to communicate only if so inclined; otherwise, 'each follows his own path'.

In research, universities and academies formed a scientific community and networks. In the eighteenth century there were competing conceptions, with unanimity in Newtonian science, but division in medicine and law. In the nineteenth century, the community drew together owing to ease of communication through conferences and journals. Science was more cohesive, though some issues were controversial, such as Darwin's theory of evolution. Theology remained split by differences of creed, opinion and school. Disciplines became minutely specific; chairs and fields of research multiplied. The academic community divided into interrelated sectors. With the creation

of new research centres, their members – whether or not of professorial rank – were admitted to the scientific community. In 1887 the Imperial Physical and Technical Institute was founded at Berlin, which in 1910 became the Kaiser Wilhelm Gesellschaft, encompassing other institutions.

Student numbers grew in the nineteenth century, particularly in law and medicine. Germany had numerous theologians, the clergy being university-educated. Estimates of social background are hazy: parents' occupations offer an unconvincing guide. Matriculation fees and living costs kept out the poor, and few scholarships were available; in this, Britain's private and public aid was in the lead.

The nineteenth century was a time of revolution and unrest. Students partook of politics: in Poland,

Entrance of the Lycée Condorcet, Paris (19th century)
The *Lycées* were the core of the public education project set in motion by Napoleon. Founded in 1803, the Lycée Condorcet is one of Paris' oldest and most prestigious. Throughout most of the nineteenth century, under various names (Bonaparte, Bourbon, Fontanes), this was the 'great liberal lyceum' of the *rive droite*. The novelist Émile Zola evokes the arrival of schoolboys to the Lycée Condorcet in *The Kill*.

after the second partition of 1793, they vindicated nationalist claims. In Germany, Fichte's writings appealed to students and the old *Burschenschaften* brotherhoods called for a unified nation state. The third centenary of the Reformation stimulated more radical groups and secret societies: banned by Metternich at Carlsbad from 1819 to 1848, they remained active regardless. Student brotherhoods operated in Vienna, too, grouping the various nations of the Empire. Students held conferences at Uppsala and Copenhagen.

The demonstrations and strikes seen in the French universities from the 1820s were harshly put down by the later Bourbons. Student agitation returned with the revolution of 1830, which elevated Louis Philippe of Orleans to the throne.

In the Netherlands, students clamoured for freedom and volunteered against the Belgian rebels. Belgian independence found student support, with echoes even in Warsaw, where Polish scholars feared the Tsar would put down the uprising. Belgian students rebelled in Louvain and moved to the Free University of Brussels (1834). Student movements gained strength in 1848 from the proclamation of the French Second Republic, the fall of Metternich and the gathering of the liberal parliament at Frankfurt,

***Jules Michelet and Edgar
Quinet Resume Lectures
(1848)***
One of the earliest student riots
took place in Paris in 1848.
Students came out in protest
against a ban on lectures by
the writer and historian
Jules Michelet.

where several professors had seats, despite ultimate
failure. In Paris, a great demonstration protested the
ban against Jules Michelet's lectures. At Bologna, restored by Innocent XII in 1824, over the following
decades students demonstrated for unity, prompting
intervention by Austrian troops. In 1859, students
supported the provisional government; the poet and
tribune Carducci, a literature professor, had ministry
support to celebrate the eighth centenary of the
Commune and the Province. Conflict faded in the
second half of the century, universities modernised
and governments grew more tolerant.

STUDENTS IN THE EIGHTEENTH CENTURY

From its beginnings to the eighteenth century the university landscape underwent far-reaching change. After a moment of splendour in the sixteenth century, in which the numbers of both universities and of students surged, in the eighteenth century universities did not notably multiply, and student enrolment languished. The demand for education shifted in nature, and the so-called 'major' centres of learning – Alcalá, Salamanca and Valladolid – no longer attracted students from so far afield: this meant higher demand for the outlying regional universities.

Salamanca had 7,000 students on its roll in the sixteenth century; it started the seventeenth century with under 1,500 students, and rose again to 2,500 scholars by the midpoint of the century's opening decade. Alcalá reached its peak in the late sixteenth century, with around four-thousand enrolled students, and never again attained to this size. Valladolid, however, managed to raise enrolment, though perhaps not the numbers of students genuinely hearing lectures. Its student body was greater than two thousand in the academic year 1621–22, but by 1699 had shrunk to 430. Oddly, the figure rose during the War of the Spanish Succession, but was not to exceed one thousand until 1771, reaching 1,500 towards the end of the century. The reforms introduced by Charles III plainly encouraged matriculations, probably by tightening admission requirements.

Matriculation meant one was a member of the university and enjoyed all the privileges of a scholar. But not all universities had the same prerogatives. In that litigious society, the privilege valued the most was the availability of an exclusive jurisdiction administered by a 'judge of schools', which disposed of any need for the ordinary royal courts. Other attractive perquisites were exemption from lodging fees, exemption from conscription into the army and entitlement to church stipends as an absentee, under a bull of Pope Eugene IV. The student body was male, young (the average age upon enrolment being seventeen to eighteen) and typically clerical, though not to the extent that it had been in its medieval beginnings or in the Renaissance. All these exemptions were intended to enable masters and scholars to concentrate on the business of study, without having to leave it aside 'with delay and undermining of their wealth and knowledge'; but in the eighteenth century these privileges were encroached upon by royal prerogatives.

Martín de Cervera, *Lecture Hall* (1614), Library of the University of Salamanca, detail
One of the doors of the manuscripts room is decorated with this painting of gowned scholars taking notes at a lecture.

Students were prone to distractions regardless. University rectors set curfews and banned behaviour such as bearing arms, riding on university premises or playing cards. The academic authorities would enforce their rules by going on a nightly round of the town, watching streets and lodgings – innkeepers were bound to allow inspections under the rector's warrant.

Commoners had to be identifiable by their outward appearance. Their uniform consisted of a 'decent habit' in the clerical – as opposed to the military – fashion, with a soutane and mantle in dark flannel, *bayeta negra*, of up to the second-finest quality and 'manufactured in these kingdoms'. It was by so dressing that they were marked out from townsmen as privileged students.

Uniformity of dress survived well into the eighteenth century, but then came under pressure from 'womanly' French fashions (wigs, queues and powdered hair) and the criticism of Enlightenment intellectuals like Olavide. The habit was doomed. By the end of the century, students were expected merely to refrain from extravagant attire, such as 'boots, trousers, bows on shoes, a tie instead of a collar, hair in a queue, the frock worn open down to one's calves, so as to show off coloured breeches, waistcoat and ribbons'.

The academic year ran from St Luke's Day (28 October) to the *Virgen* (Day of Our Lady) in August. Scholarly status was retained all throughout one's studies, and university marked one for life: a successful graduate was given the prize of a job in the civil service or the Church, and was styled 'bachelor', 'licentiate' or 'doctor'. In the modern age Spanish graduates came to be called *letrado*, 'lettered'.

Margarita Torremocha Hernández

Students were prone to distractions. University rectors set curfews and banned behaviour such as bearing arms, riding on university premises or playing cards. The academic authorities would enforce their rules by going on a nightly round of the town

George Knapton, *Portrait of a Scholar* (18th century)
The painting depicts a young man dressed in academic garb – black gown, mortarboard and white tie – as prescribed by Oxford protocol.

Ceaseless Reform in Spain

Napoleon, bestriding Europe with his victories, invaded Spain on the pretext of conquering Portugal. He forced the Bourbons to give up the throne to his brother Joseph. On 2 May 1808, Madrid and other Spanish cities rebelled. Patriotic juntas of notables mounted a resistance, supported by the army and the Duke of Wellington's British troops. In a letter dated 22 August, Ferdinand VII congratulated the Emperor for 'seeing his beloved brother King Joseph installed upon the throne of Spain'. Joseph I did not get as far as making any change to the universities. At Salamanca, Thiébault introduced a curriculum prescribing the Napoleonic Code as a subject in jurisprudence; he was rewarded with an honorary doctorate.

In September 1810, the Cortes opened in Cadiz and proclaimed the sovereignty of the people. On 19 March 1812, there was approved a Constitution, establishing new political and government bodies, and promising education for all under uniform curricula. Reform was entrusted to the directorate general of studies, formed by a group of 'wise men', subject to parliamentary decrees and government orders, and chaired by Manuel José Quintana, a poet and revolutionary intellectual. The 'Council of Regency' – the government – appointed an advisory committee, again chaired by Quintana. The Condorcet-inspired report became a parliamentary bill that was printed and distributed to the House, but never discussed. By his decree of 4 May, Ferdinand VII abolished the Constitution and repealed parliamentary decrees contradicting his sovereignty. He drafted his proclamations with the aid of Captain General Elío from his base in Valencia, where he had returned from exile amid popular clamour, but only released the order in Madrid days later, after dissolving parliament. He reinstated the curriculum of 1807, but in 1818 introduced a new one, inspired by the Salamanca scheme of 1771, fixing orthodox subjects and textbooks. So much upheaval left education in disarray, and assemblies were disrupted by tension between liberal and absolutist lecturers.

The insurrection of Rafael Riego in the garrisons and provinces returned the liberals to power. The king swore allegiance to the Constitution and convened the Cortes. The plan of 1807 was reinstated, with a subject on the Constitution and another on natural and international law, according to liberal textbooks. Reform followed, based on the bill of 1814, and a general law of public instruction was enacted by decree on 29 June 1821. The matter was barely disputed: complaint came only from universities condemned to disappear, since the scheme sought to have universities evenly distributed. Oviedo, Huesca and Valladolid were to disappear, and a new university to be created at Burgos. Funds were a concern, given peasant reluctance to pay tithes, which parliament had in any event halved. The law forbade the expropriation of property relating to public instruction and ordered an inventory; any shortfall was to be made up by the public purse.

The enactment of 1821 made far-reaching changes both in the metropolis and the Americas and Philippines. The directorate general of studies and the Academia Nacional lay at the core; the former comprised five commissioners selected by co-optation. The directorate general made provision for elementary schools entrusted to city and provincial authorities, and framed rules on course dispensations, commutations and requirements that reshaped the curricula of many secularised monks and clerics. The Academia Nacional was composed of three sections of academics: physics and chemistry, moral and political sciences, and literature and the arts, absorbing the old academies of Philip V. Half of its 48 members were American colonials.

The new law of public instruction created three levels of education – primary, secondary and tertiary, which comprised the universities and the special schools. Primary education was compulsory and free, though this was not effective until much later. Private education was allowed even at university level – again, this has only recently become a reality. Secondary schools were termed 'province universities', but were mere high schools. Some did provide higher education and were called 'universities of third teaching' by analogy to the French lyceums. There

were ten in Spain: Huesca was dissolved and Alcalá was moved to Madrid and Cervera to Barcelona. The Central University of Madrid, like its counterparts in Mexico City, Lima and Santa Fe de Bogotá, taught mathematics and physics, literature, history, Arabic and European public law. The other universities were limited to theology and law, while other professions were taught at special schools of medicine, surgery and pharmacy or of veterinary medicine. Engineers trained at the polytechnic school and at 'application' schools. Before the new law was fully implemented, Alcalá and Cervera started their moves. In his inaugural address at the Central University on 22 November 1822, Quintana deplored the previous state of affairs – its backwardness and persecutions – and hoped for an Enlightened era. Ferdinand VII regained absolute power by the intervention of a French army sent by Louis XVIII, the 'hundred

thousand sons of St Louis'. He repealed the Constitution and parliamentary decrees, and purged the army, bureaucracy and academia. In 1824, he enacted a university curriculum that buttressed orthodoxy and centralization. Rectoral appointments rested with eight delegates selected by lot from the congregation of doctors, who then made a list of three from which the king made his choice. In 1830, universities closed for two years in response to the revolution that deposed the Bourbons in France. Chancellors were suppressed in 1831. This curriculum prevailed for over twenty years, because the first liberals made only light changes.

In August 1836, the 'sergeants' coup' at La Granja forced María Cristina, mother of Isabella II and regent during her minority, to reinstate the Constitution of Cadiz and appoint as prime minister Martínez de la Rosa, a moderate liberal. The directorate general

Eugenio Lucas Velázquez, *Revolution of 1854 at the Puerta del Sol* (1855)
In the reign of Isabella II, there was a military coup or *pronunciamiento* known as the *Vicalvarada*. The revolt was joined by the working classes and students demonstrating in front of the central post office building and the former church of Buen Suceso in Madrid's Puerta del Sol square.

of studies was restored and Quintana rearranged curricula to allow academics to teach and choose textbooks as they pleased. The time seemed right to revive the Law of 1821 – as other decrees had been – but, this being the time of the Carlist War, a heavily indebted treasury could not afford it. The Law also purported to regulate education in the American possessions, which since Ayacucho in 1824 were de facto independent, though not yet so recognised by treaty.

General Espartero ended the Carlist War with the 'Embrace of Vergara' sealing his agreement with General Maroto. Army risings and *pronunciamientos* continued until Espartero replaced María Cristina as regent. He joined the law and canon law faculties in a single faculty of jurisprudence, and introduced a philosophy faculty comprising higher education in sciences and letters.

After his fall, the provisional government suppressed the directorate general and concentrated decision-making power in the ministry, while a council of public instruction dealt with consultations and case files. Pedro Mata's medical curriculum was adopted, leaving only two faculties of medicine, surgery and pharmacy, at Madrid and Barcelona: the rest were 'schools of the art of curing', awarding lesser qualifications. In 1843, the Battle of Torrejón de

Ardoz gave power to Narváez and the moderates. Juntas and garrison revolts again ensued: this mechanism of changing government had become ingrained. The absolutist curriculum was in force and reform was in order. But no bill was passed into law by parliament. The development minister Pedro José Pidal imposed reform in 1845 by a cabinet decree, soon superseded by fresh decrees issued by Pastor Díaz in 1847, Seijas Lozano in 1850 and further tweakings by later ministers. Change was funded by increased enrolment fees as shown by the national budget, which itemised university income and expenses separately from 1842 to 1854. Over time, the State raised spending, and subsidised the middle and upper classes' university training. In 1854, corruption near the throne sparked a new uprising, involving students, led by General O'Donnell, who called upon the progressives. The constituent Cortes debated the public instruction bill drafted by Alonso Martínez. Finally, with the moderates in power, Moyano pushed through a primary statute, *Ley de Bases*, in 1857, the implementing instruments of which remained in force for almost a century, subject to constant variations by the Marquis of Corvera (1858) and the Marquis of Orovio (1866). Rules made by one minister were reversed by the next.

Features of the Spanish University

The inaugural address of 1857 at the Central University fell to Julián Sanz del Río: 'We now have the law,' he said, 'all that is needed is for this grand building to breathe in the spirit of knowledge, which its harmonious organism attracts and invites, but cannot create... Teaching must conjoin with the law in an intelligent and active enterprise in which each rivals the other in fulfilling its intellectual mission'.

Moyano introduced a strict centralisation that depended on the government and the development minister, with the director-general under him. The council of public instruction, formed by professors and bureaucrats, decided on books and syllabuses, competitive examinations for chairs and various other proceedings. Rectors were ministerial appointments signed off by the monarch. As the highest authority in a university district, they also ruled over primary and secondary education funded by city and provincial authorities. A rector was advised by a university council, thus following the French scheme of single-handed decision-making and collective advice.

To save costs and in consonance with liberal elitism, there were only ten universities: the Central University at Madrid and nine district universities, namely Barcelona, Granada, Oviedo, Salamanca, Santiago, Seville, Valencia, Valladolid and Saragossa. Murcia and La Laguna were created in the twentieth century. Madrid stood above them all, because it had the full complement of faculties and special schools; the rest remained a step behind, with varying degrees of endowment. Madrid had a monopoly of doctorates and professors who taught highly specialised subjects to cultivate a given discipline; sometimes a chair was created with a particular individual in mind. The outcome was mediocre: doctoral theses were mere exercises in rhetoric. From the twentieth century onwards, a thesis was a hurried and ill-supervised paper, which, with few exceptions, mirrored the poverty of Spanish higher education.

Moyano established six faculties: theology (abolished in 1868), law, medicine, pharmacy, sciences, and philosophy and letters. After foundational subjects, study bifurcated into specialities. In many district universities only the first few years of sciences and letters were taught, as entry qualifications for medicine or law. They had few students of their own, but survived. Degrees took five years, medicine somewhat longer. Halfway through, one took examinations for the bachelor's degree, discontinued in 1868. At the end of five years one took finals for the licentiate degree, which enabled one to practice professionally. In 1917 the graduation examination was dispensed with, and merely passing the component subjects sufficed. A doctoral degree was a requirement of professorial appointment.

Lecturers and students are the protagonists of the transmission of knowledge, the ability to inquire and ascertain. Professors became civil servants; the 1846 list names about three hundred, and this figure rose to 466 by 1900. Formerly, each was a member of a single university and could not move, but now transfers were possible to vacancies elsewhere. The other two routes into tenure involved competitive examinations among doctoral graduates – or among auxiliary lecturers only, except in periods when they were barred. Ministers regulated competitive appointments, time and again seeking to entrench their own pet solutions. Proceedings were conducted in Madrid before a tribunal of seven or five members, depending on the period, selected by the ministry, subject to certain quotas of academicians and professors in the same subject area. Examination exercises were old-fashioned, guarding promotion from one category to the next. Mateo Orfila, a native of Minorca and a professor of forensic medicine and chemistry at Paris, criticised this twofold examination procedure for frustrating legitimate claims to tenure. Later, proceedings were rigged: auxiliaries were named by their own faculty, then tried for a chair. The competitive appointments regulations of 1864 placed tribunal composition in the discretion of the directorate general, which chose among professors and academicians or other prominent scholars in the domain of the given vacancy, with no requirement that they even hold doctorates. A paper was submitted upon entry. The first *viva voce* exercise

BOLETIN
DE LA INSTITUCION LIBRE DE ENSEÑANZA.

La *Institucion libre de Enseñanza* es completamente ajena á todo espíritu é interés de comunion religiosa, escuela filosofica o partido político; proclamando tan solo el principio de la libertad é inviolabilidad de la ciencia, y de la consiguiente independencia de su indagacion y exposicion respecto de cualquiera otra autoridad que la de la propia conciencia del Profesor, único responsable de sus doctrinas.—(Art. 15 de los *Estatutos.*)

Este BOLETIN, fundado en conformidad con el par. 5. de los *Estatutos*, se reparte por ahora gratuitamente á los Socios de la *Institucion*, así como á las Corporaciones científicas y redacciones de periodicos análogos; esperando que unas y otras se servirán aceptar el cambio con sus respectivas publicaciones.
La correspondencia se dirigirá á la Secretaría de la *Institucion*, Esparteros, 9.

AÑO I. MADRID 7 DE MARZO DE 1877. NUM. 1.º

NECESIDAD DE RECONOCER LEY EN LA HISTORIA,
POR EL PROFESOR D. NICOLÁS SALMERON.

Si en los tiempos de transicion en que vivimos más nos espanta y aterra la oscuridad que aún nos rodea, que nos reanima y fortalece la claridad que de lejos presentimos; si observamos frecuentemente aún que la indiferencia alterna con la supersticion, la guia engañosa de las conciencias, en el imperio de los corazones; si este desconsolador espectáculo ocasiona desfallecimiento en unos, deja sueltas en otros pasiones egoistas, y en todos siembra confusion y siniestra ansiosa inquietud, que en la vida exterior política aparece como revolucion de un lado, reaccion de otro, oscilacion impotente en medio y por resultado—obligados estamos, si no hemos de perder el último derrotero que nos resta en este cáos, la ley de la razon en nosotros y el sentimiento de la Providencia sobre nosotros, cayendo de aquí en manos del accidente y en el goce egoista de la herencia de siglos, á indagar los principios que determinan el desenvolvimiento humano y la ley á que obedecen los momentos de crísis, como el presente, en nuestra vida. Preciso es tambien, si no hemos de caer en la duda y la desconfianza moral y religiosa de la vida ante la larga série, aun no terminada, de dolores y de martirios, y de sangrientas luchas que apenas han dejado al hombre espacio para reconocerse y pensar en sí, precisa

ne constituida desde muy antiguo y su índole ha sido desde entonces y es hoy exclusivamente filosófica; la segunda empezó á formarse con carácter general en tiempo de Romé de l'Isle y Haüy, y recibió su nombre de Goethe, que la extendió, de los minerales, á otros productos y séres de la Naturaleza. Las partes hoy más constituidas de la última son: la «Cristalografía» y la llamada «Morfología de los organismos.» Cada una de ellas se distingue luego en dos miembros, teórico ó general y práctico ó especial. Llevan estos, en la Cristalografia, los nombres de «Cristalografía pura, teórica, matemática, geométrica,» etc., el primero; y el segundo los de «Cristalografía aplicada, especial, práctica, descriptiva,» etc. En la llamada «Morfología de los organismos,» recibe el primero, cuando se le distingue del segundo, la denominacion de «Promorfología, ó Doctrina de los tipos, de las formas fundamentales, de los *promorfos,*» y el segundo es llamado en ese caso «Morfografía;» fuera de raras excepciones (Carus. Bronn, Burmeister, Jaeger, Haeckel) suelen confundirse todavía ambos miembros en la designacion general de «Morfología.»

De suerte que, prescindiendo de las partes aun no constituidas en la Morfología natural relativas, tanto á séres como á productos naturales, se puede ya dar por extendido este nombre á todo el concepto que envuelve, y decir que se llama así la «Ciencia que estudia en teoría y aplica-

First issue of the newsletter of the Institución Libre de Enseñanza, Madrid (1877)
Founded in 1876, the Institución Libre de Enseñanza implemented the most liberal and innovative educational plan Spain had ever seen. Wholly independent from officially sanctioned schooling, the Institución took a more practice-oriented approach than the established norm.

Lecturers and students became the protagonists of the transmission of knowledge, the ability to inquire and ascertain. Professors became civil servants

144

was to give a lesson – common to all candidates – and meet objections fielded by fellow aspirants in one's same *trinca*. One then spoke his own lesson on a randomly selected topic, and was tested on miscellaneous items from the tribunal's questionnaire. Sometimes – in medicine, pharmacy or languages – there would be a practical exercise. Memorisation and sheer mass of knowledge carried weight, as did friends in high places.

Academics rarely engaged in research or even wrote books. They gave conferences and compiled lecture handbooks. In 1854, Manuel López Gómez, professor of canon law at Valladolid, said a teacher's duty was to pass on an up-to-date version of the legacy, exercise intellectual tolerance and respect for reasonable opinions, and engage in common effort. In the second polemic on science, Manuel de la Revilla and Gumersindo de Azcárate insisted on Spain's unimpressive contribution to human knowledge. Menéndez Pelayo replied with long lists of sixteenth and seventeenth-century authors.

Professors recited lectures and lessons; facilities and laboratories were scarce and most universities remained in old buildings or took over refurbished convents. Ministerially endorsed textbooks were central. Francisco Giner de los Ríos complained that 'in addition to pressuring students fairly directly, as if the inevitable anxiety of examinations were unfortunately not enough, they exact a budgetary supplement in the form of a monopoly over a voluminous and expensive text, which is accordingly doubly pernicious'.

Enlightenment curricula had designated one textbook per subject. The liberals refused to allow a free choice and published lists of eligible texts for each topic until the late 1860s; from then on, books were authorised by the council of public instruction.

Low-paid lecturers often practised at their own clinics or law offices. Many wrote for the press, and spoke at athenaeums and the old provincial friends' societies to build their reputations and fulfill hopes of political office. The Constitution of 1876 encouraged this by giving a senate seat to a representative of each university, elected by all doctoral graduates. Some even reached ministerial rank; Segismundo Moret became prime minister. Sainz Rodríguez,

Francisco Giner de los Ríos (1839–1915)
Philosopher, teacher and essayist, Giner de los Ríos was the founder and principal of the Institución Libre de Enseñanza. He and his colleagues advocated academic freedom as a fundamental right essential to the transmission of knowledge.

Franco's first education minister, boasted of reaching both professorial and ministerial rank: 'I have attained all the ambitions of the average Spaniard of my time, except being a general or a bishop', he noted wryly.

Students were middle class and dropped their former aspirations to being rogues, sages or saints. Their studies were confined to lectures and textbooks; they hoped to join the professions or get civil service jobs. They sought out fun and friendship, as evoked by Pérez Lugín in *The House of the Troya*. They might strike over academic issues or demands for longer vacations, and started to form student societies.

In 1865, Isabella II ceded all royal wealth to the State, keeping back one quarter for herself. Emilio Castelar wrote an article, 'The Feature', in his newspaper *La Democracia*, in which he argued that the property of the old monarchy rightly belonged to the liberal State. He was forthwith deprived of his tenure, and, on the Eve of St Daniel, students demonstrating in the Puerta del Sol square were harshly repressed by the army. Two years later, Orovio demanded from lecturers an oath that they would not teach 'pernicious doctrine in the religious, moral or political spheres'. About 30 academics – mostly Krausists – refused to sign, and lost their posts.

September 1868 saw a new military coup, termed the 'Glorious Revolution' in remembrance of England's. General Prim, Admiral Topete and progressive politicians formed a government. Isabella II fled to Paris; Amadeus of Savoy was elected king. Upon his abdication, the Spanish First Republic was proclaimed; it ended when General Pavía entered the Cortes on horseback, and was followed by the provisional government of General Serrano. In *Leaves of Grass*, Walt Whitman lauded the Republic, emerging in a Europe shattered by the Prussian Wars: 'Spain.../ Out of the murk of heaviest clouds,/ Out of the feudal wrecks, and heap'd-up skeletons of kings,/ Out of that old entire European debris—the shatter'd mummeries,/ Ruin'd cathedrals, crumble of palaces, tombs of priests,/ Lo! Freedom's features, fresh, undimm'd, look forth – the same immortal face looks forth.../ Shall the clouds close again upon thee?'

On 21 October 1868 a decree of the minister Ruiz Zorrilla allowed the creation of schools and universities: 'The greater the number of those teaching, the greater the number of the truths propagated and of the intellects cultivated'. He wanted freedom in professional practice, freedom of academic doctrine, and student freedom of attendance – liberated education. The Krausist Fernando de Castro, rector at Madrid, backed his vision in his inaugural address: 'Nineteen centuries ago divine wisdom thus proclaimed: only the truth shall set you free (John, 8:32). This is the motto of the new education, the new right, the new life'. In the assembly hall, the queen's portrait was replaced by the words *veritas liberabit vos*. In a bid to spread education to the people, the rector organised popular lectures in mathematics, reading and writing, and even Sunday conferences for women on dance, feminism, marriage, free trade and religion.

Ruiz Zorrilla repealed Orovio's law, dissolved the public instruction council and allowed some independence. Rectors were to be professors, sometimes even elected by the university. Competitive examinations were held in the university where the vacancy arose, before a tribunal of the dean, four professors in the given subject and four lecturers named by the university. Giner de los Ríos deplored the survival of this proceeding, which he described as 'China's ideal of abstract intellection, but, seen from the outside, it still seems to many the acme of democracy and impersonality in the assignment of office'; and yet it was the legacy of 'the Scholastic tradition of the Church and a naive reaction against the favouritism that corrupted and continues to rot the innards of our public life'.

Academics were required to swear allegiance to the Constitution of 1869. The canon lawyer Vicente de la Fuente and others tried to qualify their oaths on religious grounds. Rome relented, and most took the oath; those refusing were expelled, and reinstated later by the Republic. These years were darkened by the intransigent federal cantons and the Carlist revolt, and the first Cuban War. But its remembrance inspired hope of progress. Giner claimed universities had acquired an inner life, knowledge was deeper, assemblies more poised and institutions more open to society.

At the end of December 1874, General Martínez Campos rebelled in Sagunto and proclaimed Alfonso XII as king. Antonio Cánovas del Castillo gave the development ministry to Orovio, who restored the former status quo. He ended the private schools but recognised their teaching, subject to examination before a tribunal. He accepted liberated education for students and the public instruction council reinstated by Serrano. For competitive examinations, Orovio sometimes appointed the second or third member of the three-man list; the terna system was abolished by Albareda in the Sagasta government of 1881. He required lecturers to submit their programmes and teach 'no religious doctrine other than that of the State'. He feared the Darwinism taught by Augusto González Linares. Giner de los Ríos, Pérez Pujol and other Krausists were dismissed; they founded the Institución Libre de Enseñanza, a parallel institution of learning that held the group together, and were later reinstated by Albareda. Orovio was succeeded in office by the more tolerant Count of Toreno, who regulated appointment examinations – these were rules no minister left untouched, going through all permutations of tribunal membership. The faculties

suffered several reforms and curricula and detailed bureaucratic prescriptions. Unamuno perceptively compared the shifting situation to Penelope's loom. The faculty selection process continues to be woven and unwoven even today, although the present Constitution recognises autonomy.

In 1898, Spain was shaken by the loss of Cuba and the Philippines. Joaquín Costa and others wrote on how to 'regenerate' Spain. Rafael Altamira, in the inaugural speech at Oviedo, suggested ways of improving research. Bartolomé Cossío wrote 'Who can now doubt that the foremost cause of our catastrophe is ignorance?' Politicians did what they could. In 1900, Silvela created the ministry of public instruction. García Alix, its first minister, laid before parliament a bill allowing at least minimal autonomy to universities: rectors elected by university assemblies unanimously or, failing this, chosen by the minister

from the three leading candidates. Competitive appointments and financial matters remained centralised. The bill failed to pass, despite support from the liberal Romanones and resubmission by Santamaría de Paredes. Autonomy had years to wait yet, though demanded by a gathering of academics at Valencia on the fourth centenary of the university: they later met in Madrid and Barcelona. The situation improved in the following decades, which earned the name 'Silver Age'. Universities were beginning to catch up, but were interrupted by the Civil War, Franco's dictatorship, persecution and exile.

Miguel de Unamuno (1864–1936)
The leading exponent of Spain's Generation of 1898, Unamuno was made rector of the University of Salamanca in 1901. He was dismissed for political reasons in 1914 and reinstated six years later, when he was appointed dean of the faculty of philosophy and letters. After exile during the dictatorship of Primo de Rivera, he returned to his position as rector at Salamanca and stayed until 1933, when he retired as an honorary lifelong rector.

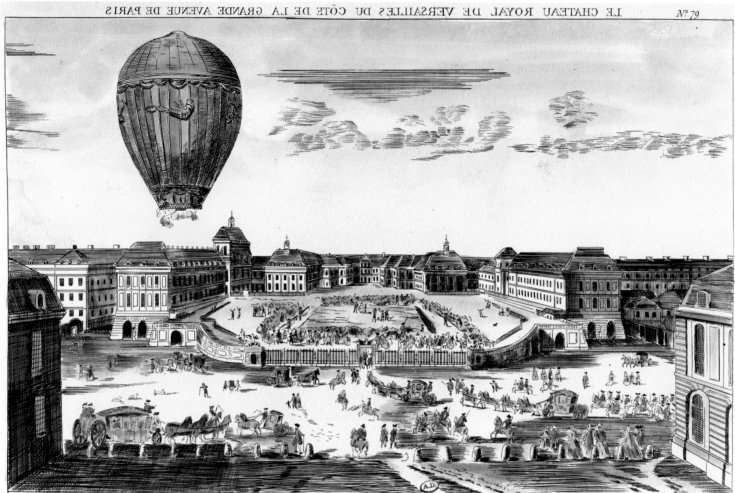

Expérience de l'Aérostat nommé la Montgolfière faite par M.ʳˢ Pilatre du Rozier à Versailles, le 23 juin 1784, en présence de la famille R.ᵉ et de M.ʳ le C.ᵗᵉ d'Haga, et grand nombre de Spectateurs. Cette Superbe Machine la plus brillante que l'on ait encor exécuté par le procédé de M.ʳ Mongolfier, de 86 p.ᵈˢ de haut sur 74 de large. Après l'espace de 35 minuttes de feu l'ascention se fit avec majesté à 5 heures moins ¼ au son d'une grande Musique et d'un applaudissement general. M.ʳ Pilatre du Rozier et M.ʳ Pronts sont les voyageurs qui dans l'espace de ¾ d'h. ont parcouru 12 lieues et est descendu sans accident entre Champlâtreux et Chantilli. S.A.S. M.ʳ le Prince de Condé leur envoya ce qui etoit necessaire pour les transporter au Chateau et de la a Versailles le Champ ou cette machine a pris terre n'ayant point de nom. S.A.S. la nomme Pilatre de Rozier

Balloon flight by Jean-François Pilâtre de Rozier over the Palace of Versailles (1784), Bibliothèque des Arts Décoratifs, Paris
On 23 June 1784, there took place the first hot air balloon flight carrying passengers. The Montgolfier brothers were the inventors of the contraption. Its swift acceptance by the public bears witness to how scientific inventions quickly gained popular currency from the Enlightenment onwards.

In the eighteenth and nineteenth centuries science made a giant leap. The astronomy of Copernicus, Kepler and Newton was now standard, mechanics was further refined, chemistry started with Boyle and the evolutionary theory advanced

Knowledge, Science and Technique

In the eighteenth and nineteenth centuries science made a giant leap. Theology lost its crown. The Catholic universities – Rome, Paris, Cologne or Salamanca – preserved the scholastic tradition. The Jansenist current, emerging at Louvain, was condemned by Clement XI's bull *Unigenitus* (1713) and persecuted by Louis XIV, a story told by Racine in his *Abrégé de l'histoire de Port-Royal*. The Jesuit expulsions enabled the Dominicans to shape opinion. In Leo XIII's encyclical *Aeterni Patris* (1879) St Thomas remained the doctrinal core. But some modernisation followed, at Protestant universities particularly. Emphasis was placed on biblical studies, moral theology and ecclesiastical history. Canon law looked to history, to the ancient discipline and councils. Regalism scoured the past for arguments to combat papal power. Lecture rooms heard the works of Zeger Bernard van Espen, who, having taught at Louvain, took shelter in a Jansenist community in Holland and died under excommunication for his adherence to the schism of Utrecht.

In the nineteenth century, theology faculties survived for training clergymen at the Anglican universities, the Lutheran universities of Germany and Scandinavia, the Presbyterian centres of Scotland, the Netherlands and Switzerland, and the Russian and Balkan Orthodox schools. Schleiermacher, the liberal theologian, taught at Berlin and combined rigour with religious sentiment. His seminary, headed by a dean, was divided into sections: two philological departments, for the Old and New Testaments, and a third area devoted to ecclesiastical history, where Adolf von Harnack taught. A practical homiletics and catechism section emerged later. Hegel's influence is visible in David F. Strauss, who identified Jesus with the World or Divine Spirit, and in Ludwig Feuerbach, who wrote on the essence of Christianity.

The French Revolution, by contrast, abolished theology faculties. Napoleon restored some at Paris, Bordeaux, Lyons and Rouen, but bishops refused to recognise their degrees; they were suppressed in 1885. Theology had earlier disappeared from Spain and unified Italy. When La Sapienza became part of the kingdom of Italy, theologians were not convened with the rest of academics to swear allegiance to Victor Emmanuel II (14 out of 48 professors stepped down). Pius IX rejected liberalism in *Syllabus Errorum* (1864), which condemned the following proposition: 'LXXX. The Roman Pontiff can and must become reconciled with and accept progress, liberalism and modern civilisation'. In his encyclical *Pascendi Dominici Gregis* (1907), Pius X opposed 'modernism', source of all heresies. Clerical training sheltered in seminaries and monastic novitiates, and the new Catholic or pontifical universities, first Louvain, where the liberal Catholicism of Lamennais reigned, and later on Angers, Lille, Lyons, Paris, Toulouse, and Dominican Freiburg in Switzerland.

Catholic theology faculties in Germany survived at the universities of Munich, Bonn, Mainz, Tübingen, Münster and Strasbourg. They taught exegesis and dogmatics, philosophy and Church history, and opened to modern ideas. At the turn of the century the Church condemned Morin Hermes, a lecturer at Bonn. Ernest Renan, author of a *Life of Jesus*, was expelled from the Collège de France, then readmitted by the Third Republic. Ignaz von Döllinger, a Munich professor, rejected the papal infallibility proclaimed by the Vatican Council and seceded with his Old Catholics; Ludwig II of Bavaria made him life president of the Academy of Sciences.

Philosophy attained high importance. Descartes had drawn it close to science, as did Leibniz and Kant, who examined critical reasoning and the rational possibility of metaphysics. In Britain, too, philosophy was beholden to science, but taking an empiricist stance. John Locke relinquished theology and took up medicine and chemistry. A fellow of All Souls College, Oxford, his continental exile ended only after the Glorious Revolution of 1688. His *Letter Concerning Toleration* and his *Treatises of Civil Government* laid down modern principles on citizens' individual rights and the right of property, heralding the political future of Europe and America, as later rounded out by Montesquieu – who looked to the British constitution – and Jean Jacques Rousseau, who hailed from Geneva. Both opposed the absolutist apologia of Jean Bodin, a lecturer at Toulouse, and Thomas Hobbes. In *An Essay Concerning Human Understanding* (1690), Locke vindicated inductive logic against rationalism and innate ideas. Close to Locke's thought was David Hume, a merchant who had retired to France. Voltaire and Diderot continued on this path, perhaps more lightly and incisively and with an eye on the politics of France and Europe. In the south – Italy, Spain and Portugal – the Church condemned them all.

In the nineteenth century, rationalism and empiricism both flourished. Kant's disciples constructed idealist systems: Hegel and Krause in Berlin, Schelling in Jena and Leipzig. Philosophy was central in Germany. Jurists and theologians were required to pass a preliminary philosophical *tentamen* test. Idealist notions extended to science and medicine, the so-called *Naturphilosophie*. France adopted empiricism – in the sensualism of Cabanis and Condillac, although Victor Cousin then developed an eclectic vision. Auguste Comte famously argued that, after religious and metaphysical phases, humanity's crowning moment was positivism. Widely translated and influential, Comte's followers formed a sort of church. He was an external examiner at the École Polytechnique. At the turn of the century Henri Bergson, of the Collège de France, sought to embed positivism within an idealist system.

In Spain, any glint of European philosophy was condemned by the fundamentalist Menéndez Pelayo in the final volume of his *History of the Spanish Heterodox*. Inveterate scholasticism now competed with Krause, imported by Julián Sanz del Río. Having travelled in 1842 to Belgium and Germany to meet Heinrich Ahrens and other disciples, he formed a Krausist circle on his return. Unamuno first admired Comtian positivism, then wrote his brilliant works – straddling theology and philosophy – inspired by wide reading of Kierkegaard, Nietzsche and Bergson. His books were prohibited by Rome in 1957.

European research achieved a high standard. Mathematics and sciences, after the fading of the French universities, took refuge in the Collège and the Polytechnique, where Joseph Louis Lagrange taught. Alexander von Humboldt visited these institutions on his Paris trip. The refounded French university had good lecturers to choose from. Mathematics later shone in Germany at Königsberg, where Karl Gustav Jacobi formed a seminar. Georg Cantor lectured at Berlin. Probability theory was partly developed by the St Petersburg School. Karl Pearson created modern statistics in London.

The astronomy of Copernicus, Kepler and Newton was now standard. In Spain, the Salamanca constitutions of 1561 recommended Copernicus, among others. But, after condemnation, his vision could be taught only as one among many theories, as practised by the Jesuit José Zaragoza at the Imperial College of Madrid and Valencia, and by the Oratorian Tomás Vicente Tosca in his mathematical compendium. Full acceptance had to wait for Jorge Juan's *Estado de la astronomía en Europa* (1774).

Enlightenment mechanics was further refined by Lagrange and D'Alembert, Euler and Bernouilli. Watt built the first steam engine. Electricity entered the stage with Franklin's lightning conductor and the Leiden jar of Kleist and Musschenbroek, a Utrecht lecturer. Galvani discovered electricity in animals, Volta made the first battery. Coulomb perceived the unity of electrical and gravitational attraction. Around 1800, the academic Laplace drove astronomy forward with his explanation of the solar system in terms of his nebular hypothesis, and Sir Frederick William Herschel provided a description of the Milky Way and the galaxies. Distances to the stars were later measured by Friedrich Wilhelm Bessel at Königsberg and the new astrophysics characterised their chemical composition. Measurements were now made of mechanical energy, heat, electricity and the speed of chemical reactions. Thermodynamics, founded by Mariotte and Gay-Lussac, was developed by Joule, Carnot, Clausius and Kelvin; electricity, by André Marie Ampère of the École Normale at Paris, by the Englishman Michael Faraday at London, by Hans Christian Oersted and, above all, by the Scotsman James Clerk Maxwell at Cambridge, with his theory of electromagnetic fields. By the end of the century, Ernst Mach, who taught at Graz and Prague, and Henri Poincaré – Caen and Paris – raised doubts about classical mechanics, later resolved by Einstein's theory of relativity (1905).

Chemistry started with Boyle. Empedocles' water, air, earth and fire gave way to chemical elements. The discovery of hydrogen, oxygen and nitrogen led to accurate quantitative formulation and laws of combination framed by Antoine Laurent de Lavoisier of the French Academy (he died under the guillotine). His disciple Louis Proust taught in Spain at Vergara, Segovia and Madrid. John Dalton formulated the atomic theory of matter and atomic weight, which Gay-Lussac and Avogadro harmonised with the theory of gases. Jöns Jacob Berzelius created modern chemical analysis at Stockholm. In 1869, Mendeleev at St Petersburg proposed the periodic table, while the Curies discovered radium. Organic chemistry emerged with von Liebig at Giessen. The gradual unification of chemistry and physics owes much to the Norwegians Maximilian Guldberg and Peter Waage of Oslo University.

Linnaeus classified plants into classes, orders, genera and species under a fixed taxonomy. He corresponded with the Spaniard José Celestino Mutis, who sent him a specimen of cinchona. Mutis introduced Newtonian science to Colombia, catalogued American flora and improved silver metallurgy, collaborating with Fausto de Elhuyar y Lubice, a mineralogy lecturer at the friends' society of Vergara. Botany was researched in France at the Jardin des plantes with Georges Cuvier, an anti-evolutionist and creationist, and Isidore Geoffroy Saint-Hilaire, and by Robert Owen at the London College of Surgeons. Zoology shifted from an Aristotelian to a mechanistic vision of comparative anatomy. Buffon stood at the summit, entertaining some evolutionist notions. Evolutionary theory advanced from Lamarck to Darwin, finding confirmation in the comparative anatomy undertaken by Thomas Henry Huxley, Ernst Haeckel and Carl Gegenbauer, both at Jena, and the geologist Charles Lyell, a Darwinist convert, in a movement quite remote from the speculative and idealist evolutionism of Alexander von Humboldt and Lorenz Oken, who lectured at Göttingen, Jena, Munich and Erlangen.

Critical historiography began with Mabillon's *De Re Diplomatica* (1688). Large collections were published of documents, patristic writings, church councils. Interest remained keen in kings and barons, saints and friars, but also in famous writers – for instance, Nicolás Antonio's surveys *Bibliotheca Hispana Vetus* and *Bibliotheca Hispana Nova*. Voltaire summarised world history in his *Essay on the Customs and Spirit of Nations* (1763). Herder's view was more philosophical. In the nineteenth century, history broadened its scope to entire peoples and nations. Thiers in France and Macaulay in Britain saw in it a thread of nationalistic progress; more academicc and rigorous were the histories of Mommsen and Niebuhr in Germany, who published the *Monumenta Germaniae Historica* series from 1826 onward. Other German historians were Heinrich von Treitschke and the famous Leopold von Ranke. Jules Michelet taught at the Sorbonne. At century's end, with Lamprecht at Leipzig, the history of civilisations superseded political and military chronicling. New fields opened up: Egypt, through the Rosetta Stone deciphered by Champollion, who followed Napoleon on campaign. An amateur, Heinrich Schliemann, excavated Troy and the Euphrates, driving back the historic horizon.

Modern philology emerged in Germany. The classical languages and Hebrew were rivalled by Germanic studies, with Joseph von Görres at Heidelberg and the Schlegel brothers at Vienna and Berlin. Savigny's interest in history spread to other jurists, like the brothers Grimm. Karl Lachmann and Moritz Haupt, classicists at Berlin, prepared critical editions of old texts, such as the *Nibelungenlied*, published grammars, and improved methods. They also took an interest in the Romance languages and English. In mid-century, the discipline arrived to Rostock, Halle and Bonn, and reached Spain with Menéndez Pidal. The study of Slavonic languages began at Berlin and Vienna.

In medicine, Hermann Boerhaave systematised the various currents of thought. A mechanist, he was acquainted with the classics, botany and chemistry and was an outstanding clinician. He thought of health as a properly functioning body; disease was a malfunction brought about by an anatomopathological lesion. His influence and textbooks prevailed across Europe. At Halle, Friedrich Hoffmann was a mechanist who befriended Boyle and learned chemistry. The vitalism of Van Helmont inspired Georg

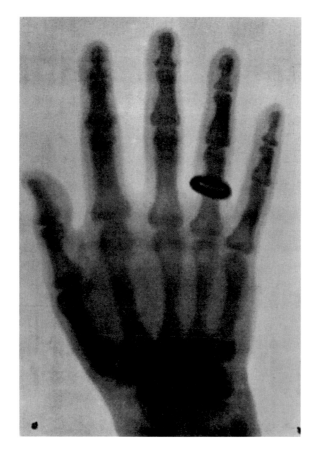

Early x-ray (1896)
The physicist Wilhelm Conrad Roentgen, the first ever Nobel prizewinner for physics, discovered x-rays in 1895. An x-ray is an invisible electromagnetic ray that traverses the body and leaves a trace on film: a radiography. This enables medical practitioners to detect otherwise unidentifiable internal lesions and disorders.

Ernst Stahl. He thought bodily processes were ruled by an anima that had curative properties, while mechanism explained external causes. Vitalism spread to Montpellier with Sauvages, who, influenced by Sydenham, classified diseases in Linnaeus' manner.

Leiden was the centre of medicine until Boerhaave's death in 1738. His teachings were diffused to other universities. At Vienna, his disciple Gerhard van Swieten founded a school, and his alumnus Johann Peter Frank taught at Pavia. Another of Boerhaave's followers taught at Göttingen, Albert von Haller, whose knowledge ranged from botany to medical bibliography and the edition of classic works. A firm anatomist, he saw the body as behaving mechanically and chemically and used the concepts of the sensibility and irritation of bodily fibres, but allowed the existence of a neuro-vegetative *anima* separate from the rational and immortal soul. Vitalism was advanced at Edinburgh by the noted clinician and taxonomist William Cullen and the more

simplistic but influential John Brown, commended by the French Convention.

In the early nineteenth century German medicine was contaminated by the philosophy of Hegel and Schelling. In France, René Théophile Laënnec, of the Necker Hospital, and Claude Bernard perfected the positivistic method of experiment and observation using new and refined instruments to uncover the lesions underlying disease. Late in the century, Roentgen discovered x-rays, a great step forward in detecting hidden lesions. Claude Bernard, before teaching at the Sorbonne, worked at the Hôpital-Dieu, where his colleague François Magendie conducted animal experiments and concentrated medicinal active ingredients. Bernard succeeded Magendie at the Collège. They were opposed by the then famous vitalist Broussais, an advocate of bleeding. But most turned to the positive method and the search for the lesion: William Stokes at Dublin, and, at London's Guy's Hospital, Robert Bright, Thomas Addison and Thomas Hodgkin. Karl von Rokitansky lectured at Vienna and Jean Martin Charcot at Paris.

The vitalist vision survived in Germany, but experiment and observation of lesions was adopted nonetheless. Two great masters, Johannes Mueller at Bonn and Berlin and Carl Ludwig at Leipzig, headed the schools that framed modern physiology, the study of bodily movement and function. Rudolf von Virchow succeeded Mueller in the professorship, having taught at Würzburg. He shared the anatomopathological outlook of Claude Bernard, and made a huge contribution with his *Cellularpathologie* (1858). Fallopio, Borelli and Baglivi had viewed the body as consisting of fibres: in the eighteenth century, Caspar Friedrich Wolff introduced the idea of 'atoms' or 'globules'. Bichet, of the Hôpital-Dieu, spoke of 'tissues', Philippe Pinel of 'membranes'. Virchow, preceded by the botanist Matthias Schleiden and especially by Theodore Schwann, developed the theory of the cell. Years later, Camilo Golgi and Santiago Ramón y Cajal extended the theory to the nervous system. Cajal elevated Spanish science; he undertook research at his Institute and formed a following that faded with the Civil War.

Progress was made with inquiry into the causes of disease: the aetiopathological approach. Magendie

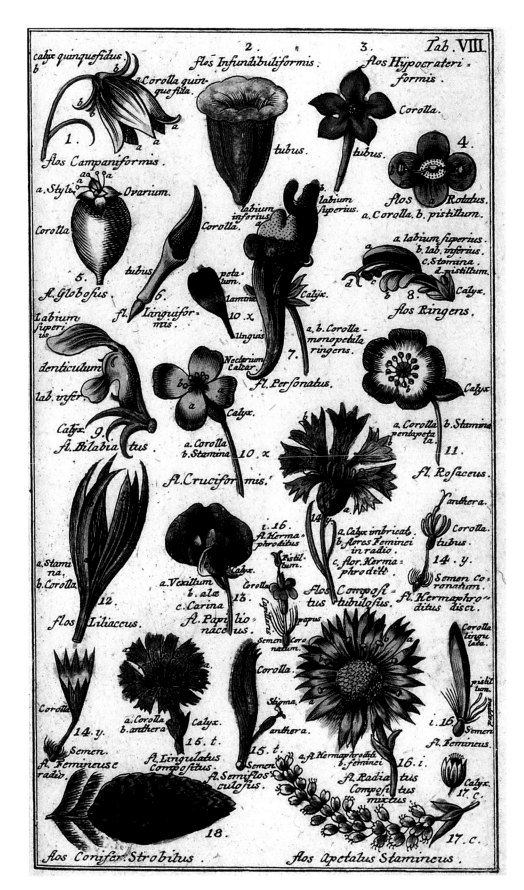

Carl Linnaeus, *Botanical Classification* (18th century) The Swedish naturalist Linnaeus (1707–1778) created a taxonomic scheme for botanical classification. His best-known works were *Systema Naturae*, in which he classified the mineral, animal and vegetable domains, and *Philosophia Botanica*, his masterwork.

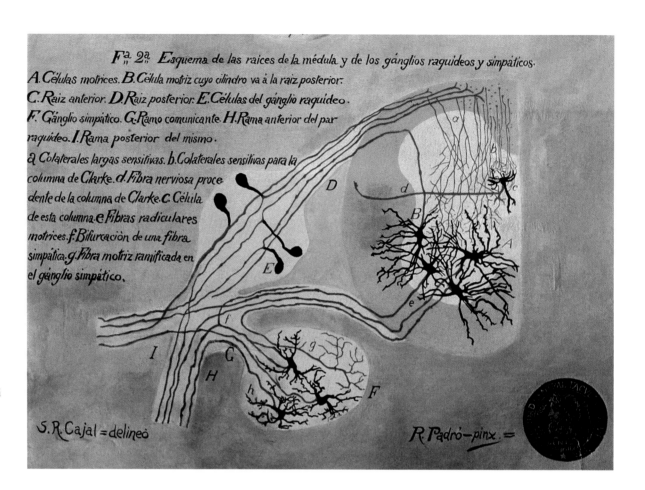

Fª 2ª *Esquema de las raices de la médula y de los gánglios raquideos y simpáticos.*
A. Células motrices. B. Célula motriz cuyo cilindro va à la raiz posterior.
C. Raiz anterior. D. Raiz posterior. E. Células del gánglio raquideo.
F. Gánglio simpático. G. Ramo comunicante. H. Rama anterior del par
raquideo. I. Rama posterior del mismo.
a Colaterales largas sensitivas. b. Colaterales sensitivas para la
columna de Clarke. d. Fibra nerviosa proce-
dente de la columna de Clarke. c. Célula
de esta columna. e Fibras radiculares
motrices. f. Bifurcación de una fibra
simpática. g. Fibra motriz ramificada en
el gánglio simpático.

S. R. Cajal = delineó   R. Padró-pinx =

Santiago Ramón y Cajal,
Neuronal Scheme (c. 1900)
A physician and histologist,
Ramón y Cajal used the Golgi
method to discover the unity
and cellular complexity
of the nervous system. The
importance of his discoveries
won him the Nobel Prize for
medicine in 1906.

and Mateo Orfila had studied poisons and their effects. The chemist Louis Pasteur brilliantly studied fermentations and contagious disease in animals and humans. Tenured at Strasbourg and Paris, he then headed an institute funded by the Academy of Sciences. Robert Koch rivalled him in Berlin.

The nineteenth century saw the rise of new academic disciplines. Forensic medicine, mooted by Zacchia in the seventeenth century, was enriched by Fodéré and Orfila. Psychiatry progressed with Philippe Pinel, a judicious clinician, and later with Jean-Etienne Dominique Esquirol and Wilhelm Griesinger in Berlin. Freud started writing at the end of the century. Johann Peter Frank and Max von Pettenkofer founded public hygiene, Chadwick created medical statistics. In law, at the begining of the eighteenth century Scipione Maffei expounded the new currents: Roman civil law was to be joined by natural and international law, regal and customary law, public law and criminal law. Penal law accommodated the Enlightenment principles of Cesare Beccaria and Jeremy Bentham, which found governmental favour. At the

end of the century, Cesare Lombroso won resonance with his ideas on the born criminal.

The *Corpus Iuris Civilis* remained the core text. The *Mos Gallicus* continued the history of Roman law – Heinecke at Göttingen. Salamanca ended the seventeenth century with Francisco Ramos del Manzano and his disciples, but the current faded, with only José Finestres at Cervera and Gregorio Mayans at Valencia. The European jurists were fond of historic adornment, but needed a Roman law in consonance with the present, the *Mos Italicus*. In central Europe, lawyers prepared a wide-ranging doctrine, the *usus modernus Pandectarum*, which systematised the Roman legacy with references to customary law. Thomasius and Wolff continued the natural law tradition which later acquired liberal principles with Burlamaqui and Vattel. Public law and governmental science intervened in the training of civil servants, the 'cameral science'. Initiated at Göttingen by Johann Pütter, it then became 'State science' by the hand of Justi at Vienna. Enlightened codes were drafted by order of Maximilian Joseph II of Bavaria, the

Empress Maria Theresa and her son Joseph II. Samuel von Cocceji's Prussian project (1749–51) was enacted in modified form by Frederick II. Piedmont and the Two Sicilies produced further codes, while in Spain the Marquis of Ensenada commissioned one from Mayans which never came into force.

In France, Louis XIV created chairs of royal law in 1679. He had renovated it with extensive ordinances of civil law and for trade by land and sea. Louis XIII had already partly organised the various bodies of local custom of France. Robert Joseph Pothier, an Orleans lecturer and magistrate, systematised Roman doctrine and customary law in his vast oeuvre, which facilitated the future drafting of the *Code civile des Français* (1804). Napoleon created a commission and attended many sessions himself. After enacting his Code, he dismissed academics daring to criticise it. There were introduced the criminal code, the commercial code and the two procedural codes, which were imitated and adapted across Europe and the Americas. The Napoleonic Code prompted voluminous commentary from lawyers and judges, including the Sorbonne lecturer Duranton.

Imitations of the French civil code included the Piedmont code of 1865, prevalent throughout unified Italy, the Portuguese code of 1867 and the Spanish code of 1888–89, drafted by the politicians García Goyena and Alonso Martínez. Lecturers used the Code in their textbooks, the longest being the *Elementos de derecho civil y criminal de España* (1841–42) by Pedro Gómez de la Serna and Juan Manuel Montalbán.

At Heidelberg, Thibaut proposed a German version of the Code, but came up against Savigny's resistance. These were times of nationalism and war against Napoleon; Austria and Prussia did not give up their codes. Following Savigny, the German professors built up a valuable technical doctrine through a new interpretation of the *Pandects* and customary law: 'Pandectistics'. Prominent among them was Bernhard Windscheid, who lectured at Munich and Berlin and helped draft the German civil code introduced by Kaiser Wilhelm II in 1896. The influence of the Pandectists was felt in Italy and France. Marcel Planiol imported the current to the Sorbonne, while the Madrid professors Felipe Sánchez Román and Felipe Clemente de Diego were responsible for bringing it to Spain.

These centuries witnessed the emergence of economics. Genovesi had held the first chair of commerce and economics at Naples and taught the old mercantilism. But the modern science originated with Adam Smith's *Wealth of Nations* (1776), in which this moral philosophy professor at Glasgow advocated free trade against interventionism. His concepts were further developed by the banker David Ricardo, John Stuart Mill and others. In France, Jean-Baptiste Say taught economics at the Collège, from where it spread across the faculties. Economics attained maturity with Alfred Marshall at Cambridge and William Stanley Jevons at Manchester and London. Exiled in England, Karl Marx, trained in Hegelian philosophy, gave an alternative version of economic thought in *Capital* (1867–94), deeply influencing the twentieth century. In Germany, economics took the form of 'science of the State', the heir to public law and cameral science. Knut Wicksell, lecturing at Lund, headed the Swedish school. In Spain, chairs were founded early, in 1807 and under the later liberal curricula. Sociology, founded by Comte, also penetrated legal studies, and was further divulged by the British philosopher Herbert Spencer. This was a discipline embracing highly varied approaches, including those of the Frenchmen Gabriel Tarde and Emile Durkheim, the Germans Schäffle and Max Weber and the Italian Vifredo Pareto.

Science and knowledge grew apace into the twentieth century, despite two world wars, the communist revolution, Nazism and totalitarianisms.

THE GERMAN AND ENGLISH MODELS

The German Model of University

The founding of the University of Halle in 1694 was the outcome of Christian piety, an interest in the physical and natural sciences and an ambition to reform the State. In 1727, Halle became home to the first chair of 'cameral science' (public administration). Particular attention was paid to the emerging natural sciences, already regarded as an engine of economic and social development.

In this same innovative spirit, the two contributions of the University of Göttingen, founded in 1737, were a university library – which twenty years after its creation had brought together the then impressive figure of over 60,000 volumes – and the invention of the 'seminar', the key institution underlying the organisation and teaching method of this new model of university. Its three pillars were the library, 'seminars' in the humanities and 'laboratories' in science departments.

As part of the drive for reform prompted by Prussia's defeat at the hands of Napoleon, the University of Berlin was founded in 1810. As against the traditional notion that the purpose of a university was to train professionals, the new Berlin model sought to form scientists. Following in the footsteps of the Enlightenment academy created for the sole purpose of expanding the frontiers of science, the university, too, was thought of as 'a community of masters and disciples, wholly dedicated to the search for the truth'.

It was only in a community of equals – from which the 'argument from authority' was banished – that knowledge could flourish. The principle of 'unity of teaching and research' blurred the difference between instructor and student: the one now learned by teaching, the other taught when learning. 'One cannot teach philosophy,' said Kant, 'but only how to philosophize'.

Academic freedom became the underlying tenet of the university community. It implied both freedom for teachers – *Lehrfreiheit* – whereby a lecturer was unrestricted in his choice of content, scope and methods of teaching, and freedom for students – *Lernfreiheit* – which meant a student studied whatever he wanted, in whatever manner he pleased and with the guidance of whomever he chose.

Being forced to learn something the meaning of which we are not qualified to understand is a waste of time and a pointless ordeal. You can only learn what you are interested in learning. And, since it is possible to master only limited areas of knowledge, nobody other than ourselves is

Humboldt University, Berlin (1900)
It is located in Unter den Linden boulevard. Its lecture halls have seen famous German philosophers, scientists and poets, including Schopenhauer, Hegel, Einstein and Heine.

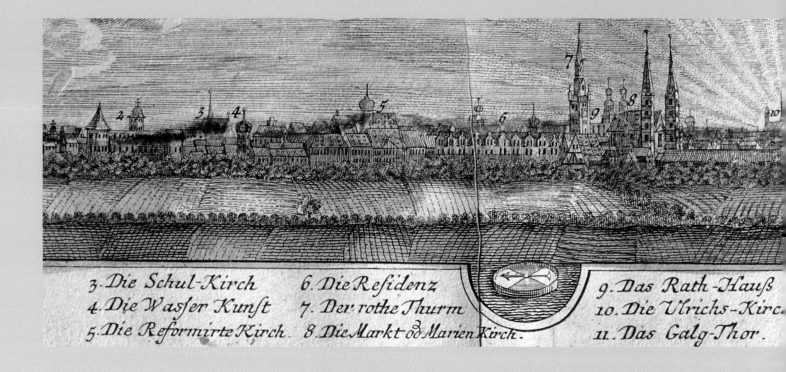

3. Die Schul-Kirch   6. Die Residenz   9. Das Rath-Hauß
4. Die Wasser Kunst   7. Der rothe Thurm   10. Die Ulrichs-Kirc.
5. Die Reformirte Kirch. 8. Die Markt od Marien Kirch. 11. Das Galg-Thor.

entitled to choose what we should learn. Freedom to choose what we want to learn is inseparable from a freedom to choose our teacher. We stand to learn little from someone we do not admire intellectually or do not respect as a human being.

The purpose of the Humboldtian university is to initiate a tiny elite in the cultivation of the sciences. This means acquiring a critical stance able to question established beliefs, and building a particular kind of character. Dedication to scientific research requires certain practices and strengths – a moral stance – that correspond to the virtues that entire societies need if they are to develop under conditions of freedom. The ultimate end of university is thus to equip an Enlightened minority with the moral and intellectual wherewithal for it to guide the fate of the nation.

This new model of university would have been unfeasible without broad-ranging reform embracing primary and secondary education. The Humboldtian project accordingly started with elementary schools, adopting the ideas of Johann Pestalozzi (1746–1827), for whom the main goal at this early stage was to build character (moral education) and teach people to think for themselves; reform continued with secondary education, which was to instil the linguistic and scientific foundations required for partaking in the search for truth. Whereas university education consists of a critical questioning of the known so as to uncover the unknown, secondary education must endeavour to pass on the confirmed rudiments, mastery of which is a prerequisite of the arduous labour of engaging with the new. So the nineteenth-century splendour of the German university was built upon the excellent standards achieved by secondary schooling.

Created to equip an Enlightened minority with the intellectual and moral wherewithal to guide the fate of the nation, the Humboldtian University was built on the foundations of a broad-ranging reform of Germany's elementary and secondary schools

12. *Die Morizer-Kirch.*
13. *Hoch-Gericht.*
14. *Pædagogium.*

View of Halle, **Germany (18th century)**
The city of Halle in Saxony stretches out
along the banks of the river Saale. In 1694,
Frederick I of Prussia founded a university
here, which in 1817 merged with Wittenberg's.

The English Model of University

The classic English model is embodied in the universities of Oxford
and Cambridge, both of which have retained their high prestige
from the thirteenth century to our own time. Their most striking
achievement is that, while adapting to the circumstances of each age,
they have preserved many of their old traditions – this being a
distinctively British strength.

   In the sixteenth century, the break with the Roman Catholic
Church and the dissolution of the monasteries enabled the
universities to secularise, an essential step towards developing
a modern institution of learning. Even so, attendance at church
services remained compulsory until 1871, and it was only as late as
1915, at Cambridge, and 1920, at Oxford, that the last religious
strictures were finally removed. English universities are remarkable
for the survival of medieval institutions: communal college life,
time-honoured privileges and relics – some merely amusing, others
deeply annoying. But they are also distinctive for a precocious
opening up to modern values. Cambridge specialised in
mathematics and the physical and natural sciences as early as the
seventeenth century, while Oxford devoted itself to the classics.

   In addition to this bonding of the new and the old, a
characteristic trait of the English university is its independence
from the Crown, the civil service and the Anglican Church, an
independence that extends even to each individual college with
respect to the university's central institutions. It would be hard to
exaggerate the extent to which the salient feature of the English
university is this robust autonomy of its constituent parts.

   Whereas in its origins the university was an institution of the
Church designed to train its qualified staff, from the sixteenth
century onwards, while retaining that role, it became increasingly
concerned with the education of the country gentry, and thus
developed into an institution of higher education for the
aristocracy. The community life of the colleges served to acquaint
a young man with the patterns of conduct and values of a
gentleman. The English university was a school of good manners
and taste, which aimed to shape its scholars' character, beliefs and
ideals in an aristocratic mould. This was the process that
transformed the old *noblesse d'épée* – 'nobility of the sword' – into
a new *noblesse de robe* – 'nobility of the gown'. Even today, Oxbridge
graduates gain privileged access to the highest reaches of power
and society.

   Another special feature of the British university is that it both
shaped and was shaped by the aristocracy. Had country gentry
of 1688 *not* been educated as the ruling elite of a modern state,
the outcome of the Glorious Revolution would have been quite

different. The compromise struck between the aristocracy and the rising middle orders cemented noblemen's willingness to acquire the behavioural norms that befitted a modern ruling class.

And what characterises the English university as a university of the aristocracy is a notion of education that embraces both body and mind. Along with the formal learning of an elite (notably the classical languages and mathematics), this education passes on the manners, practices and values of a class destined for the highest positions in ecclesiastical and lay government. Certain values – self-control, fair play – are fostered both in sporting pursuits and in purely academic activity, and prevail everywhere as the essence of interpersonal relations.

No other university model has cleaved so closely to the original meaning of *universita*s as a form of community life: the English university is an institution at which teachers and students literally live under one roof. A fundamental aspect of education, in some sense a 'cohabitation', is realised only in the personal relationship between educand and educator. The originality of the university college thus lies in the bond between scholar and tutor, one of the most fruitful relationships ever achieved in higher education. The English university, unlike its medieval forerunner, does not verbally transmit a 'belief-knowledge'; rather, cohabitation communicates a 'know-how', a sense of how to live and act as a ruling class.

Ignacio Sotelo

Students in the dining hall at Christ Church, University of Oxford (20th century)
Gatherings in college dining halls are a deeply rooted tradition of the British university, which has, in exemplary fashion, preserved the original meaning of the *universitas* as a form of community life. At these events students observe a time-honoured dress code and etiquette.

National Autonomous University of Mexico (UNAM) (2009)
UNAM became autonomous in 1929. As Mexico's leading institution of higher education, it has spearheaded the development of the university system in Latin America and the Caribbean.

V

THE UNIVERSITY IN THE AMERICAS

Battista Agnese, South America, in *Atlas of the World in Thirty-Three Maps* (1553)
The maps made by this Genoese cartographer are regarded as the finest of the sixteenth century for their geographical accuracy and mass of detail. His nautical charts, showing existing navigation routes, were an invaluable aid in an age in which knowledge of the South American continent was still tentative: here, for instance, the Atlantic coast is intricately charted, but the greater part of the Pacific coast is left blank.

Three Centuries of Founding Universities in Colonial Latin America

Iván Escamilla González

One of the most notable areas of the history of culture in colonial Spanish America is the emergence throughout this period of dozens of universities in the entire vast area of the Spanish Indies. From the founding of the University of Santo Domingo in 1538, less than half a century after the first voyage by Christopher Columbus, to that of León in Nicaragua, established by the Cádiz Cortes in 1812, the American university institution came to faithfully reflect the evolution of the Spanish Empire, from its beginnings as a conquering and evangelising project, to its consolidation as the largest Catholic monarchy in the world, and its demise amidst liberal revolutions and the emergence of Atlantic nation-states. Similarly, during the course of those centuries the university was confirmed as one of the first and foremost channels for the expression of intellectual flourishing and the search by colonial American societies for an identity of their own.

When the university first appeared in America, it had already been in existence for four hundred years elsewhere. It had been one of the most representative institutions in European medieval civilisation and the birthplace in the West of what we now call 'the intellectual', in other words, the individual devoted to cultivating sciences and letters, and socially recognised for this. As seen in earlier chapters, universities were born at the height of the Middle Ages, when, thanks to the ascent of cities, Europe experienced a time of demographic, economic and cultural growth known as the 'twelfth century Renaissance'. Following centuries in which the preservation and transmission of knowledge had become confined to monasteries,

cities offered the right medium for students and teachers wishing to cultivate the ennobling study of the liberal arts and to meet freely and independently to create study establishments and learn civil and canonical law, theology, medicine and the arts or philosophy. This is how, among others, the University of Bologna was born, created by jurists, or that of Paris, founded by theologians. However, this was not enough to obtain the security needed for intellectual work, and in the likeness of the social solidarity among groups such as the powerful urban craftsmen's associations, many of these institutions began to constitute themselves into bodies, consortia or *universitas studiorum*. And just as the trade associations used examinations to control access for craftsmen wishing to attain the category of master, universities began to offer the qualifications of bachelor, master and doctor to those showing sufficient levels of proficiency in various areas.

Thereby afforded legal status, the new universities sought to preserve their regime of independence by confirming their privileges through the papacy, which saw in these institutions efficient doctrinal seedbeds to contain the spread of heresy. To a lesser extent they were sponsored by the princes and municipal governments, who confirmed their bylaws and statutes, and afforded them incomes that would ensure their material subsistence. During the golden age of the medieval university (twelfth-thirteenth centuries), study corporations had their own jurisdiction in cities where they were located, and they governed themselves through a complex system of *claustros* (faculties) that shared out the various tasks

Philiponus Honorius, *Nova Typis Transacta Navigatio: Novi Orbis Indiae Occidentale* (1553)
Caspar Plautius, the real name of the Austrian Benedictine abbot behind this work, narrates the journey of the first Benedictine missionaries, who accompanied Columbus on his second voyage to the Indies under the protection of the legendary St Brendan. Plautius recounts and illustrates what they encountered on their arrival: native customs, landscapes, farming practices, ceremonies and the rest.

within the institution, such as the provision of chairs or professorships, the appointment of authorities and the administration of funds. Students and professors had equal weighting in the university structure. A system of colleges to house the different 'nations', in other words, the foreign students who attended classes at the major universities in large numbers, accentuated their cosmopolitan nature.

However, the independent model based on *claustros* – which was precisely the model from which the first universities in the Iberian Peninsula were born, like the failed University of Palencia, or the universities of Salamanca and Valladolid – entered a crisis in around the fifteenth century, due not to the disappearance of the universities, which had multiplied throughout the previous century in the entire continent, but because of the transformation of the political and social context of the university institution itself. In the midst of a series of disconcerting circumstances, such as the break-up of Christianity, the threat of Ottoman expansion, and in particular the new ideas and power structures on which modern states should be built, the new universities increasingly responded to the interests of their creators

and protectors, mainly secular princes and ecclesiastics. In late-medieval Castile this translated into the biased intervention of the Crown to varying degrees in the financing and governing of these institutions, especially when, from the reign of the Catholic Monarchs onwards, universities were seen as the nurseries of learned men who would join the increasingly large and specialist royal bureaucratic apparatus. And while some of the oldest universities in the Peninsula, such as Salamanca, emerged stronger from the crisis and equipped with considerable academic prestige, it is also true that during the sixteenth and seventeenth centuries part of their fame and influence derived mainly from the roles of their alumni as members of the Councils (of Castile, Italy, Flanders, The Indies, Finance, etc.) through which the Spanish monarchy governed during the period of the Habsburgs. Such was the university's outlook prior to the emergence of the New World in the Western consciousness.

Evangelisation and Rewards: the First American Universities

It is impossible to understand the ascent and meaning of the university in the Latin-American colonial world without considering that, since the Conquest, Spain's presence in America was special in nature due to the early integration of New Spain, Peru and its dependencies, as de facto and de jure kingdoms, dependent on the Crown of Castile. They were thereby, connected to a vast monarchy, which from the sixteenth century onwards comprised a number of territories in Europe, Asia, Africa and, of course, America. Such vast dominions had only two features in common: they obeyed a single leadership, the Spanish sovereign; and professed a single religion, Catholicism. These circumstances conditioned the process of exploration and conquest of the New World, and converged with different driving forces and needs befitting the beginning of the colonial order in the creation of the first American universities. The most important of these driving forces, as it constituted the main justification of the sovereignty of the Crown of Castile in the Indies, was the conversion of the indigenous population to Catholicism. In effect, the adequate preparation of missionaries was one of the reasons given by the Dominican monks when they asked the pope to create what some consider to be the first university in America, that of Santo Domingo in the island of Hispaniola in the Antilles, created by the papal bull *In apostolatus culmine* issued by Paul III on 28 October 1538. There has been some debate as to whether this papal foundation really took effect, or whether in fact the first university on the island was the one created in 1558 by Philip II with the bequest of the wealthy landowner Hernando de Gorjón. In fact, the Dominicans already had a well-organised general study institution at their monastery in Santo Domingo, so that with the papal bull what they were actually asking the pope for was the power to award degrees in accordance with the custom at the universities of Alcalá and Salamanca. There is no doubt that in the early seventeenth century a small university was working normally in the Dominican monastery of Santo Domingo.

In Lima and Mexico, in the next two (and the most important) colonial universities, the missionary purpose was coupled with the purpose of consolidating Spanish domination. To understand this it is vital to recall that in both the Andes and in Mesoamerica, where they had met with highly cultured hierarchical societies, the *conquistadores* had built an initial model of colonisation based on the *encomienda* system, in other words a royal trusteeship or concession entitling its recipient to a compulsory workforce and part of the tax paid to the Crown by the Indian peoples in exchange for support in their evangelisation. The pre-Hispanic governing elites were incorporated into this scheme as contributors in the organisation of tax collection and work of the indigenous masses, and in the missionary work of the members of the religious orders.

The idea soon emerged of establishing universities as a way of protecting and promoting the interests of these groups. As well as wanting to perpetuate their *encomiendas*, the *encomenderos* wished to see their descendants ennobled by studies and placed in honourable positions at the service of God and the king, an adequate reward for the services of the *conquistadores*. Meanwhile, the members of the religious orders thought that the university could help realise their dream of forming an indigenous priesthood, as well as stimulating cooperation from the sons of Indian lords in governing the land. Not in vain did they cite the precedent of the creation of the University of Granada in 1531, which helped underpin the conversion of the former Muslim kingdom. That is why in New Spain, as in Peru, the requests multiplied in this connection from civil and ecclesiastical quarters, each with their own particular agenda. For example, the Spanish councils or municipal authorities governing the capitals of both kingdoms, since they were filled by the families of *encomenderos*, were great promoters of universities. In 1550, Lima sent its solicitors to express to the king their concern that due to the lack of means to study in Spain the sons of the city's inhabitants would 'remain ignorant'; not very distant were the arguments used by the council of

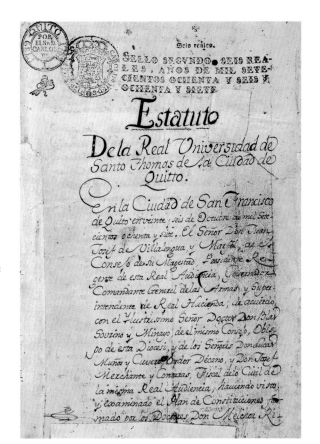

Charter of the Royal University of Santo Tomás in the city of Quito, Ecuador (1786)
Since the sixteenth century, the Ecuadorian capital saw the foundation of three institutions: the College of San Fulgencio, founded by Augustine friars in 1586, the University of San Gregorio Magno, created by the Jesuits in 1651, and the University of Santo Tomás de Aquino, a Dominican institution formed in 1681. After the expulsion of the Jesuits and the dissolution of San Fulgencio, the University of Santo Tomás was made a royal public university, as reflected by its charter of 1786.

Mexico, supported by the Viceroy Antonio de Mendoza. Meanwhile, the monks continued to consider the prestige which they might be afforded by their association with a university project, as evidenced by the central role of the Dominican friar Tomás de San Martín in dealings to create the University of Lima, or the interest shown by the Augustinian friars of Mexico in participating in local university life as soon as the institution had been established.

The final outcome of this clamour (and without doubt, the Crown's desire to appease the *encomenderos* and mitigate their tendency towards insubordination, which had just surfaced in Peru) was the issuance of founding charters for the University of Lima in Valladolid, on 12 May, and for that of Mexico in Toro on 21 September in the same year of 1551. Each of these charters had specific characteristics that are worth highlighting.

The Lima charter emphasised the suitability of the general study institution of the Dominican monastery to establish there a university where 'the children

of its neighbours' could be educated. Consequently, the university was required to be established in the monastery of this order unless a decree were issued for it to be moved elsewhere, and it was afforded 'all the privileges, freedoms and exceptions' enjoyed by the University of Salamanca, save for jurisdictional autonomy and the exemption from levies and taxies on its members. It was not assigned an income, since it was implicitly understood that it would depend on the Dominicans for its maintenance. In contrast, the charter for the University of Mexico included the Indians, albeit nominally, in the university project by indicating the suitability of a study institution to cover the 'natives and sons of the Spanish'. It was also afforded an annual income of a thousand gold pesos taken from the Royal Treasury for the institution's incorporation and maintenance. Furthermore, it was granted the privileges and exemptions enjoyed by the University of Salamanca with the same exceptions established for the University of Lima.

The inauguration of the new universities took place two years later. On 2 January 1553, with the assistance of the city and cathedral councils, the University of Lima was opened in a solemn ceremony in the chapterhouse of the monastery of Santo Domingo. The university's first chancellors were the Dominican priors of Lima until 1571, when Viceroy Francisco de Toledo awarded it independence from the monks and ordered the appointment of the first secular chancellor; it was then that it was renamed after the Evangelist Saint Mark. In Mexico the inaugural session took place on 3 June 1553, and was presided over by the humanist Francisco Cervantes de Salazar, who also provided a famous and colourful description of the early times of this new institution. Since in this case the university did not depend on any religious order, its first chancellor was an *oidor* (judge) from the Royal Court of Mexico, doctor Antonio Rodríguez de Quesada, a legal expert and alumnus of the University of Salamanca.

Dominican convent, Santo Domingo, Dominican Republic (1511)
From early on the Dominican Order had a *studium generale* within the convent of Santo Domingo on the island of Hispaniola, Antilles. The friars soon applied to the pope for permission to raise the *studium* to the status of a university able to award degrees. A licence was duly granted in 1538 under a bull of Paul III. Santo Domingo has since been regarded as the earliest university in the Americas.

The adequate preparation of missionaries was one of the reasons given by the Dominican monks when they asked the Pope to create what some consider to be the first university in America, that of Santo Domingo

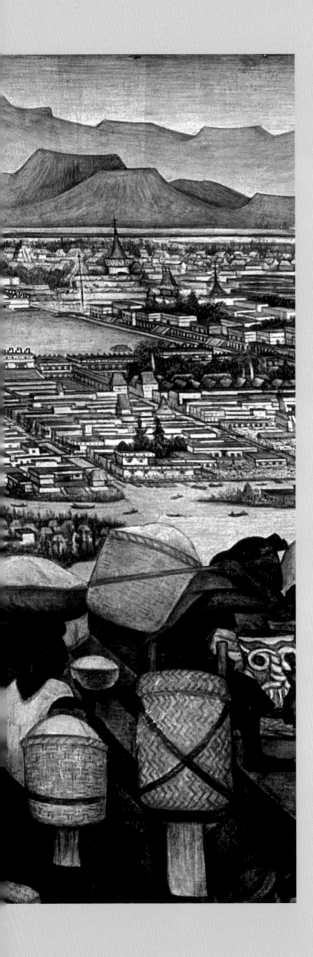

EDUCATION AND KNOWLEDGE IN PRE-COLOMBIAN AMERICA

Education in Ancient Mexico

With regard to education in pre-Hispanic Mesoamerica, sources reveal more data for the Nahua and Maya cultures than for the rest of the indigenous peoples of this major cultural area. Miguel León Portilla has said that, through the concept and reality of education among the Mexicas, it is possible to learn about their culture. By training children and young people, the Nahua world revealed not only the intellectual legacy of its ancestors but the importance afforded to the development of the group in society. Education was compulsory and, furthermore, there was not only an education system for these peoples, but also, and even more importantly, a 'concept' of education.

As for the Nahua concept of education, the importance of the Sahaguntine corpus has been highlighted. Emphasis was placed on moral, intellectual and physical education, on 'giving wisdom to the face of others' (*ixtlamachiliztli*), as Sahagún himself put it. In the discourse of the wise Nahuas or *tlamatinime*, great importance was given to the integral individual, and will and understanding were identified as something essential to the human being. Humans should have hearts as firm as stones and as resistant as trees. The goal was to attain maturity and wisdom, and at the same time be skilful and understanding. The latter was a definitive characteristic of plenitude of personality. Meanwhile, the teacher, or *temachtiani*, was respected in society for teaching people to live, obey, respect, behave honestly and overcome evil and perversion. The teacher was considered someone who enlightened, a guide showing the way, teaching prudence and good sense; someone who admonishes and teaches people to become 'sensible and careful', but also who comforts, helps and looks after his fellows. The figure of the teacher was, then, extolled in the Nahua world for his extraordinary attributes, since his mission was, literally, according to Sahagún's linguistic interpretation, to give people a face.

Father Joseph de Acosta, in his *Natural and Moral History of the Indies*, describes the education of children in a family setting, another interesting facet of Mexica society. Parents had clear roles as educators. Children were obliged to perform useful and honest activities. As well as receiving moral

Diego de Rivera, *The Great City of Tenochtitlán* (1926–45), Palacio Nacional, Mexico
The great Mexican muralist Rivera painted the frescoes of the Palacio Nacional in Mexico City. The imagery retells the history of Mexico from its pre-Columbian past to the Spanish conquest.

education, they were taught to be well-mannered and respectful of their elders, to serve and obey, to sing and dance, and also to be practised in the art of war, to have good aim, and to use shield and lance. Furthermore, they were given board at temples, houses and seminaries. The Mendocino Codex also reveals how parents educated their children, with discipline, sacrifice and, sometimes, corporal punishment to make them stronger and improve their self-control and self-governance. They were given a 'code of moderation', as Jacques Soustelle called it in a work on the daily life of these peoples. Children were forced to help in the daily household chores, carrying water and firewood or sweeping the house.

As regards Mayan education prior to the Conquest, and although the sources are more limited compared to those of the *Altiplano*, it has been deduced that it had highly distinguishing characteristics, such as the prevalence of religious aspects. According to Ana Luisa Izquierdo, the educated Mayan man was one whose personal life was constantly linked to the gods and who was alert to the manifestation of all things divine. With this significant religious bias, he was devoted mainly to adoration and religious cult, but also distinguished himself in the values that Mayan society appreciated: solidarity, obedience and temperance. He was ethically oriented towards respect for his elders, and wisdom was granted considerable importance. The family influenced the individual's primary training.

The lower classes were taught technical and practical skills, while the nobles were given intellectual and scientific education. At schools, young people performed recreational activities such as ball games and board games with dice. Recent studies have shown that among the Maya there was institutionalised state education, with pedagogical functions and responsibilities. To prepare people for religious and political power, there were houses for young people and schools at reserved temples. The priests' speeches and songs reflect a system of educational values and mechanisms to train the community. The paradigm of the mature man was the old man, considered so based on his life experience and moral authority.

Young people and children needed to be guided and educated to obey their elders and authority. They were taught good manners, to show respect to their peers and to behave decently. Moreover, men and women received different training. Men's education focused on certain skills and qualities. Women's education was very strict in regard to their treatment of men, based on stringent rules for the household and for their behaviour *vis-à-vis* the group. They were relegated from intellectual knowledge, but their training was distinguished by the rules of courtesy, living harmoniously together and social conduct. They learned to cook, to look after the domestic animals, to make textiles and clothing and to model clay. They were also given notions of agriculture and certain trades, so as to be of help to the men.

Alicia Mayer

Nahua education, in its urge to shape morals, intellect and body, strove to 'lend wisdom to the faces of others': this was the teacher's overarching purpose

El Caracol astronomical observatory, Chichén Itzá, Mexico (*c.* 1050)
Built during the Toltec era of the last Mayan period, the Caracol ('snail') observatory was used to observe astronomical phenomena, to which the Mesoamerican cultures accorded high significance. It was designed as a round tower with a series of terraces oriented specifically for stargazing.

Places of Learning of the Mexica and Inca Peoples

The two most powerful kingdoms in America prior to the Spanish conquest, the Mexica and the Inca, were based in two cities, splendid, fully urbanised and inhabited by numerous groups of specialists in all the crafts, as well as the priesthood and government. Colonial sources tell of the importance of education in both kingdoms: they were rigorous in the teaching of children and young people, and careful in the transmission of the knowledge of crafts that comprised a long-standing tradition spanning many centuries. Furthermore, in both Mexico-Tenochtitlán and Cusco there were special schools for boys who belonged to the nobility.

POPULAR SCHOOLS

Mexica children spent their childhoods with their parents if they lived in villages, and were also helped by nannies and tutors if they were children of noble families. All sources point to a rigorous education, in which language, urbanity and, naturally, respect for elders were of the utmost importance. Reprimands and corporal punishment were frequent. From the age of ten or twelve, the time for staying at home was over and the time for schooling began. The plebeian boys would go to the *telpochcalli* and the noble boys boarded at the *calmécac* or 'house of lineage'. There were hundreds of the first kind of school in Tenochtitlán and dozens of the second kind.

At the *telpochcalli* boys completed religious tasks, especially cleaning temples, but the emphasis was mainly on military teaching and participation, in work-gangs, in the city's major public works. In the evening, the youngsters from the popular districts would go to the *cuicacalli*. The working-class girls would also attend. In general, they did not go to school in the morning. Towards midnight, they would dance with their arms linked, boy and girl alternating, to the sound of drums and trumpets, to learn the rhythms and choreographies of the lavish state rituals in which they would be expected to participate periodically.

PLACES OF LEARNING

In the *calmécac*, life was very austere and the boys were obliged to remain there without being able to leave and visit their families as the plebeians could. Fasts, sleep deprivation and the practice of self-sacrifice were very important, since the Nahua nobility boasted of its capacity to mediate with the gods and ability to unleash divine reciprocity through sacrifice and offerings. It was indispensable for young people to learn to live this life of mortification as their parents did, and to learn the techniques linked to the presentation of offerings and in particular blood sacrifices. The young boys of the *calmécac* would climb the nearby mountains at midnight and there they would puncture their tongues, shins and other parts of their bodies to obtain the blood which they would then burn in balls of straw to make it reach the gods.

In the *calmécac*, language was important. Young people were taught to speak correctly and were reprimanded for using bad words; furthermore, they were taught the procedures of the delicate Nahua rhetoric, which included memorising long allocutions and adequately expressing anger or sorrow to enable them to convey with drama the most significant news for the workings of the State.

The *calmécac* was also a place of study, one of the most important places for conserving and transmitting knowledge in ancient America. According to colonial sources, students studied the *amoxtli* (in other words, the book) and the *tlacuilolli* (the art of pictography). Among the books young people were expected to study were the *tonalámatl*, the 260-day divinatory almanac, which usually included astronomical cycles and prediction tables. There was also the *xiuhámatl*, as the historical record of the kingdoms was known.

When their period of schooling concluded, the boys who became priests needed to refer to the almanacs often, and anyone joining the administration and government would need the genealogy and history books. Furthermore, we know that in the palaces another codices were used, such as warehouse lists, cadastral pictography and maps that were indispensable in planning military strategy.

EDUCATION AMONG THE INCA PEOPLES

Among the Inca, the variety of specialist knowledge was huge, as it was in Mexica society: there were carpenters, weavers, embroiderers, gold and silversmiths, painters of walls, painters of *queros* (ceremonial vases made of wood), masons and architects, to name but a few. There must certainly have been systematic transmission of these crafts, from masters to apprentices, in most cases probably from fathers to sons. However, as well as the crafts, records suggest that there was another complex body of knowledge relating to administration, history and politics.

Two specialist areas linked to the function of government were historical narration and accounting. At the start of his reign, the Inca or supreme leader assembled a group of elderly specialists in memorising, composing and narrating historical events. It was this group's task to compose stories about what happened during the Inca's reign, but they were banned from reciting or singing these stories while the Inca was still alive. Their task was to adequately compile the history of the reign and transmit it to the next Inca. This practice required extraordinary memory training, as well as being an exercise in singing and oratory.

But the empire built by the Incas was too complex for its administration and government to be described in detail in the songs of the royal historians. Just as the Mesoamerican codices enabled a

'Stone of the Sun', National Museum of Anthropology, Mexico (n.d.)
This basalt monolith depicts the 'Legend of the Suns', which tells that there were four 'suns' or epochs, culminating with the advent of a fifth sun, the sun of movement, which heralded the splendour of Mexico-Tenochtitlán.

precise record to be kept of genealogical data, government actions and taxes in the provinces, the system of *quipus* allowed a record to be compiled of the taxes crossing the entire vast empire. A *quipu* was a system of bundled strings hanging from a horizontal master string. Each of the hanging strings had knots or stones, and a specific length and colour. The lower knots generally represented units, the following represented tens and so on. The colours of the strings of the *quipu* were linked to various issues: yellow represented gold and white silver, for example. But in different contexts the meaning of the colours might change; if the *quipu* was used to tell the story of a war, the red string represented the Inca army and the green string the enemy army. The most recent studies indicate that the *quipu* was not only a way to count men and goods, but, in general, a highly significant support for the procedures of memorising and for the Inca oral story-telling tradition. *Quipu* scientists were called *quipu camayoc*. Although there must have been hundreds of them in Cusco, they had to be dispersed throughout the provinces for the administration of the imperial wineries or *tampus*, which were located on all roads, from Chile to Ecuador.

The 'Houses of Wisdom' and the 'Amautas'

There were no schooling systems for village-dwellers in Cusco or the other cities of the empire, but there were schools for the sons of nobles. The *yachay wasi* or 'house of wisdom' was the place where the sons of nobles were trained to work in the administration and government. Some sources suggest that their training lasted four years. The first year was spent learning how to correctly use the Quechua language, which was especially significant considering that the nobles in the provinces spoke other languages. The second year was spent learning about Inca religion, and the third in studying *quipu* science. In the fourth year, according to sources, they studied history. There is every indication, then, that these wise men whom the Incas needed to preserve the history of their reigns and who were also probably used by the *curacas* or provincial lords, were trained at the *yachay wasi*; the *quipu camayoc* would also have studied there.

The masters of these schools were called *amautas*. The word *amauta* is equivalent to 'wise man' and, in truth, these masters must have accumulated a variety of knowledge: not only did they know about history and *quipus*, but also about the weather, the agricultural cycles, the stars and, in particular, the comets.

The *amautas* were very strict with their students and were authorised by the Inca to apply corporal punishment, with the only restriction that it be once a day and no more. The prestige of the *amautas* was such that the leaders, many years after having themselves studied at a *yachay wasi*, continued to seek their advice on important matters.

Pablo Escalante Gonzalbo

Students studied the amoxtli *('the book') and the* tlacuilolli *(the art of pictography). Among the books young people were expected to study were the* tonalámatl, *the 260-day divinatory almanac*

Science in Inca Culture

Given a dictionary definition of science as 'a branch of knowledge or study dealing with a body of facts or truths systematically arranged and showing the operation of general laws', it can safely be asserted that science was practised in Inca culture. Inca astronomy was undoubtedly the product of observation, reasoning and the use of principles drawn from prior systems of classification; it brought into being a calendar and measured time in accordance with an imperial scheme that ruled throughout the various regions of the Tahuantinsuyu. The Incas had no alphabetic script, but did use counting instruments – methods by which to preserve patterns of beads, and, though subject to severe constraints, ways of passing on words and remembrances of the past.

The 'Quipu'

The native American chronicler Felipe Guamán Poma de Ayala, in his *Nueva crónica y buen gobierno* (1615), speaks of a character named *Tawantin suyo runa quipoc Yncap haziendan chasquicoc*, 'he who keeps account of the people of the Tahuantinsuyu' or 'he who receives the revenue of the Inca': a state official. Displaying his deep knowledge of the vestigial Inca culture, the chronicler Guamán distinguished between two types of *quipu*-using functionaries: those who simply recorded numbers of people, chattels and property, and those able to perform mathematical operations.

As an instrument of accounting, classification and organisation of data, the *quipu* remained in use in the Andean regions into the twentieth century. The Dutch historian Reiner Tom Zuidema, in his thesis *The Ceque System of Cusco: The Social Organisation of the Capital of the Incas*, cast doubt on the universal applicability of the conjecture advanced by Jack Goody to the effect that rational thought emerged of a piece with writing: Zuidema suggested that the *quipu* may have fulfilled the role that writing played in other ancient cultures, in Europe, Asia Minor and the Far East.

Machu Picchu, Peru (*c.* 1440)
In Quechua, 'Machu Picchu' is the name of the ancient Inca settlement located between the mountains of Machu Picchu and Huayna Picchu. Its past uses remain open to debate, but the prevailing theory is that it was a religious sanctuary, or the palace of the Inca Pachakuteq, the founder and first emperor of Tahuantinsuyu.

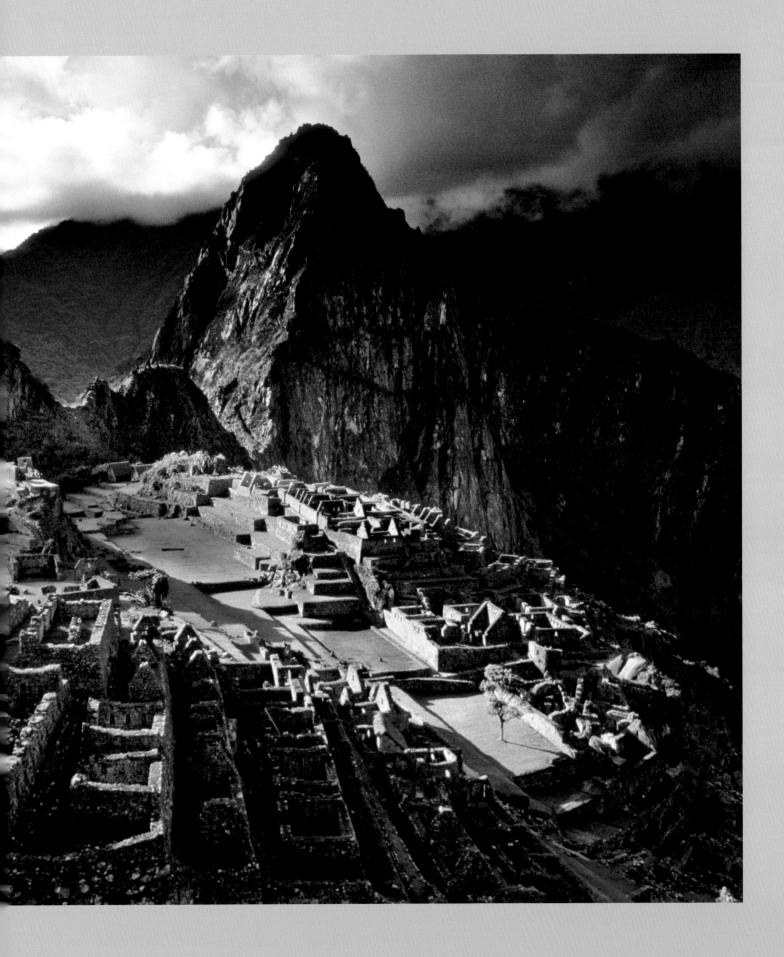

THE SYSTEM OF 'CEQUES' IN CUSCO

Zuidema detected a close but mysterious link between a set of 41 imaginary lines (*ceques*) that radiated out of the Temple of the Sun – Coricancha – towards the four points of the compass.

The lines comprised 328 *huacas* (shrines), each divided in turn into two halves, *hanan* (up) and *hurin* (down), which were again split into four groups – *Chinchaysuyu, Antisuyu, Collasuyu* and *Contisuyu*. This division of Cusco into two parts and four districts had its counterpart in the structures of kinship: the various groups of family relations were organised on the basis of ancient principles of duality, tripartition and quadripartition.

The new organisational pattern was first essayed in the capital, but, with the spread of the empire throughout the central Andes, later extended to vast territories brought under the rule of Tahuantinsuyu. This real and imaginary pattern also governed the rites that marked the passing of the Inca year and were the responsibility of the noble clans resident in Cusco and in the provincial towns.

'CEQUES', 'QUIPU' AND THE CALENDAR

The Empire of the Tahuantinsuyu crowned a long cultural and political process in the central Andes. Before it, there had flourished the Chavin horizon and the old Wari Empire, a great number of technical conquests – megalithic architecture, irrigated agriculture and intensive llama-farming – and the core principles of a redistributive state based on a rule of reciprocity. The rise of the Inca Empire brought with it an unprecedented size of state organisation in the Andes.

The Inca polity – the Andean political culture as a whole – was neither understood nor even wholly perceived by the Spanish conquistadors and government officials. The history of the Spanish encounter with the Incas was chronicled in the seventeenth century at the city of Cusco by the Jesuit Bernabé Cobo, who spoke of an ancient document that he termed the 'list of the *huacas* of Cusco', describing the shrines in and around Cusco in the Inca epoch, which, as Cobo himself testified, were still places of worship for the local population. And this was not even the first mention of this document. In 1610, the Mercedarian chronicler Martín Murúa, and, five years later, Guamán Poma de Ayala, described shrines strung along the *ceque* lines of other Andean settlements. And Juan de Matienzo, in his *Gobierno del Perú* (1567), also makes mention of this early document describing the organisational structure of Cusco: he had seen the same pattern among all the Andean peoples that he had come across. Cristóbal de Molina, who described the rites and fables of Cusco in 1573, also mentioned the cryptic system of *ceques*.

A *quipu*, Peru (n.d.)
The *quipu* was an accounting mnemonic tool, which remained in use in Andean regions into the twentieth century.

In the Andes, the quipu *filled the role that in the ancient cultures of Europe, Asia Minor and the Far East was played by writing*

Recent research appears to have found the missing pieces of the puzzle. We now know that the author of that anonymous document was Juan Polo de Ondegardo, the *corregidor* magistrate of the city of Cusco from 1559 to 1561, who discovered those 41 lines or *ceques* issuing from the Coricancha outward to the horizon. The lines ran through 328 *huaca* shrines, the rituals of which were in the charge of the royal Inca dynasties of Cusco. Zuidema, in his book *The Inca Calendar: Time and Space in the Ritual Organisation of Cusco: The Idea of the Past*, suggests that the system of *ceques* constituted a twelve-month year measured in rituals. The *huacas*, many of which had been brought in from newly conquered lands as proof of subjection, friendship and allegiance, were still worshipped according to an Inca calendar that lent coherent meaning to the doings of an empire and the authority of a single state.

The Coricancha, which lay at the centre of the 41 *ceques*, was in fact an astronomical observatory from which the culture's sages followed the movements of the sun in its travels from north to south. At the summer solstice, when the sun was at its zenith, there was held the feast of *Inti Rayme*; the winter solstice, when the sun returned to its zenith, was the occasion for the feast of *Capac Rayme*. In between the two, the rest of the rituals were calculated to steer the course of time by organising farming activities and fixing the record of the past. The Incas developed Andean astronomy through their observations taken from the Coricancha and their use of pillars built on the hills of Cusco to watch the rising and setting of the sun. Their observations were arranged into a twelve-month year that subtended the ceremonies of the 328 *huacas* scattered along the 41 *ceques* issuing out from the Coricancha.

The system was a sort of great *quipu* deployed over the site of the city of Cusco and its environs. Reading it meant one could control the passage of time, comprehend the role of the twelve noble houses of Cusco and pinpoint their location in space and time. The Incas had a passion for astronomical observation. When Gomez Suárez de Figueroa, also known as the Inca Garcilaso de la Vega, in his *Comentarios reales* (1609), retold the northward expansion of Tahuantinsuyu during the reign of Guayna Capac, who annexed the kingdom of Quito, he pointed out that the purpose of conquest was not merely to increase territory but to find better sites for astronomical observation: to reach the place where shadows disappeared when the sun crossed the equatorial line, and from where the sun headed north and southward. The yearning for astronomical knowledge, consubstantial with Inca culture, was nothing less than a passion for science.

Manuel Burga

The King, the Friars and the Bishops: Models of the Indian University

Since their launch the universities of Lima and Mexico were characterised by a rare contradiction. At the express request of their developers and also because many of their first professors were alumni of the University of Salamanca, the new institutions were shaped on the bylaws and customs of that university, to which they referred until they had their own. However, because they had been created through an express charter issued by the monarch, and because they depended on him for their material survival, they became institutions of royal protection. This meant that, although as corporations they adopted for their internal and day-to-day governance the *claustro* system on which Salamanca University was based at the height of its autonomy, they were also subject to constant intervention and controls by the representatives of the Crown, such as viceroys, *oidores* (judges) and *visitadores* (inspectors).

The medieval origins of the *universitas* had been left behind. The new universities were incorporated fully into the organisational system that governed relationships between the various bodies and states constituting the Spanish monarchy, as well as other corporations such as municipal councils, royal tribunals, cathedral councils, religious orders and trade associations. All of these institutions contributed efficiently to shape the upcoming American societies. At the same time, they were gradually altered by the peculiarities of a natural, ethnic and cultural environment that had nothing to do with Europe.

Universities were not an exception in this process. At the end of the sixteenth century, the colonising model of the *encomienda* declined rapidly throughout the continent because of the demographic decline of the indigenous population caused by the epidemics imported from Europe, and with it its former beneficiaries, the *encomenderos*, also declined. However, the university survived the demise of its initial sponsors. In the following decades, while the American descendants of the first colonisers weaved alliances with members of the new economic power groups, such as the major traders, literary studies and qualifications from the universities were consolidated

as the starting point of an advantageous career, whether in the judiciary, the royal administration or in the regular and secular clergy.

The native population's drive for individual and family success through studies may partly explain the second wave of American universities in the early seventeenth century. This time around, though, the initiative did not correspond to the Crown, which lacked the funds to create new study institutions, but to the religious orders. In the previous century there were already establishments run by regular clergy empowered by the pope to grant degrees, like Universidad del Estudio Dominico de Nuestra Señora del Rosario, in Santa Fe de Bogotá (1580), and the Augustinian College of San Fulgencio in Quito (1586). In addition to these orders, traditional cultivators of knowledge, the Jesuits joined the new wave of university launches, having arrived from the Spanish Indies from 1572 onwards; their pedagogical and humanistic work is well known. Two briefs by Paul V and Gregory XV in 1619 and 1621, issued respectively in favour of the Dominicans and the Jesuits, enabled no fewer than a dozen of their schools spread over the entire continent to begin awarding degrees according to the system used in Salamanca, although they were subject to the jurisdiction of their respective religious orders.

These were small institutions, which did not formally have all the powers of universities and where generally students only read theology and arts. Furthermore, the Crown had stipulated in all cases that they should cease to function when a royal university was created in their vicinity. In fact, many of these new foundations responded to the need for studies in areas located far from the major viceroyal capitals, as happened with the university colleges of the Jesuits in Córdoba, Rio de la Plata, Charcas and Cusco. In some cases, however, the new universities were established in cities where other regular study institutions were already in existence, and this triggered open and hostile rivalry between the orders running them. This was the case in Guatemala and Santiago de Chile, where Dominican and Jesuit universities existed side-by-side, and in Bogotá and Quito, where these two orders' institutions also competed with that of the Augustinians.

The increasing number of new university launches and the resulting conflicts between the different orders indicated transcendental changes in the Church in the Spanish Indies. The importance of the regular clergy in America was due to the extraordinary powers given to them at the start of the evangelisation, in view of the absence of a solid diocesan structure and a secular clergy well prepared to look after the spiritual well-being of the indigenous people. However, in the middle of the seventeenth century, with the possible exception of the Jesuits, the former missionary fervour had been lost and the religious orders had focused on the urban environment, where they competed with each other for the devotion and favours of the elites, and for the minds of the indigenous young. In view of this situation, the bishops, appealing to the Crown for it to use the powers granted to it by the *Regio Patronato* on the American Church, were increasingly vocal in their demands for the delivery to the secular clergy of the Indian villages where they imparted their doctrine, and for a general strengthening of an ecclesiastical project centred on episcopal power.

The founding by royal charter of San Carlos University in Guatemala in 1676, following the closure of the Dominican and Jesuit establishments, is illustrative of the change already at work in that direction in the second half of the seventeenth century. In a notable report on the matter delivered to the king a few years earlier, in 1659, Bishop Payo Enríquez de Rivera, a firm backer of the creation of the new institute, discussed the multiple benefits to be reaped for his own diocese and the Republic. In the institution it would be possible to train clergymen able to undertake the doctrine of the regulars, and it would be possible to teach the indigenous languages so that both parish priests and doctrinarian friars could exercise their ministry competently. In time, jurists graduated from the university with degrees enabling them to serve the king in various posts, and subjects were well prepared to occupy prebends in the cathedral council and to work in the administration of the diocese. Lastly, there was the no less significant academic benefit of publicly teaching all subjects, not only theology

Unknown artist, *Antonio de Mendoza* (1535) Born in the late fifteenth century, Mendoza was the scion of a powerful Spanish family and held multiple offices at the court of Charles V. In the Indies, he was the first viceroy of New Spain (1535–50) and viceroy of Peru (1551–52). During his mandate in New Spain, he supported the *cabildo* guilds and *encomenderos* – Spanish settlers – in their aim of founding a university in the Mexican capital: the plan came to fruition in 1551.

and art, at the existing colleges. At the new university the dialectic battle between various positions and schools (something that could not happen in the small colleges run by the regular clergy, where only the doctrine of the theological current identified with each order was taught) gave rise to a positive advance in knowledge.

After the creation by royal charter of San Carlos University in Guatemala, institutions run by the regular clergy continued to be established, and as well as those previously mentioned, in the eighteenth century the Jesuits renamed the former College of Gorjón in Santo Domingo as University of Santiago de la Paz (1703), while the Dominicans converted their *studium generale* of Havana into a university in 1721. However, by that time there were already new universities founded directly by the bishops, such as San Cristóbal de Huamanga (1677), San Antonio del Cusco (1692) and Caracas (1721), where the first studies planned and financed by the sponsors were also the arts and theology. Although scant and not always well provided for, the significance of these incorporations is better understood if one takes into account that in the late seventeenth and early eighteenth century in many American dioceses the first conciliar seminaries were established for the education of secular clergy, sometimes in connection with existing universities and sometimes with newly-created ones, as in the case of Huamanga and Caracas.

University of Havana, Cuba (1958)
As they had done elsewhere, the Dominicans transformed their *studium generale* of Havana into a university in 1721. Under the name of Real y Pontificia Universidad de San Jerónimo de La Habana, the earliest faculties were those of arts and philosophy, theology, canon law, law and medicine. In 1850, the institution changed its name to Real y Literaria Universidad de La Habana.

In the middle of the seventeenth century, the former missionary fervour had been lost and the religious orders had focused on the urban environment, where they competed with each other for the devotion and favours of the elites

From Royal Corporation to Seminary of the Nation: The Last Colonial Universities

The eighteenth century brought to the Spanish Empire major changes that would end up by affecting, among many other institutions, American universities. The ascent to the throne of the Bourbons in 1700 accelerated the transformation of the decadent Spanish monarchy already underway since the end of the seventeenth century, bringing among other novelties the disappearance of the system of government by councils and the implementation of the executive authority of the Secretariats of State. Accordingly, a new caste of lawyers and administrators rose gradually to power, many of whom came from modest social origins and had studied precariously in Castilian universities, outside the privileged circles tucked away in their famous *colegios mayores*.

When, from 1759, under Charles III this new bureaucracy finally reached the main commanders of the monarchy, it was almost inevitable that the university would be the target of their plans for reform. Because of their recalcitrant scholasticism and their elitism they were accused of being, along with the Jesuits, the cause of the intellectual backwardness in Spain, an accusation not entirely without basis since, in general, the knowledge that had emerged in the scientific and philosophical revolution of the eighteenth century was only to be found in the Peninsula outside traditional academia. With the Society of Jesus expelled in 1767, in 1769 a royal charter was issued to appoint the directors of Castilian universities, genuine *visitadores* who would seek their academic and administrative modernisation. For the reformists, the university should ideally become a public corporation, vertically managed and devoted to the education of professionals in sciences that would be useful for the economic and social progress of the State, according to the absolutist guidelines; unfortunately, the old institutional pattern did not easily admit the incorporation of new knowledge or the relinquishment of former privileges. Nevertheless, between 1771 and 1786 new study plans for the main Spanish universities were indeed approved.

Following the political and generational shift triggered by the ascent of Charles IV to the throne, in 1807 the first single study plan was approved for the universities in the Peninsula.

Although the establishment of a royal university in Santiago de Chile in 1738, to replace the institutions run by regular clergy, appeared to usher in a new era, the biggest impact on the American university in the eighteenth century was certainly linked to the expulsion of the Jesuits by Charles III. From 1767 onwards, the Jesuits' universities were definitively removed or replaced by those of their Episcopal competitors or of other orders, and Jesuits were banned from teaching. In some cases this was merely a first step towards their complete transformation into royal universities. Accordingly, the University of Córdoba passed into the hands of Franciscans, and in 1800 became a royal university under diocesan authority. Having had its activities suspended with the expulsion, the University of Charcas reopened in 1772 as a royal university. In Quito, the disappearance of the Jesuits and the suppression of the Augustinian College of San Fulgencio led to the transformation of the Dominican University of Santo Tomás into a royal public university in 1786. Finally, having overcome the resistance of the University of Mexico to losing its monopoly in granting degrees in the new-Spanish viceroyalty, in 1792 the royal University of Guadalajara opened its doors in Nueva Galicia, located in the former Jesuit College of Santo Tomás.

As one can see, the echoes in America of the renovation of Spanish universities appeared limited, at least compared to the decisive reforms in regard to tax, administration and military matters implemented on the continent from the mid-eighteenth century. Notwithstanding the expectations of the most conspicuous representatives of the American Enlightenment, the forces of tradition never lost political and academic control of the institutions in the Spanish Indies, perhaps more due to the fear in university *claustros* of losing their corporate privileges as a result of an open intervention by metropolitan authorities than to the wholesale rejection by their members of the philosophical and scientific advances of the time. Similarly to what happened in Spain, and except for the isolated initiatives of enthusiasts like Bishop José Pérez Calama and his failed plans to modernise the University of Quito, the enlightened spirits did not find haven in the old or new American universities. Their place was in new social spheres, like the Sociedades Económicas de Amigos del País, or in scientific establishments promoted from the city, such as the Royal Mining Seminary or the chair in botanical studies created in New Spain at the end of the century.

This kind of initiative almost always met with the support of the viceroys, quartermasters and other reformist civil servants who grasped, as the founders of the Spanish American Republics would a few decades later, that the historical time for universities, as they had hitherto existed, was over. It was time to sketch a new ideal for public instruction, free of the ideological shackles of the religious orthodoxy and the old corporative traditions, a task which absolutism did not have either the time or the capacity to perform.

In this regard, it is no coincidence that the very last colonial universities to be launched in Spanish America were established by institutions that filled the void left by the old monarchy when it was overthrown in 1808. Accordingly, the San Buenaventura Seminary in Mérida, Venezuela, was made into a royal university by the Council of Caracas in 1810, and it was by a decree issued by the Cádiz Cortes in 1812 that the former tridentine seminary of San Ramón became the University of León in Nicaragua. In effect, it would henceforth be the nation that would decide the meaning and mission of the university, and the place in which it would build a future of its own.

College of Santísima Trinidad, Guanajuato, Mexico
This Jesuit college was closed down in 1767 when the Society of Jesus was expelled from Latin America. In 1798, under the new name Real Colegio de la Purísima Concepción, the school was refounded by the priests of the Oratory of San Felipe Neri, one of the city's leading churches.

Jesuit Universities in Latin America

In 1767, the King of Spain expelled the Jesuits from his American dominions with the dual accusation (among other more general allegations) that they had taught intellectuals the 'right of just rebellion' against tyrannical governments that sought to legitimise their despotism through 'the divine right of kings', banning subjects from questioning them, whether tyrannical or not. The other accusation was that the Jesuits had vast treasures hidden in the reductions of Paraguay and that they had plans to form, under a Jesuit theocracy, an indigenous kingdom independent of Spain.

Between that expulsion and the Jesuits' modern university presence in Latin America there was a interval of 170 years, since all the current Jesuit universities except for one were founded after 1940, making them very young in comparison to their European or North American peers. Born from national circumstances and in a variety of legal forms, they all coincide in the conviction that quality higher education based on the secular educational tradition of the Jesuits was a good service to Latin American societies that were modernising and transforming from rural into urban. The Jesuit universities tried to transplant into Latin America the manner of training elites and professionals to spearhead modernisation typical of universities in the Western world. Without much discussion, this was the current of opinion until the start of the 1970s, when, stemming from the contradictions in Latin American societies, the criticism and controversy about the university's mission began.

November 2009 was the twentieth anniversary of the brutal murder of Ignacio Ellacuría, chancellor of Central America University of José Simeón Cañas (UCA), run by the Jesuits in El Salvador. In the midst of the civil war, he and five other Jesuits from among the university's leaders were dragged out of bed and riddled with bullets by the army under the presidency of Alfredo Cristiani, himself a former student of the Jesuit college. The UCA, and in particular its chancellor and directors, were highly critical of the unfair structure of Salvadorian society and the pro-military government, but at the same time they advocated peaceful dialogue between the government and guerrillas, in the wake of a long and bloody war. The university was caught between its desire for dialogue to achieve social justice, and the radicalised conflict in a society that excluded the country's poor majority. This massacre, an attack on a way of understanding the university, was preceded by the monstrous murder in 1980 of the Archbishop of San Salvador, Óscar Arnulfo Romero, to silence his inspirational and courageous voice

Father Florián Paucke, drawing of a Jesuit mission and vegetable garden in South America (18th century)
The Jesuits took it upon themselves to educate the American native peoples from the sixteenth century until their expulsion in 1767. Their missionary settlements were designed to survive self-sufficiently.

that refused to use Christianity to legitimise injustices and which, in the name of God, ordered the soldiers not to shoot their own people.

Finally, in 1992 in El Salvador an agreement was reached between the government and the Farabundo Martí National Liberation Front to end the deadly and sterile war and, through dialogue, to enable the country's development based on social justice. Although it is by no means easy, this is the only possible way forward and the universities have the duty and opportunity to play a major and clear role in the process.

It is true that not all Latin American societies experienced poverty and social conflict to the same degree as El Salvador, but in 1990 Latin America was emerging from two decades of brutal right-wing dictatorships and, a 'lost decade' from an economic standpoint, when neo-liberal simplicity sought to reduce everything to leaving the market to its own devices and reducing the role of the State. In the 1990s it was recognised that a democratic change involving citizens' participation must be brought about, with economic and social development and the clear aim of overcoming poverty in a continent with the biggest gap between rich and poor in the world. The Soviet bloc had collapsed and many communist experiments in the third world had failed. The right combination between market and State could work to channel national aspirations towards success.

SOCIETY AND UNIVERSITY NETWORKS

The AUSJAL (Latin American Universities Entrusted to the Society of Jesus) was established in 1985. At the beginning it was an association without any great authority or pretensions, which was content for chancellors to meet every two years. However, this situation has changed radically in the last ten years, following a reappraisal of both the future outlook of Latin American societies and the best way in which universities can contribute to the achievement of their aspirations.

In 1995, AUSJAL published a text entitled, 'Challenges in Latin America and the Educational Response of AUSJAL', in which it outlined the serious problems undermining Latin American development and defined the role of the Jesuit university against this backdrop. On the basis of this analysis, six years later the '2001–05 Strategic Plan' was published, containing four shared strategic guidelines. In these documents Latin America is seen as a dual society with massive poverty, a scandalous gap between rich and poor, and a damaging loss of prestige for its political parties and, more generally, for its governments' public policies. Dictatorships and their recent failures are also condemned, as are the broken promises of the 'neo-liberals'. This is combined, however, with praise for the many policies devised to redress macroeconomic imbalances, and to trim and scale down public bureaucracy and state-run business activity. The Strategic Plan establishes – always based on the question of what the Jesuit universities can do to contribute to the solutions – the following common action lines: understanding and solution of the problem of poverty in dual societies; social and democratic rule of law and human rights; entrepreneurs,

Jesuist professor lecturing at the blackboard (1995)
After their expulsion by the Spanish Crown it was over a century and a half later, in the 1940s, that the Jesuits returned to Latin America to found new universities in which to train the emerging urban classes.

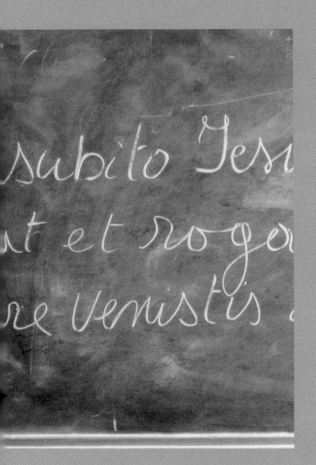

ethical management and social commitment of business; and the education system and universities. These four aspects of the issues affecting the region are interlinked with the need to achieve a systematic increase in social, economic and political productivity, and to create well-paid quality jobs. Without good employment it is impossible to escape poverty and without radical growth in education in Latin America, and in the quality of business and public management, there will be no dignified employment sufficient to pull people out of poverty. New leadership is required to rescue public policy and ensure its adequate synchronisation with more creative and responsible private initiative. This brings us to the questions: 'What is the university for?' And 'What university for what society?'

The Jesuit universities of Latin America, after decades of work training professionals and expanding to meet growing demand, now ask themselves (as they did in the 1995 publication) whether they are training 'successful professionals in failed societies'. Consequently, the Strategic Plan proposes to make the training of students and future professionals more comprehensive, thereby improveing their ability to take on a public role in their societies. This means really understanding the society as a whole and its place in a globalised world, as well as the challenges posed by the particular studies being followed. The ethical commitment of future professionals must be integrated into their lives: their personal success must contribute significantly and be linked to and the success of society as a whole. The entire university must become a permanent forum for the major issues in society, and one of its core 'subjects' should include the ability to convert university studies and research into a vital driving force for the population at large. It is a critical examination of society, but also of the university as we know it. Instrumental knowledge may be applied to unleash either war or peace, to either increase business with no regard to national development, or enable companies and governments to produce a democratic and social society for all.

The AUSJAL comprises thirty universities, with around 250,000 students in fourteen countries. Numerically speaking, this may appear insignificant, since it accounts for less than two percent of Latin American university students. But these universities share a common inspiration and are understood to be public-service, privately-run and not-for-profit institutions, which makes agreement on the aforementioned lines much easier. The Association enables work to be shared, and strives for a common goal inspired by the essence of Latin American Christianity, committed to overcoming poverty and to making human development compatible with democratic freedom and social justice. However, these basic agreements are not enough to act together; it is necessary to overcome a tradition of excessive independence, to create a new culture of cooperation and to innovate in the use of information and communication technologies.

Luis Ugalde

Emerging in different national circumstances and legal forms, the Jesuit universities in Latin America aspired to train an elite of forward-looking professionals

Juan O'Gorman, Central Library of the National Autonomous University of Mexico (UNAM) (1950–56)
The Mexican architect Juan O'Gorman designed the library as a functional building, a large concrete rhomboid covered with mosaics of intricate iconography. Each façade depicts scenes relating to the history of Mexico: the pre-Spanish past, the colonial era, the modern world and the current image of the university and of Mexico itself. Its singular architecture has made the library an icon of the Mexican university; it was declared World Heritage in 2007.

The University in Latin America and the Caribbean

Juan Ramón de la Fuente
with contributions from Alma Herrera and Nadia Villafuerte

The university is still the critical entity in which societies' most sweeping transformations are reflected. This is the case of the university in Latin America, which has always played a central role in the history of the continent. The Latin American university is currently at a defining moment with regard to not only its identity but also the role it must assume to achieve its goal of reviving humanism and driving scientific development in a complex and necessarily global context.

In Latin America and the Caribbean, the university has played a decisive and far-reaching role. While it is difficult to visualise a single concept of university in the region, it is still the legitimate generator and disseminator of knowledge, complicit in the ideal of 'America' as a land with a social conscience aspiring towards justice, equality and sovereignty of its peoples as a condition of a much desired balance.

In addition to the reflection on social engagement that characterises higher education in Latin America and the Caribbean, the twenty-first century university has brought to the debate new issues emerging in a society marked by the impact of the scientific-technological revolution and the new approaches to the concept of the nation-state and geopolitical borders, as well as the attempts to commercialise higher education and reduce it to nothing more than a trade transaction.

Since it is impossible to give a fully comprehensive account, this chapter offers an overview of the most significant aspects of the university institution in Latin America and the Caribbean.

According to the World Bank, the region currently comprises twenty-nine countries. Characterised by being heterogeneous, multi-cultural and multi-ethnical, Latin America encompasses various levels of development, significant differences in growth and modernisation between the nations that comprise it and, in many cases, profound differences between regions of a single country.

The literature on the impact of the university in Latin America and the Caribbean is extensive, but two recent publications give a good account of much of the history and the current state of higher education in Latin America: *The History of the Union of Universities of Latin America and the Caribbean* (UDUAL), and the *Report by the Interuniversity Development Centre* (CINDA).

The UDUAL (founded in 1949 through an agreement of the First Congress on Universities in Latin America, held at San Carlos University in Guatemala) is still, to date, the university organisation with the longest-standing tradition in the region. In the last sixty years, however, other regional organisations, federations and networks have consolidated the task of coordinating and unifying institutions with similar academic projects (see Appendix). CINDA, meanwhile, focused on the task of updating the available information on higher education in Argentina, Bolivia, Brazil, Colombia, Costa Rica, Chile, Ecuador, Mexico, Panama, Peru, Puerto Rico, the Dominican Republic, Uruguay and Venezuela. This work, involving leading specialists, was conducted with the support of Universia which, in an unprecedented

Rectorial residence, University of Simón Bolívar (USB), Caracas, Venezuela
The USB is Venezuela's leading public university for science and technology degrees. The rectory is one of several buildings making up the campus in Sartenejas valley.

effort, has managed to bring together one thousand universities on the American side of the Atlantic.

The UNESCO International Institute of Higher Education in Latin America and the Caribbean (IESALC), headquartered in Caracas, has also undertaken significant work in this connection. Many of the improvements, limitations and concerns of higher education institutions in the region were expressed in a document presented in Paris, during the World Conference on Higher Education organised in July 2009 by UNESCO, the final communiqué of which included two recommendations which are particularly sensitive with regard to the university scenario in Latin America and the Caribbean: on the one hand, that higher education be maintained as a public good; on the other, that countries be encouraged not to cut investment in higher education, despite the current economic recession.

For historical reasons and due to the socio-economic conditions in the region, both points take on some significance. Firstly, because in modern-day society, which is no longer the society of work in the traditional sense, but a knowledge society, education is closely linked to welfare. Secondly, because in view of this situation, the public university is still the best instrument for social inclusion, not only forging links with science and culture, but also as the focus of intellectual debate, and the political and economic concerns of our era.

Background and Autonomy

As seen earlier, the university in Latin America and the Caribbean is rooted in Spanish universities, in particular that of Salamanca, although some general study institutions also took their inspiration from the University of Alcalá de Henares. The first known royal charter issued in respect of the university in America corresponds to Santo Domingo in 1538. Subsequently, royal charters were issued to establish universities in the cities of Lima and Mexico. In the following three centuries, similar institutions were set up in Quito, Santiago de Chile, La Plata and Córdoba (Argentina), Santa Fe de Bogotá, Cusco, Guatemala, Havana, Caracas, Buenos Aires and Panama, as well as in the Yucatán and Nuevo León, in Mexico. In 1812, the Cádiz Cortes established the university in Nicaragua, and it was not until the early twentieth century when Brazil saw its first university built in Rio de Janeiro (incidentally, despite its relatively late arrival, the Brazilian university has managed to make significant headway in research, development and innovation).

During the colonial period there were thirty-three universities in America. Some survived, others disappeared, and only a few managed to consolidate their position. However, it was with the independence of the American republics that new universities began to develop, adding another fifty institutions in the following hundred years. Towards the second half of the twentieth century the wave of expansion in higher education in Latin America and the Caribbean began. In 1950, there were around seventy-five universities with just over 250,000 students. Today, registered tertiary students total around seventeen million.

One of the distinguishing characteristics of the university in Latin America and the Caribbean is its autonomy. The university revolution in 1918 in Córdoba, Argentina, inaugurated the reformist tradition of Latin American universities. Since then, the ideology of 1918 university reform began highlighting Latin American regional unity. The background for this concept stems directly from the independent movements, although the term 'autonomous' acquired,

Students at the library of the University of Córdoba, Argentina (1964)
After the revolution of 1918, the main events of which took place at this university and give rise to the 'ideals of Córdoba', the conception and structure of Latin American universities changed radically. The new paradigm sought closer involvement with regional politics and recognition of the autonomy and democracy that ought to characterise academic life.

One of the distinguishing characteristics of the university in Latin America and the Caribbean is its autonomy. The university revolution in 1918 in Córdoba, Argentina, inaugurated the reformist tradition of Latin American universities

Students at the University of Concepción, Chile (1960)
The founding of this Chilean university was the outcome of several visits by Chilean government officials to the United States to research American academic methods. In 1919, the University of Concepción opened its doors to train professionals in the liberal and technical disciplines in accordance with the country's state of development. From its beginnings, the institution was concerned with fostering a humanistic and philosophical outlook.

in the university context, a special social and progressive meaning that has endured ever since. It would be difficult to understand the nature of the university in the present day without knowing what that reformist movement meant for the Latin American university at the time.

The Córdoba ideology included the 'coordination of writers, intellectuals and teachers of Latin America in the struggle to reaffirm democracy, abolish economic privileges, remove the Church's influence on public life and education, and extend free, secular and compulsory education'. This vital link between the university and politics also explains the ideological link between the university in Latin America and the Caribbean and the Spanish Republic during and after the war, and European anti-fascist positions in the 1940s.

In a way, it was the university of Córdoba's reform that paved the way for today's public university and from which concepts such as 'public good' or 'social investment' derived. It was also the starting point for the idea of identity in the Latin American university: the rebellious, critical, democratic, citizens' university inspired by the values of free thinking and by the development and autonomy of peoples. This nurtured the ideal that the university must contribute actively in defining and executing public policies, with authority to make decisions not only regarding its forms of government and administration, but also, and perhaps most importantly, regarding the curricula, research lines and granting of degrees and qualifications, in other words, regarding the establishment of an academic university, which is its essence.

The model that has emerged from this reform was incorporated steadily throughout Latin America. Peru, Chile and Mexico assimilated, each in their own way, the reformist elements which later impacted decisively on their universities' relationship with society and the State.

The autonomy laws began to proliferate during the last century. Accordingly, as the reform progressed, the university's social mission acquired a broader and more engaged meaning. Ninety years have elapsed since the Córdoba university reform, but the mark it left within a liberal and progressive tradition remains present in the region and is reflected in the

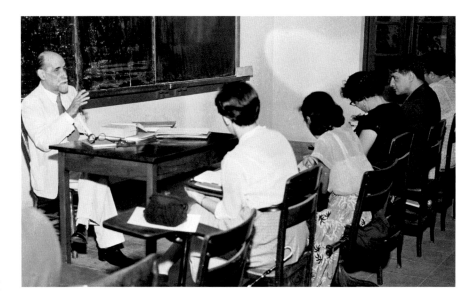

development of many countries, despite the sweeping changes in the social fabric of Latin America and the Caribbean.

Autonomy explains the size of many universities, such as that of Mexico and Buenos Aires; in some cases it also manifests the difficulty in implementing subsequent reforms and the considerable sensitivity of the university as an institution to the effects of privatisation, some of them unavoidable, others perhaps more indirect. With all of its implications, the basic and irrevocable principle of autonomy is an element without which it would be impossible to understand the identity of the university in Latin America and the Caribbean as a public, secular and popular institution, as a scientific and self-reflexive university which has historically declared itself to be against the notions of the 'denominational' university and dogmatic thought.

Today, university autonomy is fundamental to understand freedom of teaching and research. Autonomy, democracy, science, teaching and outreach are the pillars of a legacy that is not limited solely to the sphere of universities, because today's university is still expected to deliver on concepts such as social responsibility and influence on the democratisation of society, as well as rewards for the society to which it owes allegiance.

Juan Ramón Jiménez lecturing at the University of Puerto Rico (1958)
This famous Spanish poet, like other intellectuals of Republican Spain, went into exile after Franco had installed himself as dictator. Many exiles took up teaching jobs at Latin American universities. The political complicity inherent in a common enmity towards fascism eased the way for this influx of Spanish talent.

Higher Education in Mexico

The history of the university in Mexico commenced in 1551 with the issuance of the founding charter of the Royal University of Mexico, where teaching was offered continuously from 1553 onwards. This university was initially organised in the likeness of the University of Salamanca. It comprised four 'greater' departments (theology, canon law, laws and medicine), one 'lesser' department (arts) and other chairs, such as indigenous languages. Furthermore, it governed itself through a system of *claustros* (faculties) comprising the university's doctorate-holding professors. Adjacent to the university, a number of schools run by Jesuits and other orders were established, as well as tridentine seminaries, both in Mexico City and in the main cities of the Viceroyalty. These include San Pedro, San Pablo and San Ildefonso, in Mexico; San Ignacio, in Querétaro; El Espíritu Santo, in Puebla; San Nicolás, in Michoacán; and La Santísima Trinidad, in Guanajuato. Later on came universities like that of San Francisco Javier in Yucatán (1624), run by the Jesuits, and the Royal of Guadalajara in 1792. Furthermore, in the new era of Enlightenment, colleges devoted to teaching modern science were created, such as the College of Mining, or to teaching arts, like the San Carlos Academy. Those trained in letters were the heart of the bureaucracy of the Spanish monarchy in America and, in the early nineteenth century, the promoters of enlightened thought.

During Mexico's first few decades as an independent nation, its Royal University (established by royal charter) was suppressed and restored several times, until it was finally closed in 1865. Meanwhile, in the different states new education establishments were founded or reorganised. The universities of Guanajuato, Guadalajara, Nuevo León, Puebla, Querétaro, San Luis Potosí and Yucatán, all with colonial backgrounds, were transformed in the nineteenth century into civilian colleges run by the states, or scientific and literary institutes, and they were then reconfigured as universities during the first few years of the twentieth century. In 1867, President Benito Juárez issued the Public Instruction Act, which organised primary and secondary education for the Republic. National or professional schools were created: preparatory, jurisprudence, medicine, surgery and pharmacy, agriculture and veterinary medicine, engineering, fine arts and trade, as well as secondary education for women and the school for arts and crafts, among others. In 1910 mid-higher and higher education in Mexico was reorganised and reinvigorated with the opening of the National University of Mexico, comprising several national schools founded during the nineteenth century: preparatory, jurisprudence, medicine, engineering, fine arts, and the newly created School of Higher Studies.

The Monterrey Institute of Technology (1969)
The present campus was built in 1981. Since 2008, the university has offered an innovative curriculum that enables individual estudents to design their own academic plan in accordance with her interests.

The National University, which in 1929 was established as the National Autonomous University of Mexico, was the largest project in the nation's contemporary development; it has been a standard-bearer in regard to growth in the system and a leader in its process of consolidation. Meanwhile, rooted in nineteenth-century colleges or institutes, the states of Aguascalientes, Campeche, Chihuahua, Chiapas, Durango, Guerrero, Hidalgo, Michoacán, Oaxaca, Sinaloa, Tabasco, Tamaulipas and Zacatecas began opening institutions that would later become autonomous universities. In those places where institutes were not established, public universities were also created, so that by the end of the twentieth century, there was at least one public university in each of the country's federal states.

At the end of the first decade of the twenty-first century, Mexico has a broad, complex and diverse higher education system. Of the thirty-nine institutes and universities in existence in the mid-twentieth century, most of them public, which attained barely 1.3 percent of coverage by age-group, the figure has risen to 2,539, of different types and legal status which, overall, cover close to 27 percent of the young Mexican population, despite ongoing imbalances and inequalities throughout the country. In 2008–2009 almost three million students were registered on higher technical university level courses (3 percent of the total), undergraduate courses (90 percent) and postgraduate courses (7 percent), 92 percent of the registrations belong to the on-site modality and the rest to open and distance learning, in three sub-systems: university, technological and normal education. The system is subdivided into public and private categories. In the former are the federal universities (4) and state universities (56), technological institutes (239) and universities (67), polytechnics (31) and intercultural universities (9), normal schools (268), research centres (27) and other institutions (161), together accounting for 66 percent of national registrations. The private system comprises 1,677 universities, institutes, centres and schools, with just over a million students, accounting for 34 percent of registrations.

Federal and public state universities account for 44 percent of all students in the country. With more than 25,000 full-time academics, they conduct significant activities in research and dissemination of culture. The statute of autonomy, which grants them freedom for teaching and research, has enabled them to cultivate the humanities, sciences and arts in a responsible manner in the country's best interest and that of its different regions, and to foster progress in the various areas of education. Mexican universities have transformed in the last two decades, in an effort reminiscent of their historical origins, while at the same time tackling the challenges of scientific and technical progress worldwide, the constitution of cooperation networks, academic exchange and international mobility, transparency and accountability requirements, and the processes of evaluation and accreditation of their work. Furthermore, they have revitalised their commitment to the needs of broader society, to strengthening the nation and to injecting renewed momentum into a real system of secular values for society as a whole.

José Narro Robles
Lourdes Chehaibar Náder

The National University of Mexico won its autonomy in 1929 and, as the standard-bearer of the Mexican system of higher education, has spearheaded the country's development ever since

Mural *The conquest of energy*, Alfonso Caso Auditorium, UNAM, Mexico (1956)
The former science faculty, now occupied by the Alfonso Caso Auditorium and the Postgraduate Unit, is presided over by a mural by the artist José Chávez Morado, dated 1952. Titled *The conquest of energy*, the work portrays the struggle of humankind to find a source of vital energy since the discovery of fire.

First Campus Party in Brazil, São Paulo Exhibition Centre (2008)
Created in Spain in the 1990s, the Campus Party event was first staged in Brazil in 2008. The fixture is regarded as the world's largest digital technology, creativity, leisure and arts convention to be officiated over a networked platform. The latest Campus Party drew over 6,500 *campuseiros* – participants – and 118,000 visitors from twenty-two countries.

The universities of Latin America and the Caribbean today cater for around 17 million students, a considerable figure, which contrasts with the just over 36 million illiterate people in the region

The Current Situation: Figures, Trends, Contrasts

The universities of Latin America and the Caribbean today cater for around seventeen million students, a considerable figure, which contrasts with the just over thirty-six million illiterate people in the region. The largest student numbers are in Brazil, Mexico, Argentina, Colombia and Venezuela; Argentina, Panama and Chile have managed to register 45 percent of their population aged between twenty and twenty-four years, and they are followed by Costa Rica, Venezuela and Uruguay. However, the average in the region is less than 30 percent. The number of students per ten thousand inhabitants is, on average, two hundred and fifty-nine, although the breakdown is uneven. Argentina has more than four hundred and fifty students per ten thousand inhabitants, while Panama, Costa Rica, Venezuela, Chile, Dominican Republic, Bolivia, Peru and Uruguay have between three hundred and four hundred and fifty students for every ten thousand inhabitants.

The main problem facing university education in Latin America and the Caribbean, from the social standpoint, is still the inequality. There are still major inequalities depending on household income. Access to university studies is still very scant in marginal social groups, including the various ethnic groups. The graph opposite illustrates this reality.

Furthermore, it is difficult to estimate precisely the number of universities there are in Latin America and the Caribbean. According to the Directory published by the International Association of Universities there are four thousand and fifty-three, including universities and other higher education institutions. As in other regions, there are many institutions calling themselves universities, which in fact are not.

In the last few years, the countries that have seen the biggest annual rise in higher education are Brazil, Venezuela, Chile and Colombia, and registrations at private universities are responsible for a good deal of this growth. In almost all of these countries there are more women than men registered in higher education, and since the beginning of this decade the average number of women for the region as a whole has exceeded 50 percent of the total.

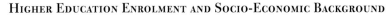

HIGHER EDUCATION ENROLMENT AND SOCIO-ECONOMIC BACKGROUND

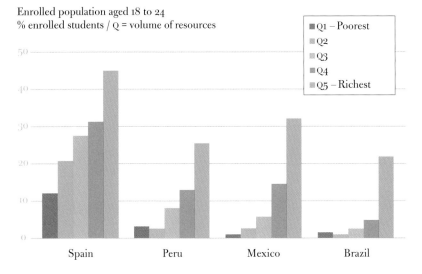

Enrolled population aged 18 to 24
% enrolled students / Q = volume of resources

- Q1 – Poorest
- Q2
- Q3
- Q4
- Q5 – Richest

Spain   Peru   Mexico   Brazil

Source: World Bank, 2008.

Public universities in Latin America and the Caribbean are currently facing major challenges deriving from the swift changes in a number of sectors, both nationally and on the global stage, which require them to update as dynamic institutions of education, science and culture. Internationalisation was slow to reach the region. This is manifested, for example, by the fact that there are approximately forty thousand Latin Americans studying at universities outside the region, compared with the five hundred thousand Asian students registered at universities outside their countries.

Despite their considerable differences, universities in Latin America and the Caribbean do share some common characteristics in relation to both their mission and their substantive functions, as well as their recent efforts to update and modernise the educational services they offer and lead the way in higher education in an international context, despite the severe financial constraints in place.

In the 1990s, the long growth cycle begun forty years previously had ended. During that period, the gross rate of higher education increased from two

Enrolment at Private Universities as a Percentage of Total Student Population, by Country

Figures in %

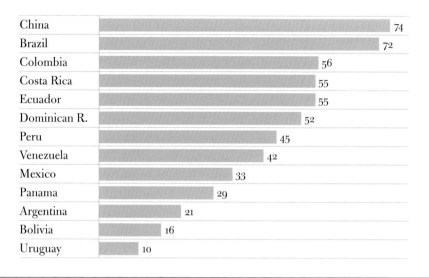

China	74
Brazil	72
Colombia	56
Costa Rica	55
Ecuador	55
Dominican R.	52
Peru	45
Venezuela	42
Mexico	33
Panama	29
Argentina	21
Bolivia	16
Uruguay	10

Source: UNESCO, Global Education Digest, 2006; CINDA Report, 2007.

percent in 1950 to close to 25 percent in the first few years of this century. The number of public universities (those financed mainly by national treasuries) increased from seventy-five to more than three hundred; and at the same time another 1,200 institutions were created, most of them private. Not all of these are universities and the education they offer is highly diverse. While it is true that relatively few universities have managed to integrate research into teaching, and to offer studies at both undergraduate and postgraduate level, many more have managed to focus their activities on the teaching itself, especially in undergraduate programmes.

The biggest growth has occurred in the private sector. This circumstance could be explained by the fact that in Latin America and the Caribbean, generally speaking, demand for university education has exceeded the State's offering at public institutions, and this has triggered a proliferation of private institutions, of varying degrees of quality. The graph above shows some data to evidence this. Private universities in Latin America and the Caribbean are characterised, in most cases and with a few known exceptions, by giving degree-level study programmes.

Few conduct basic research and this is generally limited to postgraduate courses. In countries such as Brazil, Colombia, Chile, Costa Rica, Ecuador and the Dominican Republic, more than half of students are registered at private institutions.

Because of their significance in generating new areas of knowledge, their broad offering in postgraduate studies, their potential to innovate and their association with various social sectors, public universities in Latin America and the Caribbean are still the benchmark of university education in the region. Various government policies, supported by business groups, foundations and specific education projects, have sought to establish new higher education policies aimed at reforming and strengthening the university as an institution. Despite the novel methods of institutional management and the increasing link to the productive and social sectors, universities have repeatedly come up against financial constraints that have curbed their growth in basic areas such as scientific research and technological innovation.

An interesting phenomenon in the last few years has been the establishment of networks of public universities, based on the principle of solidarity. This has derived in agreements that have enabled shared post-graduated programmes to be developed, and have facilitated student mobility as well as a dynamic virtual interconnection. The benefits of networking, in terms of grants, support for research, innovation and conservation of heritage, are encouraging.

The fundamental challenge for the university in Latin America and the Caribbean is to make technological tools into mechanisms of social integration, obviously including the humanities and social sciences, to make knowledge generation a real instrument of insertion, equality and social mobility, in a bid to redress the huge imbalances that still prevail in the region. The task of the Latin American university in such a complex era as this also involves claiming back national and regional terrain through an education project that is able to insert itself into the knowledge society with its very own stamp of identity.

Orquideorama José Jerónimo Triana, Medellín Botanical Garden, Colombia (2008)
With ties to the National University, the Orquideorama was laid out in 2006. This botanical garden has helped develop scientific knowledge and research in the country; its innovative architectural design is coupled with an important role in scientific and environmental education and dissemination.

University, Science and Innovation

Vital for progress, research is one of the drivers that contributes decisively not only to problem-solving, but also, and in particular, to social development.

Between 1996 and 2006, Latin America was posting 34.6 percent economic growth, underperforming other regions worldwide by a considerable margin. These differences are at least partly explained by the high standards of competitiveness shown by some economies as a result of their focus on research and innovation and their capacity to incorporate knowledge into the productive apparatus.

At present, a country's innovative strengths largely define its productive levels. Investment in research and development, patent registrations, the application of new technologies and even foreign investment find fertile ground in societies where broad sectors of the population have had the opportunity to complete tertiary studies. This is where the university plays a vital role.

In science and research, universities in Latin America and the Caribbean post a discreet and heterogeneous performance. Average investment in research and development in the region is approximately 0.7 percent of gross domestic product.

Universities that stand out for their scientific productivity are: in Argentina, the University of Buenos Aires; in Brazil, the University of São Paulo, Campinas State University and Rio de Janeiro Federal University; in Chile, the University of Chile; and in Mexico, the National Autonomous University. Of course, there are many others that conduct research and some of them do so to a notable standard. The ones listed are those that, according to various bibliometric studies, appear to be the 'most productive in science'.

In this connection, the various international evaluations regarding universities that stand out for their capacity in research and innovation coincide. Spain's Consejo Superior de Investigaciones Científicas [Scientific Research Council], for example, evaluates universities based on their presence on the Internet. Systematically, the aforementioned universities are listed, as well as some others: Rio Grande do Sul Federal University and Santa Catarina Federal University, as well as the University of Brasilia, Minas Gerais Federal University, São Paulo State University, Paraná Federal University, Bahía Federal University and the University of Rio Grande do Norte, all in Brazil. In Mexico, among the top-ranked in this list are the National Autonomous University of Mexico, Guadalajara University and the Monterrey Technological Institute. Others in the top twenty 'most visible' online are: Colombia's University of the Andes and Chile's Concepción University.

Because these are, in effect, incomplete parameters, these and other rankings have unleashed a flurry of intense reaction in universities almost everywhere, and Latin America and the Caribbean are no exception. However, these rankings do effectively reflect development and potential in terms of science, technology and innovation at some universities, in contrast with others whose main purpose – and one that is certainly respectable – is teaching, also decisive for local, national and regional development.

There are relatively few researchers working in universities in Latin America compared with universities elsewhere. However, it is worth pointing out that many of them have managed to stand out on the international stage and they have the added merit of having done so despite adverse conditions, by offsetting a low budget with high doses of creativity.

The contribution by Latin America and the Caribbean to global scientific production is modest, scarcely accounting for 4 percent. Chile, Argentina, Costa Rica, Mexico, Uruguay, Panama, Venezuela, Bolivia and the Dominican Republic, interestingly, have gradually increased the resources at their main universities for research activities. Brazil has made a particularly colossal effort in the last few years, as according to the United Nations Development programme it is the only country in Latin America and the Caribbean to spend more than 1 percent of its GDP on scientific research.

Universities, especially public ones, represent the best option for countries in the region to join the so-called 'knowledge society'. They are also the entry

	Biology Environmental Sciences	Technology	Agricultural Sci. and Aquaculture	Social Sciences
Argentina	INGEBI, University of Buenos Aires	Research and development area, Technological Institute of Buenos Aires	IFEVA University of Buenos Aires	Department of Economics, National University of La Plata
Brazil	Computer sci. Department, Catholic University of Rio de Janeiro (PUC)	Chemistry Institute, University of Campinas	Superior School of Agronomy Luiz of Queiroz, University of São Paulo	Graduate School of Economics of Foundation Getulio Vargas
Chile	University International Center Europe Latin America, University of Concepción	Center of Mathematical Modeling, University of Chile	Center Coastal of Aquaculture and Marine Research, University North Catholic	Legal Research Center, University Diego Portales
Mexico	Institute of Biotechnology, National Autonomous University of Mexico (UNAM)	Center of Applied Physics and Advanced Technology, UNAM	Research Center and Advanced Studies, Unit Irapuato	Center for Economic Studies, The College of Mexico A.C.

Source: IESALC / UNESCO, 2008.

point for science to be assimilated as a part of culture. This is a gradual process which must gather pace, because it brings huge social benefits in the medium and long term.

A recent survey by the IESALC examined successful experiences in various areas of research at some universities in Latin America and the Caribbean (see table above). The selection was based on the premise that Argentina and Brazil, Chile and Mexico had all worked specifically to develop scientific and technological skills as a basic element of the development of their societies. The lessons from these positive experiences show that the research teams at the universities studied were able to make major contributions to society, with high academic standards. The study concludes that these are exemplary cases which show the huge potential of research at universities in the region. The project also involved the Inter-American Network of Academies of Sciences (IANAS).

It is interesting to point out that in the case of Brazil some private institutions had been chosen, such as the Pontifical Catholic University and the Getulio Vargas Foundation. Furthermore, the Chemistry Department of Campinas University and the Irapuato campus of the Centre for Research and Advanced Studies in Mexico (CINVESTAV) were able to link up with both industry and society, enabling them to generate additional resources for their research projects.

The survey also highlights the thematic diversity and, in particular, the space devoted to social sciences at La Plata National University in Argentina, Diego Portales University in Chile and the Centre for Economic Studies in the College of Mexico.

There is a long-standing and splendid tradition of social sciences in Latin America and the Caribbean. The region has made vital contributions to universal culture and social sciences continue to focus the interest of many students. Social sciences and administrative areas account for around 40 percent of the career preferences of students in the region, according to IESALC/UNESCO data. The vocation for exact and natural sciences does not, on average, reach 10 percent.

Argentina, Brazil and Mexico account for most of the scientific production in Latin America. In accordance with their demographic dimension, and consequently on a lesser scale, the efforts of the universities of Costa Rica, Cuba, Panama, Paraguay and Uruguay are also highly admirable because of their tradition, their relation to national development programmes and the increasing resources they plough into the sciences, meeting high quality standards. All the efforts made in this connection, however modest, are deserving of praise and should be encouraged.

University Art Gallery, Central University of Venezuela (UCV), Caracas
This space was made into an art gallery in 1967. The central piece in its collection is a mural by the French painter Fernand Léger. The campus of the UCV is a UNESCO World Heritage Site.

One characteristic of the university in Latin America and the Caribbean is its humanist tradition. From its origins in the sixteenth century to the most recently created universities, it has had a distinctive vocation for preserving the cultural, natural and social heritage around it

University, National Culture and Heritage

One characteristic of the university in Latin America and the Caribbean is its humanist tradition. From its origins in the sixteenth century (Santo Domingo, San Marcos and Mexico), to the flourishing institutions created in the nineteenth century (Buenos Aires, the Central University of Venezuela and the Central University of Ecuador, Andrés Bello University and the University of Uruguay, among others, to the most recently created universities, it has had a distinctive vocation for preserving the cultural, natural and social heritage around it.

In a recent exercise led by the macro-university network Red de Macrouniversidades Públicas de América Latina y el Caribe, twenty-six universities from nineteen countries went online with an interactive document called 'Our Heritage' containing more than three thousand items including texts, video clips, slide shows, photographic collections, etc. clearly showing this mission and the extraordinary wealth of their heritage. Of course, this is not an exhaustive list or complete inventory; but overall it is safe to assert that the tangible and intangible heritage that the universities represent covers much of the very best of Latin American heritage. Appendix lists the institutions that belong to this network.

The campus of the Central University of Venezuela, in 2000, and the central campus of the UNAM, in 2007, were declared by UNESCO to be part of the Cultural Heritage of Humanity. Libraries, museums, sporting facilities, cultural venues for music, performing arts and cinemas, laboratories, workshops, protected natural areas, historical monuments, art galleries, biological collections, botanical gardens, etc., are elements that show the strength of the university in Latin America. In short, the humanist heritage of Latin American universities is a reminder of why they could not exist but for their historical legacy.

An unwavering defender of the principles of freedom, solidarity and justice, the university in Latin America and the Caribbean has undergone profound transformations which are, in turn, a reflection of all that has happened throughout the region's tumultuous history.

The university, perhaps the ideal forum for the free discussion of ideas, is committed to the objectives and interests of a society that is moving towards a change of era. The goal of education must be to form minds and reflect on our human nature and our role as citizens.

This century looks set to be the ideal time for universities to participate in designing an inclusive social project; one able to help nurture globalisation processes and that, in turn, coordinates its purposes with the needs of national development and helps curb hegemonic approaches. A model, in short, that does not lose sight of education's status as a public good, and that builds new mentalities among citizens: in other words forming independent, critical and imaginative personalities.

Today, furthermore, the university faces a tough challenge: to modernise productive apparatus taking into account the impulse from science, technology and innovation, without relinquishing societies' culture and artistic heritage, since the university cannot be understood without humanism, which is its very essence. This is the challenge which universities must overcome. Their social responsibilities must be strengthened.

David Alfaro Siqueiros,
The People to the University and the University to the People, **UNAM, Mexico (1950–54), detail**
The great Mexican muralist Siqueiros created this impressive sample of glazed pottery for the Torre de la Rectoría [rectory tower]. Symbolising the fellowship that ought to reign between university and people, the artist uses highly abstract images that nonetheless represent the need for action that he demands from society.

Higher Education in Brazil

Brazil, which was discovered by the Portuguese in 1500, did not see its first universities until four hundred years later, at the beginning of the twentieth century. A major event that contributed decisively to the implementation of higher education in this Portuguese colony was the royal family's decision to transfer the court there in 1808. The establishment of the royal court implied the need for political organisation, and required personnel to be trained to meet the demands of the government and society. Consequently, higher education was formally organised through the introduction of courses in engineering, medicine, chemistry, agriculture, economics, politics and fine arts.

In 1822, independence led to the development of higher education under the responsibility of the imperial government. At the outset of this period there were various attempts to create universities, all of which failed. A notable event was the creation in 1827, through a decree issued by Emperor Dom Pedro I, of the first law courses in Brazil (in São Paulo and Olinda). At the end of the nineteenth century, the country had twenty-four higher education institutions, in the areas of law, medicine, mining and metallurgy, agronomy and engineering, with close to ten thousand students registered.

When the Republic was set up in 1889, two developments proved extremely important for higher education: training for positions in the government bureaucracy, underpinned by the adoption of a federal system, and the need to take higher education to the decadent oligarchies as a path to preserve their social status. Higher education was destined for the elites, envisaging only professional training and omitting all activities relating to scientific research. At the outset of this period the first Brazilian universities were opened: Manaus (1912), Paraná (1912), Rio de Janeiro (1920) and Minas Gerais (1927).

Created in 1934, the University of São Paulo became the paradigmatic higher education institution in Brazil. The new university was based on the restructuring of the faculties that already existed in the state of São Paulo and on the creation of new faculties of philosophy, science and arts, the core of the new institution, where all the basic disciplines required in the training of the country's future scientists and teachers were taught.

In that post-war period industrialisation came and brought with it an increase in the demand for places in higher education and the creation

Ministry of Education, Rio de Janeiro, Brazil (1946)
The architects Oscar Niemeyer and Lucio Costa designed this building in an 'international' style. The choice of a rationalist architecture for the Brazilian capital was political. A public building had to project to the world an image evincing the modernity and openness of Brazil.

of new public universities. In 1964, there were 37 universities in Brazil:
28 public and 9 private. The dictatorial regime installed by the
military coup in 1964 (and lasting until 1985) played a major role
in defining the models of education. The military government,
perhaps to minimise the political problems generated by university
movements that opposed the interference and restrictions imposed
by the regime, implemented a vigorous policy to transform higher
education. For this purpose, it allocated considerable financial
resources to education, for use in hiring personnel and modernising
infrastructure. The controversial and desired modernisation
of education was performed based on the North American model with
the MEC-USAID Agreement (between Brazil's Education and Culture
Ministry and the United States Agency for International
Development), which was rejected by most students and progressive
professors. Evidently, they did not oppose the idea of reform itself,
since the need to overcome the anachronistic situation of universities
was widely perceived. However, they preferred a reform driven from
inside the country, rather than imposed through foreign interference.
During this period higher education spread to meet increasing demand
in society triggered by the growing middle class, resulting from the
favourable economic situation that lasted from the end of the 1960s to
the early 1980s. The university education model was no longer devised
solely for the elites, but for society as a whole. Because it was impossible
for the public sector to meet the demand for university places, the
Education Ministry facilitated accreditation processes for private
institutions, without focusing on the precepts of quality; education was
starting to be seen as a profitable investment. The number of
registrations increased significantly, especially in the private sector.
A significant event in this period was the implementation, in 1965,
of postgraduate courses, based on the models of graduate schools.

Today, higher education in Brazil is consolidated in the model of the
dictatorial period, with small changes introduced by the Federal
Constitution of 1988 and the 1996 Education Act (Lei de Diretrizes e
Bases da Educaçao Nacional – LDB). It is a complex system comprising
free public education institutions and private institutions. The system is
divided into universities, university centres, integrated faculties and
isolated institutions (faculties and schools). The universities are the only
institutions where research and dissemination are obligatory.

In the last decade, the number of registered students has increased
from 2.1 million to more than 4.8 million. However, despite this
increase, the number of students aged between eighteen and twenty-
eight years is quite low. In 2008, for a population of close to 23 million
young people, in that age group barely 12.1 percent were registered in
higher education. Looking at enrolment without reference to age
group, the percentage is 20 percent, as against 50 to 60 percent in
developed countries.

Student revolt, São Paulo, Brazil (1968)
The political concerns of the French student
unrest of May '68 were echoed at the Latin
American universities. In Brazil, students
rioted against the military dictatorship
then in power.

The military government, to minimise the political problems generated by student movements, implemented a vigorous policy to transform higher education

Qualifications at the undergraduate level are formidably complex and variegated; the postgraduate level, however, was successfully patterned into a harmonious, uniform and efficient system governed by a single and clearly drafted body of law. The Coordenaçao de Aperfeiçoamento de Pessoal de Nível Superior (CAPES), the main agency intervening in education policy and development, created a robust operating structure undergirding the growth of postgraduate courses. This success was based on: involvement of community representatives in the processes of formulating and deciding on the postgraduate policy in the country; implementation of a sophisticated system to evaluate courses, performed by the peers; establishment of a national policy to offer financial support to study programmes; a broad programme of scholarships in Brazil and abroad;

strong internationalisation policy, facilitating associations between national programmes and renowned international research centres, etc.

The system has developed quite quickly, as manifested by the increase in the number of postgraduate programmes and students registered and qualified in master's and doctoral programmes (the figure has risen from 16,200 to 46,700, divided into 33,360 professors and 10,700 doctors). In the last ten years, the number of post – graduate students has doubled (the figure has risen from 76,000 to 150,000) and the number of MA and Ph.D. students has tripled. This improved efficiency in post-graduate education is due to the continued application of a stringent evaluation process, linked to the ongoing funding of the system, and a major scholarship programme. In 2008, the system received from federal agencies (CAPES and CNPQ) 57,785 grants, of which 33,518 were for master's qualifications and 24,267 for doctorates.

Postgraduate education has played a fundamental role in scientific development in Brazil, since more than 85 percent of the country's scientific research is conducted in higher education institutions, in particular public universities. In the 1980s, Brazil's involvement in worldwide science was 0.2 percent; it currently accounts for 2.1 percent of the total. More than thirty thousand papers were published in 2008 by Brazilian researchers, ranking the country thirteenth out of a total of 183.

Finally, the Brazilian university system has grown extraordinarily in the last forty years, and especially in the last two decades. Although expansion has not managed to meet all the needs of higher education in the country, it has still come astonishingly swiftly. The Brazilian university is presently experiencing a process akin to a growth crisis, triggering the need to make readjustments not only to tackle the difficulties of the new era of globalisation, but, above all, to harmonise and render more efficient its complex mesh of structures and actions.

Adolfo José Melfi
Shozo Motoyama

Brazilian researchers, National Institute of Space Research (INPE), São José dos Campos, Brazil (2009)
Most Brazilian research sites lie within the university sphere, being designed to underpin the standards of postgraduate programmes.

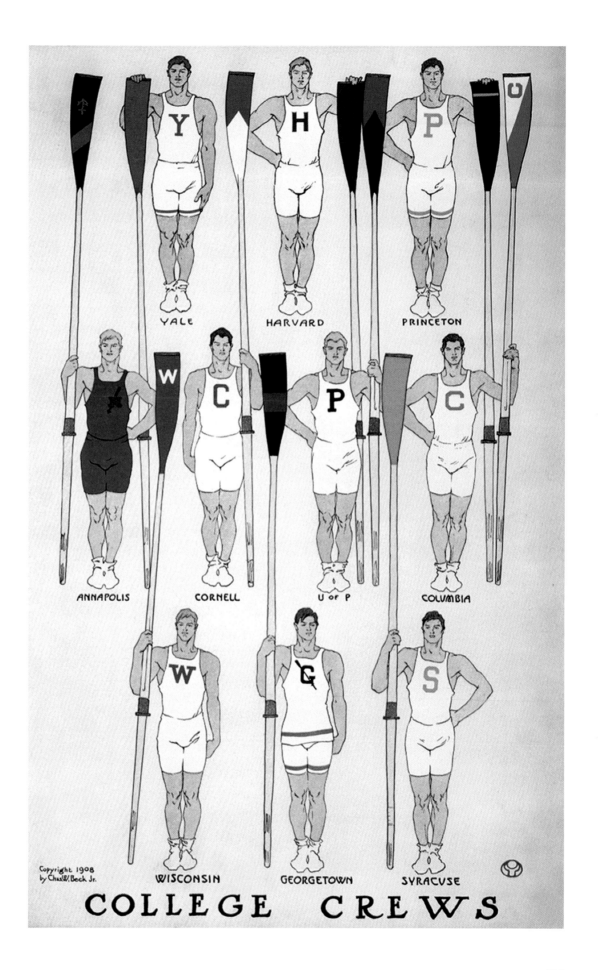

Edward Penfield,
College Crews **(1908)**
The leading American universities have preserved and strengthened the sporting tradition inherited from the English model. The most famous rowing crews were those wearing the colours of Yale, Harvard, Princeton, Annapolis, Cornell, Columbia, Wisconsin, Pennsylvania, Georgetown and Syracuse.

Universities in North America[1]

John R. Thelin

Colonies and Commonwealth: the Heritage of University Charters

The historical development of universities in North America dates back to the seventeenth century as an endeavour in colonial settlement that was unusual and complex in its hybrid character that relied on features of universities in England, Scotland and France; and, to a lesser extent, it included influence from other nations on the European continent. Although generalisations about universities in North America are part of the historical narrative, it is imperative to acknowledge differences as well as similarities in the universities in what now includes two geographically large, contiguous nations: the United States of America and Canada. Universities in each of the two nations are cooperative in their exchange of ideas, faculty, and students. On balance, they have been interdependent yet independent.

Universities in North America over three centuries have been part of the larger phenomenon of 'higher education' – and, in recent years, what has been expanded to the term 'post-secondary education'. The pattern of organisational evolution and expansion has been one in which student enrolment in North America has progressed from elite status, then to mass higher education and, since 1970, toward the goal of universal access to colleges and universities. These qualitative demarcations can be translated into quantitative terms: from the seventeenth-century origins of universities until around 1920, less than 5 percent of late adolescents in the United States and Canada enrolled in degree programmes beyond secondary school. Between 1920 and 1970, the participation rate of this traditional student age group grew persistently up to a range of 35 percent to 50 percent. Finally, since 1970, academic programmes and institutions have been expanded and diversified with the aim of enrolling approximately 60 percent to 70 percent of students who have completed secondary school diplomas, typically at about age seventeen or eighteen.

University development in North America from the mid-seventeenth century to the early twenty-first century represented a successful endeavour. By 2009 higher education enrolments in North America typically reached a level of 19 million students per year. Disaggregated by nation, this breaks out as four million students in Canada and fifteen million students in the United States. This statistical profile illustrates the growth of colleges and universities that was neither inevitable nor expected. Founding universities in distant colonies was seldom a priority of monarchies whose imperial vision for their colonies usually emphasised revenues drawn from abundant natural resources, trade routes and cheap labour. Illustrative of the emphasis on colonies as a commercial venture was a memorable episode from 1693. A delegate from the American colony of Virginia persisted in petitioning the King of England to grant a royal charter for a university because such institutions would provide an educated clergy and laity. It would be useful for transmitting Christianity and saving souls of colonists

Royal Charter of King's College (15 March 1827)
Founded in 1789, King's College was the earliest university founded in English-speaking Canada and so benefited from privileges granted by the British monarchy. It had its first seat at Windsor, Nova Scotia, where it stayed until 1920. After a fire, it moved to Halifax, the Nova Scotia capital. Granted by George IV, the charter features a likeness of the monarch.

and members of indigenous tribes. The Attorney General representing the Crown tried to discourage the petition by exclaiming, 'Souls! Damn your colonial souls! Raise tobacco!'.

In fact, the Virginia colony fulfilled its obligation to raise tobacco. And, King William and Queen Mary of England then responded gratefully by conferring a royal charter in 1693 for the College of William and Mary in Virginia. One of the most distinctive characteristics of universities in North America is that a mother country would grant a charter and dedicate funding to these institutions in the 'New World'.

In England, dedicated graduates of Cambridge University, led by prosperous merchants in London, responded by donating money and books to create a college in the Massachusetts Bay Colony in 1636, named 'Harvard College' in honour of Cambridge alumnus John Harvard. This pattern continued, as eight academic degree-granting institutions were

chartered in the American colonies by 1776. The first academic institution in Canada was founded in 1663 by the Bishop of New France as the Seminaire de Quebec – later renamed and chartered in 1852 as the Université Laval at Quebec. The University of King's College, chartered in 1789, was the first university in English Canada.

Patterns of Growth and Expansion in the Nineteenth Century

Canada and the United States have been unusual in that neither has a central ministry of education. This was less problematic in Canada as part of the British Empire and, later, as part of the British Commonwealth, because the thoughtful care associated with conferring royal charters to universities maintained responsible, orderly founding of new institutions under the auspices of the governing authority of the Provinces. The experiences in the new United States were markedly different.

The United States Constitution reserved education, including higher education, as the domain of the respective state and local governments. A peculiar historical development was that governors and state legislators often saw granting an academic charter as a convenient, inexpensive political reward for loyal supporters. Furthermore, the new state governments departed from the practices in the colonial era when both royal charters and colonial charters by custom included government commitment to support universities via taxation. The state governments felt no such obligation. The result was that starting in 1785 one finds for over a century a proliferation of literally hundreds of new colleges and universities in the United States. It included the fashionable practice of each state creating a public university bearing its name. In the late eighteenth and early nineteenth century this included several new universities in the Southern states – such as the University of Georgia, the University of North Carolina, the University of South Carolina, the University of Alabama, the University of Tennessee, and in 1819, Thomas Jefferson's innovative University of Virginia.

In the mid-nineteenth century the building of state universities moved to the Midwestern states, as one finds charters for the University of Wisconsin, the University of Michigan, Indiana University, Ohio University, and the University of Iowa.

Public higher education (i.e., tax supported institutions) in the United States gained immensely in funding from the 1862 Morrill Land Grant Act. It was one of the few times in the United States where the national government became actively involved in

higher education. It provided each state an opportunity to obtain revenues from the sale of unsettled western lands so long as the revenues were used to establish courses of study in applied fields of agriculture, engineering, and military sciences – as well as in the liberal arts and sciences. Some states opted to incorporate these new programmes and funds into existing universities, such as the University of California, Cornell University in New York, the University of Missouri and the University of Kentucky.

Other states, however, created new public universities known popularly as 'A&M' institutions (an acronym for 'Agriculture & Mechanics'), including Purdue University in Indiana, Clemson University in South Carolina, Auburn University in Alabama, Oregon State College, and Oklahoma A&M. What had emerged in the politics of higher education in the United States was that a state government had the power to chart all universities in its boundaries. Having been conferred a charter, universities tended to be bifurcated into two major groups: so-called

Interior Stanford Museum (1925)
Stanford University opened in 1891 at Palo Alto, California. Designed as a miniature city, it is endowed with its own museum. The atrium boasts statues of the founders: the industrialist and railway tycoon Leland Stanford and his wife, Jane, with their son. Flowers are left at the museum's doors every Sunday in their memory.

College pennants
Under the Morrill Land Grant Colleges Act of 1862, the Federal Government allowed states to sell unsettled land subject to a condition that the buyer found a centre of higher learning. As a result, this period witnessed a flourishing of universities and fresh statutes were given to existing ones, with a sharp dividing-line between private and public institutions.

Cornell University (1925)
In 1865, Ezra Cornell, a Senator for the state of New York, bequeathed his entire fortune for the purpose of a university bearing his name. The institution opened its doors in 1867 to offer practice-oriented training that combined technical and scientific study with history and literature.

'private' universities where the state government usually had no appointive power over the university's board of trustees; and, second, the so-called 'public' or 'state' universities that typically were subject to supervision by the governor by means of board of trustee appointments and also by annual state appropriations for university budgets.

Amidst this growth in the nineteenth century, one source of confusion in the history of universities in North America has been the lack of a formal definition as to what constitutes a 'university'. This was especially prevalent in the new United States where in the nineteenth century there was a proliferation of

academic charters granted at will by the various state governments, with little concern as to whether an institution called itself a 'college' or a 'university'. Often the term 'university' designated an entity that provided unification for a federation of units known as 'colleges', such as the 'college of liberal arts', the 'college of law', the 'college of medicine', and the 'college of engineering'. This usage is, indeed, still widspread in the twenty-first century.

However, starting around 1820 the concept of a true American 'university' started to take on a different meaning. For several decades a small but steady flow of students from the United States pursued advanced studies at universities in Germany. They were impressed by a system of higher education in which were professors were respected as experts in their scholarly fields. The visiting American students applauded the continental pedagogy that relied on lectures which were then supplemented by seminars involving a senior professor with a small group of serious students. The Doctor of Philosophy – also known as 'The Ph.D.' – represented the apex of academic degrees and licensure. Above all, the curricular idea that a university ought to be a place of new knowledge was hailed as a pleasant contrast to the dull recitation of existing material that characterised the American collegiate classroom. When the young American students returned home, they waged sustained campaigns to transplant the continental university features of libraries, laboratories, scholarly journals and doctoral dissertations to the United States. At least as an ideal if not a reality, this movement gave a new meaning to the connotation of a great university as a place of serious scholarship, characterised by research guided by the principles of the scientific method to guide systematic inquiry.

One editor who wrote about higher education framed the debate over academic institutions in the following manner: 'The essential difference between a college and university is in the way they look. A college looks backward and a university looks forward.' To fulfil this vision, aspiring universities created new administrative structures along lines of academic departments. The typical arrangement was to have a hierarchy in which a senior professor served as chairman of the department. Professors

Two college students studying in their dorm (1895)
One of the most salient characteristics of North American universities is the sitting of their student accommodation on campus, where most of the students' social life takes place. Based on the English model, this tradition continues to thrive today.

The historic universities in the New England and Mid Atlantic states tended to draw the majority of their students from the private academies known as 'prep schools'

then were organised according to rank. Most prestigious were the 'full' professors who had earned lifetime tenure. Below them in salary and prestige were associate professors and then the 'assistant professors'. Obtaining an appointment as a professor increasingly required that the applicant had completed the Ph.D. degree. Implicit in this compact was that a professor at a university was expected to pursue and publish about new knowledge. Academic departments became highly specialised so that it was no longer sufficient to speak of 'the sciences'. Instead, one had to distinguish departments of chemistry, biology, physics, geology and mathematics. The same pattern held in the humanities, with separate departments of history, literature and philosophy. Perhaps the most innovative development was the creation of new academic fields in the social and behavioural sciences. This included the disciplines of psychology, sociology, economics and political science.

What is clear, both in Canada and the United States, is that no matter which name an academic degree-granting institution called itself, it was not until after 1860 that one finds many examples of universities which offered advanced programmes of study leading to such graduate degrees as the Master of Arts and the Doctor of Philosophy, or providing facilities and time for professors to pursue scholarly research. Central to the structure of a university was the accommodation of new academic disciplines and fields, especially in the natural and physical sciences. Establishing strong scholarship with new Ph.D. programmes also included efforts to connect professional schools of law and medicine to the structure and spirit of university life.

Foremost pioneer of these initiatives was the new Johns Hopkins University that opened in 1873 in Baltimore, Maryland. Johns Hopkins University was unusual among universities because its enrolment in the entry level undergraduate college leading to the bachelor's degree was relatively small. In contrast, enrolment in programmes leading to the Master of Arts degree and, then, the advanced studies for the Ph.D. were numerically large – and also dominated the spirit and personality of this university that was known as a 'pioneer' in scholarship. The ability of

7285. JOHNS HOPKINS UNIVERSITY, BALTIMORE, MD.   COPYRIGHT, 1903, BY DETROIT PHOTOGRAPHIC CO.

the medical school at the Johns Hopkins University to attract scholars in biology and chemistry as part of education for the learned professions made its faculty distinctive. Also, Johns Hopkins University required that students entering its medical college complete a Bachelor of Arts or Bachelor of Science degree, including numerous courses in the sciences, mathematics and liberal arts. These rigorous prerequisites represented a determined effort to have new universities in the United States catch up with the established educational systems associated with the gymnasium or the *lycée* that characterised the European university model.

The Johns Hopkins University was sufficiently unique and prestigious that it became the model for attempts to reform medical schools nationwide. Abraham Flexner of the Carnegie Foundation for the Advancement of Teaching undertook a lengthy study in which he visited and analysed all medical schools in the United States. Publication of his critical study in 1910 attracted headlines in major newspapers nationwide. Its message was harsh: the education of medical doctors in the United States was judged to be markedly inferior to the standards and excellence found at universities in England and in Europe. Since most medical schools in the United States had marginal academic requirements for admission, one recommendation was that university presidents and academic deans ought to learn from – and imitate – the curriculum presented

Johns Hopkins University (1903)
Founded in Baltimore, Maryland, in 1873, from the start Johns Hopkins pursued an ambition to join the country's academic elite. Prominent in medicine, admissions were subject to attainment of a previous degree in science or the arts. Today, its nine academic divisions are spread across its Baltimore and Washington campuses.

Abraham Flexner (1929)
The author of *Universities: American, English, and German* and a member of the Carnegie Foundation for the Advancement of Teaching, Abraham Flexner undertook a comparative study of European and American universities. Having acquainted himself with the English and German models through numerous visits, Flexner's research commanded widespread influence and helped guide American educational policy.

by Johns Hopkins University. The problem was that such reforms were expensive, and many university presidents preferred to spend money on architecture and the extracurricular activities of undergraduate life, rather than invest in advanced scholarship.

Another formidable experiment in creating a great American university was the University of Chicago, founded in 1892. Thanks to the unprecedented financial support of John D. Rockefeller, this brand new institution was led by a precocious young president, William Rainey Harper. Harper was a legend for his scholarship that included fluency in several ancient languages and his study of religion. His greatest contribution to university building, however, was his organisational genius. He understood that the modern university was in large part a complex bureaucracy. Hence, he introduced an elaborate hierarchy of administrative officers who dealt with such matters as public relations, fund raising, community development, recruitment of students, and coaching university sports teams. Harper transformed the role of the university president into a highly popular figure who

associated with wealthy merchants, industrialists, philanthropists and politicians. He made certain that university events and activities were prominently covered in newspaper and magazine articles. Illustrative of his energetic, public character was that the grand opening of the magnificent Gothic revival campus of the University of Chicago coincided with the unprecedented Columbian Exposition of 1892 in which the ambitious, young city of Chicago hosted literally millions of visitors from all over the world to showcase modern inventions and developments. And the new University of Chicago was part of this showcase.

In Canada comparable signs of academic enhancement after 1860 indicated the maturing of historic institutions into genuine universities. Foremost in this progression were McGill University, the University of Toronto, Université Laval and the University of New Brunswick. The defining element of 'university' stature was the addition of new, advanced courses of study to the customary undergraduate 'collegiate' education that had long been modelled on Bachelor of Arts curricula in Scotland and England. Canada enjoyed one advantage over its educational counterparts in the United States in that it adhered to the English model of rigorous secondary school preparation as a requisite before a student enrolled at university. In contrast, secondary education in the United States remained uneven and haphazard well into the twentieth century. Not all states had adopted a system of public high schools supported by taxation. The historic universities in the New England and Mid Atlantic states tended to draw the majority of their students from the private academies known as 'prep schools'. In the United States the shortage of academically prepared students meant that institutions were forced to provide remedial instruction or, simply, to waive entrance requirements. The consequence was that even if a university aspired to offer advanced graduate programmes, it still tended to be weighted down by its obligation to accommodate many undergraduate students who were indifferent to or not ready for serious academic work. In 1890 many universities that offered Ph.D. programmes actually attracted few doctoral students – and conferred only a minuscule number of doctoral degrees.

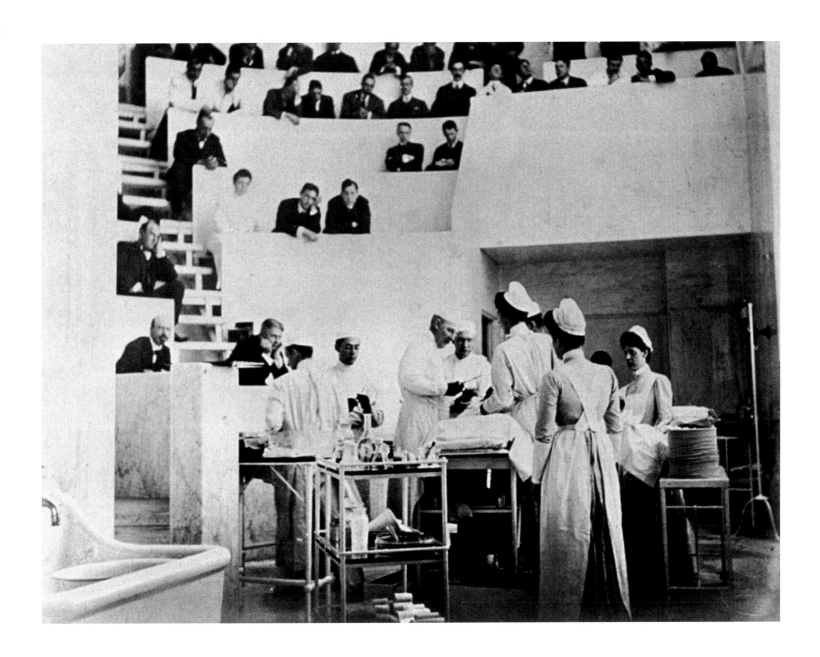

In Canada and the United States it was not until after 1860 that one finds many examples of universities which offered advanced programmes of study leading to such graduate degrees as the Master of Arts and the Doctor of Philosophy, or providing facilities and time for professors to pursue scholarly research

THE UNIVERSITY OF SCOTLAND:
SEED OF NORTH AMERICAN'S

In the middle decades of the eighteenth century, that great flowering of philosophy, science, culture and the creative arts, known as the Scottish Enlightenment, was in full flood. At the same time, the migration of Scottish teachers, clerics, physicians and officials to the colonies across the Atlantic was gathering pace. This intellectual migration had a powerful impact on the nascent American, and in time also, the Canadian system of higher education. Over the 100 years from 1680 to 1780 an estimated 818 college or university-educated men settled in North America from Europe. 211 of this total, or around one third, had been educated at Edinburgh and Glasgow universities or the two colleges in Aberdeen, King's and Marischal. The majority emigrated to the middle colonies of Virginia and Maryland with fewer making for New England, which was already relatively well supplied with university institutions of high quality. The movement was not simply one from east to west across the ocean. Several hundred colonists also came to Europe for higher learning, and of the Protestant Americans who have been traced, nearly half, especially those who sought medical training, enrolled at the Scottish universities.

The scale of this transatlantic mobility was bound to leave a mark on American intellectual life in general and the newly-founded colleges in particular because that was where many of these young Scottish *émigrés* eventually established successful careers. At the time, Scotland had five universities when England had two. Indeed, Scotland had more places available in higher education per head of population than any other nation in Europe in the eighteenth century. There were simply too many university-trained men for the professional opportunities open to them in Scotland itself. Large-scale emigration of the intellectuals was therefore inevitable. Equally, predictably, they carried with them to America the ideas and values they had absorbed as students.

The future Princeton, Yale, William and Mary College, Harvard and the College of Philadelphia (later the University of Pennsylvania)

Edinburgh University Library
Founded with a large gift of books from a lawyer, Clement Litill, in 1583, over the centuries Edinburgh University Library has attracted further gifts and bequests, enabling it to build up a priceless bibliographical collection and become one of Europe's largest university libraries.

were all influenced by Scottish professors, by Americans such as Benjamin Rush who had studied in Scotland (at Edinburgh) and by the series of seminal texts written by the geniuses of the Scottish Enlightenment such as David Hume, Adam Smith, John Millar, Thomas Reid and numerous others. Their curricula were also shaped by the generalist approach and the Scottish ideal of a liberal education that asserted the key principle of the need for interplay between philosophy, science and letters.

In all of this the influence of the University of Edinburgh was paramount. Its alumni had a remarkable impact. The legendary John Witherspoon single-handedly created the modern Princeton by transforming a provincial college into 'a seminary of statesmen' who laid the constitutional and administrative foundations of the United States after 1783. William Robertson, Principal of Edinburgh, was the most widely read historian in the new nation and his *History of America* was a staple text well into the nineteenth century. But more generally its flourishing medical school, then renowned as the world's best, the accessibility to men of all social ranks – in deep contrast to the Oxford and Cambridge of the day – and its enormous reputation for useful knowledge as an aid to professional careers made Edinburgh a model for other colleges to follow, both in the Americas and throughout the Empire. As a Princeton committee concluded: 'Athens, that commonwealth of science, of taste, and of art, though subdued by Rome, still continued to govern by instructing her masters. And in the present age, Edinburgh, by her celebrated university, lays both Europe and America under contribution from its students.'

Timothy O'Shea

The future universities of Princeton, Yale, William and Mary College and Harvard, among others, were influenced by Scottish professors, by Americans who had studied in Scotland and by the geniuses of the Scottish Enlightenment such as David Hume, Adam Smith, John Millar and Thomas Reid

The first women to graduate at Edinburgh University (1893)
Scotland's Edinburgh University pioneered women's access to higher education. In the closing third of the nineteenth century, a medical school was founded to provide women with scientific and practical training on a par with that offered by men's medical schools.

228

The Quest for Academic Standards and Standardisation in the Twentieth Century

The lax academic standards did prompt some university presidents to press for reforms that would enable a few serious universities to aspire to the quality of universities in Europe. One promising sign was the creation in 1900 of the Association of American Universities, often known as the AAU. Its original members were dedicated to raising academic standards in order to have their doctoral degrees gain respect internationally, especially when judged by the standards of scholarship at universities in Germany. The fourteen charter members were the University of California, the University of Chicago, Clark University, Columbia University, Cornell University, Harvard University, Johns Hopkins University, University of Michigan, University of Pennsylvania, Princeton University, Stanford University, University of Wisconsin and Yale University. In Canada, collective efforts to energise and coordinate expansion of research and advanced degree programmes at disparate universities encountered set-backs in 1891 but gathered momentum in the early 1900s, ultimately leading to the creation of the Conference of Canadian Universities in 1920.

In the United States the era of 'university building' from 1870 to 1910 was marked by fierce competition by presidents and donors to attract talented professors and students. A university often became a symbol of local or regional pride, called the 'jewel in the crown' for a city or for an entire state. These innovations, including the construction of magnificent, elaborate campus buildings, were possible due to the generous philanthropy of new wealthy industrialists such as John D. Rockefeller in oil, Andrew Carnegie in steel, William Marsh Rice in commerce and real estate, Johns Hopkins in railroads and Cornelius Vanderbilt in transportation.

Most conspicuous were the expenditures for building a beautiful campus whose laboratories, lecture halls and libraries were monumental and inspiring. An influential magazine editor noted in 1910 that the

Graduation, Columbia University (1930)
Graduation ceremonies lie at the heart of academic life. Upon successfully completing their studies, students are formally awarded a degree by the university's governing bodies in the presence of friends and relations. Graduands receive their diplomas in academic gowns worn for the occasion.

The architect James Gamble Rogers with the plans of Yale University Library (1926) Many of the first American universities favoured a Neo-Gothic style for their campuses. These nostalgic designs, evocative of Gothic cathedrals and castles, connected the university to the European cultural tradition and, specifically, to the British legacy.

American university was an architectural wonder because the 'campus appeared older as it got newer'. By this he meant that wealthy donors insisted on historic revivalism in the design of the new buildings. Neo-Gothic architecture was popular, as several of the great universities instantly appeared to be transplanted from the cathedrals and castles of fourteenth-century Europe. But these historic exteriors were, in fact, brand new, and also deceptive: what appeared to be a Gothic cathedral often was a skyscraper, ten to twenty stories in height, and housing a complex array

of offices for academic departments, seminar rooms, lecture halls and scientific equipment.

The AAU is significant in the history of universities in North America not only because it raised standards, but also because it increased cooperation across national borders. In 2009 it described itself as 'An Association of 62 research universities in the United States and Canada'. In 1926 two Canadian universities – McGill University and the University of Toronto – accepted invitations to become members of this prestigious group. The historical record

of the new and cumulative AAU membership starting with the original fourteen charter members in 1900 and continuing for over a century provides a good lens by which to track the appearance of universities that have ascended into the top tier of scholarly and research prestige. Between 1920 and 1960 one sees the maturing of the state universities of the Midwest, including the University of Illinois, Indiana University, Northwestern University, Purdue University, the Ohio State University, the University of Iowa and Michigan State University; and in the South, Duke University, the University of Virginia, the University of North Carolina, and Vanderbilt University who then were invited to join the AAU.

After 1960, the AAU roster continues to extend geographically to the south and to the west, as Washington University of St Louis, Rice University, Tulane University, the University of Washington, the University of Colorado, and the University of Kansas gain AAU admission.

The decentralised arrangements for higher education in Canada and the United States meant that prior to the First World War there were few linkages between universities and research funding provided by the national governments. In the United States, thanks to the land grant acts of 1862 and 1890, Colleges of Agriculture within state universities often were one of the few academic units that enjoyed external support for applied research and development. In Canada the National Research Council (NRC) was established in 1916 and henceforth has been a source of research and development projects for universities.

University of Montreal (1948)
Founded in 1878 with three faculties – law, theology and medicine – the university's original seat was in the city's Quartier Latin. At first it was subordinate to Quebec's Laval University, but in 1919 it gained independence. In 1926, the university moved to the north of the city and erected an art deco building noted for its geometrical volumes and clarity of line.

Ford Foundation (1963)
Founded in 1936 by the industrialist Edsel Ford, its philanthropic purposes range over a broad programme of social aid schemes. It pursues a commitment to support scientific and technological research in the tradition of the Rockefeller, and Carnegie Foundations, which as early as 1916 injected huge sums into the National Research Council created that year by President Woodrow Wilson for the purpose of conducting pure and applied research.

Taking Stock of the Universities
between the First and the Second World Wars

During the first half of the twentieth century those universities in the United States which sought to enhance their scholarly research enterprise were dependent on appropriations made by a distinctive organisation – the large non-profit philanthropic foundations. Instead of individual donors, the new arrangements for university support were perpetual endowments administered by a foundation director and staff. Foremost among these were the Rockefeller Foundation, the Rockefeller General Education Board, the Carnegie Corporation and, later, the Ford Foundation. Each foundation set its own priorities and goals, ranging from assisting struggling universities to improve, to stimulating academic interest in a new field of study. The major foundations also were distinctive in that they often framed a research agenda less for its impact on a particular university, and more on whether their endowment expenditures could make a substantive contribution to solving some regional or national problem. In a number of cases, the projects sponsored by the private foundations served as a pilot study or test case for programmes later adopted as permanent services administered by the federal government.

To take stock of the status of the universities in North America in 1930, a useful source is the book by Abraham Flexner, titled *Universities: American, English, and German*. Published by Oxford University Press, this volume was based on the series of lectures Abraham Flexner presented in 1929 as a visiting scholar at Oxford University in England. Flexner already had gained renown as the author of the Carnegie Foundation for the Advancement of Teaching's critical, comprehensive study of medical schools in the United States. In this 1930 project he was asked by Oxford University to comment on the universities of the United States in relation to their counterparts in Europe. Flexner commended the historic English universities of Oxford and Cambridge for their excellence in providing coherent, mature courses of study for undergraduates. However, his foremost praise was reserved for the model of

scholarship and advanced studies provided by universities in Germany. In contrast, he expressed concern that universities in the United States were hampered by their indiscriminate growth and their tendency to offer degree programmes in too many fields of study – many of which Flexner did not think were appropriate for a university to offer. Also, presidents and governing boards of universities in the United States often were tempted to place high priority on external relations, such as spectator sports and intercollegiate athletics – activities that were unknown at universities in England or Europe. To Flexner, the American university lacked a central purpose. As a result, it was compared to an adolescent that was growing by leaps and bounds each year, but without maturity or coordination.

A few years after Flexner's famous lectures at Oxford, universities in the United States started to gain a much needed cohort of internationally known professors. Discrimination often associated with anti-Semitism in German universities prompted a migration

The Rockefellers (1925)
John Davison Rockefeller (1839–1937), the famous industrialist who founded the Standard Oil Company, and his son, J.D. Rockefeller, Jr (1874–1960), gave generous funding to academic and cultural concerns. Their philanthropy came under the management of the Rockefeller Foundation, formed in 1913, which has since been a major benefactor of many universities.

Albert Einstein, Elsa Einstein and Robert A. Millikan (1933) In the interwar period, many leading academics fled the political turmoil of Europe and emigrated to the United States. The American universities welcomed the exiles with offers of teaching jobs, and in exchange received an invaluable boost to their development and standards. One such arrival was Einstein, a Nobel prizewinner who taught in California.

Dean D.L. Mordelland Gerald V. Bull (1962) These two academics at McGill University are shown discussing the *Martlet I* space vehicle prototype. Close collaboration between university and government is essential: many academic research projects are invaluable for defence purposes, for instance. During the Space Race, spurred by the Cold War, the partnership took on special relevance.

of established scholars who either were expelled or chose to flee punitive practices in their home universities. Many universities in the United States offered to sponsor these refugee scholars, inviting them to join their faculties and find an academic home. This infusion of established faculty talent substantially changed the character and profile of scholarship in the country.

A major and unexpected change took place during the Second World War when national governments in Canada and the United States each looked to their universities and their faculty as readily available partners for numerous and diverse research projects associated with the national war effort. Most conspicuous were projects in which teams of university physicists and chemists joined together in laboratories to invent and implement new weapons, including the hydrogen bomb. More surprising is that university professors whose specialities included cartography, foreign languages, physical education and engineering were effective in providing timely training and solutions. The windfall for university research was that following the end of the war, physicist Vannebar Bush of the Massachusetts Institute of

Technology, who had served as Director of the federal government's Office of Scientific Research and Development, persuaded the United States Congress that the contributions made by university scientists and scholars, which had been indispensable during the war, ought to be extended permanently as part of the peacetime economy. The argument was compelling and led to the creation and generous funding of such federal agencies as the National Science Foundation and the National Institutes of Health. In Canada, the major unifying source for lobbying was the national Conference of Canadian Universities, later renamed as the Association of Universities and Colleges of Canada.

The dominant principle of Vannebar Bush's successful case for federal government support of university research was that 'Big science was the best science'. Implicit in this credo was the following logic: if the national government wished the United States to be eminent internationally in physics, chemistry, biology and mathematics, then its formidable research funding must be awarded only to the best, most prestigious universities that were sufficiently large to provide the necessary critical mass of scholarly talent that could solve significant problems in their academic fields. This strategy was less concerned with spreading federal government research funds widely so that universities new to research might develop – and more concerned with nurturing and then harvesting the research fruits from the 'brightest and the best' institutions.

Creating the Modern Research University, 1950 to 2010

The result of these agencies and associations was that during the period 1950 to 1960 a small number of universities with a strong commitment to research were successful in receiving large federal grants for sponsored research projects – primarily in the natural and physical sciences. This created a new category of prestigious research universities – what the President of the University of California, Clark Kerr, called 'The Federal Grant University'. It was a category that overlapped closely with the members of the Association of American Universities. It also transcended the typical categories of 'private' and 'state' universities, as one could find some members of each category whose federal research grants made them increasingly similar in their missions and priorities. Clark Kerr's memorable 1963 book, *The Uses of the University*, estimated that in the United States six universities received 57 percent of federal research funds in one year. Extended a bit further, Kerr's analysis showed that a total of twenty universities received about 80 percent. Within this elite group, federal research project funding typically accounted for 20 percent to 80 percent of a university's annual operating budget. The landmark implication was that out of more than one thousand degree-granting institutions, national research resources and power were concentrated in twenty to fifty 'research universities'.

An excellent illustration of how a university could transform itself in this new environment of research funding was Stanford University in California. Since its founding in the late nineteenth century, Stanford University had been a pleasant campus with beautiful architecture and idyllic weather. It was good but not great. Starting around 1935 the academic provost emphasised competition for external grants, primarily in conjunction with commercial and industrial projects. It was a strategy that included cooperation among physicists and engineers. Among the students who graduated from Stanford were two young engineers whose inventions would be integral to creating

Frank O. Gehry, Stata Center, MIT (2004)
MIT wanted to create a new physical locus to facilitate interdisciplinary teaching. This modern building is accordingly designed as a continuous space in which each environment interrelates with the rest. As a further example of the value of advanced research, many resources discovered at MIT itself went into the building's creation.

the electronics and computer industry – and their namesake Hewlett Packard Corporation. At the same time, those departments that could not – or, would not – compete for industrial contracts were penalised. After the Second World War, the Stanford agenda emphasised federal research grants in science and engineering. It was a strategy well suited to the newly available government grants. As a result, Stanford University prospered, and was a strong partner in creating the computer industry of what came to be known as 'Silicon Valley' – a home of one of the most prosperous economies in the world.

The demographic and economic growth of the post-war decades also triggered an important change in the structure of the university. As enrolments at a university surpassed 20,000 students, presidents and board members settled on the innovation of creating a state university with multiple campuses. The University of California, whose historic and great campus was at Berkeley, eventually transformed itself into a complex system and extended itself across a geographically large state with ten university campuses and numerous research sites and extension facilities. Its numerous locations and fields led to the new term of the 'multi-versity'.

The crucial means to the end of fostering great research universities was government research funding. This is illustrated by the rapid increases in grants provided by the new National Science Foundation from its start in 1950 over the next half century. In 1952 the NSF budget was $3.5 million. This increased dramatically to $134 million in 1957. By 1983 the NSF was awarding over $1 billion in research grants. This then doubled in a decade, to reach $2 billion. By 2007 the NSF budget surpassed $6 billion.

Its companion federal agency, the National Institutes of Health, demonstrated an equally amazing record of affluence and growth. In 1940, prior to the Second World War, the NIH had a budget of $250,000 and was confined to applied research projects dealing with infectious diseases associated with seaports and naval bases. After the war the scope and size of the agency changed, as its budget increased to $8 million and was assigned to an increasing range of health and medical research topics. The trend continued, as the 1966 NIH budget surpassed $1 billion. Indeed,

health-related research in the biological sciences became paramount in sponsored university research, as the NIH budget in 2003 was $28 billion – most of which was dedicated to faculty research projects at university medical centres.

One dysfunctional or problematic aspect of the wealth of the NSF and NIH research budgets was that it created imbalances within the great research universities. It was unlikely that professors in such fields as literature, philosophy or history could compete for external research grants even remotely near the size of the NSF and NIH grants in the sciences and medical fields. As a result, research universities tended to lose their gyroscope of mission and priorities because they tended to gravitate only to those academic fields that were competitive for large scale federal research grants. External research dollars, known as 'soft money', became the dynamic source of university momentum that supplemented the regular operating budgets, known as 'hard money'. What university presidents often overlooked was that national research grants carried hidden costs because a university had to invest large sums of its own budget so that it would have the requisite high-quality facilities that its faculty needed if they were going to be competitive in the high stakes federal research grant application review process.

The 'federal grant' research university that emerged by 1960 has endured as the 'gold standard' by which university prestige has been gauged in the United States for over half a century. Talent and resources have diffused to additional universities so that by 2009 one estimates that as many as one hundred universities in the United States compete aggressively and with success for federal research funding. This is reflected in the recently added new members of the AAU, as the University of Texas, State University at Stony Brook, the University of Maryland, Tulane University, the University of Florida, Texas A&M, Emory University and the relatively young University of California campuses at Irvine, Davis, Santa Barbara and San Diego joined the ranks of well-known, historic, established universities.

Since the sixty-two universities that were members of the AAU represented the pinnacle of success among hundreds of universities in the United States and

Biologists examining X-rays, San Francisco, California (1980)
The bulk of university research is government-funded. Public funding favours the predominantly scientific research that finds immediate applications, particularly in the realm of the health sciences. But the system falls short in other branches of learning, notably the humanities.

Juxtaposed against the aggressive ambition of research universities in the United States, Canada's model has been more temperate, reasonable and realistic

Canada, this prestige had positive and negative consequences for morale within higher education. On the one hand, numerous universities which were slow to develop a research tradition now sought to make up lost ground and lost time in their own pursuit of federal agency research grants. This was good news in that it signalled a successful diffusion of scholarly talent to an increasing number of universities. It was troubling news in that one now had a tense situation where far more universities and professors was competing for limited research funds. The new, ambitious universities worried that peer evaluation of research proposals was skewed to favour scholars from the established AAU universities. At the same time the AAU members and their association leadership complained that there now was an over-expansion of the academic research enterprise that would dilute and eventually weaken the tradition of 'Big Science as the Best Science'. The tension was increased by the early 1980s when some advocates of university research warned that the federal government commitment to science research funding was waning.

Juxtaposed against the aggressive ambition of research universities in the United States, Canada's model has been more temperate, reasonable and realistic. Faced with the situation of a geographically huge nation with a relatively small population concentrated along its southern border, universities in Canada extended into doctoral programmes and sponsored research – but without the frenzy of aspiration and hubris that often characterised the scramble for academic success in the United States after the war. One estimate of the most distinguished research universities in Canada would include the historically established McGill University and the University of Toronto, joined in the past half century by the Universities of British Columbia, Waterloo and Dalhousie.

Simon Fraser University, Vancouver, British Columbia (2005)
This Canadian campus was designed in 1963 almost single-handedly by the architect and urban planner Arthur Erikson, who conceived of the project as a small city integrated with its surrounding landscape. The university began to admit students two years later. Today, it is spread across three campuses in Vancouver, Burnaby and Surrey.

Research Universities in the Twenty-first Century: The Paradox and Problems of Success

To gauge the growth and improvement in the universities, it is useful to contrast their profiles from 1910 to 2010. Among the so-called 'Great American Universities' of 1910, the largest enrolment at a single institution was slightly over 6,000. The highest number of doctorates conferred per year was 50. Some of the allegedly 'great' universities showed little record of success in graduate degree programmes. A century later, the prototypical research university enrolled between 30,000 and 50,000 students and conferred about 300 to 500 doctoral degrees per year.

One indicator of this growth is provided by a profile of research and development expenditures in engineering and in the sciences among the prestigious universities. The rankings from the 2006 fiscal year include the following (figures in US dollars):

Johns Hopkins	1,499,977,000
Wisconsin	831,895,000
Los Angeles	811,493,000
Michigan	800,488,000
San Francisco	796,149,000
Washington	778,148,000
San Diego	754,766,000
Stanford	678,196,000
Pennsylvania	676,052,000
Duke	657,080,000

Another important measure of the magnitude of university resources were the endowment figures and rankings for 2007 (in US dollars):

Harvard	34,634,906,000
Yale	22,530,200,000
Stanford	17,164,836,000
Princeton	15,787,200,000
Texas	5,613,672,000
Massachusetts IT	9,980,410,000
Columbia	7,149,803,000
Michigan	7,089,830,000
Pennsylvania	6,635,187,000
Texas A&M	6,590,300,000

The quality and quantity of research universities in the United States and Canada at the start of the twenty-first century indicate that in one century this institution in North America, which had only a marginal presence in 1900, acquired scholarly influence and respect internationally. These select universities represent 'steeples of excellence' within higher education systems in the two nations.

The select research universities, for all their prestige, faced numerous problems in the late twentieth and early twenty-first centuries. Foremost was the challenge of reconciling research emphases with teaching, especially for the undergraduate courses of study leading to the Bachelor of Arts and Bachelor of Science degrees. Since research universities traditionally had been preoccupied with attracting the 'brightest and the best', numerous constituencies were concerned that these prestigious institutions did not always give attention to the priorities of social justice that gave attention to redressing inequities of race, ethnicity, gender and social class from which these institutions historically had been exempt.

Finally, one paradox of success is that the attractiveness of universities in the United States and Canada to graduate students and scholars from other nations worldwide over several decades has eventually led to their programmes, practices and talent being transplanted and emulated at universities elsewhere. This means that a new generation of universities spread across many countries now competes well with the established universities of North America.

---

1. Editor's note: The author's account of 'North American universities' embraces the United States and Canada only. Mexico, though strictly a part of North America, is dealt with in the section on 'Latin American universities' on historic and linguistic grounds.

Among the so-called 'Great American Universities' of 1910, the largest enrolment at a single institution was slightly over 6,000. A century later, the prototypical research university enrolled between 30,000 and 50,000 students

Quadrangle and chapel at Stanford University (1989)
Rated as one of the world's ten leading universities in the fields of law, economics and business science, Stanford is also the spearhead of electronic and computer engineering: its campus saw the gestation of companies such as Hewlett-Packard, Yahoo and Google.

THE FUTURE OF THE HUMANITIES IN NORTH AMERICAN UNIVERSITIES

The university landscape of the past few decades has been enlivened by a debate about the present and future of the humanities, particularly since the enactment of the GI Bill (1944) and the Higher Education Act of 1965, two statutes that raised the numbers of students on American campuses exponentially. The influx of baby boomers swelled teaching faculties, fed the creation of journals and new publications, multiplied conferences and symposia; but it also meant that academics in the humanities – particularly scholars of classical and modern languages – came under a ghostly cloud of suspicion. It fell to them to justify the legitimacy of work that dwelled almost solely on the past and had an air of strangeness and eccentricity. By way of contrast, science, the 'new learning' of the future, enjoys and always has enjoyed authority and outward prestige. Science often makes headlines beyond academia and attracts generous public and private funding. Science is the social and economic capital of universities, and many deans and principals cherish it as their crown jewels. Literature, art history or film professors – to mention only three examples – may have taught generations of students to approach a text in a critical and imaginatively resourceful way; but the threat of budget cuts and the acrimony engendered by blind allegiance to one or another school of thought have poisoned the atmosphere in many departments to the point of shattering any semblance of unity. The embers of these harmful disputes are regularly stoked from outside by leaders and opinion-formers – politicians, administrators, philanthropists – whose tone ranges from the critical to the bitingly sarcastic. Henry Kissinger, for example, allegedly said that 'academic politics are so vicious because the stakes are so small', while the prominent English literature professor Stanley Fish wrote a piece titled 'The Unbearable Ugliness of Volvos' in which he lamented the quenchless rancour of American faculties.

Be that as it may, until very recently the humanities had an almost privileged status. Its practitioners, especially those comfortably installed at leading institutions, enjoyed an enviable lifestyle. Pressure to publish built careers and cemented reputations, in step

Beinecke Library, Yale University (1986)
The Beinecke Library holds a major collection of rare books and manuscripts, ranging from Egyptian papyri to the first edition of the Gutenberg Bible. Its various sections bring together about thirteen million volumes.

with the growth and apogee of the university presses, which up until the recent publishing crisis remained financially robust. Mark Bauerlein, a critic and professor at Emory University, perceptively points out that the figures released in the Modern Language Association's *International Bibliography* have run parallel to this exegetic explosion: in 1956, the yearbook listed 10,056 entries in the field of literature, whereas by 1970 the figure was 36,158, which became 58,260 by 1980. Given that philology in its various forms is a millennial discipline, Bauerlein rightly wonders whether there is any genuine benefit to be had from such a disproportionate inflation of papers in a relatively short timespan, particularly for those who have yet to become acquainted with classics such as Shakespeare, Cervantes, Dante and Lope de Vega.

Still, despite the labours of institutions like The American Council of Learned Societies, The American Academy of Religion, The American Historical Association, The American Political Science Association, The College Art Association, The Linguistic Society of America or The Modern Language Association of America, the number of humanities students is relatively small. The proportion of humanities graduates is now less than half what it was in the 1960s, according to the Humanities Indicators Prototype, a database created in 1990 by the American Academy of Arts and Sciences as part of its Humanities Resource Center Online, which compiles data from over 1,500 departments across the United States. For political, economic and cultural reasons, in 1966 graduates in the humanities numbered 91,000 students; that figure rose to 140,000 in 1971–72 (i.e., 17 percent of enrolled students), but today stands at only 110,000 (8 percent), and this level has held steady over the past fifteen years with no apparent sign of change. The institutional disconnect has meant that, in the end, the humanities are of interest only to those who teach or study them, although the occasional startling discovery in an archive, or the work of some public figure, may manage to reach out beyond the ivory tower to wider audiences. Doubtless this is partly the handiwork of film, television and even literature – one might bring to mind the amusing novels of David Lodge or the historical extravaganzas of the bestselling Dan Brown, which have perpetuated an image of the arts professor as an eccentric and neurotic bohemian, woefully cut off from the surrounding reality and lacking the glamour invested in doctors, lawyers and market traders. These are occupations that film and television regularly reinvent, dazzling viewers and awakening fresh vocations.

But the real challenge is not to change the image of the discipline, but to address highly specific features of the humanities, which in coming decades will decide its future. The ongoing budget cuts, for example, have reduced the number of humanities courses at

Humanities departments need to breathe life into the complex equation balancing rigour and pleasure that for centuries has made the humanistic disciplines the intellectual and ethical bedrock of the human being

university and so narrowed students' opportunities to engage with subjects whose attraction sometimes springs from purely demographic peculiarities, such as the rising interest in Hispanic cultures and literatures in the United States, where Spanish is no longer a 'foreign language'. But, returning to the origins of the humanities, the so-called 'civic virtue' of future generations depends on the survival of the study of literature, art, religion, languages, history and philosophy. In an increasingly connected and mutable society, exposed to the shifts and pressures of the 'globalisation of knowledge', the humanities will stay relevant only if they adapt to the rise of new technologies that compete with the conventional book as a traditional format with an entrenched prestige. Humanities departments should insist – in language teaching especially – on foreign study and exchanges with other universities, and embrace the cultural output falling outside the 'canon' or hailing from outside the West. Teaching staff should continue to diversify in terms of geographical origin, race and sexual orientation; alliances and partnerships should be sought with embassies and consulates, cultural centres, museums, galleries and other institutions from which humanistic materials can be divulged in a living, tangible form. Fieldwork should be encouraged in subjects such as theatre, film and the more recent television studies. Higher versatility should be sought in forums of debate such as libraries and lecture rooms to make the past relevant to the future. Above all, we need to breathe life into the complex equation balancing rigour and pleasure that for centuries has made the humanistic disciplines the intellectual and ethical bedrock of the human being. If technology enables us to engage with the humanities in new or even 'futuristic' languages, coining terms – Google, Kindle, Apple – that function at one and the same time as words and tools, means and ends, there is no reason why humanities scholars cannot dream up new ways of reinventing themselves, of surging ahead of the present.

Enrique García Santo-Tomás

Morrison Library,
University of Berkeley, California (1996)
Opening in 1928, the Morrison Library retains the air of an old reading room that lets students take a step back from the demands of college life. One of its jewels is the famous private collection of the philanthropist Alexander F. Morrison, ten thousand volumes donated by his wife May Treat Morrison.

Professor Jack Steinberger teaching at CERN (the European Organisation for Nuclear Research), Geneva
Twentieth-century teaching methods encourage a two-way exchange between teacher and student, and debate is of high importance in the learning process. The physicist Jack Steinberger, who won the Nobel prize in 1988, uses a blackboard as a lecture aid.

VI

THE MASS UNIVERSITY

University examinations, London (c. 1995)
Twentieth-century higher education has become a mass pursuit. In response to enrolment demand, universities have been forced to adopt selection filters such as entry tests. The huge influx of candidates is a sign of heightened educational attainment across the population. Primary and secondary education is compulsory in most countries: the proportion reaching higher study is accordingly greater.

The University in the World and the Modern University

Josep M. Bricall

The University in the Higher Education System

Within the academic community, it is sometimes supposed that the university stands apart from the flow of history and society. This, for some, is one of the distinctive traits of the institution. Others, however, see an ongoing exchange between the university and the society in which it is embedded, such that, regardless of what academia might intend, a university's development is shaped by its societal setting. And the university, in turn, exerts some influence on society. The relationship is not always obvious. Quoted in the first volume of *A History of the University in Europe*, originally published by CRE (the Conference of Rectors, Presidents and Vice-Chancellors of the European Universities), Peter Classen puts this same point in the following way:

> The schools of the twelfth century and the universities of the thirteenth century never set themselves the goal of providing the courts and municipalities with specialised experts. Nevertheless, the new social pattern that took form in the university was in part shaped by society, since it was the lively interest of wider social groups, which made it possible for the higher schools to become enduring and independent institutions. From the very beginning, education was subject to the tension between the fundamental and primary impulse to seek the truth and the desire of many persons to acquire practical training. Conversely, without really wanting to do so, the schools formed the new academic stratum and changed the whole structure of society, enriching it and making it more complex.

The effects of social and technological change on education in general, and on the university in particular, became especially conspicuous after the Industrial Revolution. The emergence of myriad new lines of economic activity created a demand for increasingly skilled workers, and, accordingly, a greater need for secondary schools. Later, the technological and research requirements of the economy were felt in higher education as well. New technical subjects were introduced that went beyond the traditional vocational training of physicians, lawyers and clergymen.

Ever since, the standard of education prevalent among the population at large has steadily risen. Primary education and the first few years of secondary education have been made universal by law. The proportion of the population in education at all levels has greatly increased; the scope of studies has widened, as has the range of research.

Expectations of improved job and salary prospects have encouraged a constantly rising number of students to continue their studies beyond the compulsory stage. Post-compulsory secondary education has accordingly taken on a wider role. While preserving its original place as a corridor to higher education,

Stenography students in a classroom improvised on the roof of Southern University, California (n.d.) New market needs prompted students to continue study after completing secondary education. Superior and tertiary education raised chances of getting a job.

it has also become an end in itself: preparation for direct entry to the world of work. The new conditions prevailing in the labour market have meant that a far greater proportion of the population now hold post-compulsory secondary qualifications. And those job market conditions, of course, have been shaped largely by social and economic change, particularly in those countries where growth has been swiftest.

After the Second World War, technical progress and the rise of the welfare state created a still greater need for qualified workers, while affording a wider range of students the opportunity to remain in education. The skills now required in the job market went considerably further than those conferred by secondary education alone. The need for routine manual work receded, and the sophistication of tasks increased. The economic system now required new kinds of knowledge. It was against this background that education systems were called on to expand technical training in higher education beyond the traditional

schooling of engineers and administrators. Previously unknown qualifications were created – specialists in automation, robotics, and more – embodying a new approach to higher education. University study was becoming commonplace, and many courses were now closely tied to the new needs of the economy and society.

The upshot of these trends was a far-reaching change in the nature of higher education. Whereas in the past secondary education was simply a bridge from compulsory education to university, it now shifted its strategic position. The notion that post-compulsory secondary education should be continued in more sophisticated form by higher education drove university education to take on a greater mass of technical content.

This may go some way towards explaining the distinctive features of the Spanish system of higher education, where further training outside the confines of the university has played a minor role. This is not

252

Students in a medical university laboratory, Brazil (1947)
Social change demands a new kind of knowledge that is more closely integrated with society. Theoretical study continues to be important, but the exponential rise of practical training with immediate applications in the world of work has opened up new areas of intellectual endeavour.

solely due to a different approach or to some national idiosyncrasy. It follows from the fact that Spain has taken a different path from its European peers towards achieving some measure of social and economic progress. The case of Spain, then, can be described as an incomplete progression from a scheme of pre-university secondary education to a scheme of post-secondary higher education. Viewing the landscape of Spanish higher education and research from this angle may provide the insight required to prevent it from turning in on itself, and to guide it towards a closer alignment with modern society, perhaps by emulating its European peers.

Among member countries of the Organisation for Economic Cooperation and Development (OECD), in 2007 the average proportions of the population aged from 25 to 64 who had achieved post-compulsory secondary education and higher education were 44 percent and 27 percent, respectively. These proportions varied from country to country. The percentages were 60 and 24 percent in Germany, 48 and 40 percent in the United States, 42 and 27 percent in France, 39 and 13 percent in Italy, and 36 and 32 percent in the United Kingdom. However, the proportions were 22 and 29 percent in Spain and 14 percent for both levels of education in Portugal. It is a surprising fact that in Spain the proportion of people achieving university education matches the OECD average, but for non-university further education it falls far short. This Spanish disproportion between higher education and the rest of the educational system is an anomaly.

In Spain, the boundaries between the various levels of higher education have come under pressure owing to the complexity of the legislation. The succession of laws have tended to organise university and non-university studies as forming one and the same sphere, with no clear distinction and without reference to any systematic vision of the whole. In France, however, the *Instituts Universitaires de Technologie* are given special status despite forming part of the university system; in Germany, the universities operate side-by-side with the *Fachhochschule*; and in the English-speaking countries universities coexist with liberal arts colleges. In Spain, the Education Reform Law of 1970, a highly salutary piece of lawmaking when compared to the wider backdrop of Franco's educational policy, paved the way for university rank to attach to a far wider range of technical and vocational training. Before then, vocational training had been imparted in non-university institutions. The new law was widely welcomed, because so far it had proved difficult to assure both quality and efficient management. This cannot be said of all Spain's institutions of further education. In Catalonia, a long industrial and commercial tradition had prompted many to choose studies involving the applied skills and professional aptitudes then required on the job market. These schools were more practically organised than the universities and better able to meet demand from small and medium enterprises.

As a corollary of the 1970 statutory reform, the rules and structures by which higher education was organised became more uniform. However, the possibility of creating shorter courses of study was passed up, owing to the dubious view that a longer course made for better academic quality. The traditional programmes run by university faculties earned wider social recognition than non-university studies, even if taught by the universities themselves.

In 1983, however, the University Reform Law conceived of Spanish universities as forming an independently managed system. The new enactment, followed in 1986 by the Science Law, reinforced the role of research at Spanish universities. This policy was genuinely innovative, given that the time-honoured approach of Spanish governments to research had been neglect. However, in addition, the 1983 statute confirmed the presence of non-university studies – defined as 'short-cycle studies' – within the university system in contrast to the 'long-cycle studies' taught at the faculties and higher technical schools. The changes introduced by the University Law of 2001 left the significance and purpose of the short-cycle courses unaltered. Adaptation to the European Higher Education Area has brought about a single curricular scheme for both cycles, thus vindicating the approach already prevailing in Spain.

The Education Law of 1990 substantially reformed the earlier system of vocational training to bring it into step with the new needs of the Spanish economy. Higher-education status was conferred on the system of occupational training. In order to reach this new level, students had to have completed their post-compulsory secondary education. Yet a further Education Law was enacted in 2006. Unlike the 1990 statute, this law was not particularly innovative. However, it made provision for the conditional recognition of transfer routes between vocational training and university study.

Continuity and Changes in the Role of the University

The university is historically distinct from other institutions of higher learning. Over the centuries, the university in the European mould has taken on a range of functions that have become widely recognisable and given shape to a definition so entrenched that it is now hard to imagine it being otherwise. These functions include preparation for professional life, the advancement of learning and the stewardship of a broadly humanistic tradition.

In what way do these functions live on at the modern university, and in what ways have they changed? We shall now address each of the university's roles, and highlight new developments.

Higher Education and Training

The transmission of learning is closely bound up with preparation for professional practice. The universities have traditionally combined general education with specific training for the proper exercise of the professions. The general component follows in the footsteps of an illustrious tradition first seen in the medieval *trivium* and *quadrivium*: these disciplines lie at the foundations of modern faculties of arts and science. Historically, specific training came later; it was taught in the so-called 'major' schools, which prepared one for the practice of law, medicine or theology. The Industrial Revolution brought with it the addition of a new range of disciplines in the realm of engineering, and the nineteenth century saw the rise of the technical universities.

How have the changes brought about in the twentieth century influenced the university?

Preparation for the new professions now spills over the bounds of the university, given the strong rise in demand for professionals in modern economies. The world of work has become increasingly sophisticated, abreast with the spread of secondary education – one of the distinctive features of the welfare state.

But this widening of the range of skills that higher education is called on to impart has not been confined to the range of university degrees. Teaching, too, has changed, with the use of the tools furnished by modern technologies of information and communication.

Specifically, the European Commission's Communication of November 1997, *Towards a Europe of Knowledge*, spoke of:

> Developing employability through the
> acquisition of competencies made necessary
> through changes in work and its organisation.
> This means that it is necessary to promote on
> a lifelong basis creativity, flexibility, adaptability,
> the ability to 'learn to learn' and to solve
> problems.

All of these new concerns are directed at the way studens conduct themselves, whereas previously it was purely their intellectual development that educational institutions hoped to cultivate. Could there be a gap between societal expectations and academic ambition?

The starting-point of these new priorities is the so-called 'knowledge society'. Since the Industrial Revolution, knowledge has been a decisive factor in economic activity and social development. Today, the application of knowledge has become all the more urgent, to the point that it is now regarded as a society's or an individual's most valuable asset. The knowledge society creates knowledge through scientific and academic progress; transmits knowledge through education and training; promotes the dissemination of knowledge by the techniques of information and communication; applies it to technical innovation; and, finally, creates and uses new frames of reference through the operation of international networks (European Commission Communication of February 2003).

One of the corollaries of this is that individuals must replenish their stock of learning over their lifetime, and therefore return to education at times of her life that fall outside the traditional learning stages. The conventional learning periods are now the mere springboard, and cannot encompass the ceaseless change of reality. As defined by the European

Solvay Conference, Hotel Metropole, Brussels (1911)
The conferences sponsored by the chemical industrialist Ernest Solvay, starting with the 1911 conference on radiation and quanta, drew together the scientific elite of the day. From left to right, seated: Nernst, Brillouin, Solvay, Lorentz, Warburg, Perrin, Wien, Curie and Poincaré. Standing: Goldschmidt, Planck, Rubens, Sommerfeld, Lindemann, De Broglie, Knudsen, Hasenöhrl, Hostelet, Herzen, Jeans, Rutherford, Kamerlingh Onnes, Einstein and Langevin.

conventional first-degree studies, for their part, must evolve so as to contemplate the long-term horizon of continuing training.

Responding to this demand has not been easy. It has called for a transformation in the format and organisational structure of academic disciplines and a shift even in what qualifications mean. With the emergence of 'specific experience of an educational nature' – whether provided by a company, a trade union or other social organisations, or earned informally through life experience without reference to any express educational intent – an academic degree may now have to be seen as bearing a somewhat different significance. It remains the case that formal education at an institution is capable of creating a kind of value that still lies outside the reach of purely occupational activity and on-the-job learning. Occupational learning may nonetheless add value to academic study, and this is the ground on which it is now being recognised.

By taking increasing account of vocational considerations and societal demand, curricula have tended to become more diverse. The flexibility students now has to shape their academic itinerary means there is a need for more extensive guidance and supervision from institutions.

Commission, lifelong learning is a form of continuing education designed to enhance knowledge, skills and competencies.

Lifelong learning, largely aimed at fulfilling the requirements of the economy and society, has also made it possible to make use of higher education studies that do not focus exclusively on the job market but are designed to enrich personal education: a better understanding of social issues, one's own personal encounter with the arts and culture.

Lifelong learning has done more than merely swell the number of students at universities. It has also heralded a new kind of student. The OECD distinguishes here between 'young adults', 'second-biters' and 'new-chancers'. Young adults are students who stay on at university beyond the usual age of graduation; second-biters are students who return to university to flesh out or update their existing knowledge or to learn new subjects; finally, new-chancers are students recouping an opportunity they did not grasp when it first came up.

These new circumstances have made the design of study plans a complicated matter. Consideration has to be given to part-time study and interruptions in what used to be conventional itineraries. And

Research

The second important calling of the university is research. Alongside their educational role, the universities have been decisive for scientific and academic progress. The crisis of the European universities in the sixteenth and seventeenth centuries led, as a result of the reform introduced in Prussia by Wilhelm von Humboldt, to the introduction of experimental science to the university. This development enshrined what has later come to be seen as a defining feature of the university: the intimate tie between education and research. By playing this role, universities have endowed society with an institution capable of fostering, adapting and disseminating the progress of knowledge and of lending rigour to technical discoveries. It is widely accepted that funding given over to satisfy intellectual pursuits such as research ultimately creates knowledge and wards off the possible alternative: an intellectual desert. Moreover, the universities have ensured that the knowledge garnered by research remains public, which is essential for its effects to be widely enjoyed by society at large.

Research has attracted special attention in modern times. For example, universities now employ 34.4 percent of all European researchers (the figures being 15 percent in the United States and 37.1 percent in Japan) and undertake 80 percent of all European fundamental research.

The pairing of research with education has meant that the universities have nurtured a mindset that regards all knowledge as provisional. Scientific conduct is characterised by doubt and rigour, and remains subject to the verification and improvement of acquired knowledge. Professor Laurent Schwartz has said that innovation and creativity are attainable only by the practice of research – even where such practice does not always rise to the heights of dedication and thoroughness. Anything else would soon lead to conformism and routine.

Given the present importance attached to the creation and application of new knowledge, research has become a core element of development policy. Investment in research, it has been claimed, earns returns three times greater than investment in physical property. Universities have seen new prospects open up, while their traditional concerns have remained in place. In Finland, for instance, where companies invest 11 percent of their turnover in research and development, Olli-Pekka Heinonen, the education minister in 1996, recognised the role of higher education institutions as drivers of the regional and national systems of innovation. He underscored that the quality of a university can be assessed only with reference to international standards; absent international comparison – at least within a given discipline – an institution cannot be regarded as useful even in its regional or national dimension.

So universities are engaged in the mechanisms of knowledge transfer as full participants in the process of innovation. Today, technology transfer is no longer viewed as the bottom rung of a ladder that descends from the heights of science down to economic and social workaday bustle. Today, application and

development and so-called 'fundamental' science are intertwined in a dialectic process the boundaries of which are hard to draw. Whereas some research is conducted without reference to external aims, a significant portion of the research undertaken in modern society is directed at specific goals and measured out in specific schedules of performance. As a result, universities operate at several levels simultaneously. In the domain of research, they must be willing to compete with a wide variety of other institutions. The increasing diversity of players in research has led to internal stresses that might undermine the traditional idea of the university. At some institutions, the tasks attempted have become so widely different that there is a danger of fragmentation. A loss of internal consistency would detract from the public face of the university and make it hard to explain to the wider community what it does.

And there is an expectation that universities should find a balance between allocating funds to the pursuit of intellectual curiosity alone and attracting external funds for research directed to the performance of

Sergey Brin and Larry Page, founders of Google (2002)
In 1997, Brin and Page, who met as students at Stanford University, founded Google, now the Internet's largest search engine. The name is a play on the word 'googol', a term designating the number notated as 10 to the power of 100. In its beginnings, Google was a data search algorithm. From this starting point, the firm developed and refined a technology that has since attained ubiquity.

specific goals. To meet this challenge, universities have tried to create their own centres of excellence as venues for research towards innovation. They have had to draw up their own scientific policies, embracing issues such as research authorship, use of research results, patents and so forth.

Research today is becoming more complex. Research institutes, research and development centres, companies based on or near university campuses – all of these have acquired agile structures and cultivated networked relations with universities. Michael Gibbons has dubbed this pattern 'socially distributed knowledge production'. Negotiation between a university and its partners is now a key aspect of its science policy and, in the long term, manifests its ability to manage itself independently or, as the case may be, the extent to which it is dependent. There is a risk, of course, that universities end up being merely the executive arm of a research programme decided on elsewhere, the results of which speak to economic concerns alone.

Critical Role

Finally, the third function typically attributed to universities is the preservation of the humanistic tradition. From the Renaissance onwards, there took root in Europe an intellectual preoccupation with the significance of the human condition, and with its social aspects in particular. This concern permeated the universities and eventually gave shape to a number of initiatives to serve society – hospitals, libraries and other forms of engagement with their host communities.

The emergence of humanism at the university was a process of problematic assumption of classical culture – essentially Greek and Roman – and signalled a change in the way that any given question was approached. From 1500 to 1800, a major shift took place. From the pursuit of truth alone, the university became preoccupied with the conflicts of life in society. This explains why the centre of gravity of the European university system swung from Bologna and Paris to Padua and Leiden, for their proximity to the commercial hubs of Venice and Amsterdam.

This change also demonstrates a revolution in the kind of humanism that universities were practising.

After an initial stage of absolute trust in classical authority, there opened a second stage. Now, attention focused on applying the results of the humanistic disciplines. It was no longer a matter of imitating the classical authors, but of bringing the achievements of the ancient world to bear upon the issues of the present. The response to a given problem was no longer regarded as correct by reference to the authority of classical texts alone; it now entailed a confrontation of the classics with a state of affairs that also drew on one's own experience and knowledge.

Today, too, some of the issues faced by universities relate to their humanistic tradition, as noted by Rodees:

> The growth in importance of professional studies has been paralleled by a decline in the influence of the traditional liberal arts [...] Part of the decline in the influence of the liberal arts reflects the lack of internal cohesion within their own traditional core disciplines. The sciences have become powerful, but increasingly unintelligible to non-scientists. The social sciences, entranced by microanalysis and quantification, have become increasingly irrelevant to social issues and public policy. The humanities, embracing fragmentation, otherness, and unreality, have neglected the great overarching issues of human commonality in favour of partisan advocacy.

These words, though sensible, are only partly true. In fact, human knowledge and human resources are recognised today as the central factor in economic and social development. They are the only elements able to give society an awareness of common values and a sense of belonging, according to the report 'The New Economy' from the Organisation for Economic Cooperation and Development (OECD):

> Although the information economy is accompanied by an increasing codification of knowledge, large amounts of knowledge remain tacit, embodied in people's skills, experience and education.

It is the set of all these functions that must undergo a process of adaptation. Universities are responsible for ensuring that that adaptation does not undermine their original calling. The humanistic tradition and research practices have breathed life into a critical stance that remains vital to the preservation of democratic values.

The humanistic function of the universities has benefited from a number of experiences, such as the recruitment of students to provide social services (Mexico), actions to help the long-term unemployed to return to work, environmental initiatives, and support for culture and the arts. Universities have often been decisive in opening up their host localities to salutary international influences.

Michel Foucault at the Technical University of Berlin (1978)
Major twentieth-century thinkers like Michel Foucault used the universities as a platform for a critical stance towards the established system. These attitudes aligned themselves with political currents on the Left, sparked frequent protests against government-imposed structures and won broad-based student support.

Soviet Regime and the University

Even before the Second World War ended, the European continent was divided into East and West at the conference in Yalta, the Western leaders quietly complying with Stalin's will and plans. The division was a political and ideological one, but economic and also cultural division was soon to follow. Also the 'Western' universities of Eastern and Central Europe – including the ones of Prague and Kracow which date back to the fourteenth century – were absorbed into the Eastern reality of the Soviet bloc.

What were the immediate consequences? A considerable number of teachers were fired and many students were expelled on the basis of difference in political views. Divinity schools were closed down as religion was deemed incompatible with 'scientific' education. Departments of philosophy were drastically reduced and the dogmatic ideology of Marxism-Leninism was imposed on the curricula in practically all fields of study, above all in social sciences and humanities.

With the progress of the Cold War, the isolation of the Eastern countries and their institutions gradually deepened; for universities it meant very limited access, if any at all, to new knowledge published in the free world. Textbooks in most disciplines were rewritten according to the new political requirements. The university in Brno could no longer be even called after the founder of the modern democratic Czechoslovak state, President Masaryk; it had to be renamed. Academic freedom became an empty phrase to such an extent that when we wanted to renew the academic liberties after the Revolution of 1989, we hardly knew what they should represent and where to begin in the process of restoring them. Indeed, it was generally true that after decades of totalitarian rule we knew better what we wanted to get rid of than what we wanted to achieve and how to proceed.

When democracy was restored, it took us a while to recognise that we needed to change not just the overtly political content of education, but also the ways in which studies had been organised in the Communist period. The curricula had been overloaded with positivistic facts. Heavy class schedules amounted up to 36 hours of compulsory classes per week, allowing little time and opportunity for independent study. Students did not have a chance to depart from rigid study programmes or modules. Exams were mostly based on repeating 'truths' included in officially approved textbooks. Libraries and reading rooms were very poorly

M.V. Lomonosov Moscow State University (1959)
Moscow University was founded in 1755. The present building was erected in 1958, during the Stalin era, and remains the Russian capital's largest university.

equipped and computers were still non-existent. Thus, the course of education was a well-guarded, indeed, well-controlled corridor.

In addition, the Soviet-inspired educational policy kept teaching at the institutions of higher learning separate from research, which was reserved for the Academies of Sciences. (This, of course, violated the principle of unity of learning, teaching and doing research in pursuit of knowledge.) In 1981, the regime had changed doctoral studies in Czechoslovakia to a mere formality, awarding the titles mostly as a reward for political loyalty rather than for any intellectual and professional performance of merit. By that time, higher-ranking university teachers (professors and associate professors) who were not members of the Communist Party were becoming a species threatened by extinction. The positions of university authorities (rector, dean) were filled with loyal Party hacks and by appointment of the regime authorities whose consent was needed for any major decisions taken on campus, as well as for trips abroad, participation in international conferences and also professional or academic promotion of faculty members.

Nonetheless, education was something valued by people in Eastern European societies and families continued sending children to universities despite the fact that the salaries of university graduates could actually be lower than those of blue-collar workers. However, there were too few positions available. Only 14 percent of the age cohort of 18 to 25 was lucky enough to be accepted. (This has ceased to be a problem because the number of students admitted to institutions of higher education is at present at least three times as high as it used to be before 1989.) Then high demand for few openings created ample space for political manipulation as well as for simple corruption. There were standardised entrance exams, but their results were rarely decisive. In the earlier stages of the regime, preferences were given to children from working class backgrounds or from underdeveloped regions; this could still be somehow justified, but later it was the parents' membership of the Communist Party which would weigh in favour of some applicants – while those whose parents had been 'blacklisted' for political reasons found themselves rejected from university studies as late as spring 1989.

Notwithstanding these efforts of the regime to breed and reward conformism, university students became major actors in the Velvet Revolution. Obviously, totalitarianism rarely enjoys total support of the population. In spite of totalitarian propaganda, students – helped by some teachers – learned to 'read between the lines'. And in November 1989, the students (along with actors, singers and writers, mostly dissidents) played a key role in spreading the message to the broadest public, launching a massive protest movement that could no longer be stopped.

Boris A. Zelensky, *Economics and Education Policy* (c. 1940)
Poster bearing the slogan 'Produce more to have more. Know more to produce more.'

In the Soviet bloc, the dogmatic ideology of Marxism-Leninism was imposed on the curricula in practically all fields of study, above all in social sciences and humanities

Mathematics lecture at Tashkent Teaching Institute, Uzbekistan (n.d.)
The restrictive Communist regime regarded any hint of criticism of the Party as an act of dissidence. Many academics were barred from lecturing for political reasons.

They manifested their power to bring about democratic changes, including applications of some principles of university autonomy. Revolutionary senates were created, with 50 percent representation of students, and for the first time in decades, they could freely elect their university authorities – the rector (president) of the university and the deans of individual schools.

Transforming the inherited universities into more democratic, more academic and efficient institutions was and remains a difficult process, but certainly a gratifying one. The fact that the division of the continent is no longer a reality and East and West have met again in the project of a common European future is very promising and encouraging. It also represents a commitment. International exchange programmes and international cooperation in general do help to overcome the heritage of our totalitarian past, but they are also an invitation to the former 'Eastern' universities to join the 'Western' ones in facing up to the current challenges of higher education, which are by no means small.

Josef Jǎrab

The Velvet Revolution, Prague (1989)
The former Czechoslovakia was the stage
for mass protest against the Communist
regime. Students and intellectuals
demanded an opening-up towards
a democratic system and university autonomy.
The movement was peaceful but effective,
setting off a transition from a totalitarian
regime to a democratic system.

Central library of the Spanish National University of Distance Education (UNED), Madrid (c. 1995)
The UNED was created in the 1970s in aid of equal opportunities and widened access to university. Learning units are circulated to enrolled students in printed form, and partner institutions provide tutorials and guidance. Today, UNED is the Spanish university with the largest number of enrolled students.

New Trends in University Systems

Public and Private Universities

University systems have developed new forms that coexist with the classical structures. Public and private universities have always operated alongside one another. Save regional exceptions – such as in the Far East – public universities predominate. This is the case in Germany, France, the United States (where 80 percent of students are enrolled at public institutions, universities or colleges) and Europe as a whole. The Netherlands and Belgium have seen the flourishing of a major tradition of private universities, but they are barely distinguishable from public ones, in so far as they attract public funds and are integrated within the national system.

However, in Japan, Korea, Taiwan or the Philippines, universities are private (accommodating 80 percent of university students) and depend on private funds alone. In Latin America, the oldest universities were established by the Catholic Church, although the weight of the public sector grew in the twentieth century.

The founding of private universities has been a recent phenomenon in Eastern and Central Europe after 1989. But Portugal and Spain are perhaps the only countries in Europe where private institutions have enjoyed a measure of expansion. Out of Spain's 75 universities, 25 are private, teaching somewhat over 12 percent of the country's university students.

It is difficult to generalise about private universities. Though highly prestigious in some countries – notably in the United States – they have no distinct reputation elsewhere. Their limited access (in Eastern Europe especially) to public research funds renders them dependent on enrolment fees, with the funding problems this implies.

Private universities are subject to a fairly flexible regulatory framework in the Far East. In the United States, they are overseen by private regulatory agencies. The new private universities in Eastern Europe come under an as yet poorly defined statutory framework.

The Influence of Information and Communication Technologies

Technological change has had a powerful influence on universities and presages future transformations. One of the interesting aspects of the present state of technology is the opening up of possibilities for the service sector, formerly organised to a hands-on scheme and heavily dependent on personal dealings. The technological revolution of the second half of the twentieth century has successfully spread to the non-industrial field and influenced those structures, however, and this development has of course touched upon universities, in their capacity as suppliers of teaching and research services. New technologies have enabled the universities better to cater to the prodigious rise in the number of students and in the diversity of study options.

This technical transformation is underpinned by the new information and communication technologies (ICTs). The use of ICTs creates major advantages in the provision of university services and in the institutions' internal management and administration.

At the close of the twentieth century, an Australian paper 'Learning for Life', April 1998, from the Department of Employment, Education, Training and Youth of the Australian Government, stressed that ICTs were helping to lower organisational costs and the burden of processing academic documentation.

Leonardo da Vinci University Centre, Paris
This private centre of higher education was founded in 1995. It comprises three faculties: the business management school (EMLV), the higher school of engineering (ESILV) and an international multimedia institute (IIM).

The paper warned, however, that the introduction of ICTs itself entailed high risk and cost. The spread of the new technologies has enhanced teacher-student communication and enriched global relations among researchers.

Universities have reacted in varying degrees. They have had to spend large amounts on installing the telecommunications infrastructure itself, training university staff to use it and producing teaching materials. By the end of the twentieth century, the United States had spent over $3 billion on introducing ICTs. This has paved the way for their increasing use in education and their gradual incorporation into universities' institutional strategy. At that time, too, 54 percent of courses were using e-mail in support of teaching and 39 percent were using Internet-based resources. It is reasonable to suppose that these figures have been amply exceeded by now.

The availability of new technologies has forced the universities to make a number of decisions. The use of ICTs is an obvious step forward for distance education, but traditional institutions have come up against a fair measure of resistance. Strategic planners have had trouble estimating the various costs attendant on these technologies, such as maintenance and asset depreciation.

It is not an easy proposition to strike the right balance between face-to-face and distance teaching. The personal development of students would appear to require that they become integrated with a given educational environment. Activities away from the lecture hall and the laboratory are critical. Distance education universities have had to find ways of replacing real campuses, just as in-person systems have had to integrate the use of ICTs.

Now that services are provided on an industrial scale they have drawn the attention of the GATT negotiations (General Agreement on Trade and Tariffs). Education forms the subject-matter of multilateral negotiations on the liberalisation of international flows, just like any other service. Australia, New Zealand, the United States and Japan originally put forward proposals to the World Trade Organization (WTO), while underscoring the need to leave governments' power to regulate educational policy untouched. The European University Association (EUA) and the European Student Union (ESU, formerly ESIB) and certain American bodies have viewed this development with suspicion. They fear it may threaten the public nature of education. The European Steering Committee on Higher Education and Research (CD-ESR) urged in 2002 that the GATT deals abide by the terms of the Lisbon Convention of 1997, based on co-operation and trust among national education systems.

As was to be expected, the revolution in the service sector has permeated the world of the university. Some universities – the so-called 'entrepreneurial universities' – have attempted to follow business principles and practices. However, unlikely it may seem, this trend has been at its keenest among public universities. Fearless of any loss of their academic tradition, they have hoped to generate a return on their creative capacity and enhance the value of their teaching and research services. They have streamlined their organisational structure on a goal-oriented basis, have closely watched the changes in their economic and social settings and have diversified their income streams so as partly to wean themselves off public funds.

Another new – and related – phenomenon has been the rise of new providers of higher education outside the universities, making intensive use of ICTs. More widespread in the United States than in Europe, this trend has been led by for-profit institutions – so-called 'corporate' universities – and by alliances between big leisure and communications firms and certain conventional universities. The more aggressive players, such as the University of Phoenix, create multidisciplinary working groups (designers, teachers, content experts, IT specialists, etc.) to target market demand and sell online courses around the world.

Diversification

The growing social and economic importance of universities has driven them to diversify. Other than the higher technical schools, until well into the twentieth century there was only a single model of the university, which accorded priority to research. The creation of new universities during the second half of the twentieth century, following the gradual spread of higher education, generally recreated the structure

In Germany, France or the United States, 80 percent
of students are enrolled at public institutions,
universities or colleges. However, in Japan, Korea
or Taiwan, universities are private, accommodating
80 percent of university students

Taiyuan University of Technology, China (2009)
Today, university study is closely tied to the job market. Companies provide lists of vacancies to students who are about to complete their training. In China, the growth of university study has kept abreast of the country's economic development. Holding a university qualification is the most effective way to secure a contract of employment.

Some universities have acquired the status of international benchmarks for the quality of their research or their special have preferred to focus on certain fields. Other universities focus on their immediate social and economic environment

of existing universities. Little heed was paid to the arguments in favour of breaking up the structures of higher education across a given territory. All the same, their founding aims and their territorial loyalties were quite different from those animating the formation of the old European universities.

In practice, the demand universities have encountered has prompted them to diversify. This has been most visible in the United States. Diversification is not a matter so much of specialising in a given subject as engaging in a wider variety of practices and activities. These ventures should be assessed and rated in accordance with the quality of the contribution they are making in their chosen roles, at a remove from the benchmark of excellence that would apply to more conventional institutions.

Diversification within a single university and across various institutions reflects the trend towards dissolving the boundaries among the various kinds of institution through a more flexible approach to their roles. Higher education institutions generally provide two types of courses: some are general, particularly in the first years of study, tending towards growing specialisation in later years. Another kind of course, however, focuses more tightly on vocational training from the outset, supplying the basis for learning certain skills. Despite the variety of purposes, boundaries are overcome by a system of walkways, credit transfers, etc. Even the curricular prescriptions of the university authorities have been largely evaded by the use of broader international spaces for education.

Some universities have acquired the status of international benchmarks for the quality of their research or their special have preferred to focus on certain fields. Other universities focus on their immediate social and economic environment. This is the case of many of the recent institutions. Falling somewhere between the two, most universities steer a middle course between local engagement and distinction in other countries.

Competition and Cooperation

The diversity of independent institutions intensifies competition among themselves and other higher education sites. But the fact that they work in similar fields encourages them to collaborate so as to make use of their complementary features; they thus share costs and advantages and essay a form of division of labour. It is precisely this need to cooperate that has given rise to agreements to form university networks.

These arrangements are common in Europe: the Coimbra Group, the League of European Research Universities, the Confédération européenne des universités du Rhin supérieur (EUROCOR) which brings together faculties of the Rhenish universities of Mulhouse, Basel, Freiburg and Karlsruhe, and others. The network has also been the chosen pattern for the alliances forged with non-university institutions, such as businesses and regional and national authorities, to deal with specific issues or create a stable basis of contact.

It is rarer to see pre-existing universities merge. But experiments of this kind have taken place in the United Kingdom and Switzerland, and there are likely to be more. Sometimes mergers have responded to a perceived over-specialisation in certain disciplines – such as the specialisation drive seen in France since 1969. Elsewhere, in Central and Eastern Europe, mergers have sought to reverse the dismembering while under Soviet control of what was originally a single university. Historically – examples being London or California – dispersed and independent university centres have melded within one system.

University and Technological Development

The technological development of the modern age would have been impossible without the universities. The steam engine, which drove the Industrial Revolution, was invented by James Watt (1736–1819), a Scots engineer with ties to the University of Glasgow – he had a shop there, and made and sold mathematical instruments. His association with the university enabled him to meet other scientists who undoubtedly helped him on his way to creating the new machine, which sparked the great leap from an agricultural society to a new, industrial one.

From the University of Glasgow to UCLA and Stanford

Where the University of Glasgow was central to the original Industrial Revolution, the latest revolution – ushering in the age of the Internet – revolved around two Californian universities, UCLA and Stanford.
In 1969, Leonard Kleinrock, after taking a doctorate at the Massachusetts Institute of Technology (MIT) and joining the ARPANET project, designed the technology that now underpins the Net. Its first node was located at the University of California at Los Angeles (UCLA), while the second node was installed at the Stanford Research Institute. Vinton Cerf, regarded as the inventor of the Internet, also has links to both these major American universities.

In the interval between these two technological leaps, which have so deeply influenced the way we work, the way we learn and our cultural practices, universities played a central role in the development of new technologies.

From 1815 to 1870, the universities of France and Britain made major contributions in the field of electricity; Germany, with the first properly scientific university, Humboldt University at Berlin (1840), instituted organic chemistry, and so humanity's ability to create synthetic substances, opening up fresh horizons in the industrial economy and society. Universities have had a decisive effect on two of the four main stages of the history of humanity: industrial society, and the post-industrial society of today.

That role did not spring from a static model. There has been a clear evolution from classical, vertically structured universities, home to individual researchers and inventors, to the modern pattern, in which

MIT, Cambridge, Massachusetts (2004)
The campus is spread over several sites in Cambridge. The building designed by the architect Frank Gehry has transformed the face of the city. Wavelike volumes, unusual materials and the importance of colour give Gehry's architecture an unmistakable stamp.

universities seek to produce rapid responses to the emerging needs of society.

The universities have moved on from being 'habitats' that merely encourage innovation to their present role: purposely designed engines of economic and social change.

FROM THE EUROPEAN TO THE AMERICAN UNIVERSITY

From the mid-nineteenth century to the Second World War, the European universities were the main suppliers of applied technology to satisfy the needs of the traditional industry of the age. However, after the war, this role faded. The universities became part of great national systems of education, and adopted values remote from the needs of regional development. The difficulty was not so much a lack of resources or funding as a shift in systemic structure and values. A gap opened up between regional development policy and the universities until the industrial crisis of the 1970s drew attention to the importance of science and knowledge as key factors of the new scheme of development. The British and Swiss universities were perhaps the exception to the model prevailing elsewhere.

In the United States, however, after the war universities became the world's major centres of scientific and technical output. A network formed of open-ended, competing universities intent upon encouraging merit and excellence: prestige became an obsession. And this model, allowing full university autonomy and a free choice of academic faculty and students, was tightly focused on pushing out the boundaries of scientific knowledge and technological innovation. Silicon Valley, Route 128 and the Research Triangle are all outcomes of this pattern, which many countries and regions now seek to emulate.

The contribution of American universities to development was not entirely new. From the 1920s onwards, many were already engaged in technology transfer. But it was in 1945 when, in a report to the president, Vannebar Bush formally recommended the creation of the National Science Foundation. In 'Science, the Endless Frontier', he wrote that fundamental research was the road to technological progress, and urged that all government bodies across the United States undertake research.

One of the outcomes of this policy was a debate in the 1960s and 1970s about the ownership and use of research results. The United States government owned 30,000 patents, of which only 5 percent made it onto the market. The debate ended with the passage of the Bayh-Dole Act of 1980, which gave control of inventions and patents to the universities and other academic institutions, thus decisively reinforcing the major technology

Universities have had a decisive effect on the last two revolutions in human history: the Industrial Revolution, and the age of the Internet, which emerged at UCLA and Stanford

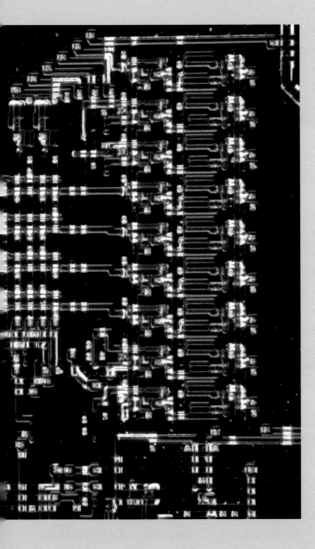

transfer centres of American universities, science and technology parks and other platforms for relations among universities and enterprise.

THE PRESENT DEBATE IN EUROPE: CHANGES IN THE UNIVERSITIES AND THE EIT

In Europe, the technology transfer system – coupled as it is to a certain conception of university – does not really work. The EU has in fact admitted that 'universities should develop structured partnerships with the world of enterprise in order to become significant players in the economy, able to respond better and faster to the demands of the market and to develop partnerships that harness scientific and technological knowledge.' Europe is knowledge-productive, however: the challenge is to improve the way that publicly funded research and development is put to use.

Some countries have already made progress in changing the university model. Finland recently created Aalto University: termed the 'Innovation University', it is a merger of the former Helsinki University of Technology, Helsinki School of Economics and University of Art and Design Helsinki. Other countries are also moving towards models patterned after the British and American fashion, and are developing their interfaces with enterprise in the form of technology transfer offices, science parks and patent offices.

The recent creation of the European Institute of Innovation and Technology (EIT) is Europe's latest effort to find the right way to harness the outflow of knowledge from its universities in close cooperation with businesses and market trends.

Francesc Santacana i Martorell

Microchip (n.d.)
Universities are the leading outposts of research and technological innovation. The development of semiconductors of minimal size is constantly evolving towards increasingly sophisticated devices.

Sources of University Funding

In recent years, universities have found it harder to make ends meet. The rise in the number of students going on to higher education and new statutory demands have coincided with a policy of budgetary containment which since 1980, however futilely, has attempted to rein in public expenditure.

The diversification of university activities has itself made it expedient to vary the sources of funding. Universities are funded by three main income streams: enrolment fees, public subsidies and other public and private funds, such as donations, service provision income and so forth. The reforms undergone in the second half of the twentieth century reflected a greater relative weight of private sources of funding (fees, research contracts, advisory services, continuing training, patronage, alumni donations). In most countries, however, government subsidies remain by far the biggest source of funds. Hybrid funding models, partly based on a higher proportion of fees, have become common both in countries where such models were already entrenched (United States, Canada, the Netherlands) and in countries where tradition had removed fees from the scheme of public university funding (Australia, New Zealand and the United Kingdom).

Other forms of funding have been tried. Under an income loan, for instance, students can put off paying fees during their studies. After completing their degree and once they have attained a given level of income, they begin to pay off the loan. Donations have been encouraged by tax breaks. In the United States and other countries where the welfare state is only weakly present, a large proportion of funds come from private foundations and from alumni.

Universities have promoted an active policy of cooperation with the economy and society. This has brought in funds through professional services and applied research. Government subsidies are now retreating at least partly from their traditional role. They are now subject to the achievement of certain goals or targets. Total expenditure per annum and higher education student (in a strict sense, not including research and development or additional activities)

ranges from $5,000 to $10,000, the average being $8,000 ($7,200 in Spain). Research and development spending and supplementary outlays usually account for 4 to 24 percent of expenditure per student.

The proportion of public to private funds mirrors the practice of the various governments. Public funding is generally predominant in those countries where public spending has the greatest weight in the economy: Scandinavia and most of Western Europe (and in some of the Central and Eastern European countries), where public spending as a proportion of gross domestic product is close to or above 50 percent. In the United States the lower proportion of public spending correlates with a lower proportion of public funding for education. But exceptions are fairly common. In Korea, Mexico, Chile or Slovakia, where public spending forms a relatively low proportion of gross domestic product, there is a highly significant public funding effort for the education system as a whole. As regards universities, public funds generally exceed 90 percent in Scandinavian countries and make for a considerable proportion of university funding in Western Europe. In France and Germany, the figure is somewhat above 80 percent, and this is the pattern also of the Central and Eastern European countries. In Spain, the proportion is 77 percent, ahead of Poland, Portugal and Italy. The lowest percentages are found in the United Kingdom, the United States and non-European OECD members.

The public or private nature of universities' income is not subject to precise boundaries – this again reflects the complexity of university funding. High enrolment fees do not always signal low public funding, because government may fund higher education indirectly through transfers to households and students (grants, accommodation services, etc.).

The OECD has classified four groups of countries by their systems of public funding. The first group is characterised by waiving enrolment fees entirely or charging only a token amount. They provide universities liberally and directly with the funds they require. This certainly is the case in Scandinavian countries (where almost all people of university age are enrolled at university) and also, to some extent, in the Czech Republic and Turkey.

English-speaking countries, the Netherlands and Chile form a second group in which enrolment fees are high (above $1,500) this is coupled with the distribution of a large amount of direct aid to students. The proportion of these transfers to all funds allocated to higher education is close to 40 percent – but only about 25 percent in the United Kingdom and the United States. Thirdly, in Japan and Korea here are very high enrolment fees but these are unaccompanied by any evolved system of student support. This means, of course, that university entry rates are lower than the OECD average. Finally, in the fourth group of countries – which includes Austria, Italy, Belgium, France, Spain and Poland – enrolment fees are relatively low (not above $1,100); and the systems of support to students and their families are weakly present; in so far as they exist, they focus on specific groups. Such aid as there is sometimes comes from non-central government.

The considerable rise in university autonomy has been coupled with an effort by some universities to supersede traditional modes of management and endow themselves with a modern structure in order to acquire an improved awareness of what their activities cost. A contributory factor here has been competition for attracting funds for research, particularly from other countries and institutions. A recent research paper conducted by the European University Association on a sample of universities showed that international funds account for barely more than 10 percent of total funding, and mostly come from European programmes. The efficient allocation of resources and a more accurate knowledge of the costs of potential projects have been largely the outcome of the wider management autonomy that universities have been given. The quid pro quo for this greater freedom is that universities are now more rigorously accountable to government. The new models of university funding require regular monitoring by supervisory authorities, periodic assessment of teaching and research, use of programme-contracts and the full complement of other measures that help build trust in the higher education system and its use of public funds.

James William Fulbright
An American senator (1905–1995), Fulbright was the force behind legislative amendments appropriating government funds to support university exchanges among different countries and seek world peace through education. Since 1946, Fulbright fellowships have been coveted among graduates hoping to complete their studies overseas.

The Spread of University Autonomy

From the nineteenth century onwards, the governance of European continental universities and British universities – which had enjoyed broad-ranging autonomy – remained largely unchanged.

In continental Europe, the universities were largely administrative institutions: in other words, ministerial appendices. This was a shared feature of both the Napoleonic and the Humboldtian traditions, although dependence on government took various forms. The relevant ministries exercised tight control over the universities by setting the status, level and content of studies, regulating student admissions, selecting academic staff, allocating funds, and so forth. Except in periods where democracy yielded to autocratic regimes, this was no obstacle to academic freedom, widely accepted as academics and researchers' right to produce knowledge and express their opinions free from external strictures.

The reform of the universities that followed the events of May 1968 was calculated to nurture involvement by the student body and the various echelons of academia in a bid to democratise university governance. This reform ushered in a further change, when in the closing third of the twentieth century university autonomy spread throughout the continent. Autonomy, it was hoped, would raise each institution's ability to respond to a rapidly evolving environment. The new conception of autonomy openly questioned government intervention and modified the composition of both the governing bodies of universities and the authorities to which they were accountable.

This did not invariably mean that universities were self-managed, and this is not a necessary corollary of autonomy. For example, English and Dutch universities cannot be said to be self-managed, and yet they are probably more autonomous than their counterparts in other European countries. The University of Barcelona had a certain measure of autonomy granted in 1933 – which it has never enjoyed subsequently. Its main decisions were entrusted to a board of

Students at the Sorbonne, Paris (May 1968)
General De Gaulle's France faced a mass protest movement involving university students, workers and intellectuals. Demands varied widely, but all sprang from a revolt against the established political and social system. Demonstrations often degenerated into riots, violently broken up by the police.

trustees the members of which came mostly from outside the university. Autonomy involves the transfer of power from legislative and executive public authorities to the central bodies of a university.

By way of summary, the spread of university autonomy means that by the responsible exercise of this new independence the universities can achieve a better fit with their social and economic settings. It is a functional improvement. And it is no new craze: the autonomy granted by Gregory IX to the University of Paris under the papal bull *Parens Scientiarum* in 1231 was intended to shield the faculty masters from the designs of the cathedral chapter. At the University of Bologna, by way of contrast, it was students who achieved the greater share of power. The reason for this is that in Paris the students were younger, and devoted to the study of philosophy and theology, being destined for careers in the Church. Bologna, however, drew in older students who trained primarily for the professions, law and medicine.

This robustly functional aspect of autonomy is set out in the *Magna Charta Universitatum* of 1988, which says:

> The university is an autonomous institution [...]
> it produces, examines, appraises and hands
> down culture by research and teaching. To meet
> the needs of the world around it, its research
> and teaching must be morally and intellectually
> independent of all political authority and
> economic power.

Claude Allègre, the mind originally behind the European Higher Education Area, said in 2001 that:

> The university seeks freedom of thought. This
> is entirely legitimate. But if academic freedom
> leads to total isolation, as has happened on
> occasion, universities fold in on themselves and
> become unable to develop new disciplines or
> new fields of research [...] If autonomy means
> the capacity to be responsible, then the
> university in Europe or anywhere else must
> open up to society. This bond must be reflected
> in the universities' organisation. The modern
> way must be found of creating a tie with society
> that expresses dialogue with all partners. The
> conditions of this dialogue are the foundations
> of this autonomy.

It is hard to imagine that the general rules laid down by government authorities, with their inevitably static nature, can accurately accommodate the changes to come. Those responsible for managing universities are therefore expected to do more than simply mediate between academics and civil servants; their governance and policy for the universities should be guided by a long-term strategy.

The exercise of university autonomy rests with the central organs of the university. The institutes, departments, faculties and other bodies making up the institution constitute its internal structure, which is modifiable in accordance with an overarching policy. The exception to this practice (of which there have been examples in Eastern Europe, particularly in the universities of the former Yugoslavia) have been seen to be a divergence that ends up endangering autonomy itself – as it turned out in those countries. The social environment of the modern university inspires it to connect with the outside – with government bodies, businesses, and so forth. This engenders centrifugal stresses that may lead to a loss of internal cohesion, adversely affect the university's mission and undermine the general criteria of resource allocation.

In parallel to the spread of autonomy, governments have changed their university policy so as to influence research priorities and fields of study by indirect means. These initiatives are persuasive if supported by funding. Governments have introduced schemes to gauge university performance. Political action has tended to replace the former framework of *ex ante* regulation with a strategy of *ex post facto* oversight and verification. The growing trend towards autonomy in continental universities is now converging with the British government's rising interest in university policy in a country were universities were autonomous by dint of historic tradition.

The extent of such autonomy depends on the rules prevailing in each country, and tends to differ as regards selection of staff, student admissions or the configuration of curricular itineraries. Autonomy is

The spread of university autonomy means that by the responsible exercise of thisnew independence the universities can achieve a better fit with their social and economic settings

Henry Ford Building, Free University of Berlin (1952–54)
The construction of this building was funded by a donation of over 8 million German marks from the American industrialist Henry Ford. In the hall hang the portraits of illustrious scientists and intellectuals who have passed through its doors.

Encaenia ceremony, University of Oxford (2007)
Keeping faith with tradition, Oxford annually holds this academic ceremony in recognition of graduates, emeritus professors, benefactors and prominent figures in the arts and sciences. The Greek word *encaenia* means 'consecration' or 'renewal'. The ceremony follows a strict protocol and comprises graduation, conferences and a procession of the university's dignitaries.

coupled with a global transfer of funds allocated to no specific purpose, although the original sum springs from predetermined indicators.

The laws regarding university autonomy, after legislative changes of varying scope, have strengthened the executive bodies of each university and encouraged the recruitment of decision-makers from outside academia.

The universities of England, Wales, Scotland and Ireland have preserved their traditional system of governance, based on a mixed board that elects a vice-chancellor for an indefinite term. French universities have developed their autonomy, although the role of government is still strongly predominant. Independent trustees are still few, sitting on the three boards created by the 'Savary Law' – particularly on

the most important of the three, the Conseil d'Administration. Relations with the ministry are carried on individually by each university through the office of the *conseiller détablissement*.

German universities are under the aegis of the federal regions or *Länder*, and depend on both the education and finance councillors of their specific region. The Federal Law of 1998 made considerable changes, but left the reform of the internal governance of universities to the Länder. In practice, the novelties have been marginal. The formerly hegemonic role of academics has been somewhat curtailed, while the influence of external trustees and government bodies has risen.

Change in the Dutch universities has been very considerable and appears to have exerted some influence on the systems of other countries. The spate of reforms of the 1980s and 1990s – creating a board of three trustees, formed by a chairman, a rector and a third official – crystallised in the reform of 1997. This statute created a supervisory board made up of a small number of government appointees, the decision-making powers of which include the appointment of the rector. The rector, in turn, appoints the faculty deans. The other boards are merely consultative, although their resolutions may carry considerable moral weight.

Although it had a forerunner in the timid reforms in Sweden of 1983, the Dutch system, with slight variants, appears to be the main influence behind the Austrian law of 2002 and the Danish law of 2003, where boards with a majority of non-academic trustees carry on the management of the university and make managerial appointments.

In Spain, university autonomy was recognised in the University Reform Law of 25 August 1998. This was the first statute making provision for a general pattern of university autonomy (other than the royal decree of 21 May 1919, which allowed for the adoption of some university statutes, though this was later reversed by the royal decree of 31 July 1922). The government of the Spanish Second Republic granted autonomy to the faculties of arts of Madrid and Barcelona in September 1931. Finally, however, the Decree of 1 June 1933 gave autonomy to the University of Barcelona only, and this autonomy was suppressed in 1939.

The deregulation brought about by the spread of university autonomy has enhanced the accountability of universities to society and government.

Assessment – mostly conducted by private agencies in the United States and by public agencies in Europe – has been calculated to implement quality assurance in the university system. The assessment of universities is not limited to the various programmes and special fields of the academic faculty, but ranges over university policy and decision-making procedures as well.

The launch of the European Pilot Project for Evaluating Quality in Higher Education (1994–95) demonstrated the value of sharing and developing common experiences in this key area. The initiative inspired the idea of an association, formed in 2000 as the European Network for Quality Assessment in Higher Education, which then became the European Association for Quality Assurance in Higher Education, ENQA, in 2004.

Assessment of universities and their programmes often leads to courses earning accreditation from independent bodies. Assessment results also serve to confirm whether funds received have been used properly. The assessment system is not equipped with a system of penalties; rather, it provides the opportunity for making improvements on the basis of assessment comments.

The Changing Territorial Scope of the Universities

European universities, originally founded by the Church and recognised by the popes, came under government authority in the wake of the reforms set in motion by the French Revolution. With this change of master, the universities began to play a 'national' role for the training of civil servants and the social and economic elites of the nation states, thus relinquishing the universal nature they had enjoyed in the Middle Ages and the Renaissance. This explains why the European universities have mostly remained under state ownership.

In recent decades, however, this starting-point has seen a number of changes. The emergence of new providers of higher education, and the rise of English as an alternative to other official languages in the provision of higher education and the dissemination of research activity, has meant that national education systems have gradually become more exposed to international competition and have lost their monopoly over higher education. The frontiers imposed by the demarcation of the various nation states in the organisation of higher education have become blurred by phenomena such as student mobility. Given this competitive environment, universities have deployed networking as a strategy to face these challenges in a cooperative way.

However, the fading of boundaries has coincided with the rise in the value accorded to the role of universities in their territorial settings – even beyond those boundaries. The various levels of government have become involved in the universities' contribution to regional development. This is now one of the objectives of public authorities hoping to promote the comparative advantages in their territory by reason of its collective and public services, including its universities. Policy-making practice has tended to reinforce the presence of universities in the regional systems of innovation.

The concern is to mitigate some of the problems of adopting a new technology without sufficient entrepreneurial support. For example, France has created the PRES (*Pôles de recherche et d'enseignement supérieur*) as a territorial tool for cooperation and the sharing of actions and resources of research bodies and higher education institutions. The goal is to foster a territorial logic that strengthens the effectiveness, visibility and attractive force of the system of training and research. This kind of body has aided the territorial fixing of international capital movements and nurtured loyalty in the availability of human resources.

A recent publication of the OECD, *Higher Education and Regions: Globally Competitive, Locally Engaged*, 2007, has drawn a distinction between three aspects of the issue: the production of knowledge by research and the fertilisation of knowledge by technology transfer; the capacity to absorb available knowledge; and, finally, cultural and communitarian growth towards a framework favouring innovation. At the Forum 2000 promoted by the European Commission, based on the experiences of the universities of Bordeaux and Amsterdam, the growing importance was emphasized of local and regional authorities in assisting universities to take the initiative in this field.

Bologna and Lisbon

Governments have always jealously guarded their university policy. It is unsurprising that this policy domain was not addressed by the Treaty of Rome. However, reality has intervened to change this. For example, one of the working parties formed in the wake of the adoption of the Declaration of Bologna drew attention to anecdotal evidence brought to light by the principal of a Dutch *hogescholen*, a non-university institution of further education. Students at *hogescholen* were barred in their own country from undertaking doctoral study. However, they would bypass the difficulty by gaining admission to a doctoral course at a university in a neighbouring country where their Dutch *hogescholen* studies had been accorded recognition. This specific case study was symptomatic of a trend that modifies the territorial scope of higher education in a framework of increasing internationalisation.

Barcelona Supercomputing Centre, BSC (2005)
Housed in a former chapel, the Mare Nostrum supercomputer is one of Europe's most powerful, and the first to have been installed at a public research centre. Glass wall protec it from environmental damage and preserves the right temperature and humidity for the computer's more than 10,000 processors to run at top performance. Mare Nostrum is capable of 94 million of trillions floating-point operations per second.

Assembly Hall of the University of Bologna
This Italian university gave its name to the European plan or convergence in higher education. The Declaration of Bologna aims to support freer student mobility and enhanced university quality. With its signing on 19 March 1999, twenty-nine European states undertook to create a European Higher Education Area by 2010.

In the Magna Charta Universitatum, *endorsed in September 1988 on the occasion of the ninth centenary of the University of Bologna, universities advocated the values of freedom, autonomy and accountability, defining themselves as institutions for research and teaching*

The European Union's first attempt to address education was in 1987, when it adopted a programme for student and academic mobility within the Community – the Erasmus programme. Though problematic in some ways, the Erasmus programme laid the foundations for cooperation among independent institutions and shaped the instruments that were later to be adopted by the European Higher education Area (EHEA), such as the European Credit Transfer System (ECTS).

In the *Magna Charta Universitatum*, endorsed in September 1988 on the occasion of the ninth centenary of the University of Bologna, universities advocated the values of freedom, autonomy and accountability, defining themselves as institutions for research and teaching. The events of 1989 gave the *Magna Charta* a new dimension, because the Central European universities took it as a benchmark in the new stage they were about to embark upon.

The rectors' stated aim of strengthening ties among European universities eventually culminated in government-driven initiatives. The crowning event was instigated by the French minister of education, Claude Allègre, who on 25 May 1998 held a meeting at the Sorbonne with his Italian, British and German counterparts. The meeting produced the Declaration of the Sorbonne, the forerunner of the Declaration of Bologna of 19 June 1999, in which 29 signatory states – even from beyond the borders of the EU – undertook to create a European Higher Education Area by 2010. This space was to be achieved through university autonomy. Other governments soon followed, and at present the number of signatories stands at 46. To achieve its ends, the EHEA has sought to set in motion a voluntary process to make the various itineraries and courses that make up higher education in Europe comparable and compatible, while avoiding bland uniformity and allowing for flexibility.

Three formulas were put forward: the creation of an itinerary of three successive cycles (bachelor, master, doctor), with the bachelor stage required to last at least three years; the reference frame of a system of credit equivalence based on the ECTS scheme and the use of a diploma supplement detailing curricular content.

Since then, a number of meetings have been held among European universities and government officials, at Prague, Bergen, London and Leuven, serving to round out the scope of the EHEA, particularly as regards assessment of university performance. The EHEA is not a European Union initiative. However, at the European Council of Lisbon in March 2000 (as confirmed by the Barcelona summit of 2002) the European member states defined a strategy so as to achieve, by the end of the decade, the world's most competitive knowledge economy, based on sustainable growth and social cohesion.

The Lisbon Strategy involves bolstering the triangle of education, research and innovation. To this end, European policy focuses on university reform. Unlike the Declaration of Bologna, which seeks to encourage student mobility and improve the quality of higher education in itself, the Lisbon Strategy hopes to reform the university so as to enhance the competitiveness of the European economy and society. This entails a broader vision of the role of the European universities, and in practice means that there is some friction between the two strategies. Not all countries view their society and their universities in the same way.

The Lisbon Strategy, after the Council meeting in Copenhagen in 2003, has been broadened to create the 2010 Education and Training Programme, which covers vocational training (including at university) and proposes a European table of qualifications.

In 2000, there was created the European Research Area (ERA) to support careers in research, apply research for social and economic policy purposes, and optimise the effectiveness of European and national programmes.

The Erasmus Programme, a Keystone in European Cooperation and Exchange

The Erasmun scheme, launched in 1987, is one of the most visible and positively perceived programmes of the European Union (EU), promoting the academic mobility of over one million students and thousands of academic staff. The European Action Scheme for the Mobility of University Students was named after the Dutch Renaissance philosopher Erasmus, reflecting a time in history when scholars and students moved from one university to another around Europe.

Up to the early 1980s the notion of exchange of students with foreign universities as part of their home degree programme was still rather unknown. Organised programmes for the exchange of students and staff did exist, such as bilateral cultural and academic agreements of European countries, but these programmes were limited in both funding and scope and primarily focused at the postgraduate level. In the 1970s programmes were created in Sweden and the Federal Republic of Germany to promote cooperation and exchange. In 1976 the European Commission established a Joint Study Programmes Scheme (JSP), aimed at the promotion of joint programmes between institutions in the member states. The focus of this experimental programme was primarily the stimulation of academic mobility within the EU. In 1984 the Commission added a budget line for student grants into the JSP Scheme, which was the pilot for the Erasmus Programme of 1987.

The creation of Erasmus coincided with other programmes, such as Comett, a programme for cooperation between higher education and industry (1986) and Lingua, a scheme for the promotion of the learning of European languages (1989). The Commission at that time still lacked a legal basis for action in the field of higher education. Ironically, this gave the European Commission a great deal of freedom for creative action in the field of education in that period. Erasmus in particular could develop into a significant programme, that in the first six years already allowed more than 200,000 students and 15,000 staff to be exchanged in the framework of 2,200 Joint Study Programmes, in which 14,000 departments of 1,300 institutions of higher education worked together.

In the 1990s the creative and informal period of education policy came to an end. The Maastricht Treaty, ratified on 1 November 1993, gave the European Commission its legal basis for actions in education. One of its

Library of the University of Dijon, France
The Erasmus, which has operated since 1987, supports university exchanges across Europe. Originally available only in EU member states, it gradually opened up to the rest of the continent.

results was the merger of several of the small programmes into two large framework programmes: Leonardo da Vinci, in the area of vocational training; and Socrates, including Erasmus for higher education. In 1993 Erasmus moved from a decentralised scheme with active involvement of faculty and departments into an institutional contract. The requirement to write a European Policy Statement stimulated the development of institutional strategies for internationalisation. A European Credit Transfer System (ECTS) was established to make it easier for institutions and students to transfer credits in the framework of exchanges.

In 1999 the Europeanisation of higher education made a next big step forward through the Declaration of Bologna, which in the following years was signed by nearly all countries in Europe. The Director for Education of the European Commission, David Coyne, stated in 2004, that the EU academic mobility programmes – Erasmus in particular – have 'created an indispensable foundation for the European Higher Education Area'. The promotion of mobility of students and staff, the elimination of remaining obstacles to mobility and the establishment of ECTS as the credit system for European higher education are among the key objectives and measures of the Bologna Process. In the 2009 Bologna Communiqué it is stated that in 2020, at least 20 percent of those graduating in the European Higher Education Area should have had a study or training period abroad.

Originally, Erasmus was limited to the member states of the EU, but in 1991 the EFTA countries (at that time Austria, Finland, Norway, Sweden and Switzerland) were allowed to take part in the programme. In 1998 and 1999 the programme was gradually opened to countries in Central and Eastern Europe, which had previously been supported by another scheme, Trans European Mobility Programme for University Studies (TEMPUS). Other countries, such as Turkey, Cyprus, and Malta were also allowed to participate. Now most of these countries have become part of the EU, but those which are not, such as Norway and Turkey, are also actively involved in the programme.

There is some concern that the introduction of three cycles (bachelor, master, doctor) under the Bologna Process, and the increased opportunities for travel, study and internships outside the Erasmus programme and outside of Europe, will have a decreasing impact on the numbers. But the impact of the programme is undeniable, both in quantitative and qualitative terms. Erasmus has allowed large numbers of students and staff to acquire a European experience, both academically and socially; it has placed internationalisation on the higher education agenda; it has influenced the development of the European Higher Education Area; it has inspired other countries and regions in the world to develop similar initiatives; and it has been exemplary to other European programmes for cooperation and exchange with the rest of the world, such as Alpha and Alban for cooperation with Latin America, and Erasmus Mundus.

Hans de Wit

Hans Holbein the Younger, *Erasmus of Rotterdam* (1523)
The Erasmus programme is named after the famous Renaissance humanist and academic. This choice of name invokes an age in which European students travelled freely from one university to another.

Erasmus was limited to the member states of the European Union, but during the 1990s it was extended to the countries in Central and Eastern Europe. Other countries, such as Turkey, Cyprus and Malta, were also allowed to participate

University of Coimbra, Portugal
The Erasmus programme, besides implementing academic exchange among students from different countries, fosters fundamental experiences for all-round personal development.

45 nanometer microprocessor (2007)
Innovation in information technology is constant. 45 nanometer processors have recently outdone the 65 nm chips that so far ruled the market. This new microprocessor, barely 300 millimetres across, provides higher efficiency within a smaller space.

VII

TOWARDS A
KNOWLEDGE-INTENSIVE SOCIETY

Entrance hall of the main building on Sichuan University campus, China (2004)
Sichuan University, originally founded in 1896, is the result of the merger of three of China's leading universities: the historic University of Sichuan, Chengdu University of Science and Technology, and the West China University of Medical Science. The present-day institution operates faculties of arts, foreign languages and cultures, mathematics, chemical engineering, and pharmacy, and the West China College of Stomatology.

The University in the Twenty-first Century: Challenges and Uncertainties

Manuel J. Tello

The twenty-first century began with a tumultuous process of change. However, we were already familiar with this trend; there have been changes in the past, probably just as sweeping as the current ones: The Renaissance, Industrial Revolution, etc. In this connection, Ortega y Gasset wrote:

> The current crisis is deeper and came more suddenly. Furthermore, its quality is, in a way, inverse to what we observed in the great mental drama that is commonly known as the Renaissance. Then, Thought felt that progress was from less to more [...]

> [...] While no-one has even formulated this as a programme [...], it so happens that the best of the intellectual elite of Europe and America are, without realising quite how, thrown together in the closest possible coexistence. Perhaps the most surprising aspect of this phenomenon is the speed and spontaneity with which it has taken place.

However, what distinguishes the present moment from previous eras are new circumstances that render the process much more complex. We highlight four of these, because of their significance. The first is the speed of change. We no longer talk about centuries, but now refer to decades or even years. The second refers to what we will call the influence of globalisation. We must make an important distinction here between the concept itself, which as such is not new, and its instantaneous influence on the social,

economic and cultural fabric of all countries. The third has to do with the transition from a knowledge economy to a 'knowledge-intensive' society. This term serves to highlight the incorporation of the world of ideas as part of the broader information society. The fourth is the most recent factor, the emergence of instability as a commonplace feature. We are probably commencing a century in which the only stable thing will be instability itself. This latter factor is due to our having made the transition from a simple world to a complex system, and instability is an intrinsic property of complex systems.

Universities, like companies and other public or private institutions, must find their feet in this new global social environment in which the unpredictable will be the norm. Accordingly, from the conceptual standpoint, universities will have to show, their capacity to cope with unpredictability, and, their ability to respond swiftly. In the past, universities have changed, but they have done so gradually. There have

Detail of the back cover of an e-book, Princeton University Library (2005)
Princeton University Library was among the first ten such institutions in the United States to sell e-books. Students can buy 'new' and 'used' electronic books, or get an electronic prepayment card that entitles the holder to download books from the Internet.

been times when it took them more than a century to change. However, in this new century, in which the economic driver will be knowledge, obsolescence will roll in relatively quickly.

Furthermore, as we shall see below, it is important to keep in mind that the university will be subject to increasing and intense pressure from political, economic and social spheres. Consequently, universities must respond swiftly, without losing their historical essence; and these responses must not be uniform. In this regard, one might say that the quest for uniformity has probably been one of the mistakes made by universities in many countries. This has been one of the causes of the scant influence universities have had in developing countries in accelerating the social, political and economic change they need. We must therefore believe that universities' response to the demands of the twenty-first century will have a general framework, as befits a globalised world. However, this framework will have to be adapted by each institution to its own location, socio-economic environment and history.

In the new scenario, the main asset for countries' economic growth will be quality higher education. The importance of the university stems from the fact that the twenty-first century has inherited from the last few years of the twentieth century rather more than what was called the 'knowledge economy'. As we have said, we are really entering what is being called the 'knowledge-intensive society'. In this regard, universities must be aware that their response cannot be confined to the scope of applied science and technology. It must also cover the world of ideas and culture in a global context. So if the university wants to spearhead change, it must act as a critical and free conscience, able to rise above political and economic interests. This means that universities will have to gain in strength. Suffice to recall that the less respect there is for knowledge in the society outside universities, the greater the pressure on them. There are countries that believe in their possibilities and act accordingly, and there are others that, to a greater or lesser extent, talk the talk but fail to walk the walk. Consequently, universities will have to create an awareness of the need for change in those societies where this is lacking.

Universities traditionally establish or maintain a social contract with the citizens in their environment. As part of this contract, in the past they were required to pioneer countries' creativity and innovation. The question universities must ask themselves now is: can the institution continue to be fundamental in generating creativity and innovation in the twenty-first century? This can only be answered positively if universities are able to find quickly an adequate way to respond to the challenges arising from the uncertainties. Some of these challenges are already on the horizon and are currently the subject of reflection. Others might be guessed at, but still others will appear in the future that are neither guessed at or known, and they will be the children of unpredictability.

What can be easily foreseen is the considerable pressure which indeed is already being exerted on universities by market as well as political and social forces. On the one hand, these forces generate competitiveness between universities, but they are also clamouring for the implementation of knowledge led by the economic needs of countries, regions or localities. This pressure may pose a danger when only a short-term view is taken, or, what amounts to the same, when these external and internal forces manage to undermine the universities' mission. This poses much more of a danger to universities in countries with average or low levels of technological progress than in countries with a longer academic or industrial tradition. In these latter countries, society, politicians and the business community have significantly more respect for the creation of knowledge and see it as an asset in the short, medium and long term.

On top of this, there is now a new factor, which may become permanent: the economic or economic financial crisis. There are plenty of examples worldwide of public powers in times of crisis, and indeed in the absence of crisis, failing to see higher education as a national priority, as evidenced by the trimming down of budget allocations in some countries. In addition to this, in many countries there is a strong tendency towards government interventionism with the apparent aim of gaining political control of universities. What is truly perverse about these approaches is that they are being implemented in the full knowledge that societies that deny their universities

autonomy and academic freedom move inexorably towards economic, social and cultural decline.

All the signs suggest that the university is at an interesting and highly significant crossroads. The future university will be different to the one that has existed and evolved over the last thousand years, including the one we have known in the last century. On the path towards this future there are two options: to lead or be led. This means that if the uni versity does not change under its own initiative, its transformation will be managed for it. If it is unable to reinvent its mission, a new mission will be imposed upon it. The smart approach would be to abandon resistance, jump over the barricade and from the other side play a central role in changing twenty-first-century society. A change in which many new factors such as complexity, diversity and sustainability emerge. These and other factors must be considered, directly or indirectly, in the university's response to the challenges of the present century.

Oscar Niemeyer, Mentouri University of Constantine, Algeria (1968)
In his design for this university, the Brazilian architect aimed to facilitate and improve the students' relationship with both the campus and the academic institution. The hallmarks of Niemeyer's style, such as the use of reinforced concrete, purity of form, the combination of curves and prismatic shapes, the creation of open spaces and sensitivity to the surroundings, are all adapted perfectly to the context of the Algerian university.

RESEARCH INSTITUTES AND KNOWLEDGE TRANSFER: A SCANDINAVIAN PERSPECTIVE

In the past forty years there has been a rapid growth in the collaboration between research institutions and industry as well as government, reflecting the changing character of the knowledge society. With their strong emphasis on research and education, the universities do not necessarily address all forms of interaction. Although they produce knowledge, the universities' main 'product' is human capital, in the sense that knowledge primarily migrates from the academic world to society in the form of well educated professionals.

But since the universities mostly work with education and 'free' research, there is also a niche for research institutes that do not get involved in education, and substitute free research for focused contract research. They can also work with topical studies that are 'non-academic' in the sense that they do not fall into the usual departmental categories associated with the typical university organisation. Such topics could be of interdisciplinary character, or aim at applied research with a focus on a narrowed-down area of strategic relevance or importance to infrastructure or government.

Whether research institutes outside the universities have a niche or not depends on whether they can provide research and services that the academic and industrial worlds cannot provide themselves. Industrial R&D needs to be commercially viable and focused, as it is an investment and typically works with strict time constraints. Academic research, on the other hand, primarily focuses on developing knowledge and competence, at a pace governed by the capacity for intellectual growth and the general progress internationally in the field of study. Although there are all kinds of research institutes, covering everything from plain academic research to industrial contract research, it would appear that this form of research has its real niche in non-academic topics, and at a more basic, long-term level than the time scale of typical industrial R&D efforts. For example, there is sometimes a need for government-induced research that is neither academic nor industrial in character, but addressing other issues in society.

Research institutes in Scandinavia have a quite long tradition, but their focus and funding has changed considerably since 1970. The aim of this

Global Seed Vault, Svalbard archipelago, Barents Sea, Arctic Ocean (n.d.)
The government of Norway, which has sovereignty over Svalbard, is one of the main sources of funding for this reinforced vault, which stores seeds from all over the world.

contribution is to give a brief sketch of their development and project a possible future, with a focus on the situation in Sweden.

A Multitude of Research Institutes

Internationally there are many research institutes or organisations that are devoted to what is basically academic research but in a non-university environment. The Max Planck or Fraunhofer institutes are excellent examples. This model is, however, rare in Scandinavia, where there is a strong polarisation between academic research, which is carried out at the universities, and commercial R&D carried out in industry. Research institutes in Scandinavia have typically aimed at bridging this gap.

The number of research institutes in Sweden has varied considerably. There are currently some 30 institutes devoted to applied or industrial research covering areas as diverse as cement and concrete; microelectronics; forestry and wood industry; computer science; metallurgy; surface chemistry; defense; environment; transport, etc., reflecting a cross-section of the country's economic life, from basic industry to high-tech development. About half of the institutes are organisations operated by the state, while the remaining are owned either privately or by foundations, often in the form of joint ownership and operation by industry.

In Norway and Finland a similar approach has been taken, although, especially in the technical sector, with a considerably stronger centralisation. Thus the well known institutes SINTEF (Norway) and VTT (Finland) are huge organizations, with 2,000 and 3,000 employees respectively, and a scientific breadth and competence that indeed make them part of a scientific–industrial infrastructure, where they take on a broad role in research, innovation and knowledge transfer. There is no counterpart to these research organisations in Sweden, where the institutes are always rather small organisations, devoted to special research areas. They typically have fewer than 100 employees. Thus Swedish spending on sector research (research institutes) is relatively small, according to OECD statistics, with most of the research taking place either at the universities or in industrial R&D. The role of the institutes is significantly different from that found in Germany, Holland, France and Italy, for example.

Forty years ago, the typical operation of the Swedish institutes was that part of the funding was provided by the state (say one third), and part by industry (two thirds), with the condition that the state support would be payable if industry chose to participate in the research programme. Thus it was in effect a form of state

The time from basic research to industrial application appears to grow ever shorter. Many areas of research do not only generate new knowledge but also produce potential innovations

subsidy intended to promote long term research that had industrial relevance, although the research usually did not have the character of an industrial R&D project. This model had various degrees of success, depending on the role that long term research played in the various areas. Some highly focused institutes were very successful and developed into today's operations, while others eventually were closed down or merged with academic institutions. An example of the latter was applied and industrial mathematics, which had few industrial partners that identified distinctly with that area. Its state support was finally withdrawn in 2001 and the institute instead became a semi-academic Fraunhofer Institute, which undoubtedly was a more viable format.

The institutes usually work in close collaboration with industry, and may often have a character of providing research consultancy work to the industry. A similar situation can be seen in institutes focusing on government investigations, although the expertise provided there is not aimed at knowledge transfer.

THE FUTURE ROLE OF RESEARCH INSTITUTES

The time from basic research to industrial application appears to grow ever shorter. Further, many areas of research do not only generate new knowledge but also produce potential innovations, and last but not least, modern high-tech industry relies on using cutting-edge technologies with a high R&D content. These factors are typical for the knowledge-based society, and they call for a rapid knowledge transfer.

Research plays a different role under these circumstances, as evidenced by most high-tech industries being located in the vicinity of university environments. In such environments there is often also an emerging industry, growing in research parks or clusters that benefit from being close to a good supply of knowledge and human capital, as well as business opportunities. This means that the research-based infrastructure has become much more dynamic. To some extent this is modelled on the extremely successful Silicon Valley region in the United States, a concept that has also proven successful and vital elsewhere. A rich and complex research infrastructure is believed to be a key ingredient in the knowledge-based society's potential for economic growth.

Do the research institutes fit into this picture? It is a safe guess to suggest that they do, provided that they can find a niche that is not already occupied by the classical university or the already commercialised R&D efforts. They can strengthen academic research by focused efforts, while not having to be involved in the educational duties of a university, and they can assist industry with innovation and long-term industrial research of a more general character. A key question is openness. While the universities are open environments publishing their results, and industry usually considers their R&D proprietary, research institutes can have it either way, depending on the nature of the projects in which they participate. It is

The Phoenix Mission, Arizona (2008)
Cooperation between scientific institutions is becoming increasingly common. This project in Arizona involves research centres and universities from the United States, Switzerland, Denmark, Germany and Finland.

likely that such concerns will play an increasingly important role in the future.

The potential difficulties lie, at least in Scandinavia, with political involvement. Because private universities are rare, and most research funding agencies are government agencies, public research policy plays an extremely important role, and affects the research institutes at least to the extent that they are partly state funded. The present view in public policy appears to push the universities into a more direct involvement with innovation. This seems to reduce the niche for research institutes.

However, whether this line of thought will prevail in a longer perspective is uncertain. After all, it is not realistic to expect universities to take on a role as regional motors of growth in the knowledge-based society. On the contrary, the main tasks of the university remain unchanged: education and open research.

It is the author's present belief that universities will benefit from focusing on these two tasks and excel in their efforts, in order to provide the knowledge and human capital that is needed in the wider context of the knowledge-based society, while efforts directed towards innovation and direct interaction with economic life at large is better left to the research institutes. Nevertheless, the enormous differences in goals and organisations of research institutes throughout Europe indicate that there is probably not one ideal type, size, organisation or goal of a research institute, but that regional differences play a central role in making a research institute effective in its local economic and scientific environment.

Gustaf A. Söderlind

Universities will benefit from focusing on education and open research, in order to provide the knowledge and human capital that is needed in society, while efforts directed towards innovation and direct interaction with economic life at large is better left to the research institutes

The housing 'village' of the student union of the School of Science and Technology, Helsinki (1968)
In Finland there are a number of institutes of technology or centres of applied research. While they are linked to a university, they work on specific projects in close partnership with the world of business.

A Change of Scenario

As we have seen, universities in the twenty-first century must fulfil their mission in a social framework that, almost certainly, will be radically different from the present one. Adoption of this new framework will require from all universities in the world an unprecedented cultural shift which they must effect using a teaching faculty trained in the twentieth century and who, generally speaking, tend to be rather conservative. In this new society, which in many aspects we are incapable of imagining, changes will come in decades or years, instead of over centuries, as happened in the past. Consequently, response time is a new and important variable.

We are in an entirely uncharted scenario in which the most advanced countries are those that are in line with an idea put into words thirty years ago in a report 'Global Competition: The New Reality' by the President's Commission on Industrial Competitiveness in the United States (1985): 'Our universities must play a pivotal role in revitalising our nation's competitiveness [...] Without strong higher education institutions the United States will not be able to capitalise on key strengths in technology and human resources.' This notion is not materialising in the countries where it is most needed, namely those with medium technological levels, and more especially developing countries. As a result, it is fair to say that the new scenario is not general, but depends on the degree of economic development in each country or region. Accordingly, in the most economically advanced countries, the universities have already started to feel emphatic outside pressure to play a more active role in economic development at local, regional and national level. This pressure stems from a belief in the capacity of their university institutions to navigate through uncertainty, their skill in generating advanced knowledge, and their creativity in orienting it, directly or indirectly, towards technology – all in the context of a global world in which the university already feels at home.

In the second half of the twentieth century the so-called 'knowledge economy' emerged, with two new paradigms: intangibles and intellectual capital.

Depending on those two categories, henceforth economic development will be understood in general terms as a process that increases the capacity of individuals and organisations to produce goods and services that generate wealth that, through an adequate social structure, spreads to all the citizens of a country. Against this backdrop, without relinquishing their traditional role, universities must play a pivotal part in the process. A new need has also arisen: lifelong higher education. This is because the productive private sector will need to train its professionals continuously. In short, one might think that, with the necessary changes, education, research and public service actions that are at the heart of the university's mission will persist, as necessities, in this new century. However, although this is true, when defining their national priorities even some developed countries are curbing universities' real capacity to influence their economic development more efficiently by cutting their budget allocation. This is based on a political discourse of demagogy that is frequently aimed at obtaining very short-term results.

Training, Research and Innovation

The chart on the next page schematically depicts the economic development model towards which all countries are moving. Most evidently, knowledge is taking over from commodities. The exception to this rule is energy, the future of which is subject to a worldwide debate at this time. Furthermore, it is a proven fact that in this paradigm, when an adequate rate of development is reached, education ceases to be a social conquest. It becomes a requirement and is needed to maintain and increase the standard of economic development. This is because in the new industrial growth model this is not achieved merely by increasing the size of companies. Older and more recent companies must all use new manufacturing and information technologies. Furthermore, the new sector of companies specialising in high-tech products like advanced materials, biotechnology, robotics, future housing, transportation, etc., is here to stay. In the more developed countries, the new circle is rounded off with the appearance of a large number of services and engineering companies. This ensemble makes up an industrial sector with considerable knowledge-based added value.

In the above analysis we must not forget that the services include so-called cultural, leisure and other services. But neither should we forget that the need for cultural, anthropological and linguistic training has also emerged as a result of globalisation. Furthermore, since much of this change rests on small and medium-sized companies created around cutting-edge technology, the need arises to permanently maintain high creative standards. This means keeping creation (research), knowledge acquisition (training) and speed of response to competitors and clients as active as possible, and in many cases it means a shared use of equipment that is extremely expensive and sophisticated for a small enterprise. Evidently, we are talking about functions to which universities must provide an adequate response. For example, let us overview some of the changes in the productive sector that underlie the ideas sketched here. These changes are triggering the transition from what is now known as a traditional economy into the new framework of the twenty-first century.

Overall, from a technological standpoint, the situation has evolved from one in which a company's founding technology remained active for two or three generations to another in which the technological changes are so swift that living on the knife-edge of obsolescence is normal. Tackling this challenge will require graduates in the productive sector to undergo continuous training throughout their careers. For this new situation, countries and companies need an education and research system of a high standard and with technological transfer capacity. We must not forget that there is currently a progression from a productive sector based on highly differentiated technological fields to new demands deriving from the appearance of so-called emerging technologies. Moreover, these new technologies are based on inter-disciplinary programmes.

There is now a new concept of education which must bring on board professors who, as we indicated above, were themselves trained in the twentieth

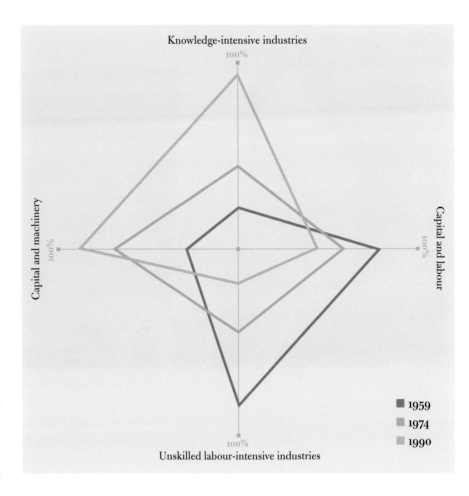

century. This new concept also encounters difficulties when it comes to being accepted by business leaders, who are used to being organised into well-defined specialties. In short, we are talking about the progress from an economy in which human resources were the main production factor to a entirely new scenario in which human resources are the main competitiveness factor. This is a new situation in which people to be recruited are no longer examined according to what they know but according to what they can learn. Those countries that are able to visualise this new scenario will be the front-runners in this century.

In this new framework scenario, higher education must avoid the reductionism associated with science and technology. We are entering an era in which, as a good deal of economic development is linked to technology-based SMEs, the education system will have to generate an innovative, creative and entrepreneurial

Economic development of Japan
The diagram represents evolution towards a sustainable economy based on knowledge-intensive industries. Three stages are shown of Japan's development, identified with the milestones 1959, 1974 and 1990.

***Pikarin* humanoid robot, Tokyo University of Science (2007)**
An increasing number of businesses are specialising in new fields of high technology such as robotics. Research continues to make progress. Professor Hiroshi Kobayashi has developed a robot capable of expressing emotions like happiness, sadness, anger, fear and surprise. Made in the image of Hikari Asano, a student, the robot is invested with a layer of muscles that give it expressive abilities, in a bid to make a machine appear believably human.

mentality among graduates. We are in an environment in which new technologies are being marketed, growth hinges on the development of new businesses and sales are carried out in new markets that require we learn about these new cultures and languages. In conclusion, we are entering uncharted territory: an era inextricably associated with technology, globalisation, rapid change and unpredictability.

As well as the pressure from the productive sector on universities, in this new scenario there is pressure from other spheres, including politics. Governments need a competitive industry to generate new businesses and jobs and to boost voters' wealth. The smaller or more local the context, the greater these needs are. Because universities impact directly and indirectly on these aspirations, governments urge them to engage more directly with these needs, often in exchange for maintaining part of their financing. In parallel, in a lighter form, universities are feeling some social pressure stemming from an entirely superficial analysis of their mission. This pressure is analysed below in relation to the changes that must come in higher education institutions. In any event, it is a public responsibility to prevent these pressures from becoming excessive. If this happens, we run the

risk that the mission of higher education institutions will be left devoid of content, which would jeopardise economic development in the medium and long term. Exactly the opposite of what it is governments' duty to guarantee.

Universities must plan their response to this and other demands analysed below. The smart course of action is to view them as being within the sphere of new opportunities, rather than to position themselves reactively against them. An example of this is the requirement on universities to participate in regional development. Against this backdrop it is vital to create effective strategic alliances between universities, governments and industry. These must generate new dimensions in technological areas and design unexplored teaching and research areas in the field of languages or cultures associated with globalisation. However, it should not be forgotten that there are also some dangers posed by these pressures on universities. Regional commitments must not be allowed to lead to universities performing tasks that are not appropriate; otherwise we can safely say they will irremediably compromise their quality. Lastly, it is worth noting that in some countries governments are taking a very negative, albeit highly tempting, course: to undermine the objective and critical position of university institutions. If they do this, there will certainly be a grave democratic deficit in twenty-first-century society, in which governments administer much of countries' gross national product and control, either directly or indirectly, much of the media.

Seoul National University Museum of Art (SNUMoA), South Korea (2006)
Seoul National University (SNU) is one of the world's fifty leading universities and ranks seventh in Asia, according to the 'World University Rankings 2009' released by *The Times Higher Education Supplement*. With a focus on scientific research, it has taken the innovative step of lending its support to the arts and the world of ideas by founding this art museum, funded by the Samsung Group.

In this new framework scenario, higher education must avoid the reductionism associated with science and technology

African Universities
in the Twenty-first Century

Modern higher education in Africa has its roots in colleges that were created and affiliated to universities in Europe during the colonial period. Right from the start they were patterned on the European higher education system. They were staffed by Europeans or Africans trained in Europe. After independence of the colonies in the 1960s, these colleges became universities and again, their academic structure, curriculum, governance mode and language of instruction were modelled on European universities. Most of them were set up in the major cities and were meant for the minority elite of African society. As a result, they were completely alienated from the rural areas where the bulk of the African population lived and where the needs for development were greatest. Many observers of higher education in Africa today believe that this initial alienation from the rural mass is the core reason why African universities have in the past been unable to contribute fully to the development of their respective countries.

For a couple of decades after independence, the African universities thrived as they received generous support from Europe, and they soon developed into centres of excellence as judged by European university norms. This was true for Makerere University in Uganda, the University of Ibadan in Nigeria, University Cheikh Anta Diop in Senegal and the University of Khartoum in Sudan, to name a few.

The late 1970s and eighties saw a severe deterioration of African economies. There were budget cuts as a result of externally imposed structural adjustment programmes and this affected financing of higher education. Major national and inter-state conflicts followed, accompanied by very poor governance, dictatorship and political repressions. The social unrest in many countries reached university campuses, resulting in the flight of academics to Europe and other countries in the North in order to escape persecution. At the same time, the output from primary and secondary schools started to increase dramatically, placing huge pressures on African universities to increase their student enrolment, well beyond what they could accommodate.

Another major blow came in the 1990s. Some economists came to the conclusion, which later proved to be erroneous, that the rates of return on investments in higher education were lower than in basic education. These findings guided funding and development agencies in the support

University of Cocody-Abidjan,
Ivory Coast (2005)
Professor Gregoire Kouassi Attin teaches an open-air lesson on Abidjan campus. Most university courses display the influence of European methods of higher education.

they provided forAfrican governments, and the latter accordingly made no further investment in higher education. However, throughout the 1980s and nineties, despite being neglected by their own governments and in spite of so many hurdles, universities in Africa survived and managed to do more with the same, sometimes even with less. The resilience of those institutions is truly remarkable.

The turning point in their fate came with the holding of the UNESCO World Conference on Higher Education in 1998. The Conference Declaration strongly emphasised the crucial importance of higher education for all aspects of development. The reform and revitalisation of African universities, with the support of African governments, development partners, and regional and international organisations, then started as from the beginning of the twenty-first century.

What then are the challenges that higher education in Africa faces in the twenty-first century, and what are the key issues that need to be addressed in the revitalisation process?

First, there is an acute shortage of professionals in Africa, and the situation is exacerbated by brain drain. African universities must increase their efforts in the development of human capital, which is crucial for Africa's development. The paradox is that African universities have doubled or even trebled their student enrolment over the past couple of decades and yet, from a regional perspective, Africa has the lowest higher education student participation rate than any other world region. African universities must also develop greater linkages with the world of work to facilitate the employment of their graduates. They must, in particular, give special attention to teacher training and assist in achieving the Education for All (EFA) goals. It is estimated that Sub-Saharan Africa would need well over one million additional teachers in order to achieve universal primary education by 2015. This is a mammoth task, especially because of the loss of teachers as a result of HIV/AIDS and brain drain. There is need for a real partnership to be established between universities, Ministries of Education, development partners and the civil society to address this crisis. Several regional and sub-regional teacher training initiatives have been put in place in Africa, including UNESCO's Teacher Training Initiative for Sub-Saharan Africa (TTISSA) and the International Institute for Capacity in Building Africa (IICBA).

Research plays a key role in the socio-economic development of any country and, in Africa, the bulk of the research is carried out at universities. The statistics show that the research output from Africa is lower than any other world region. The reasons are known and include: poor research infrastructure, including ICT; severe shortage of research-strong (Ph.D.) staff and heavy teaching load of academics. It is also vital for African universities to undertake research that is directly relevant to Africa's development. This requires a multi- and trans-disciplinary approach. It is also very important for the research results

Library of the University of Khartoum, Sudan (1992)
The development of African countries calls for encouraging higher study. The training of academics and the teaching body and a closer connection with the world of work are both of crucial significance.

It is estimated that Sub-Saharan Africa would need over one million additional teachers in order to achieve universal primary education by 2015: a mammoth task, especially because of the loss of teachers through HIV/AIDS and brain drain

to be widely disseminated, through national and regional publications, to all stakeholders, including policy makers, rather than being published in internationally-refereed journals or as monograph theses that are inaccessible to those in real need of the findings.

Poverty alleviation, the first of the Millennium Development Goals, is fundamental to Africa's development. Poverty is worse in Africa's rural areas where about 70 percent of the population live and whose main economic activity is agriculture. Generally, most departments of agriculture of African universities place emphasis on crop and animal production and produce graduates that eventually seek employment in urban areas. The focus of African universities should be promoting rural agricultural development such as food security and life-long learning of farmers and extension workers. Indeed, universities should mainstream rural development in all their teaching, research and community engagement

Departments of agriculture in African universities should allocate most of their resources to promoting rural agricultural development, and thereby emulate the examples set by the University of Development Studies in Ghana and the University of Bakhat Alruda in Sudan

Laboratories at Zimbabwe University (n.d.)
At African universities, research remains at a low standard of achievement. Academic underperformance is largely a function of precarious political and economic frameworks.

activities. Several universities, such as the University of Development Studies in Ghana and the University of Bakhat Alruda in Sudan, have successfully done so and their examples should be emulated.

The development of Africa has been severely hampered by armed conflicts. There has been a noticeable improvement in the twenty-first century but conflicts have left deep scars of suffering, abuses and mistrust which can easily cause resurgence. African universities have responded positively to promoting peace and assisting in resolving conflict over the past two decades. Centres or institutions for peace have been created in several universities in, for example, Sudan, Rwanda and Nigeria. Peace programmes or undergraduate modules exist in universities in most sub-regions of Africa. The University for Peace (UPEACE), a UN-affiliated institution, launched its Africa Programme in 2002 and runs short courses and workshops on conflict resolution and management and has developed materials and resources for universities. All these efforts must be relentlessly pursued and extended.

Good governance, both of nations and institutions, has emerged as a major issue in Africa. Universities have a fundamental role to play here. They must endeavour to produce graduates that are responsible citizens, imbued with ethics and values. And universities themselves must set the example by managing their affairs in an open, fair, democratic and consultative manner.

While African universities have to concentrate on their national and regional priorities, they cannot ignore the fact that they now operate in an increasingly globalised world. Also, higher education has now become a global, tradable and competitive commodity and this can threaten the development of national publicly-funded universities. At the same time, African universities must recognise that they form part of the global knowledge society from which they can benefit and to which they need to contribute. Their challenge, then, is that they have to be globally connected and locally relevant. In this process, the African Diaspora can be immensely helpful.

To meet all these challenges African universities need considerable financial resources, both within and outside the continent. Since the beginning of the twenty-first century the international community has expressed willingness to assist higher education in Africa and has mustered appropriate resources. The danger is that, with the recent economic downturn, national education budgets and external development financing are coming under increasing pressure, which can threaten the whole revitalisation process of Africa's higher education. African universities, in consortium with universities around the world, must therefore continue to advocate for the development of higher education, all the more so in developing countries, as it is critical for national and global sustainable development in the twenty-first century.

Goolam Mohamedbhai

Students at an economics lecture, Harvard Business School, McCollum Hall, Harvard University (c. 1985)
Harvard University tops the league table of the world's ten leading institutions of higher learning. Founded in 1908, its prestigious Business School has trained world leaders in business, finance and politics. Harvard opened its first off-campus research site in 1997 in Silicon Valley, California, followed by further sites in the Asia-Pacific region, Latin America, Japan, Europe and India.

If the university wants to continue to be true to its mission, it will not be enough to simply cut costs and increase productivity. There must be a sea-change in the financing model for higher education that will need greater independence in the case of public universities, as well as a different way of running and managing them

A New Model: Entrepreneurial University

In the wake of the euphoria generated by the economic prosperity at the end of the twentieth century, the start of the twenty-first looks set to be an era in which higher education ceases to be a public priority, even in developed countries. Indeed, in some of these this has already been the case in the last twenty-five years. A good example of this is what has happened in the United States. First, a great government effort was made, spurred by the successes of science in the Second World War and the desire to maintain the country's international leadership. As the echoes of triumph faded, governments' contribution to university budgets began to shrink, and has been declining steadily for more than two decades.

Accordingly, in this new century universities will suffer the consequences of a major contradiction. The new economic development model has generated an increase in demand for higher education services. In addition to this trend, politicians are managing to bore their compatriots with a repetitive discourse in which they depict training as the core of economic development but, in many countries, there is a degree of demagogy in this message. On the one hand, they assert that they have the largest number of trained youngsters in history; a situation that involves an increase in costs for universities if they are to maintain their quality standards. On the other hand, and in stark contradiction, all the signs point to a decline in the public contribution to sustaining higher education. This is because politicians, notoriously obsessed with the short term, when it comes to allocating priorities are hardly going to wonder seriously about the possible repercussions of the financial strangling of higher education for the future of their countries. It is evident that if budgets are trimmed, public universities, unless able to obtain other funds, will have to reduce the number of activities in which they are involved and, more importantly, the quality thereof. In this likely scenario they will have to implement new initiatives or strengthen some of the existing ones. Although this point will be returned to later on, a preliminary comment is introduced here in regard to one of the initiatives already

being applied in some places. We refer to the option, for universities with significant independence, to maintain quality standards by raising student fees. This measure, applied at many prestigious private universities, has little chance of prospering at public institutions, since it could fuel a not inconsiderable social conflict. However, as we shall see, it might also be considered within the social framework of equal opportunities.

In this foreseeable new financial scenario, if the university wants to continue to be true to its mission, it will not be enough to simply cut costs and increase productivity. There must be a sea-change in the financing model for higher education that will need greater independence in the case of public universities, as well as a different way of running and managing them. Leaders will also be needed who combine a high standard of academic and professional qualifications with organizational skills to match those required in a business environment.

Before discussing this new model it is first necessary to devote a few lines to explaining the origin of financing in public universities. Today, broadly speaking much of the activity at universities is financed by the various public administrations in each country. Funds are also obtained from public programmes and private R&D activities, donations, contracts and private aid for activities other than the two most classic ones (regulated education and basic or fundamental research), and lastly from the fees paid by students, which in some countries are symbolic. The weighting of each of these contributions varies considerably between public and private universities, and even more so from one country to another. In this regard, the latest OECD report indicates that the part of the cost of university teaching covered by the government ranges between 97 percent in Norway and 34 percent in the United States. Fees paid by students vary accordingly: from 36.3 percent in the United States to 3 percent in Norway and 5.4 percent in Austria. However, in the case of the United States a sizeable 29.7 percent is raised through grants and private subsidies. In the United States, in 1998 there were thirty-one universities with revenue from interest on endowments in excess of one billion dollars. Evidently, this is not the general rule in the United States and much less so in the rest of the world. Many universities have increased their efforts in other actions linked to technology transfer, consultancy, health centres or continuing education, to cite a few examples. In this regard, it is fair to say that universities are starting to open up to a culture that was previously distant from them: entrepreneurial culture.

This entrepreneurial culture has a much broader meaning in the university segment than in the productive private sector. It includes actions ranging from recruiting the most able students to competing for funds available in the R&D market, whether private or public. In some countries there is even competition to secure endowments, which, as we have seen, can play a highly significant role in a university's budget. In fact, we are faced with a new and highly complex scenario. It implies a transition, from a financial standpoint, from a university formulated under a social and cultural umbrella to one in which the activities that have more to do with the economic component are increasingly important. It is a model that strengthens the university's own skill and ability to attract public and private funds from various sources. It is a model which, in the first place, must adapt to the new management and organisation methods of the chancellorships, faculties, departments and professors. It is a model which must eliminate the present fragmentation. This will make it much easier to market the results of research or the supply of new services (educational, senior consultancy, advisory services to public administration, etc.).

However, the danger of this new culture is that, taken to the limit, it might make the university into a 'marketplace' in which programmes and activities are implemented in line with their financing, instead of being inserted into a country's strategic planning, and, even more worryingly, the essence of what a higher education institution is might even be lost. A clear example of this is the diminishing offering in humanities and even in some sciences and engineering specialities in favour of more popular courses relating to business, trade and natural sciences. The reduction in the number of students skilled in physics and mathematics and those focusing on technological areas triggered a major rethink by the United States government and measures were implemented during President Clinton's time in office. The same situation is being observed throughout Europe, and this led the European Union to commission a study on the loss of competitiveness and its relationship with the reduction, in terms of quality and quantity, in the number of science and engineering students. This study has unfortunately only had repercussions in some, but not all, European countries and, therefore, only in some, but not all, universities. Returning to the humanities, it is worth keeping in mind their significant contribution to a country's GDP.

However, if the model is taken to the extreme, we would be left with an entrepreneurial university, even a public one, that would cease to programme any activities in which, to put it crudely, 'the figures don't add up'. This would run the risk of completely undermining the uncompromising demand for high standards that, through legacy and tradition, the university has had in its commitment to society. This is what makes it so relevant to conduct a weighted analysis of the positive factors and the risks of the new model. Although many will become clear over time, it is important to try and foresee them as far as possible. Accordingly, although we are only at the outset of the debate, there have already been some highly thought-provoking discussions in relation to the new model. The first to emerge, pushed into the limelight by the academic world in particular, is the possible loss of the culture of *open science*. There is no overlooking the need for a balanced commitment between the effort to generate knowledge and the effort to apply it. This challenge will require, among other things, changing the parameters of merit in the systems used to assess teaching staff. A second focus of debate is related to the loss of independence of institutions, research and professors, due to the requirements imposed by contracts with private institutions. Another important issue is the possible concentration of private financing in a small number of higher education institutions, a situation which could bring highly negative consequences on regional economic development. Another immediate problem, already indicated in the discussion of open science, has to do with the effort that an entrepreneurial university must make in basic or fundamental research. This is actually an issue of the medium and long term versus the short term, or research and teaching areas more tailored to the needs of the productive sector versus those that are far-removed from it. Last, but by no means least, it is vital to distribute time between research and teaching in a balanced manner.

This discussion is important enough to merit additional examination. Due to social image issues, the budget alternative that is winning most support is that of financing a substantial part of university costs with contracted research, and with public aid for fundamental research. This may tip the delicate balance between education and research in the latter's favour, as is already the case in basic research. This has implied that today questions are being raised about the role of research, starting with basic research, as part of a university's mission. The arguments indicating that the major educational needs of tomorrow no longer point to research but to teaching are no longer anachronistic. It is tantamount to asserting that the university must make sure that its teaching faculty spend much of their time on what is the essence of their mission, namely teaching. The risk of losing this will be avoided if, in the case of a reduction in the public contribution to the budget, the alternative includes a balanced increase in fees and the hiring of services (research, knowledge).

There follows a discussion of this last point, which will no doubt become the subject of extensive debate in all developed countries. In view of this new situation, which is already the reality in some countries and is likely to be in others, the paradigmatic change put forward in the 1990s takes on new relevance. At that time it was suggested that the prices of universities be assigned in the same way as food or clothing prices were set. However, the university is not a consumer good with an expiry date. It is a long-term investment, based on the capacity to learn, which university graduates acquire for the rest of their lives. From this standpoint, higher education might be seen as the most important investment in a professional's lifetime, more so than a car or a home. From this perspective it is possible to see the financing of university studies in a similar way to Social Security,

public healthcare or a home purchase. One might even consider passing on the cost of higher education from one generation to the next – although only those citizens who have themselves visited the classrooms would be expected to finance them. They would also be repaying the funds at a time of their lives in which they are able to do so. In short, higher education is being seen not as a public good but as a private commodity with social repercussions. This model does not clash with the classical social approach, subject to the principle of equal opportunities, since access to higher education would depend on students' efforts, not on their parents' financial resources. One way or another, this debate will enable developed societies to overcome this challenge and the final solution will represent progress, even in social terms. The problem is greater for developing countries. For these nations, not only would the access of many able young people to classrooms be genuinely limited, but this limitation would be catastrophic for their economic development. They therefore need to find and implement creative measures to enable them to make the next step forward that they so badly need.

The above comments are but modest proof of how important it is to begin this debate as soon as

Student protest, Sydney (2005)
In the twenty-first century, university protests and demonstrations tend to voice dissent regarding university funding. Here, the faculty and students of an Australian university are demonstrating against the Government, which they accuse of seeking to create a two-tier system of education.

318

possible. Institutions that fail to begin a process of reflection as time flows on inexorably may find themselves in situations that are almost irreversible. Perhaps the first subject of reflection is how to incorporate entrepreneurial bias into an institution where this has not hitherto been part of its cultural reality. Traditionally, universities are, broadly speaking, non-profit organisations. This has had and continues to have a significant impact on administrative, organisational and cultural aspects. Due to its antagonism with the entrepreneurial option it is evident that it will need to adapt to the new challenges. Another fundamental need in the economic sphere is to banish the idea, more widespread in public universities, that all activities conducted by universities are necessary and worthwhile. Their governing structure makes it very difficult, if not impossible, to relocate resources in order to undertake new activities that might, in turn, generate new funds and offer new services. But the most important change must come in how the institutions are managed, organised and governed. It cannot be overlooked that the shift from a traditional university to a more complex institution has not been accompanied by the incorporation of some of the tools that make business institutions work.

In conclusion, it is safe to say that sooner or later the model will be changed. This change will be triggered not only by a reduction in public contributions to the budget but also by the need to respond to the new demands of twenty-first-century society. As regards the costs generated, laboratories, salaries, infrastructure, maintenance, etc., in general, they are quite well defined in all the universities of the world. Nevertheless, these expenses have outpaced inflation in the last few years at most universities. Another different aspect is that, in budget terms, there are major differences from one university to the next and, in particular, from one country to the next. At all events, looking ahead, the main cost hikes will be imposed, increasingly so, by the so-called market forces. These will force in new programmes, higher quality and, in general, a better service.

Quality, Excellence and Innovation: The University's Watchwords

To further the analysis, another factor that looks set to be pivotal in the new model of the university in the twenty-first century is quality. From the standpoint of knowledge, many universities have traditionally employed prestigious professors specialising in quality subjects. However, while in the productive sector quality has been associated with industrial competitiveness and reducing costs, at universities this has scarcely come into play and quality has actually been associated with an increase in spending. In this new century, one of the challenges facing higher education is to understand what quality means for the university. The institution must identify its customers, learn from their needs and expectations, and, based on the conviction that it must implement a specific quality system, it must make every effort to apply what has been learned.

With this new approach the university will be able to trim off unnecessary costs, in other words, to achieve higher quality in its mission at a lower cost. It will do this by eliminating those activities that do not impact directly on the customer or consumer, as well as those others that contribute little added value. Furthermore, due to the special characteristics of the university, implementation of a quality system must generate internal services at a much better price than in the open market. In order to attain the highest possible degree of excellence, the analysis must pinpoint all those critical activities that help to achieve this goal. At the same time those institutions worldwide that best perform these activities should come under analysis. Success can only come if the leaders of each university see quality as something central to their institutional strategy. The idea is to be the best at what we want to do or, what amounts to the same thing, to treat quality and excellence as a strategic opportunity.

The following illustrates what we have said so far. If a university wants to compete for the best students, it needs to have the best professors. In the Anglo-Saxon world, this amounts to budget. It is an example of the impact upon costs of the increase in knowledge. Furthermore, we should not forget that the

Analysing a palimpsest projected onto a screen (2003) Lecturers at Johns Hopkins University scrutinise a palimpsest using digital projections onto multiple screens. The text appears under normal light on the left, ultraviolet light in the centre, and, to the right, under a combination of both – the image thus achieved does not accurately recreate the colour of the original but is ideal for making out the writing. This research forms part of the Archimedes Project, concerned with the study and decipherment of ancient manuscripts.

quality of professors and students is the factor that weighs most heavily in the rankings of university excellence. In countries where the universities' mission is respected, these league tables have a fundamental impact on their revenues, both public and private, as well as on the number and quality of students that apply to study in them. The most highly ranked universities are those which wield the biggest budgets and receive the most funds, public and private. They also happen to be the ones with the best laboratory, library and services infrastructure.

In any case, it should not be overlooked that, unlike in the productive sector, there is no road map to ensure implementation of quality in higher education. There is a major difference in this regard between, for example, industry or healthcare and the university. In the first two, quality has been a necessity and a requirement for some time. In universities, we are still in a phase of convincing those who are not yet convinced. The main problem is that some of the critical elements for implementing quality, such as team work, discipline and hierarchy are, in principle, incompatible with some of the universities' more special characteristics, such as individuality, creativity and innovation. The challenge is to render these qualities and factors compatible with each other. To tackle this challenge and other similar ones – that are directly or indirectly linked to universities' economies, but also to their missions – a vital step is to choose leaders who are well trained for their posts. Here we return to an area that must necessarily change: the way universities are governed.

We must not forget that universities have always been the institutions of innovation, so it would be a failure for them and a serious setback for society if this characteristic were to be erased. To prevent universities from losing this initiative, public administrations cannot and must not trigger a financial collapse. At the same time they must stop trying to exercise control of the public universities through limiting and stringent legislation. With regard to future innovation, universities must cease to seek support solely in budget increases from the administration. They will also have to be more demanding and careful in choosing their priorities, something that, if they do it well, will show those who manage public and private financial resources that universities are serious about tackling cost and efficiency issues. Innovation must also be evidenced through management, organisation and government. In reference to these factors one might say that in this new century universities must use innovative ideas to tackle three major challenges: cost cuts, productivity increases and quality enhancement. Although this may seem like an arduous task, we should not lose sight of the fact that these objectives have been successfully achieved in other spheres of society.

In the case of universities, the basis of this change is found in a new line of argument for decision-making. Until now, decisions emanated from an introspective approach, whereas in the future it is vital to add the perspective afforded by a lucid understanding of the needs of the world around us. The start of this century will see the end of an era in which it was enough to have high-quality academic staff and students. We are in a new era now, in which it is indispensable to think about students' productivity, what they need to learn and what society requires from education and research. At all events, we must be aware that, due to its complexity, the process might fail even if it is tackled with the utmost professionalism once the mission of the institution has been reformulated.

The universities of the twenty-first century, due to the now-confirmed erosion in government contributions to their budgets and to the external demands of the new society, can no longer simply draft their budgets as they do now, in other words based on those of the previous year plus an increment for a handful of specific new actions, which, in general, are not subject to any strategic planning. There must be a substantial change in the way budgets are drafted in the future. They must be much more innovative and implemented as part of a broader strategic plan. Accordingly, universities will have to learn to define priorities and seek the funds to cover them. There can be no repeat of something we have seen in the last few years: cost per student, even at the best-funded universities in the world, has increased faster than the consumer price index. This is partial but nonetheless significant evidence of the inefficiency in the way the university system is run. Within the framework of an entrepreneurial university, this cost will be calculated according to the level and quality of the academic programmes offered by the institution; a parameter which is already being used in some public universities in some countries. However, in most, costs are still being allocated in accordance with the budget transferred from the administration.

In places where the government totally or partially accepts the cost per student in line with the level of academic programmes, the public budget allocation is performed directly or indirectly. In the first case, an amount is transferred directly to the university, while in the second case it is the student who receives the funding. The second option introduces a considerable factor of competitiveness. The aforementioned paradigmatic change in reference to considering higher education as a public or private good will have a significant impact here.

As a preliminary conclusion, one might say that in the framework of the entrepreneurial university, the current system, which is the prevailing one in so-called 'Latin' countries, where the university management structure is highly centralised, will no longer be valid. Another quite innovative option is that of some private universities, in general those offering the greatest standards of excellence, in which the management of funds is entirely decentralised. This is an option whose general validity is highly problematic, since it depends on a large number of exogenous and endogenous factors. Since the first option is entirely inadequate, and the second difficult to apply, it seems reasonable to assume that universities must evolve towards an intermediate solution, applicable at both private and public universities. In this option, decision-making must involve academic and administrative units as well as the central government. In short, it is a quest for cooperation based on affording much greater authority and independence to those responsible for academic units. They would be involved in strategic decisions and, from a practical standpoint, they would take responsibility for the funds they generate or obtain. In this alternative, since it will be more participative, the university governing system will be more complex and will have different repercussions on professors and structural units (faculties, departments, institutes, etc.). There is again a palpable need to undertake the analysis of how universities are governed, a path on which some institutions have already embarked.

In short, universities will be faced with three possible options to secure the future of their mission. The first is for governments to think that higher education is a public good and therefore all members of each generation will pay for the studies of those privileged to study at university in the next generation. The second is for the price increases in university education to reflect the real costs. In this case, some people suggest that an attempt at reducing fees is no more than highly regressive social policy that subsidises the rich at the expense of the poor. Lastly, in the third option only part of a generation, the part that has actually studied, pays for the next; this will be the prevailing option if, as many people expect, there is a significant decline in the public financing made available to higher education.

WORLD-CLASS UNIVERSITIES

Society has changed and the transformations, mainly in the contemporary world, point to an intense globalisation process. According to *The New York Times* columnist Thomas Friedman, 'the world is flat', and this is the result of globalisation in which diversity has been highlighted as an important factor that must be managed. This involves participation in a more competitive world than ever, where knowledge assumes a higher relevance than before and where quality is the main requirement for differentiation.

According to UNESCO, living in a 'knowledge society' implies 'increasing technological capacities by combining traditional and modern methodologies to stimulate scientific creation and lead to sustainable human development'.

Higher education must be a permanent concern in this society and its social responsibility must be always emphasised. There are many challenges to be faced in this field, especially in underdeveloped or developing countries. The 2009 World Conference on Higher Education held in Paris on 5 to 8 July, emphasised the responsibility of each country to 'invest in higher education as a major force in building an inclusive and diverse knowledge society and to advance research, innovation and creativity'.

Internationalisation, regionalisation and globalisation were also discussed in the Conference and questions arose about the role for international cooperation and the need for international, regional and national dimensions in teaching and research in the institutions. Those features lead us to think about the role of 'world-class' universities in the higher education agenda.

According to Simon Schwartzmann, a Brazilian sociologist, 'world-class universities are the only intelligent way of dealing with the globalisation trends of higher education'. His concept implies that those university categories are not only responsible for science and technology development, but also for culture, general formation, knowledge and the ability to understand what is going on in the country and in the world as well. Besides, the quality with which they

Lawrence Hall of Science, University of California, Berkeley (*c.* 1991)
Two scientists work with the periodic table of elements with the aid of a huge backlit panel. World-class universities go to great lengths to provide academics with all the resources they need to conduct their research effectively. The latest and most sophisticated technologies are introduced on a continuing basis.

develop those activities must be considered a standard for other institutions.

But what is the definition of a 'world-class' university? This is not an easy question to be unequivocally answered. Although Altbach has pointed out a paradox in world-class universities (in his words 'everyone wants one, no one knows what it is and no one knows how to get one'), he stated the main characteristics of a world-class institution as follows: research excellence, freedom in research, education and expression, academic autonomy, infrastructure, financial support, cosmopolitanism and diversity.

With the purpose of setting out a more 'manageable' definition, Jamil Salmi, the author of the *Challenge of Establishing World-Class Universities*, has considered three groups of factors that are complementary and summarises the features mentioned above: high concentration of talent among faculty and students; abundant resources, to provide suitable conditions for learning and developing research at advanced levels; and favorable governance, which comprises strategic design that stimulates future vision and innovation, besides systems that avoid the undesirable influence of bureaucracy in academic activities.

Although world rankings are generally limited and may vary significantly, they are able to recognise the world-class universities due to their outstanding performance in the qualification of graduates who are well-placed in the market and in the development of high level research. Depending on the institution, the contribution to patents and licences can also be considered, as Salmi notes.

THE UNIVERSITY OF SÃO PAULO AS A WORLD-CLASS UNIVERSITY

According to Salmi, an institution cannot declare itself to be a world-class university. On the contrary, this depends on external classification following strong international recognition. The University of São Paulo (USP) has deserved this status.

USP is amongst the two hundred top universities in the world, according to the most authoritative world rankings of the best universities. It is the 196th in *The Times Higher Education Supplement* 2008 ranking; the 121st in Shanghai Jiao Tong University's 2008 ranking; 78th according to the Higher Education Evaluation & Accreditation Council of Taiwan, 2009; 38th in Webometrics Ranking of World Universities, July 2009; and 16th in the 2009 World Report of SCImago Institutions Rankings (SIR). In the 2009 rankings it is the leader in Latin America.

The prominent position USP occupies in the world accounts for its growing international visibility in different activities, mainly

World-class universities distinguishes between high concentration of talent, abundant resources, and favorable governance

in research activities. This is based on its position in the most accepted world rankings, especially in the Higher Education Evaluation & Accreditation Council of Taiwan, whose criteria include an institution's performance, the impact of its research and its scientific productivity.

The internationalisation of USP has been a priority in the last four years and it has involved mainly students' and professors' mobility, international partnerships and international shared graduate programmes as well as cotutelle doctorates.

Thanks to the significant investments made between 2005 and 2008, an increase of almost 61 percentage in foreign undergraduate students at USP and of about 97 percentage in USP undergraduate students in foreign institutions was registered. At the graduate level, an increase of around 104 percentage and 40 percentage respectively was observed in the same period. Meanwhile, an increment of approximately 138 percentage of visiting professors at USP was derived from institutional programmes promoted together with the graduate and research pro-rectorships. This interchange has been strengthened considerably and is also responsible for the increase in reciprocal international agreements and partnerships. In December 2008, 435 international academic agreements were signed with institutions all over the five continents and more than 300 were under discussion. A 38 increase in the partnerships since 2005 was then observed as a result of the strong commitment of the institution to its internationalisation.

International shared graduate programmes have been stimulated and the first was launched in 2007. This is a tripartite doctorate programme – the students will be titled by the three institutions – on Molecular Plant Biology, created by Escola Superior de Agricultura 'Luiz de Queiroz' in conjunction with Rutgers University and Ohio State University.

USP's high scientific productivity and its impact have been highlighted in publications that reflect the excellence in research developed at the University by its more than 1,800 certified research groups, which include undergraduate and graduate students as well as researchers and doctors. About 26 percentage of the indexed papers published in Brazil from 1996 to 2006 were from USP which experienced a 200 percentage increase in its publication rate during this period. Moreover, from 2005 to 2008, there was an increment of about 58 percentage in indexed publications. A policy of multidisciplinary research has been formulated and strategic networks have been created for the study of Bioenergy, climate change and unrecognised diseases.

Part of the financial resources of the University comes from the São Paulo government and comprises about 5 percent of state income tax, which amounted to around 1.2 million US dollars in 2008. About 270 million US dollars came from public state and federal agencies and

The University of São Paulo from the air (c. 1980)
The University of São Paulo (USP) is the public university of São Paulo state, Brazil. Created 75 years ago, the university operates 40 faculties, seven special institutes, two hospitals and their ancillary departments, and seven associate institutions across the state. The student body – which numbers 80,000, undergraduates and graduates combined – is taught by a staff of over 5,000 lecturers.

from other sources, including private ones as well, and are only directed to research development.

Having decided that institutional planning and administration are essential for a governing body to operate efficiently, the USP implemented a programme of strategic management (called GESPUBLICA), which removed unnecessary bureaucracy from the University's administration and thereby made the system more streamlined.

In conclusion, it can be said that USP has the key features of a world-class university and the responsibility of advancing its academic leadership both nationally and internationally with the aim of contributing significantly to the sustainable development of the country.

Suely Vilela

Butantan Institute, São Paulo (2008)
Associated with the University of São Paulo, the Butantan Institute has built up a century of experience classifying and studying snakes from across the South American continent. Its facilities store close to 75,000 meticulously classified snake specimens preserved in formaldehyde: undoubtedly the world's largest collection. The Butantan Institute's research plays a leading international role in the study of poisons and development of antidotes.

Changes to Meet New Demands

At present, there is every indication that the university of the twenty-first century will need to bring some business philosophy into its culture. It must be able to respond to the needs of society with new educational services or to compete to recruit the best students, professors and researchers and to secure the most promising research projects. However, an entrepreneurial model taken to the limit could jeopardise some of the essential elements that, historically, universities have contributed to society. These include, most notably, because of its frame of reference, the education of citizens. This point is fulfilled by those universities that are able to offer their students, as well as specialist teaching, the cultural legacy and, above all, the adequate critical capacity to live and work in a democratic society. Universities will therefore have to courageously and imaginatively undertake the changes which this new framework will require, but at the same time be aware that there is a fundamental aspect of their mission which simply cannot be buried.

Open Learning Environments

Consequently, change must fundamentally transform those methods that are rooted in internal and personal motivations. For example, the twentieth-century university in many countries has exercised iron-fisted control over the subjects available for study and the academic qualifications that governments officially validated. The downside of this is not the control in itself, but the fact that it maintains closed training systems, which in many cases have even determined the number of professionals who have exercised their profession during the course of the century. In short, a monopoly was established that in many cases stemmed from the desires and needs of institutions and professors instead of catering for the requirements of students and society at large. In fact, to obtain the certificate that signified official recognition from governments and professional associations, students had to learn more than their professors decided to teach them. Evidently, we are looking at a

university that is teaching-biased instead of learning-biased or, what amounts to the same, biased towards what students should nurture and cultivate. However, entry into a new century is causing people to question this monopolistic approach with the emergence of open learning environments and the deregulation of so-called 'official qualifications'.

Open learning environments are creating a growing knowledge industry linked to the need for training throughout people's professional career. Consequently, expert consultancy firms, postgraduate schools and knowledge networks that have nothing to do with higher education institutions are starting to emerge. This knowledge industry is already acting as an external force in the university environment. It is a good example that validates the need to change the approach of institutions offering higher education in this new century. This change will come despite the resistance of a good many academics, who have always exercised tight control in universities, especially public ones.

Governments have also had a huge controlling influence through both budgets and legislation. This control is an added risk since, in general, it limits the independence of public universities to begin their transformation. One example of the constraints derived from this dual control is a long-standing and interesting proposal linked to the teaching-learning binomial. During the 1990s a university teaching model was put forward that involved students as an active learning element. Students would be able to choose from different options in the learning environments of various faculties. In other words, under certain guarantees, students could design their own curriculum. Something approaching this model had been applied and experimented thirty years before at the various sites of Spanish university. We can now find another example in Europe, as university programmes are adapting to the new Bologna Process. This was a great opportunity to reflect calmly as the twenty-first century unfolds. Instead, most countries regressed to the same old twentieth-century approaches. The habits acquired by professors and, in some cases, the interests of professional associations, have prevailed over the needs of modern society and the interests of students.

Need for a Strategic Approach

We have seen that in universities change is driven mainly by three forces: social, economic and technological. For example, with respect to the position described by Lobkowicz in reference to German universities – where the professors decided what was to be taught, how it was taught and even when and where it was taught – the aforementioned forces demand a new focus in which universities basically consider the needs of students in this century. At all events, it is evident that a swift and adequate response to the new demands will show that higher education institutions are able to serve the needs of a changing society, indeed a changing world. This response should not pose a problem for universities, since other sectors of society with significantly less innovative and creative tradition have already been able to tackle it. The danger is when the transformation is conducted as a reaction instead of a strategic approach. In the first case, universities will lag behind change, and in the second they will spearhead it.

However, the strategic approach widely disseminated in industrial sectors, has traditionally been met with opposition in universities. Despite this, a large number of universities are making an effort in this connection; but the methodological rigour and, in particular, the degree of implementation, are still a long way off what has been achieved in the industrial sector. Anyway, it is a proven fact that universities that have made the effort are presently much better prepared to tackle the challenges of the twenty-first century. Having reached this point, it is interesting to analyse some of the factors that hamper universities in devising and, fundamentally, implementing strategic plans. The first of these has to do with personal attitudes among professors and academic authorities. Both segments believe that the university is not susceptible to major change due to the constraints upon it linked to its tradition, culture and complexity, which make it difficult to run and even ungovernable. Underlying this idea is a certain passivity towards

working to objectives, which constantly leads to discussion about *how* to do, instead of *what* to do. This leads to countless empty debates that are far removed from the real needs of society. This manner of operating was less obvious in the past, when society changed more slowly. However, it cannot be maintained now, in which society is undergoing swift and sweeping transformations. Indeed, the university must not content itself with adapting to the demands of change, but must be able to keep one step ahead in order to influence the content of that change. Universities that have in the past set up strategic planning units that have earned the respect of their academic community have already achieved a lot. These institutions are working with priorities defined by pinpointing the activities that are likely to disappear, to be strengthened or to be newly launched. All of these aspects enabled many universities in the United States to overcome the crisis of the 1980s, and the same is likely to be true of the current crisis.

Students at a conference, University of Pretoria, South Africa (2007)
Founded in 1908, the University of Pretoria is South Africa's largest. Spread across six campuses, the largest being Hatfield, its associated institutions include Pretoria Central Hospital. The university currently offers over 1,800 courses taught in the two official languages of South Africa: English and Afrikaans. In 2008, enrolment stood over 57,000 students.

Universities Spearheading Change

If universities are to spearhead change they must implement courageous and flexible strategic planning that establishes qualitative objectives in the framework of a new university culture. Basically, we are talking about a revision of the mission of universities, adapting it to the requirements of a new society that calls for the definition of a new social contract. Within this framework, the institution must plan in the short, medium and long term, based on quantitative actions. To overcome the intrinsic difficulties, this process means that each university must have a number of skilled leaders. The latter must convince all those who are reticent (generally speaking, this may be a numerous group). Furthermore, they must take risks in the less productive part of the s-curve. And it will be precisely risk, unpredictability, participation and questioning of classical paradigms that constitute the most appealing intellectual elements to encourage the most prestigious academics to come on board.

The difficulties in this endeavour are compounded by the impediments, as we shall see later, to exercising real leadership in universities. In addition is the conservative nature of the institution itself and of many of its academics. Accordingly, there are not many examples of institutional transformations led by strategic decisions and planning deriving therein. More common are transformations due to reactive changes. Evidently, this does not mean that the university is not capable of defining its own destiny: it is amply skilled to do so; it simply has to want to. This will require a new kind of organisation that includes some of its many talented people and incorporates a new way of governing. It will also require a major intellectual transformation to eliminate certain millstones from the past, useful once, but no longer serving any purpose in the new environment. Due to the rapid changes – some almost disjointed leaps in time – the university must establish new relationships with the external elements with which it interacts, and this will require a deep-rooted cultural change inside the institution itself.

Strategic planning has been the subject of a number of publications, related mainly to the business world. Since it is a highly technical and extensive area, we will not delve into its content but cite it succinctly. Here, we will make reference only to those special aspects that relate most closely to higher education institutions. As a general rule it is safe to say that the early phases are shaped by resistance to change and even disputes born of serious disagreements. At all events, the starting point is to set up a team able to lead the process. In this team, as well as the chancellor and vice-chancellors, it is vital to include deans, directors, some administrative personnel and some academic leaders. It is also vital to create a consultancy group comprising academic experts in these areas. The first challenge is to include in the debates the largest possible number of members of the university community, in particular the best professors and students. For this purpose, the team leading the process must make an exceptional effort to integrate them.

In parallel, all the activities performed by members of the institutions anticipating change must be identified. For example, institutes, laboratories, departments or academics with significant external connections (corporate, administrative, cultural, linked to the demand for training, etc.) will be the right bodies or people to lead universities into new markets or design the new array of knowledge-based services. And it will be no less vital to expand the range of services offered. In both cases, for what already exists and for what is newly generated, a generous allocation of financial resources and incentives must be put in place in order to consolidate them. In this process leaders must be in possession of moral, as well as administrative, authority. Where this is absent it is often due to universities being governed in a centralised, closed and isolated manner, wasting the huge intellectual riches they might otherwise use to trigger change. As a final remark, it is worth taking into account that any renewal at universities often runs considerable risks. It is the transition between two stable states through one that involves disconcerting instability.

A good example of strategic planning is the one conducted over two tranches by the University of Michigan. The first came in the period 1980–91, and was called 'Vision 2000'. The leaders of this plan managed to create a campus culture in which excellence and innovation were the priorities. Furthermore, they managed to show that a public university can secure a major private contribution to its budget. The success of this effort was confirmed by entry of the University of Michigan into the worldwide elite. Since at the time the plan did not clearly entail entry into the twenty-first century, it has recently begun implementing 'Vision 2017', in order to take on the new challenges of a period of great upheaval and to maintain the excellence and leadership it has achieved.

Change as a Learning Process

Realistically, it has to be said that the transformation of universities – which is inevitable, and indeed at some universities is already underway – must be seen as a learning process, since change is more sweeping than was thought and the response time required is unprecedented. There is even talk of a theory of institutional change. Along this road, the first thing to do is to make a list of everything that needs changing at what might now be called the 'traditional university'. For example, at the present time undergraduate education, regardless of country, is obliged by regulations to include certain academic disciplines that are offered at a professional school or faculty. If an open learning system is implemented, where students can choose, this approach becomes completely obsolete. Similarly, a long list must be compiled of activities and rules at traditional universities which must mutate. The next step is to analyse the changes towards the twenty-first-century university. There follows, for illustrative purposes, a list of some of those which appear to already be incorporated into the process of transformation. Furthermore, there are others that have not yet even been proposed but that will emerge in the future. This is why the transformation must be understood as a continuous and ongoing process.

Open Geographical Sphere

Many universities have a local or regional catchment area. Some have managed to reach nationwide scope, but very few become universities of the world. However, increasingly, culture, the economy, politics, technology and the international order are transcending local or national borders to become part of the greater human heritage. And we can go further. If a small, even a large, community is not appealing to students from other places, it is a community that is moving inexorably towards its own cultural, technological and economic impoverishment. The most active communities in the world are those that retain the best and attract the excellent. With the international dimension, the university enters into the framework of diversity, which ensures education for tolerance and intellectual freedom. Another aspect of a university's international dimension is the possibility of establishing campuses in different parts of the world, linked up by information technologies. This initiative, which at present can be described as small-scale, will grow notably in the future. This opens up an interesting realm of competition with the traditional universities installed in each location.

The Creation of a Knowledge Economy: The Role of Universities in India

In ancient times Indian universities were created by Buddhist monasteries primarily to promote teaching of religion, theology, ethics and philosophy. The two best known universities of India in those days, namely Nalanda and Takshila, attracted a large number of students from both within India and abroad. Nalanda offered high quality education, and perhaps by international standards it was one of the best universities in the ancient world. During the medieval period there was a gross neglect of higher education in India. As a result there were virtually no universities in India for about 1,000 years.

The modern universities in India were founded during British rule. The British created universities primarily to produce public servants. The stress was on liberal education. The British educationist Lord Macaulay opined that the British Empire needed educated Indians to perform public duties and therefore these universities focused on general education, and in particular the teaching of English. Originally three universities were created in 1857, namely Calcutta University, Bombay University and Madras University. Later some more universities were founded during British rule, mostly through state funding. During the later period of British rule some large universities were created through private initiatives, notably the Banaras Hindu University and the Aligarh Muslim University. All universities in India during the British period, whether public or private, followed the traditional model of education.

After independence, universities were created not only in big but also in small towns. India has at present about 450 universities. With a few exceptions, all of them are created by the government with state funding. Among the private universities, only a few offer broad-based liberal education in basic sciences, humanities and social sciences. The others concentrate mainly on professional

Indian Institute of Management (IIM), Bangalore (2003)
Created in 1970, this institute is notable for the quality of its education programmes, which are among the best in the world. Its mission is to train executives by means of a holistic education that is both formative and innovative.

courses, such as engineering, business, medicine etc. There is no
foreign university in India, at present. There is, however, a proposal
to allow foreign universities in India in future.

Pandit Nehru, the first Prime Minister of India was a visionary
in education and science and technology. He realised that
post-independent India could develop through science and
technology only. He encouraged the creation of many scientific
teaching and research institutions. Some of the best known
Indian educational institutions today, namely Indian Institute
of Technology (IIT), Indian Institute of Management (IIM), All
India Institute of Medical Sciences (AIIMS), Tata Institute of
Fundamental Research (TIFR), Indian Statistical Institute (ISI) and
Indian Institute of Science (IISc) emerged from the Nehruvian
vision of scientific knowledge and temperament. Nehru also
nurtured universities and research institutions created earlier.
The large private universities like Banaras Hindu University (BHU)
and Aligarh Muslim University (AMU) were also brought under
the state sector.

At present, India offers high quality education in practically all
disciplines of knowledge. We have some general universities which
are well known abroad, such as Jawaharlal Nehru University (JNU)
Delhi University (DU), Hyderabad University, Bombay University
and Calcutta University. Apart from these, we also have a wide range
of technological universities, medical schools, law universities and
business schools which have high international reputations. Each
year, we are now producing millions of highly skilled professionals
in subjects ranging from liberal arts and humanities to the most
sophisticated branches of science and technology. Many of these
highly skilled professionals have settled abroad, because of better
service conditions and globalization.

After independence India began to focus on industrial
development. While industry continues to be the key sector in
our development strategy, services have overtaken industry as the
leading sector in the economy. Unlike in most developed countries,
services became the largest segment of the economy at an early stage
of development in India. While China has expanded its
international trade by exporting mainly manufactured goods, India
began to export heavily its professional services. India has two
advantages in this respect. Firstly, education in India is conducted
in most well known universities in English, the lingua franca of
modern world education, business and communication. Secondly,
the Indian professionals are fairly internationally competitive
in terms of salary and professional services. As a result the
services sector grew both in terms of exports of services and
also out-sourcing of services from developed countries to India.
Professional services like finance, banking, insurance, medicine,

**Student filling out application forms,
University of Delhi (2009)**
The University of Delhi was created in 1923
from the merger of three existing colleges.
Today, it enjoys a distinguished academic
reputation, operates over fourteen faculties and
has a student body of over 2,200,000.

education and research and development now contribute a significant proportion of gross domestic product in India. The value added in these services is much greater than traditional economic activities. These services are also growing very fast, probably faster than anywhere in the world.

Investment in education and in particular skill formation takes a long time to yield returns. From around the 1960s professionals educated in top Indian universities and research institutions began to make their impact in the Indian economy. By the 1970s young professionals graduated from Indian universities helped in creating our knowledge-based services for the domestic economy as well as for exports. Today, if India has a comparative international advantage in professional services in information technology, finance, banking, insurance, medicine, education and varieties of other professional services, a great deal of credit for this must be given to Pandit Nehru and the universities and institutions created and nurtured by him.

Unfortunately, however, all top universities and research institutions in India are over dependent on state funds. From time to time, they suffer severe budget constraints due to fiscal crunch. In the post-Nehruvian era, policy makers also devoted comparatively less attention to higher education and research and development. The growth of universities has, therefore, lagged far behind the rise of the young population. Thus, large numbers of Indian students go abroad to pursue their studies at a high cost. Very recently, the government has realised this and initiated steps for creating more universities in the state sector. While the federal government has become very conscious of this limitation, the provincial governments are yet to show equal concern.

The university system in India is well known for good teaching of advanced subjects in almost all disciplines of knowledge and in particular in science and technology. The research output, however, suffers due to poor infrastructure and paucity of funds. Thus many Indians prefer to go abroad to do their research. Moreover, even those who do research in the Indian universities often sell their patents to foreign establishments. The corporate-university connection in India is very weak. The Indian economy therefore does not derive full benefits from the educated professionals in India. Intellectuals in India are now greatly concerned that if these anomalies are not corrected, then India might lose its prominence not only in professional services but also in the creation of knowledge economy.

The biggest problem in higher education in India is how to expand university education without compromising quality. For a population of more than one billion, 450 universities are too few. Less than 5 percent of the population has undergone university education in some form. Among the young the total enrolled in universities is even now about 10 percent. The ratios are much worse among socially backward

The biggest problem in higher education in India is how to expand university education without compromising quality: 450 universities are too few for a population that exceeds one billion. Less than five per cent of the population has undergone university education

communities and women. To promote the knowledge-based economy, the higher education base should be at least double in the near future. The Knowledge Commission of the Government of India recommended that there should be another 1,500 new universities within the next decade. The problem, however, is paucity of funds and skilled people to teach in universities. At present, public spending on higher education in India is one of the lowest in the world: about one percent of gross domestic product. It is felt that it should be raised to at least three percent immediately. But this is a Herculean task given the low priority of higher education in state budgets.

The corporate sector in India has now become very large. Unfortunately, however, the corporate participation in higher education, in the form of endowment and research funding, is very low. With a declining tax-GDP ratio due to ongoing liberalization and privatization, there is very little prospect for a quantum leap in state funding for higher education. This can be the major lacuna in the growth of universities in India. Secondly, because of limited universities in the past, we do not have a large number of highly qualified faculty to teach in universities. The exodus of highly educated people to the corporate sector and abroad has accentuated the problem further. This is already felt in well established universities and research institutions in India.

It is now well accepted that the future of India would depend crucially on expansion of the knowledge economy. We are currently reaping the benefits of our past investments in higher education. China and other emerging economies have realised the importance of knowledge economy and are investing heavily in universities and research and development (R&D). It would be interesting to see how India faces competition from these countries in professional services in the coming years.

B.B. Bhattacharya

Students on the Hyderabad campus, Andhra Pradesh (2009)
Since opening its doors in 1974 as the Central University, this institution has won prominence in research and postgraduate training in both the humanities and sciences.

Stimulating Creativity and Integrated Knowledge

One of the most notable characteristics of the change will be how creativity is fostered. In this regard it is necessary to go beyond the moulds imposed by leaders with a background in law, business or politics and unlock the value of those deriving from people with qualifications such as art, music, architecture and engineering: qualifications that not only transfer knowledge but introduce students and professors to the creative process itself. Speaking of creativity, it has been shown that teaching based on highly specialised disciplines considerably limits students' inventive capacity and also places constraints on their freedom. Consequently, the new programmes must focus on integrated knowledge, training that will permit a better professional integration of students in the productive sector in the twenty-first century. This is a difficult change for the academic community and, in many countries, for the professional community.

The academic community is not always favourable to those who are truly creative and innovative, either among teachers or students. But in the professional world it is almost worse still; especially in countries with low or mid-scale technology levels, the trend is to find someone who knows how to do a particular thing (short term), rather than someone who has the ability to learn to do many things over the course of their professional career. In the twenty-first century the countries leading the field will be those with professionals who are able to learn, to switch from one theme to another and to maintain their desire to go on learning. This is achieved by teaching that focuses on integrated knowledge rather than on specialisation. As indicated, one of the difficulties for this change comes from the academics themselves. They are often more loyal to their disciplines than to their students' futures, societal needs and the requirements of the institution itself, which means that we repeatedly and permanently see absurd clashes between disciplines, and the problematic distinction between basic and applied science or between science and engineering. This is a far cry from the future university that is integrated through new real or virtual structures.

Another aspect impacting on creativity is the presence of information technologies. Some universities will become knowledge servers. If they do not assume this new role then private enterprise will. All of them will go online for a major part of their activities. This will introduce important modifications to the current concept of the campus as a place where students live together and to which those that do not live there travel daily. It will also require a good deal of experimentation in order to find the best possible conditions for education in this new framework. The idea of the virtual university will reach its peak in its application in continuous education and in so-called adult universities. Professionals of the twenty-first century will commence the process of acquiring knowledge with graduate training and they will complete it on retirement. Combining learning with one's professional life is problematic if it involves travelling to a physical campus. The new virtual university will overcome this serious difficulty. This approach poses a danger to local universities, which, if they fail to adapt their competitive standards, risk losing their potential postgraduate students to institutions able to offer more attractive prospects. The other option linked directly with the virtual environment is university for adults, who are only seeking to enrich their lives with the university options they choose. Adult students in both categories, specialisation or life-enrichment, may double the number of ordinary students, according to estimates. This activity will contribute significantly to universities' budgets in the twenty-first century. But this opportunity also represents a challenge. Each university must show that it has sufficient quality, competency and organisational structure to offer a range of postgraduate courses that are in line with market needs. They must prove to students starting their careers that they are entering a university for life. Evidently, this is a question of model and function.

In the twentyfirst century the countries leading the field will be those with professionals who are able to learn, to switch from one theme to another and to maintain their desire to go on learning. This is achieved by teaching that focuses on integrated knowledge rather than on specialisation

Digital Stradivarius Project, MIT (*c.* 2000)
The aim of this project is to construct a digital model whereby a violin can convert human movement into sounds emitted by one of the world's finest musical instruments.

Ciutadella campus, Pompeu Fabra University, Barcelona (1996)
One of the sites of Barcelona's public university is this department building designed by the architect Juan Navarro Baldeweg. Recent major projects at Pompeu Fabra include the Communications Station, which seeks to combine creativity and technology, and the Barcelona Biomedical Research Park.

Leadership Capacity, Pivotal in the Transition to the New Model

With regard to the quest for a new model, we must return to the same old question: is the traditional university capable of changing? And, above all, is it capable of implementing major changes? Despite the reticence, which is not inconsiderable, as we have mentioned, there is a capacity for change. The problem may arise when spectacular leaps are required. As we have seen, this change has been the subject of discussion for years now. Consequently, in many countries, including Spain, there have been some novel initiatives, in some cases looking ahead to the twenty-first century, in others with a more limited view. In the latter cases, after a time, the new institutions do not differ in the least from the traditional universities. Anyway, it will be extremely useful for promoting and effecting the change if each university takes the initiative to create and fund a research group, comprising prestigious academics, devoted to exploring new methods of education for the future, promoting new educational services and orienting research in a balanced manner, as well as encouraging enterprising approaches, to cite a few objectives.

It is also fundamental to include experimental aspects, in other words, specific applications. This kind of initiative has already been implemented in some universities or university consortia. We must not forget that the best way to predict something is to invent it and that is what can be achieved through research. The second part is the application by universities of the findings derived from research. This process is the cleverest way to move into the future, especially considering that we can only guess at what that future will look like. In this and other aspects of change, it is once again confirmed that the linchpin of success resides in the leadership ability of the institutions' governing bodies. After all, one of the main tasks for a leader is to show that new challenges in fact represent new opportunities. This makes it clear how vital the role of the chancellor or president is. Universities have undergone major transformations, like those of Singapore and Michigan, led by aggressive, innovative leaders able to assume risks and enjoying

huge intellectual prestige. This demand has always been central to the future of higher education institutions, but it has now become a necessary and sufficient condition to meet the challenges of this century.

One report concerning the role of the university in economic change states, in this connection:

> The role of the chancellor or president is especially important. Enterprising chancellors surround themselves with true leaders and set up a coherent team comprising deans and directors, enabling them to develop new relations and roles for the university, without losing sight of its traditional mission. In cases with greater regional involvement they have been able to articulate the university's mission within the framework of regional economic development, fostering a campus atmosphere that is favourable to establishing the necessary relationships.

Therefore, having a good chancellor or president is a necessary, but not sufficient, condition for change. This highlights the importance of changing the systems for electing academic-administrative heads, especially in those places where the capacity to exercise the true leadership that is so badly needed takes on a secondary role in elections. In many countries, this lack of leadership among university heads has undermined the university in its relations with political leaders and, furthermore, is actually delaying the start of the necessary transformation.

Students at the ballot, Yonsei University, South Korea (2002)
University students have traditionally engaged with politics, recording high turnout figures at elections. Ballot boxes are often set up at universities themselves, since most students are living away from the electoral district in which they are registered.

Towards New Models of University Cooperation and Technology in the European Union

The multifaceted role of universities requires them to combine the training of professionals to an adequate standard of competence with the generation of new scientific and technological knowledge. More recently, universities have also been called on to support the valorisation of that knowledge by actively transferring it to industry and society, and to foster an entrepreneurial spirit in their teaching and student bodies. These three main roles are now accompanied – though timidly – by the mission of supporting scientific and technological dissemination to the wider community, this being one of the duties of a university aspiring to exercise public leadership.

The significance and visibility of these four roles of universities have changed over time. Internally, staff promotions are now decisively influenced by research considerations; externally, research weighs heavily with public decision-making on the funding and recognition of universities. The trend is further reflected in the creation of new research sites and science and technology parks. The overarching aim is for universities to become key elements in the sustainable development of advanced societies – thus regaining their former role, which in an increasingly complex society has lately been drowned out.

Many of the key features of modern universities need to be reconsidered accordingly: models of governance, interactions between teaching and research structures, relations with other socio-economic actors, and the manner in which they outwardly account for their achievements and activities to the wider community. This is the basis of the 'modernisation' advocated by public authorities in recent years.

A university's process of modernisation cannot be viewed in isolation from other government measures. It is at the crossroads of higher education, research and innovation policies – at the intersection of the so called 'knowledge triangle' – where universities must play their transformative role.

Neither should a university be confined to a geographically limited 'territory'. Today it is common to see universities whose reach barely

Large Hadron Collider (LHC), CERN, Geneva (2007)
Commissioned in 2008, the LHC has accelerated subatomic particles to the speed of light. The goal is to validate and identify the limits of the Standard Model, the theoretical framework now prevalent in particle physics.

exceeds their own region: dependent on a regional or national government, their teaching faculties are locally recruited – often, among academics trained at that very university or nearby – and their students, too, are drawn from the physical vicinity. When placing emphasis on going beyond the boundaries of pure academic endeavour – in support of innovation in small and medium enterprises – government tends to assert the university's role in knowledge transfer to business sectors that, again, are tightly bound up with the local territory. But is this the best way of implementing the university's purported social role?

The creation of scientific and technological knowledge is a networked process. Institutions that contain within themselves all the knowledge required for their work exist no longer. Knowledge access and exchange requires the formation of 'active networks' of universities and other actors, which need not be geographically close. The formation and fostering of knowledge-generating, knowledge-disseminating networks is now an institutional priority, no longer a mere extension of the interests of the individual academics involved. The boundaries of universities' institutional action are being pushed outward to encompass an international context.

In the last analysis, universities should become foci for receiving students, lecturers and ideas from other countries; conversely, universities should strike agreements to project themselves beyond their territory of origin. A development of this sort would revive the 'universal' dimension of the medieval university in the form of the multifaceted vision that has become so characteristic of the twenty-first century.

The evolutionary drive sketched earlier affects all universities to one extent or another. But it is in the European Union where it has taken shape as a key element in the process of modernising universities, with both public authorities and universities themselves making significant efforts. Since 2000, the EU has set in motion two independent processes that nonetheless both address this broad framework of concern: the creation of the European Research Area (ERA) and of the European Higher Education Area (EHEA). The European Research Area is intended to end the fragmentation of research and innovation policies, create a single market in research, and so bring to fruition the so-called 'fifth freedom': the free movement of knowledge. The European Higher Education Area is directed at encouraging student and academic mobility by a system of inter-university credit recognition, bringing on a movement of far-reaching curricular reform in all European countries. Both initiatives are still incomplete. The 2010 deadline is simply an initial timeframe to provoke reflection on what has been achieved so far and direct attention towards 2020, in a more thoroughgoing process of coordination and cooperation in the European framework. European universities have still to assimilate these processes on an institutional scale. Internal systems

The EU has created the European Technology Institute, whose first grant award process aims to foster 'innovation and knowledge communities' in three themed areas: information and communication technologies, energy, and climate change

of governance must adapt to the twofold objective of curricular flexibility and internationalisation.

In parallel to the construction of the EHEA and the ERA, and in the framework of the 'knowledge triangle', the EU has also initiated long-running cooperation processes among European universities and research entities. University networks created from the bottom up on the strength of participants' own interests – originally focusing on exchanging information and aligning strategy – have paved the way to new networks with more forward-looking objectives of lasting integration of initiatives in both teaching and research. In some northern European countries, the effects of these networks are already very striking, putting one in mind of the notion of a 'federation' of universities that operates common models of governance at a far remove from those prevalent today.

As an example of these changes, alongside the developments described earlier, the EU has created the European Technology Institute. The Institute's first grant award process aims to foster so-called 'innovation and knowledge communities' in three themed areas: information and communication technologies, energy, and climate change. In each domain, university research bodies and businesses are invited to collaborate in education, research and innovation for a minimum period of seven years.

The EU is not an isolated bloc. One of the objectives of the ERA is in fact to open up European research to the rest of the world. For European universities, this means that in future it will be frequent to see them deploy a presence in other countries, typically under agreements with local entities to form joint research and teaching ventures. This process will also encourage a cross-border presence of the universities of developed EU states, breaking away from the 'protectionist' vision that still predominates. The 'universal' vocation of universities will become a reality.

The first decade of the twenty-first century has seen a far-reaching process of change in the university system that has made it more international, more closely integrated with the concerns of the wider community, more multifaceted and capable of a higher socio-economic impact on its host societies. Let us hope that this process goes from strength to strength. The success of this enterprise is the collective responsibility that a complex society like our own must assume if we are to harness the transformative power of our universities.

Gonzalo León

Examinations at the École Polytechnique, Paris (1994)
The more prestigious institutions have to set entrance examinations to uphold academic standards and prevent overcrowding from impairing the quality of teaching.
To accommodate the huge numbers of candidates seeking admission, examinations are conducted at the institutions' largest spaces, such as indoor sports facilities.

Regional Demands

In the introduction we mentioned that the concept of universities based on uniformity was probably one of the institution's foremost errors in the twentieth century. It has been also one of the reasons for their scant influence on the social, political and economic change that many countries need. The United States also made this mistake, even though it does make a distinction between so-called research universities and the rest of the higher education institutions. Nevertheless, in the second half of the twentieth century there has been a major drive in the country to transform higher education institutions into research universities.

This is what has become known as the 'Harvardisation' of higher education, a process in which all universities want to be like Harvard, which was seen as the ideal model. Evidently, we are talking about a movement with unrealistic expectations. The same process has occurred in many countries, especially those where there has been an increase in the number of universities and higher education institutions in the last century. The most surprising thing is that this initiative did not emerge solely from the universities themselves, but that it was also launched from public administrations. The same public administrations that now wish to transform it into 'de-Harvardization', a movement that is gaining considerable pace in the early part of this century.

This had to happen for a number of reasons. Firstly, because of the high cost of this elitist model; secondly, because competition requires differentiation between institutions; and thirdly because of social pressure on regional public universities to increase their active involvement in regional economic development. In short, the idea is to prevent, for example, a university located in a predominantly agricultural region from becoming a standard-bearer in high-energy physics while entirely lacking in agricultural research. This situation is more the rule than the exception in most countries.

A University that is Engaged Locally and Competitive Globally

To avoid compromising the standards of their 'elite' universities countries must actually differentiate them from what might be called regional universities, which also aspire to the elite but within a different framework. The reason is that the latter must serve at least two needs: the training of professionals and the generation of knowledge in areas linked to regional economic development. In these areas, in which the highest standards must be attained, as well as in training they must play a significant role in research. In short, they must offer high-level value-added services directly applicable to their immediate environment. It is ludicrous to envisage regional universities in which the principal areas of research have nothing to do with the needs of the surrounding region. This planning, which nevertheless is nothing new, will boost regional economic development. It will also allow regional universities to focus their human and material resources on a few areas of interest, in which they may take on a real leadership role, not just locally, but globally. Despite the evidence, the difficulties in redefining this kind of option are considerable, almost insurmountable, in countries where higher education depends entirely on regional policy. The lack of an umbrella provided by a central government capable of seeing issues from another perspective is patent.

Let us look at some of the risks that might affect what we have called regional universities. Each region will want the best professionals, since their economic development will depend on them to a great extent. The training of these professionals will depend on the standard of academic programmes offered by local universities. If this is not adequate, there is a risk that the local government might opt to finance students, rather than transferring funds to the university, so that students may study at an institution that guarantees their training. However, for a local university to compete it needs to have a competitive budget, as well as a broad-reaching autonomy for

recruiting professors and allocating their salaries. In a nutshell, the idea is to compete for the best. These considerations may be extended to include legislative and external control-related aspects. In conclusion, one might say that the opportunities and risks do not depend solely on the universities themselves, but on regional policies.

Efficiency in the regional or local approach can be derived from a smart and balanced application of the triple-helix model. This is a new, three-pronged approach based on the simultaneous involvement of the university, businesses and governments. Application of this model leads to the appearance of new structures such as trilateral networks, hybrid institutions or new alliances at mixed centres or other structures that have yet to be created. The model assumes that

the university must play a pivotal role in regional development. In fact, it is a matter of integrating knowledge, creativity and innovation, all facets in which the university is unique. This requires all three players to agree to introduce the necessary changes to adapt to the new structures. In particular, universities will have to redefine the processes associated with their mission, and, above all, how these processes are going to be handled. In short, universities not only can but must participate directly in the economic development of the region where they are located. There are very interesting examples of universities which have evolved from a local to a global catchment area, without turning their back on their immediate environment.

PA Technology Center, Princeton (1984)
The British architect Richard Rogers designed this building following the pattern of high-tech architecture. The technology centre attached to the famous Princeton University is calculated to fulfil several functions: hosting a complex scientific programme – necessitating laboratories, workshops, a library – while adapting flexibly to the building's changing purposes and presenting an outward image that visitors find recognisable.

The International Reach of UK Universities at the Beginning of the Twenty-first Century

Long after the eclipse of the UK's pre-eminence as a manufacturing and trading power, universities in the UK have risen to be popular destinations for students from around the world and have gained reputations as leaders in their fields. The number of international students in the UK doubled in the first decade of the twenty-first century, and even the rate of this growth is now increasing. The UK is the second most popular destination for international students (after the United States), with more than 340,000 students currently enrolled. More and more students do not need even to leave their home countries to benefit from a UK university education, thanks to the rise of 'transnational education', in which education is brought to where the markets are. At the beginning of 2010, there are almost 200,000 international students enrolled on UK university courses in other countries. This number is certain to overtake the number of international students in the UK itself (even as the latter increases) as universities invest in new distance-learning technologies, invest in the development of overseas campuses, and form sustainable teaching and research partnerships around the globe. And as these opportunities grow in location, range and flexibility, so more students from more parts of the world will be able to take advantage of a UK university education.

So how do we account for the international popularity of UK higher education? One factor is undoubtedly the UK's continued success in the international 'league tables' – according to the 2009 the Q-S World University Rankings, four of the world's top ten universities are in the UK. However much caution one should approach these with, league tables do exert considerable influence on the choices of international students and their parents, and this applies both to the choice of country and institution. But underlying these rather fickle instruments, UK universities offer three things that underpin their continuing international success: world-class research, world-class programmes and a world-class student experience.

Universities in the UK, unlike in many other places, are autonomous and self-governing institutions, which, under Royal Charter, are empowered to

Student hall of residence, Docklands Campus, University of East London (2008)
Student accommodation for UEL is provided near the former docks, in East London. With over 1,200 student rooms, the halls offer cafes, restaurants, laundry services and other necessaries of university life.

award their own degrees. Academic standards and the quality of learning opportunities are the responsibilities of each university, but within a framework established and monitored by the UK Quality Assurance Agency for Higher Education. This balance between regulation and autonomy is the key to understanding how universities in the UK succeed – possibly uniquely – in balancing quality and flexibility and responsiveness to the demands of students and the wider economy. Whether a degree is studied full-time on a traditional campus in the UK, or studied flexibly and part-time in a student's home country, employers the world over place trust in the knowledge and skills that it represents. And prospective students can be certain that the learning experiences they receive, and the value of the qualification that they are awarded, will indeed be world-class.

UK universities offer a platform for the linking of research with innovation. Research output enhances the capacity of any country for social and technological innovation. The research output of UK universities is impressive indeed: with 1 percent of the world's population, the UK produces 5 percent of the world's scientific research and 12 percent of citations. Not only do the research and innovation activities of our universities generate significant income, but they directly underpin the quality of learning opportunities that universities provide. It is therefore not wholly surprising that more than half of the 120,000 postgraduate research students in the UK are from outside the UK. Many of these will constitute the next generation of university scholars around the world, and their experiences in the UK make a sustainable contribution to this country's arsenal of soft power.

International research partnerships are increasingly important features of the UK higher education landscape. UK universities are establishing new offices around the world every week in order to support the development of international research collaborations and other international activities. Between 2001 and 2005, international collaborative research output involving UK universities increased by 154 percent.

These collaborations are important for a number of reasons. First, world-class research is inherently international. Collaborations between the leading researchers in any field are more likely to produce solutions, innovations and insights than researchers working alone. Secondly, such collaborations serve to raise the capacity for research in parts of the world with more limited research capacity. The popularity of UK universities as collaborating partners clearly demonstrates this. Thirdly, research collaboration is one means by which international competitors become international partners. This benefits universities and the societies in which they reside. Finally, strategic international

IdeasLab, University of Oxford
Angela McLean, director of the Institute for Emerging Infections attached to the Zoology Department at Oxford, and Frances Cairncross, rector of Exeter College, share research notes.

UK *universities offer three things that underpin their continuing international success: world-class research, programmes and student experience*

collaborations are the vehicles through which UK universities already, and increasingly, contribute to solving the world's big problems. Global problems – such as climate change, famine, poverty and disease – need global solutions. Our universities, in partnership with those from around the world, generate the expertise to find such solutions.

For all of these reasons – governance, teaching excellence and research prowess – UK universities are, at the beginning of the twenty-first century, in the vanguard of the creation of knowledge and its transmission around the world.

Steve Smith

Government and Leadership

To respond to the challenge of change, in addition to what we have already seen, the governing bodies of higher education institutions must exercise true leadership. This is because we are not in the same situation that led the universities of the twentieth century to transform themselves into what became known as contemporary institutions. In that case, the transformation came during times of economic boom and, above all, under the umbrella of the euphoria deriving from the role of science in the Second World War. Furthermore, this change was more influenced by the initiative and pressure of governments than by the demands of the universities themselves. This transformation did not occur in all countries at the same time, but arrived as they entered the group of privileged countries. Indeed, in some countries the change began but, due to negative governmental policies, there has been an involution that has led to a grave deterioration of the present situation.

At present, to complete the analysis of the conditions necessary to tackle change, we must take a closer look at university governing bodies. We need to look at the conditions under which they can play a real leadership role and how they can increase their capacity to assume responsibilities and move within a complex system. However, these capacities may be limited, especially in public universities, by legislation proposed by governments and approved by parliaments. For this reason, in many countries there must be major legislative changes.

Governing Boards

The head of a university is the chancellor or president, generally elected by a governing board, in the case of public universities in the United States and some other countries, and by other kinds of voting system in the rest of the democratic world. However, the governing board or equivalent body, as well as choosing the chancellor at some universities, performs other important tasks at all the universities in the world. While their existence is not called into question, there is unanimous agreement that it

Graduation ceremony, Huazhong University of Science and Technology, China (2009)
Since academic protocol in China was standardised in 1994, the wearing of academic dress, with gown and mortarboard, has been obligatory at graduation ceremonies. Over 6,800 graduands gather to receive their degrees at the graduation ceremony of this university, renowned for its research in nanotechnology and other fields of science and technology.

should be the first subject of the necessary transformation. It seems reasonable to think that the members of the governing board should act as disinterested advisors, that they should strive to run the institution based on how best to serve society. However, the political process that leads to the appointment of board members in most countries rarely tries to identify people whose experience and capacity enables them to understand the complex nature of a contemporary university. This brings with it very negative consequences. The first is that members of governing boards tend to be occupied mainly with administrative and supervisory issues, rather than submitting proposals. The second is that they often succumb to the temptation of sustaining their parties' political positions, invalidating any possible discussion. The third is that when a qualified expert is invited to participate in the governing board, they normally refuse due to the above. In those cases in which the governing board elects the chancellor, which might be sound policy, the appointee, while independent, is hostage of the political pressure from those who had the necessary power to elect him.

It is obvious that the transformation of the governing board must come from the political sphere, which is the sphere that generates new laws. For this purpose, politicians must accept that the choice of members of the board, as in a country's other key institutions, must be made in accordance with the concept of merit and independence. It is important to keep in mind what a significant role universities play in a nation's prosperity. What makes it difficult to usher in this shift is that the consequences of political decisions concerning the university emerge in the medium and long term.

Difficulties in Exercising Leadership

As we have said, university leadership is of critical importance, especially when it comes to undertaking a process of change. In this leadership the main figure is the chancellor or president. Despite their limitations, universities in which the chancellor or president is elected by a governing board or equivalent institution have some capacity to exercise this leadership. However, elsewhere, the method of election

and legislation makes it difficult for chancellors to spearhead the change that universities need. Chancellors are obliged to form coalitions and establish compromises to remain at the helm of institutions. In any case, before discussing the changes, it is interesting to sum up the inherent constraints on the method of governance.

In general, universities are highly fragmented institutions, with little coordination and without priorities. Only in the organisation of the teaching, not in the content, is there a certain authoritative order. This is because the university organisation is substantially different from all other organisations in the lack of overlapping between responsibility and authority, something that does not take place in the world of politics. The universities' atypical situation stems from the fact that academics have two prerogatives that are unique in today's world. One of these is their so-called academic freedom whereby, in something of a caricature, academics may say, teach and study whatever they like. This is not necessarily negative in itself, indeed thanks to that freedom whole new areas of knowledge are opened up, new interdisciplinary fields established, etc. The other is linked to their job security. These two prerogatives lead academics' loyalties to be strong in relation to their specific subject areas, weaker in relation to their immediate administrative environment (department, institute, faculty or school) and entirely unstable when it comes to the institution. As one might expect, there are a great many bonds that must be taken into account when analysing academic-administrative authorities' real possibilities of exercising leadership.

As regards chancellors, regardless of how they are elected, their tasks are so varied and complex that under current legislation it is difficult to find the right person for the post; and the larger the university, the more complex it is. In general, chancellors are the administrative, executive and academic heads of an institution, although frequently their most important role (sometimes their only role) is to secure funds from public administrations and to keep the university's administrative system in good working order. In the rest of the activities related to academic issues, or the receipt of other funds (intellectual property rights, licences, research lines or projects), the chancellors of most universities have only limited influence. Accordingly, the new horizon – in which there will be a reduction in public funds and an increase in private ones – will pile on more problems of leadership for chancellors unless legislation is changed.

In order to examine the main factors limiting the leadership scope of chancellors or presidents, let us begin by distinguishing two differentiated groups. On the one hand are those factors deriving from inter-actions with other organisations, and on the other those inherent to the institution itself. Among the first group, the most important is linked to the legal and economic control exercised by governments. The second is a result of the organisational dualism stemming from the co-existence of two parallel struc-tures. On the one hand is the conventional bureau-cratic hierarchy on which the chancellor exercises all of his authority, and on the other is the academic structure that sees any intrusion from the governing bodies as illegitimate. This leads to endless discus-sions regarding the mission and purpose of higher education or concerning responsibility, quality and competitive growth, to cite but a few examples. On top of this is something that has become fashion-able of late: accreditation from non-university bod-ies. These have become very prolific, and in some cases are of scant quality and highly opaque. They are even used by governments as elements of exter-nal control over universities' independence. One for-mer chancellor defined them as 'a straightjacket of many colours'. With regard to this point and others, it should not be forgotten that legislative regulations and internal factors also affect private universities, to an extent.

Chancellors subject to these contextual conditions must make a huge effort to exercise leadership. This means that achieving the broadest consensus possi-ble in every decision that is made comes at an enor-mous personal cost. If their university also has con-flicting factions, the pressure can even affect their physical and mental health. There is no doubt that it takes excessive dedication to achieve anything, and this will affect the time chancellors can devote to their families and their own intellectual activity. This means that when a university is lucky enough to choose a

Graduation ceremony, Universidad Autónoma de Chihuahua (UACH), Mexico (c. 1990)
UACH actively promotes the social and economic development of the indigenous community of the Tarahumara, who have their ancestral home in the sierra of the same name. In partnership with New Mexico State University, UACH has set in motion an effective programme of scholarships funded by the United States Agency for International Development to open up higher education opportunities for indigenous young people.

chancellor with the capacity to lead, very few feel encouraged to use it. If they do, as well as the person-al cost, at the end of their tenure they will be left with a degree of dissatisfaction at how little they have achieved despite the monumental effort.

It is evident that if the leadership universities need to tackle the challenges of the twenty-first century is to be achieved, there must be a fundamental change in the structure of governance, in the way academic-administrative appointments are made, and in the content of each. A first step would be to strengthen the office of the chancellor and other governing bodies via legislative reform. However, this will do no good unless a merit-based election system is introduced. The better the process to elect governing board members, the more viable the US model is. The model of appointment by vote requires some substantial reform. At heart it is a question of conferring ration-ality to the anarchy of university organisation. As we have already indicated, another helpful factor would be to have governing boards exert greater intellectual and professional quality demands on their members. This would enable them to broaden their attributes which could be equivalent to those of a Board of Directors. In this framework, they could promote the necessary changes and support the chancellor in the difficult task of transformation. However, there is no overlooking the fact that there is a reluctance from various quarters to bolster chancellors' capacity for decision-making and leadership.

In any case, if chancellors are appointed without being motivated to serve the institution, they will govern from isolation and, even more importantly, they will refuse to involve the real academic leaders of the institution. Evidently, when this occurs there is absolutely no chance of change. Chancellors who leave a legacy of any kind are those with limited ambitions for the power and prestige that the post offers. They see their tenure as something temporary, they set themselves few and limited goals to which they will devote the utmost energy, they seek the cooperation of all university leaders (deans, directors and academics) and they pay attention to the needs of the institution and not their own. They accept that the university is a decentralised structure, fragmented to an extent and full of conflicts of authority. They are the ones who really understand the culture of the institution and the symbolic aspects linked to the position they adopt. They are chancellors who do not hide away in their offices, but who walk through their campuses, observe and are observed and take into account that change comes with participation, and that it cannot be imposed from some regulation or from some office. They are the chancellors who accept disagreement and the mutual enriching influence between people. In general, unless legislation is changed – which is by no means certain at present – the successful chancellors in the world are those who have accepted that they must lead in a complex system. It is important to never lose sight of the fact that we are talking about a unique institution, in which professional considerations prevail over administrative ones. The mistake made by the governments of most universities is that over the years they have tried to reverse this premise in a bid to centralise power. However, those universities that have had real leaders have proved that administrative weakness can be a source of organisational strength.

What we have said so far is aimed at emphasizing the superhuman effort required to make even just a few changes under current legislation. But this legislation must evolve to ensure that the appointment of university chancellors is a careful, well thought-out and rational process, rather than something approaching a political campaign. This is the first challenge for transformation. Based on this premise, the next step – the incorporation to university governing bodies of talented and experienced academics – is far easier. The third has to do with the inertia of the institution. In society and also in universities there is a very limited perception of the challenges and opportunities for higher education in the twenty-first century. Consequently, resistance to change, which in many cases is due to an attempt to keep petty privileges, is justified with very subtle arguments. For example, in justifying their reticence, some sustain that it is necessary to defend the values of universities (knowledge, excellence, service, truth and justice) from the mediocrity of politicians and the short-sightedness of the productive sector.

Faced with such resistance to change, innovative and imaginative actions must be devised to trigger a shift in attitudes for the benefit of universities. It has been shown that universities that in the last few years have joined the group of global front-runners are those where the majority of academics have accepted and tolerated strong leadership from a chancellor. This is the battle that chancellors must win. Yet on this journey they cannot advance alone. Authority must be restored to deans, directors of schools and directors of departments. They must be integrated into the general project, and the qualifications required to fill these posts must be similar to those required to be a chancellor. The universities that accept these premises are those that will lead the field in this new century.

The Virtual University

We deliberately left for the end of this work a more extensive analysis of the virtual university, based on the global impact of the application of information and communication technologies. Because of its implications for education, research and learning, it can be described as a real revolution that will significantly change many of the methods and forms of traditional universities as well as the work of their academics. It is also important to point out that wherever there are opportunities there are also risks. One of these is the fostering of individualism and, as a result, isolation or the dangerous trend of losing the notion of personal effort or intellectual enrichment that is nurtured by living alongside others from the university community; another is the risk that students' work will eventually be confined to the vile practice of 'cutting and pasting'. In addition to these risks is that of a steady diminishing of quality standards. In countries where this happens it will be difficult to maintain productive systems and, as a result, to maintain the standard of living of their citizens. This loss of quality may be compounded by the fact that, based on new technology, there looks set to be a proliferation of non-traditional low-cost teaching and research services. This and other similar situations will heap considerable pressure on universities to quickly adapt to the new demands. However, despite the pressures, some precaution is necessary, since experience is beginning to show us that excessively swift change in this connection is reckless since trying to predict the future is, to say the least, naive.

Traditionally, the university has been the main driver and transmitter of knowledge. At present, it should continue to perform its main mission and, for this purpose, it seems reasonable to incorporate such new tools as technology can offer. However, to use the contemporary term one might say that many universities in this century run the risk of turning into no more than 'knowledge servers'. This option is strongly driven by highly extremist proposals from many computer and IT companies. Furthermore, this kind of propaganda manages to generate enthusiasm

in quite a large number of politicians. Accordingly, in order to avoid having to take orders from the outside, universities must be the ones to lead this change. It is the only way to stay on track. The knowledge server must be something more than a storage facility and must focus on creating, preserving, transmitting and applying the knowledge needed by society in this century. Even from this standpoint, the idea of a change of such characteristics generates some scepticism in universities. But there is also the opposite extreme. At all events, those sustaining radical positions in relation to these technologies should be reminded that history has taught us a number of lessons about the effect of technology on education. Many are the doom merchants of every era who herald the complete reinvention or inevitable demise of the educational system. At best, these predictions have been proven wrong. This explains why the adoption of technology in education is shaped by unexpected failures and unforeseen successes. An example of this are the (probably) millions of pages written about the supposed revolution in the education system in the years after the emergence of television. In practice, this revolution was a non-starter. Evidently, the present situation is not the same. However, we are witnessing the emergence of such a wealth of complex technological tools that, before implementing them *en masse*, it is advisable to design methods of testing them to enable us to make decisions that are not based on improvisation, and through which we can predict the possible effects and consequences before definitively putting them into practice.

The above considerations do not aim to call into question the extraordinary relevance that new technology will surely have in education. Moreover, since citizens are amply informed about the new possibilities offered by this new technology – via suppliers, specialist journals and the media – we will focus the section devoted to this area on a few cautionary notes. Very directly, the first parties to be affected will be the knowledge services. A part of these are supported in books, oral explanations, dissertations,

***Tianhe* supercomputer, National University of Defense Technology (NUDT), Changsha, China (2009)**
Operators controlling the *Tianhe* supercomputer: China's fastest, and one of the five fastest anywhere in the world. Built by NUDT researchers for the Tianjin National Supercomputing Center, the machine is capable of over one quadrillion floating-point operations per second (one petaflop).

expositions in polished classics or static images, as well as libraries. All of these tools and methodologies will undergo a major transformation with the appearance of personal computers with increasing capacities and with the swift rise in bandwidth and the expansion of fibre-optic cabling, already used in many local networks. Libraries will soon be virtual. Some international research journals have already gone online. The traditional system of spoken classes, intrinsically inefficient for the transmission of knowledge, could be transformed into a network of computers linked to each student, and, depending on the case, operating either simultaneously or asynchronously. In other words, the professor and students will interact in real time or in accordance with any other schedule that is established. Experience so far at some universities appears to assert that learning using these media is at least as efficient as with traditional methods.

In this new scenario teachers will take on more or less the functions they performed when universities began, or even those associated with methods of transmitting knowledge prior to the birth of universities: guide, tutor, advisor, etc. Something we mentioned previously as a factor to be taken into account, namely the danger of isolation, appears to be resolved through the new methods of digital interaction, capable of generating communication and stimulating the formation of new kinds of human communities.

This way of transmitting knowledge and accessing training and information online constitutes what is currently known as a virtual university. The closest thing to this concept now are what are known as distance learning universities, although they are different in an important way: technology. In the new virtual campus, thanks to cyberspace, students who are geographically separated will be electronically connected with each other and with their professors. One might even say that information technology will act as a support for the transition to a new way of learning and teaching. This is one of the bottle-necks of universities' adaptation to the new medium: the preparation of materials, devised not with traditional teaching but with new technology in mind. This is the great challenge for the universities themselves and, in particular, for their academics.

The application of this new scenario to the teaching of postgraduates (adults) is a need that no-one denies. Adults can follow their continuous education from their place of work, in other words, without having to travel. The same is true for adults who, whether retired or not, are looking for intellectual satisfaction rather than to acquire training due to the demands of their jobs. However, the real revolution will take place in undergraduate education.

As regards the acceptance of this new scenario by young people accessing university for the first time, there is no problem: they belong to the digital generation and they will not require any process of adaptation to the new medium. Whole new forms of learning and interaction will open up for them. For example, students from different universities and different countries will be able to interact through networks created by agreements between their institutions. We might see a team comprising students from three or four different countries all working on a project proposed by the professor at one of the universities or by various professors jointly. The key if the system is to work is connectivity, and, in particular, the capacity to imagine and create adequate environments to achieve the established aims. This will initially mean sizeable investment in equipment and human capital. It is precisely these two factors that require some prudence when it comes to making acquisitions that might become obsolete very soon.

The possibility of establishing networks between universities opens up new prospects for internationalisation and the option that, for example, a university qualification might be issued by two or three universities at the same time. This may also lead to the establishment of university clubs all over the world, with membership rights. As with British clubs, this will involve a selection process based on a score system.

For some, this is a very enticing prospect, considering the 'Harvardisation' that, as we have mentioned, is currently in decline. Where it might really be interesting is for the majority of regional universities that must be more deeply-rooted in local or regional development. All of them may be enriched by establishing networks between universities or faculties with common and complementary interests. A problem of competition may arise when students have the option, from anywhere in the world, to access one or another university without the expense of attending the campus. Evidently, there are a number of possibilities that constitute a real challenge for each university. At all events it seems reasonable to assume that this journey has begun but that, for a long time, it will exist alongside traditional activities, which will be steadily enriched with new technology. There might even be a transitory situation in which students will be able to choose between 100 percent on-site education, a mixture of on-site and external learning, completely virtual education, etc. This is in fact nothing short of a revolution, but it appears likely to be applied to the world of universities through a process of progressive transformation.

THE DEVELOPMENT OF THE CHINESE UNIVERSITIES: RISING STARS IN THE TWENTY-FIRST CENTURY

Higher education in China is continuously growing, changing and developing. There are over 2,000 universities and colleges, with more than six million annual enrollments in total.

According to the Ministry of Education of China, the government authority on all matters pertaining to education and language, higher education in China has played a significant part in economic growth, scientific progress and social development in the country 'by bringing up large scale of advanced talents and experts for the modernisation of the country'.

The Chinese education system is based on legalist and Confucian ideals. The teaching of Confucius has shaped the overall Chinese mindset for the past 2,500 years. But, other outside forces have played a large role in the educational development. The First Opium War of 1840, for example, opened China to the rest of the world. As a result, Chinese intellectuals discovered the numerous Western advances in science and technology. This new information greatly impacted the higher education system and curriculum.

Because of the soviet influence in the early 1950s, the research was separated from teaching in higher education. Chinese higher education continues its struggle with excessive departmentalization, segmentation, and overspecialisation in particular.

In 1977, former President Mr Deng Xiaoping made the decision of resuming the National Higher Education Entrance Examination, having profound impact on Chinese higher education in history. During the past 30 years, China has made tremendous effort to improve its higher education. Teaching-oriented universities have transformed themselves into research-oriented ones. From just over 20,000 papers in 1998, China's output increased to upwards of 112,000 papers by 2008. By the measure of annual output, China now stands second to the USA in the world. Chinese universities contribute most of these papers. Taking Shanghai Jiao Tong University, one of the leading universities in China, as an example. In early 1990s, only about 50 SCI papers were

Students of Medicine on the basketball court, Xu Jia Huai campus, Shanghai (n.d.)
In 1998, the Chinese government picked nine universities – including Peking, Tsinghua and Shanghai Jiao Tong – which it intended to raise to world-class status.

published annually. From 1999 to 2008, 9,080 SCI papers have been cited for a total of 62,560 times.

In 2000, there were about 2,000 higher education institutions in PRC. Close to 1,400 were regular higher education institutions. About 600 were higher education institutions for adults. Combined enrollment in 2002 was 11,256,800. Of this close to 40 percent were new recruits. In 2005, student enrollment increased to 15 million with rapid growth that peaked in 2008. The total number of graduate students newly admitted by higher education institutions and research institutions was 202,600 among which 38,400 were for Ph.D. and 164,200 for master's degree.

Since 2007, China has become the sixth largest country in hosting international students. The total number of international students studying in China often ranges around two hundred thousand.

In 1998, nine universities have been targeted by the Chinese government to become 'world-class' – including Peking, Tsinghua and Shanghai Jiao Tong universities. When former Chinese president Jiang Zemin, attended the hundredth anniversary ceremony at Peking University in 1998 and the ninetieth anniversary ceremony at Tsinghua University in 2001, he emphasized this ambitious goal of advancing several of China's higher education institutions into the top tier of universities worldwide in the next several decades.

Top Chinese universities putting great emphasis on cultivating students with innovation capability. A great proportion of Ph.D. students in top universities in the world had their undergraduate education in China, especially in the area of science and engineering. On 5 February 2010, a group of three undergraduate students from SJTU won the championship of ACM International Collegiate Programming Contest for the third time.

A lot of scientists, artists, educators and students from the universities in China are making great contributions to the development of the country and the higher education. For example, with their own advantage of talents and technology, the Fourder Group run by Peking University revolutionised the printing industry of China and the HDTV Technology of SJTU measures up to advanced world standards. They have their own master and doctoral training pilots, post-doctoral mobilising departments, national key laboratories and research centres for national projects, thus the integration of industry, teaching and research into reality.

Nowadays, there are more and more Chinese universities stepping on the international academic stage. It shows apparently, that universities like SJTU, Peking University and Tsinghua University are the emerging stars in the twenty-first century and they will definitely enrich the knowledge society in the new era.

Jie Yin

Today, China is the world's sixth-largest recipient of foreign students, accommodating an annual average of 200,000. A lot of scientists, artists, educators and students from the universities in China are making great contributions to the development of the country

Graduation ceremony at Zheng Fa University, Peking (2004)
In 2005, Chinese universities attracted an enrolment of fifteen million students and produced over three million graduates. In 2008, two hundred thousand students were pursuing graduate study.

Ludwig Mies van der Rohe, Illinois Institute of Technology (IIT), Chicago (1950–56)
The famous German architect's design for the IIT's Crown Hall was an instance of the maxim that ran through the entirety of his oeuvre: 'Less is more.' Mies (1886–1969) designed a sober inspired rectangular structure on two levels. The space was lent simplicity by an austere combination of steel and glass.

VIII

THE UNIVERSITY
AND ARCHITECTURE

OMA, Shinjyuku vertical campus, Tokyo (2004)
The famous architect Rem Koolhaas and his OMA partnership have designed the building – still to be built – to house the medical, fashion and IT schools. Constrained by scarcity of space, the project adapts an existing skyscraper. Careful allocation of space means the distinct schools reinforce their own architectural identity, while conferring a unique and cohesive personality on the building as a whole.

University, Space and Utopia

Pablo Campos Sotelo

Education is a spatial event. Over the centuries, the transmission of knowledge, whatever its form, was invariably accomplished in a concrete material setting. The university, too, partakes of that spatial quality. Concerned with educating the human being as a whole – in a sense that goes beyond pure academic training to embrace values, attitudes – the university must nurture personal contact, because personal contact is of the essence in education. So education at a university, too, is a spatial experience. The history of the universites is written in the history of their buildings.

The physical dimension of higher education has two aspects. First, a university campus comprises a number of locations where its specific activities are carried on: lecture halls, seminar rooms, laboratories and all their auxiliary structures and areas. Secondly, the tangible form of the university interacts with its urban and territorial environment, in tandem with the university's calling as an innovator in the social, economic and cultural realms.

Architecture and town planning are accordingly involved in the university venture: they play host to its activities and advertise its virtues. This aspect is a distinctive trait of Western culture in particular, where the university and its city have traditionally breathed life into a mutual identity.

University, city and architecture make up an indissoluble triad directed to the integrated education of the individual in a tradition of excellence.

The long history of universities has witnessed an exciting contrast between illusion and reality; but it is also a chronicle of hope and disappointment. One of the keys here has been a certain utopianism. Utopianism has encouraged the university to embark upon renewal after every period of decay; utopianism has helped the university to cut a path towards fresh ideals. Utopia is an inexhaustible source of energy in the intellectual sphere, and has lent shape to aspirations of excellence in the architectural corpus of the universities. A university is a fully realised and tangible utopia: 'utopia in motion.'

Physical space, whether internal (the constructive elements of a campus) or external (insertion within an urban fabric) is consubstantial with a university's personality.

Shinjyuku vertical campus, Tokyo (2004)
The design utilises a concept of 'subtraction' inspired by Michelangelo's Slave group of sculptures. The Renaissance artist started out with a block of stone from which he then extracted his figures. Similarly, as against the standard constructive practice of 'addition', Koolhaas's proposal 'liberates' forms encased within the building.

The Medieval University

The university was first created as an institution in the Middle Ages. The genesis and dissemination of knowledge, of course, was a pursuit that had already been undertaken for centuries before.

Etymologically, the term 'university' designated a city guild – the spontaneously emerging community of masters and students (*universitas magistrorum et discipulorum*).

It is arguable that the first university-like institution was the Greek *polis*. This embryonic 'city of learning' comprised locales that were to have a distinguished future: the agora, the academy and the gymnasium. Here, learning was accomplished by a spoken dialogue between masters and disciples. In his *Republic*, Plato sketched out a method by which his ideal citizens would be schooled, thus framing one of the earliest precedents of what we today think of as higher education. So classical Greece was the first culture to see learning as a pursuit bound up with the city.

A leap forward in time would lead one to examine the Muslim madrassa, a forerunner of the Spanish universities. One of the most illustrious madrassas was founded in Granada by Yusuf I, hard by his royal chapel. In the fourteenth century, the madrassa was the seat of the 'house of studies'. The term 'madrassa' means both 'place of learning' and 'library'; and the madrassa at Granada, contrary to what some historians claim, served a purpose far wider than that of a library. The rich Islamic culture gave grounds for the creation of 'schools of translators', whose mission was to channel Arab erudition from Spain to the European North. In 1085, the capture of Toledo – the main seat of the schools of translators – opened the gates of Islamic culture to Western civilisation.

Among the forerunners of the university as an institution, the most important were the cathedrals and monasteries.

The monasteries inspired the tangible shape that the university later chose for itself. Its cloister was the tectonic core and the focus of everyday life. The future repercussions of this architectural element are readily visible. Through the many typological shifts of university constructive models, the cloister survives as a common denominator. Tangentially, it gave its name to certain academic bodies and authorities.

A monastery was organised as an ideal city, functionally independent from the outside and following a typical pattern in the arrangement of its various spaces. One of the most widely imitated prototypes was the plan of the Abbey of St Gall, attributed to one Einhard and built around 820. A salient component, adjacent to the head of the church, was a structure housing a scriptorium on the ground floor, and, on the first floor, one of the centres of monastic life: the library.

The original monastic purpose of the cloister as a quiet, intimate space gave way in time to its use as the symbol of the emerging university. But this change did not rob the cloister of its compositional essence: the powerful outer walls sheltering the delicacy of the garden, the gentle purling of water, the breeze brushing against a few carefully tended trees. The cloister hinted at a subtle metaphor – a fragment of nature has been prised away from the landscape and set into the heart of a robust constructive apparatus.

The Cloister and the Heart of the City

The university rose on the European scene in the eleventh century as the institution inheriting the original 'faculties', or permission to teach, granted by cathedral chancellors to those 'masters' who had earned their favour.

The university took shape through an exodus of scholars from the monasteries to the cities, where they hoped to encounter the wider community. Knowledge was disseminated in a renewed cosmo-politan spirit which encouraged exchange and consciously avoided the self-sufficiency and insularity of the monasteries and the utopian ideology of St Augustine from which they had drawn inspiration.

The first universities were founded at Bologna (1088), Oxford (1167) and Paris (1170). The Italian university (which lends its name today to the process of convergence within the EHEA) started out as a

Candida Höfer,
Stiftsbibliothek St Gallen,
Switzerland (2001)
This German photographer
is famous for her enduring
concern with the history of
culture. She has explored
academic libraries – like
the one at the old Benedictine
Abbey of St Gall – which
she views as storehouses
of timeless knowledge.

Cloister of Fontevrault Abbey, Anjou, France (1110–19)
The cloister lay at the core of monastery life. The architecture is articulated by a series of courtyards; the surrounding corridors become the monastery's circulatory mechanism and organising principle.

brotherhood of students who elected their own rector. The French university was a society of graduate masters, and this model was followed at Oxford and Cambridge too. In Spain, universities were founded under the auspices of the royal court rather than papal authority. The earliest was the *studium generale* at Palencia (1212), which soon faded away. More enduring ventures were the universities of Salamanca (1218), Valladolid (1260), Alcalá (1293) and Lérida (1297). Salamanca was to become hugely influential as the alma mater of the expansion of Western culture throughout the Spanish Americas.

At this germinal stage, the palpable embodiment of the university reflected the legacy of the cloister. This,

the setting for the transmission of an absolute truth grounded in the divine, mirrored the theological outlook of the time and enacted an early identification between the educational and the tectonic schemes. The cloister founded a spatial type that held together with the institution's ideology. It provided a uniform template for the medieval 'city of learning'.

The importance of the fit between an educational undertaking and its material locus was underscored by Alfonso X 'the Wise'. From 1256 to 1263, he personally drafted the law code known as *Las Siete Partidas*. The second *Partida* set out the first specific rules about where the activities of the *studium generale* were to be carried on.

Alfonso required that the *studium* have its own purpose-built premises:

> The town where the *Studium* is intended to be established must be of healthful air and have a fine village green, so that the masters who teach the knowledge and the scholars who learn it may live healthily there, and rest and amuse themselves in the evening when they rise from their lectures, wearied by study.

Alfonso was an advocate of having his places of study in a heathy spot in the countryside, to preserve masters and students from the bad influence reputedly exerted by the city.

These principles, conceived five centuries ahead of their time, were the same as those underlying the American campus.

The inward-looking nature of the cloister had to contend with a more powerful circumstance: university premises stood in the heart of the city. The university, in Europe especially, has always been an essentially civic fact, identifying with its host city in a way that transcends architecture and suffuses the relations among faculty, students and townsfolk.

Over the long and complex history of the foundation and rise of the university, from its medieval roots through the Renaissance and the Baroque period, an architectural form took shape that was later to set its stamp on innumerable university structures: the university seat known as the 'Palace of the Muses', '*domus sapientiae*' or 'house of learning'.

Up until the fifteenth century, university locales, scattered across the central neighbourhoods of cities, were barely adequate to accommodate educational functions. There arose in response a type of compact building equipped with lecture halls, chapel, library, ceremonial hall, theatre or academic auditorium, and offices for rectors, administrative staff and masters. The advantages of better constructive quality were none-theless outstripped by a more important factor. University buildings became symbols facing the host city, lending an image and a ceremonial form to the academic institution.

The morphology of a typical university seat was a rectangular plan, containing a quadrangle and often

Courtyard of the Law Faculty, University of Bologna (2001) This Italian university has retained its original medieval seat. The use of historic buildings for educational purposes is key: it offers students direct contact with the cultural traditions of the past and helps ensure that architectural heritage will be preserved.

presided over by a tower graced by a clock. Included here are the Bo Palace in Padua, designed by Andrea Moroni, and the splendid Sant' Ivo alla Sapienza in Rome, with its cloister created by Giacomo della Porta and a magisterial chapel built by Francesco Borromini from 1642 to 1660. This building type crystallised in the Archiginnasio at Bologna, designed in 1563 by Antonio Morandi (*Terribilia*). The university-building fomat flourihed for centuries, especially in Europe, as exemplified by the universities of Vienna, Coimbra, Berlin, Prague, Helsinki, Cracow and Basel, among others. In Spain, the architectural proposal that gained the widest currency was the university *colegio*, the foreign origins of which lay in Paris. There the chaplain of St Louis, Robert de Sorbon, founded in 1257 a men's hall of residence, which grew to become the Sorbonne. One of the best-known Spanish landmarks was the College of St Clement; it was built not in Spain but in Bologna, by Cardinal Gil Albornoz, in 1367.

The most widely imitated model in the sixteenth century was the College of San Antonio Portaceli at Sigüenza. Inaugurated in the late fifteenth century, it is regarded as a forerunner of the Colegio de San Ildefonso erected under the patronage of Cardinal Cisneros in the nearby city of Alcalá de Henares in 1499. The profusion of imposing college buildings all across Spain was one of the hallmarks of the Hispanic university, which took shape somewhat later than its European counterparts. This flourishing gained crucial support from the Catholic Monarchs. It was they who enabled the Spanish collegial system to wield its influence beyond Spain and take root in the Americas.

Another internationally prominent tradition was the model of the splendid Oxford and Cambridge colleges, perhaps the highest exponents of the architectural legacy of the cloister. Their origin and diffusion across the urban fabric became one of the paradigms of the identity between city and university.

Jean Laurent, Colegio de San Ildefonso, University of Alcalá de Henares (19th century)
In 1836 the University of Alcalá was moved to Madrid, and its original buildings lay derelict. In response, the local citizenry founded the 'Society of Joint Owners of the Buildings that Were Once a University', the object of which was to buy up the buildings to make sure they survived.

The Modern European University

The Renaissance and Baroque periods saw the rise of a new idea of university. Drawing inspiration from humanism and metaphysics, its outlook shifted from the purportedly absolute comprehension of medieval theology to a more contingent conception of knowledge. According to Auguste Comte, after the Middle Ages the medieval idea of the university as terra firma faded away. Knowledge came to be viewed as a continent of ignorance where no certainty could be had – only partial and provisional truth was ever available. Research and inquiry came to the fore in the search for alternatives. And as a result of this from the nineteenth century onwards a scientific and positivistic discourse rose to prominence.

The evolution of the university brought change to its core purposes of teaching and research, and these changes were mirrored in the adoption of structures whose features cleaved to the emerging institutional ideology. There were two major aspects in play: location with respect to the city (giving rise to a historic debate concerning the dichotomy 'integration versus segregation'), and the internal arrangement of the various independent constructive elements.

And each of the various modern models of the university chose a particular spatial form to make its own.

The English Model

The English model, so splendidly represented by Oxford and Cambridge, formalised what might be viewed as a second 'city of learning', thus continuing the concept that germinated in the Greek *polis*. The English colleges were distinguished exponents of a broader European tradition. From the seventeenth century onwards, the specific English exemplar was to exert a decisive influence across the Atlantic on the emerging American models of university campus. Institutionally, the English-speaking college was more sharply independent from both the state and the rest of the university than its European continental counterparts.

Architecturally, the square or rectangular plan of the college – hence the name 'quadrangle' given to the

A quadrangle in the University of Cambridge (13th century)
A quadrangle is a partly enclosed, inward-looking, markedly geometric space that charactristically serves as the organizing core for the buildings of the ancient campuses of Oxford and Cambridge.

emblematic empty space thus formed in its midst – bore the imprint of the monastery. The cloister, as the archetype of this inner empty space, was a crisply geometric locus within which student life could be followed closely. The Oxonian college accommodated an interesting functional diptych: teaching and residence. The design of the built apparatus, with its habitable spaces disposed centrifugally around the quadrangle, brought both activities of living and learning into close proximity and harmony.

In the English university model, the genesis and growth of the city were a direct consequence of the multiplication of the colleges. With each one operating as a 'teaching cell', the colleges arranged themselves into a geometric and orthogonal pattern. The constructions cleaved to the divisions of the city's street map, thus making the best use of the available land.

The upshot is a complex shared fabric in which the colleges are distributed over an extensive surface, connected by a system of streets that channel the characteristic to-ing and fro-ing of students and dons. At Oxford, the university district is traversed by the High Street and Broad Street. The Cambridge colleges turn on the hub of St John's Street, Trinity Street and King's Parade, which to the west is joined by the course of the river Cam, from which the city take its name.

The English university model displays an inward-looking and monumental architecture dressed with a repertory of stylistic languages that range from the Gothic to the Renaissance, and more. The proliferation of colleges gradually loaded the urban grid, which worked as an ever-present undergirding for the identification of university and city. The dissemination of the colleges from the sixteenth century onwards gave rise to one of the spatial archetypes that best represented the 'city of learning' and which survives in full vigour up to the present moment.

The French Model

Setting out from the founding moment of the French Revolution of 1789, the Napoleonic university emerged in the early nineteenth century. In 1808, the decree was enacted that established the university as the body solely responsible for public education throughout the Empire. The doctrine underlying this new academic enterprise cast aside the old preference for theory, rhetoric and intellectualism to inaugurate a more pragmatic and vocational approach. The principle of reason and rationality was its *raison d'être*; the Napoleonic university was an institution with an imperial mission: centralised, bureaucratic and dependent upon an established power, it was to control both higher and secondary education.

Whereas the English model exemplified subordination to an aristocracy, here the university was subordinate to the state. The earlier liking for a permanent interrogation of knowledge gave way to the imparting of concrete bodies of fact. The university, as a public service structured into professional schools, was now entrusted with training the technical specialists and functionaries of society.

The chosen territorial model made Paris the centre of gravity of the entire university institution.

Within the Parisian city fabric, educational structures adopted a polycyclic configuration within a narrow radius of action. A parallel arose between the diversity of forms of learning and the physical splintering of the university across multiple buidings. The tectonic result was a diffuse complex within the metropolis, the architectural vehicle for a fertile dialogue between totality (university centralism) and fragmentation (the multiplicity of scattered pieces). Though in a way quite different from the English model, here, too, the university was at one with the city. The Napoleonic pavilion structures, a consequence of subdivision into professorial chairs and departments, were the built expression of the utopian legacy of the Enlightenment.

The French university model finds in the Napoleonic university an exponent of the relationship between institutional model on the one hand, and urban planning and architectural embodiment on the other. The centrepiece is the huge Sorbonne building, based on the pre-existing complex built in the time of Cardinal Richelieu to a design by the influential architect Jacques Lemercier in 1635. When Napoleon created the Imperial university, he also set off a major typological mutation: the compact, mono-structural format of the big 'academic barn' was replaced by a multiple, scattered location across the Parisian Latin Quarter.

The Sorbonne, however, stayed on its own path, keeping faith with the university building prototype, anchored between the rue des Écoles and the rue Cujas. Its restructuring and enlargement followed a design by Henri Paul Nénot. The 'Academic Palace' of the 'Nouvelle Sorbonne' was built from 1885 to 1887 by the main wall of the precinct. The intention was to vindicate the university from the standpoint of the Republic. As the emblem of this new form of government, it expressly refused to make any kind of homage to ecclesiastical power.

The Sorbonne project exhibits three gestures that throw into sharp relief the symbolic role that attaches to the social functions of university architecture. First, the central courtyard retains the contour of the original chapel erected by Robert de Sorbon in 1326. On the pavement of the historic *cour d'honneur* the marks of the old alignment of the walls remain visible even now. Students, staff and visitors to the university can retrace the history and ongoing development of the institution through its built corpus.

Secondly, the main entrance, renovated in the nineteenth century, sought to open up the university to the city, mirroring the metaphorical intention of opening up the university to the *res publica*. Today, this solemn piece of architecture enjoys the openness of the adjoining space over which it casts its monumental shadow: the square named after the mathematician Painlevé. This ratifies the shift in the university's ideological stance. Formerly, the main entrance was channelled from the inner courtyard, where the great chapel was the vital rubric of the ecclesiastical institution. In counterpoint, the new Sorbonne displaced its point of entry to the modern main façade, thus offering itself to a civic environment that stood for the sovereign people.

As the third illustrative feature, the Sorbonne offers a beautiful lesson in urban-planning engagement

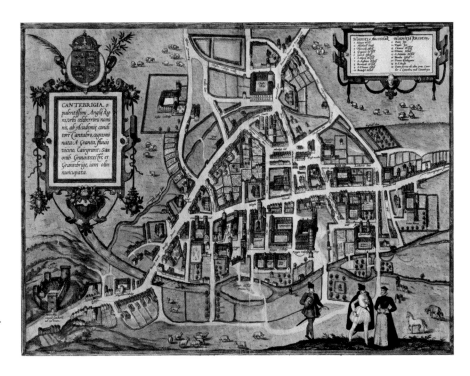

between city and university. The monumental church built by Richelieu in the seventeenth century has a large entrance from the inner courtyard, but the façade at the end of its central nave looks out onto the city, which chose to answer this token of regard by dignifying its own presence. The decision was made to knock down the old tenement housing that stood there, thus to create a small square – a 'breathing space' – adjoining the rue Sorbonne and situated exactly in front of the entrance to the university chapel. The university heritage of Europe offers two similar gestures: in Salamanca, the city elected to tear down a number of big old houses that used to stand opposite the superb Plateresque façade delineated in 1529 by Juan de Álava. This allowed room for a small square created specially for the purpose: the patio de Escuelas. And, in Alcalá, the plaza de San Diego was similarly reshaped so as to make a worthy counterpoint facing the magnificent façade that Gil de Hontañón designed in 1553 for the Colegio de San Ildefonso. In all three examples, the commitment binding university and city was given effect by a joint spatial solution evincing an admirable reciprocal sensibility.

Franz Hogenberg, Cambridge, *Civitates Orbis Terrarum* **(1575)**
The urban planning of Cambridge reflects the University's metaphorical and literal independence alike. The buildings of the University and of its famous colleges cluster near the banks and bridges of the River Cam, from which the city takes its name.

The Sorbonne, Paris
The Sorbonne is a leading example of a university taking root at the heart of the urban fabric. Its various buildings, built at different times, occupy a large part of the Parisian Latin Quarter.

The evolution of the university brought change to its core purposes of teaching and research, and these changes were mirrored in the adoption of structures whose features cleaved to the emerging institutional ideology

The German Model

The university of Berlin was founded in 1810. Wilhelm von Humboldt expressed its founding principle by calling it the 'mother of all modern universities'.

Academically, the new institution's search for truth enlisted the efforts of both faculty and students and enjoyed considerable freedom from state control, reflecting the vision of the philosopher Johann Gottlieb Fichte, its first rector, and of Friedrich Schleiermacher. As in Britain and France, in Germany the university came within the orbit of an elite minority that had sprung from the liberal middle classes.

The material embodiment first chosen was the u niversity building inherited from the Renaissance, the leading exemplar of which was the Bolognese Archiginnasio. King Friedrich Wilhelm III gave what had been the Palace of Prince Heinrich of Prussia, built from 1748 to 1766 by Knobelsdorff and Boumann. Its main façade faced the 'avenue under the lime trees' (Unter den Linden), an artery running through the heart of Berlin. The incipient university thus stood at a strategic point of the city, which even today lies close to landmarks such as the Opera, the cathedral, the Altes museum and the Neue Wache. The latter two were the work of the renowned architect Karl Friedrich Schinkel, who also transformed the private residence of Wilhelm von Humboldt, the Tegel palace.

The seat of the Humboldtian university was originally laid out on a U-shaped plan, and later (1913 to 1920) enlarged by Hoffmann, with two wings running northward in parallel. This arrangement, again, showed the inspiration of the cloister. The new rear area reinterpreted the *cour d'honneur*, which the original palace had had opposite the majestic avenue. The stylistic features of this monumental device were a tribute to rationalist Neoclassicism, the heir to the school of the French theorist Jean Nicolas Louis Durand. Its language and composition also exhibits some influence of the Italian Quattrocento in its decorative romantic elements. As an artistic and symbolic supplement, at either side of the main entrance there were put up two monuments in tribute to the Humboldt brothers – Wilhelm and Alexander – allegorising the 'sciences of thought' and the 'sciences of nature' of nineteenth-century Germany.

It was in forms such as this that the university building further multiplied in nineteenth-century Europe. Examples included the University of Vienna (Ferstel, 1884), the Central University of Madrid – a renovation of an existing structure, the Noviciado (Mariátegui, 1842) – and the University of Barcelona (Rogent, 1885), which, joining the old and new quarters of the city, was one of the earliest landmarks of the Ensanche sector laid down by the town planner Ildefonso Cerdá in 1859.

Returning to Germany, after its initial architectural formalisation as a single structure, the tangible imprint of the 'cultural urbanisation' that it brought about spread across the neighbouring area, already rich in architectural heritage. One testimony to this centrifugal outward push is the fact that in 1829 the university took over the Charité building as the faculty of Medicine. Humboldt's innovative university thus adopted a markedly urban physical model that indulged in monumentalism and hoped to engage with the essence of the city of Berlin.

The American Campus

The American university model is of special significance for its influence on generations of international educational architecture, but also because its qualities have been consistently misunderstood.

One should first unpack the etymological nuances of the term 'campus'. Used indiscriminately and sometimes quite mistakenly, it seems to have first appeared in a letter dated January 1774 at Princeton: in his description of a fire, the writer (a student) meant to designate the extension of land surrounding the central seat of the university, Nassau Hall. Other interpretations have seen a link to the Campus Martius of ancient Rome, which, if correct, would imply an allusion to the idea of a large open space rich with cultural meaning.

Leaving this terminological issue aside, the fact is that the campus, as an integrated model that defines a specific academic and experiential personality, has all too often been imitated poorly, such as to obscure its undoubted virtues. The campus is not the upshot of a single or uniform historical reality but has undergone a chequered career. The main visible forms it has taken over the centuries merit close analysis.

The Colonial Colleges

The origin of the campus was a formal and functional proposition of the English college, which, in the process of colonisation that followed the discovery of the New World, made its crossing from Europe.

The earliest settlements in New England sought to use higher education in furtherance of the conquest of the continent, a natural corollary of which was the multiplying of colonial colleges throughout the seventeenth century. The town planning that went with this abandoned the tight clusters of colleges characteristic of Oxford and Cambridge and took up a more scattered format, reflecting the idea of a gradual occupation of territory. Taking the Oxonian quadrangle as its archetype, the American college was transferred to a vast, wild natural landscape: here, the college was to be created as an isolated township. This, then, marked the beginning of a third 'city of learning',

Students playing American football, Harvard University (2001)
The English-speaking tradition of the university campus reflects an all-embracing conception of student life. The undergraduate goes to lectures, reads, lives and interacts with peers and lecturers within a closed, specially designed environment.

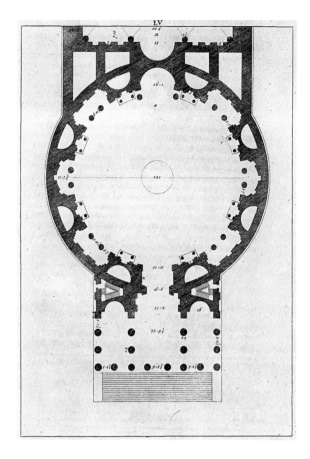

Thomas Jefferson and Henry Latrobe, plan of the University of Virginia (1817)
The third president of the United States (1801–09) took a keen interest in architecture and contributed to the design of the University of Virginia, which he founded. The plan of the Rotunda library exhibits the influence of the Italian villas of the Renaissance architect Andrea Palladio and of the Pantheon at Rome.

the formation of a self-sufficient world at a far remove from the hubbub of the city. The architectonic plan of the colonial colleges adopted a powerful spatial stance reminiscent of the pioneering design in 1557 of Gonville and Caius College, Cambridge: one of the four wings of the building was simply done away with. The consequence of this compositional change was to suggest an opening up to the social and natural setting – in embryonic form, a genuine campus integrated with nature.

The new American prototype was directed to the education of a qualified and enterprising class that would keep faith with the values of society then in the throes of winning prosperity and growth in the social, economic and educational domains.

The 'Academical Village'

Once the model of the college had been transplanted from Europe, the extension of colleges all across the United States brought about a veritable 'archipelago' of islands of learning. And yet the campus aspired to be the town-planning embodiment of the mindset of this young nation. The energy of this idea sprang from the revolutionary utopia that advocated the removal of the university to the margins of the city, as an 'academical village'.

One of the main projects that grew out of this philosophical legacy was the University of Virginia, planned in 1817 by Thomas Jefferson in partnership with Henry Latrobe. The site chosen for this ambitious enterprise was Charlottesville, near the home of the third President of the United States, his much-loved Monticello.

The University of Virginia was created in hopes of forming an academic microcosm on a human scale. The simple architecture of its parts would mark off a delicate and welcoming space, the ideal setting for the life and work of faculty and students. The plan of the complex displayed a strong compositional unity and an architectural language that drew life from the new classicism style and from the Renaissance master Andrea Palladio. These influences are accounted for by Jefferson's travels through Italy while he was the United States ambassador to France. The design of the University of Virginia was inspired by two grand notions: the Greek tradition, by which master and disciple lived together in close proximity; and the Roman tradition, imprinted on the style and arrangement of sensible space. It has been suggested that one of the works that most influenced the Jeffersonian campus was Villa Trissino.

The resulting 'imprint of learning' was a new kind of educational site that combined axiality and perspectivism with an outward-looking disposition of the pavilions, which faced the surrounding landscape. The academical village was paradigmatic of the suppression of the fourth volume of the central rectangle; it thus continued the opening-up inherited from the colonial tradition, but prompted here by a desire to bring within the campus a view of the lush woods nearby. It fixed forever the tradition of the American quad, a version of the original English quadrangle.

The Rotunda lay at the centre. With this compositional strategy, Jefferson exalted the library as the guardian of the institution's calling. It is also yet another illustration of the virtues of the bond

The campus aspired to be the town-planning embodiment
of the mindset of this young nation. The energy of this
idea sprang from the revolutionary utopia that advocated
the removal of the university to the margins of the city, as
an 'academical village'

Rotunda of the University of Virginia (1817)
The architectural distinction of this building has made the University of Virginia the only academic institution in the United States to have won World Heritage status. With his choice of a neo-Palladian style, Jefferson intended to create an aesthetics that would reflect the values of the new American nation.

**Students at the gateway
of the University of Berkeley
(1956)**
California's oldest university
was founded in 1868. Designed
as a 'city of learning', one of its
most distinctive features is the
Sather Tower or *campanile*,
built in 1914.

between institutional spirit and built embodiment, both being recruited to the furtherance of university excellence.

Nature, 'City Beautiful' and Renewal

Since it first emerged as an innovative proposal three centuries ago, the American model has undergone considerable change. Its diverse developments have engendered quite exceptional urban-planning and architectural projects. Distinguished examples of this rich and prolific tradition are the campuses of the universities of Harvard, Yale, Berkeley, Chicago, Washington and Princeton.

A selection of the more eminent examples illustrates some of the distinctive features of the American repertoire.

First, the campus exhibits a latter-day engagement with nature. One exponent of this is the University of Stanford at Palo Alto, built on a large rustic site about fifty kilometres south of San Francisco to a design drawn by Frederick Law Olmsted in 1886 in partnership with Charles A. Coolidge. At the drawing-board stage, a compromise was arrived at between the naturalistic approach advocated by the famous landscape designer and the founders, Leland and Jane Stanford, who wanted to dress up the university in monumental fashion. The treatment reinterpreted the cloister pattern in its main areas, evoking with its arcade galleries the Californian Hispanic missions.

A second form is embodied by Columbia University in New York. Founded in 1754 as King's College and first located in the southern cone of Manhattan, in the late nineteenth century it was moved to its present campus north of Central Park in Morningside Heights. The architectural firm McKim, Mead & White created in 1894 a precinct inspired by the architectural model known as 'City Beautiful', first advanced at the World's Columbian Exposition at Chicago in 1893. An unequivocally civic school, it was tightly integrated with the orthogonal net into which it had been set. The interior opens out as a prototypical central quad, the site of the famous Low Library.

A third key exponent is the Illinois Institute of Technology at Chicago, superbly designed by Mies

van der Rohe. The institution was established in 1940 after the merger of the Armour and Lewis Institutes. The brilliant German architect's creation broke new ground in the urban planning standards of the campus. The archetype of the quad, as an assembly of structures adopting a partly closed – square or rectangular – plan around a central space, was now dissolved. Mies elected to throw down the various elements quite freely in the manner of parallelepipeds scattered across the green tapestry of a flexible campus: the only regular pattern was the pervasive orthogonality to which the intrinsic geometry of each part conformed.

Architecturally, the use of steel and glass – the signature materials of the Miesian style – was a subtle wink at the technologies born of the Industrial Revolution and used in the swift reconstruction of the heart of Chicago, the Loop, after it had been devastated by fire in 1871: the campus was posited as mirroring that renewal.

This triad of examples testifies to the diversity and richness of the American campus idea. Its common denominator is a conscious link between academic model, social and urban context, and constructive arrangement as the underpinnings of excellence.

Walter Gropius, Graduate Center, Harvard University (1950)
A native of Berlin, Gropius (1883–1969) was a successful professional and academic architect who founded the legendary Bauhaus school. His doctrine, which lay at the base of functionalist architecture, was that form follows function.

Idealism, Continuity and Projection

The main contribution of the American campus to university culture is that it developed a distinctive principle of its own: the will to achieve an ideal city crystallises a modern version of the island utopia.

It is this idealistic feature that, by an apparent paradox, engages with the analogous profile of the 'island of learning' inherent to the cloister of the Middle Ages. As already suggested, the campus and the cloister both spring from one and the same ideological model, because both pay homage to a desire to escape city 'contamination'. The difference turns on the fact that the American prototype rejects the closed composition of the cloister in favour of a scattering of freestanding elements across the natural landscape.

Taking the opposite approach to the cloister metaphor, where a fragment of nature seems to have been injected into the heart of the robust built structure, it is now pieces of architecture which, like built fragments, are delicately perched along the interstices of a vast natural terrain.

Another distinctive feature of the campus is that it has preserved a historic balance between change and continuity. A general review of the repertory of American higher education premises would come across a number of different categories: the early colonial clusters inspired by the English colleges; the nineteenth-century complexes lording it over the natural environment; the park university model of the first Land Grant projects, a prime example being Berkeley, landscaped by Frederick Law Olmsted in

**Columbia University,
New York (n.d.)**
Founded in 1754 by George II
of England, Columbia had its
original seat in south
Manhattan. In the late 19th
century it moved to an
impressive new campus in
Morningside Heights designed
by the architectural firm
of McKim, Mead &White.

1866 (the victor of the 1899 competitive tender for the design of the buildings was Émile Bénard); the *beaux arts* trend, with members as distinguished as Stanford and Columbia; later proposals urging a return to the cosy character of the English quad, and, finally, the more recent plans, which, as against other organisational arguments, privilege circulation as the prime structuring criterion.

One of the main facts about the American campus is that it has been imitated worldwide. It is the university type that has won the widest international acceptance – although in recent times its emulation has given room for a trail of regrettable imitations that eiher misunderstand the idea or fail to adapt it to the relevant local reality. But one of the salutary lessons taught by the campus to the international architectural scene is the notion that judiciously devised architecture directed to the achievement of certain purposes can inspire huge interest and motivation among end users. So, when successful, it fulfils the role of a 'educational campus', a concept advocated later in this chapter.

Return to Europe:
the Ciudad Universitaria of Madrid

The entry upon the university scene of the campus as a spatial and social paradigm was echoed for a long time by the dynamics of transfer and repetition in any number of countries. Owing to rather slapdash procedures, this replicating trend sowed the university field with infelicitous projects. But it would be unfair not to

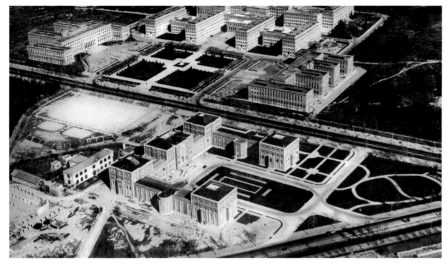

Ciudad Universitaria of Madrid (c. 1970)
The project, first mooted in 1927, developed over decades, continuing even after the standstill forced by the Spanish Civil War. Most of the campus was taken up by Universidad Complutense buildings, but in the latter third of the twentieth century the Universidad Politécnica, too, built a number of facilities, as did UNED, the National University of Distance Education.

acknowledge a few brilliant examples of educational premises the design of which exhibits an intelligent use of the values of the American model. Perhaps the best is the Ciudad Universitaria of Madrid, the first campus designed in Europe following the American blueprint.

This large academic venture started out in 1927 with the formation of the 'construction board' under the patronage of Alfonso XIII of Spain. Composed by an elite of influential personalities, the board's purpose was to renovate the entire model of the university, which was then housed in a number of unsuitable buildings in the city centre.

The decisive episode came in the autumn of that same year when, encouraged by the King's utopian enthusiasm, a commission of advisers travelled Europe and, crucially, the United States. Their hope was to find inspiration in the as yet little-known New World campus. The two-month 'utopian voyage' produced a wealth of references and documents after visits to the most famous academic complexes of the age, and its ultimate outcome was of unquestionable historic importance: the creation in Spain of the first European campus.

Modesto López Otero's master plan of 1928 was the overall result of a yearning for innovation. In some metaphorical sense, the 'space of learning' that had emigrated to the New World from the English colleges was now making the return crossing to Europe, in a new, freshly vital form, to sow its seed in the soil of the European university.

The famous Madrid campus arose from an armory of strategically intelligent arguments: a suitably understood American model was imported to Spain; that model was moulded to local constraints, which meant that the complex had to preserve a strict continuity with the fabric of the Spanish capital; finally, the buildings were fashioned to European stylistic patterns, following in the steps of the architectural avant-garde then flourishing in the Old World.

Madrid's Ciudad Universitaria was a healthily ambitious and powerfully coherent project, because it was underpinned by cultural points of reference which had been quite consciously adapted. A list of those fundamental influences would include the Academy, eclecticism, and the École des Beaux Arts; several schools had an effect on the architects' search for an overarching stylistic unity: the scheme of 'college plus sport', the Germanic organization into seminar rooms and laboratories, the philanthropy and elitism of the New World prototypes, and, in places, the design of the 1927 League of Nations building at Geneva.

Although it has suffered decades of accretions quite alien to the utopian spirit in which it was formed, Madrid's 'University City' stands today as living testimony of the power of ambitious goals when a major academic venture is in issue. Its fame and impact went beyond Spain: Europe and Latin America saw innumerable versions of the American campus, which in its Spanish interpretation had found an exponent of how a university project can be elevated into an emblem of the cultural transformation of a nation.

Ciudad Universitaria, Madrid
In 1927 there formed the grand
ambition to use land granted
by Alfonso XIII to create a
'university city' that would
bring together all Madrid's
higher education institutions
– Complutense, Politécnica
and the National University
of Distance Education – with
their governing bodies, halls
of residence, leisure areas and
sports facilities.

The 'space of learning' that had emigrated to the New
World from the English colleges was now making the
return crossing to Europe, in a new, freshly vital form,
to sow its seed in the soil of the European university

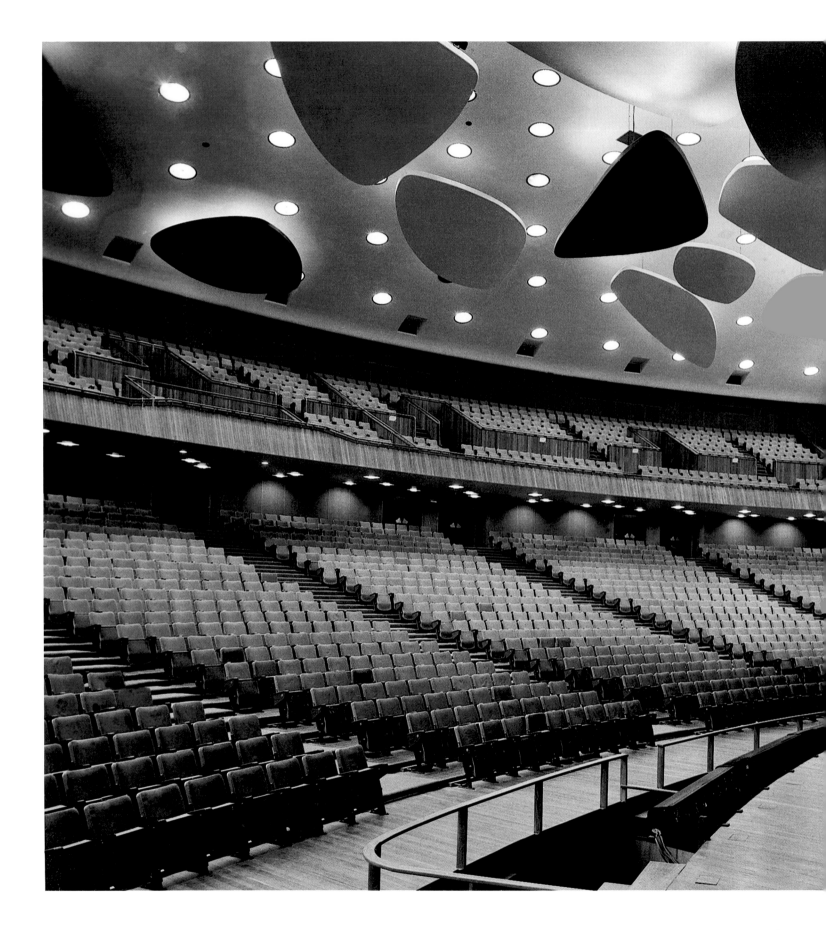

The Contemporary University

After the Second World War, universities across the world underwent considerable change in their ideals, structures and spatial configuration.

The growing complexity and size of the higher education landscape reshaped the contours of its internal structure and of its academic curricula, and shaped its relationship with the urban fabric of society, which was itself changing swiftly.

Recent decades have seen a sharp and unresolved tension between university and city. The integrated model versus the segregated model. The antithesis of university grounds anchored within the historic quarters of a city, as opposed to huge complexes built afresh on the city's edge, has sometimes acquired the nature of a dichotomy. But a constellation of examples of excellence have shown that that antagonism can be turned into a mutual and beneficial complementarity. The phenomenon has been particularly eloquent in Europe, at universities such as Utrecht in the Netherlands, Bologna in Italy, Prague in the Czech Republic, Lisbon in Portugal, Helsinki in Finland, and Alcalá, La Laguna, Santiago de Compostela and Salamanca in Spain, among many others.

The University of Masses: Macrostructures and Movement to the Periphery

One of the phenomena that moulded the social profile of the university in the second half of the twentieth century was a mass influx of students, beyond anything the institution had known before.

The multiplication of universities and the rapid swelling of student admissions brought substantial change and a number of contradictions in the ambit of what might be described as the 'utopia of democracy'. It was doubted whether a multi-social and overcrowded university would be capable of offering an adequate response to educational demand.

Mass university education, aside from its sociological aspect, had palpable consequences for the urban planning of university campuses. No model was proposed for this problem specifically. Overcrowding

Carlos Raúl Villanueva, Great Hall, Universidad Central de Venezuela (1952–53)
The Ciudad Universitaria de Caracas became World Heritage in 2000. Its high aesthetic value rests partly on its impressive auditorium, with its exceptionally good acoustics, fine architecture and a sculpture by Alexander Calder, *Acoustic Clouds*.

Alexis Josic, George Candilis, Shadrach Woods and Manfred Schiedhelm, University of Berlin (1963)
The design was conceived of as a miniature city, laid out as a pattern of horizontal circulations and low buildings. This achieved a coherence whereby each element was integrated with the whole. Photograph by Reinhard Friedrich.

After the world wars, the university revival of the 1960s and 1970s gave shape in Europe to two widely imitated urban planning models: the English model and the German. The main difference between them was that English projects made provision for student lodgings but German architects did not. The two trends unfolded across a complex international stage with a number of distinctive features.

For one thing, the creation of new institutions of higher learning formed part of an impulse towards rapid development. There was sometimes the sense that this high 'natality' of universities was more a matter of political prestige than a corollary of any rigorous academic, social or urban strategy. Moreover, there was a preference for huge architectural structures – outsize dimensions and a wide range of purposes – perhaps the heirs on a macro scale of the much earlier Renaissance 'compact' complexes, or even of the great medieval monasteries. And a third feature has been the fact that the modern university has been undercut by a woeful absence of planning. This failure of long-term or even medium-term vision is today still one of the most serious difficulties that remain to be overcome.

One of the architectural standards of this period was the design of the university in Berlin delineated in 1963 by Josic, Candilis, Woods and Schiedhelm. A composition proposing a bidirectional weave, it set off a new trend that was to inspire many other universities of the time.

The complex and prolific international repertoire offered up other efforts of distinction, and the sometimes contradictory evolution of modern universities was not devoid of gestures of engagement with urban and constructive innovation. The Finnish master Alvar Aalto brought a splendid organic vision to the campus of Espoo on the outskirts of Helsinki. One of the highlights here was the expressive volume of the auditorium, planned in 1955. The macro-project for the Catholic University of Louvain, built from 1970 onwards at Ottignies, Belgium; the extremist proposal of a linear campus dreamt up by Vittorio Gregotti in 1973 for the University of Calabria in Cosenza, Italy; and the Ciudad Universitaria of Caracas in Venezuela, the brainchild of Carlos Raúl Villanueva in 1943 – this last project, recognised by UNESCO as a

was often dealt with on the basis of pre-existing structures which were simply made denser; another option was to start afresh in large new complexes that were markedly segregated from their host cities.

In but a few years, the same Europe which had forged a strong university-civic organism, its hallmark for centuries, undertook a rapid transformation toward a hybrid system in which the university precinct was deprived of its context. This duality set off a flight of 'spaces of learning' from the city centre to the periphery. Metaphorically, the migration of universities to the suburbs can be read as analogous to the displacement of the university as an institution from the nerve centre of social power to a lesser role at society's edge.

This issue became the focus of a debate between rationalist functionalism, which argued for a zoned city, and an opposite view that preferred a superimposition of layers within the weft of the city. Functionalism advocated specialised segregation, generating counterpointed or juxtaposed university zones. The opponents of functionalism called for coexistence based on a reciprocal nurturing of identity as a way to have the university and the city entwined.

Wiel Arets, Library of the University of Utrecht (2004)
At a height of 33 metres, the reading room of the De Uithof campus is Utrecht University's landmark. It combines huge glass windows with dark colours indoors to encourage the concentration required for serious study. Photograph by Allard van der Hoek.

World Heritage Site in 2000, is the ideal of a total work of art, where architecture operates as a support for sculptural and pictorial works by masters such as Alexander Calder and Francisco Narváez. This campus is the setting for an artistic synthesis leavened by a meticulous sensitivity to the natural environment.

Innovation and Social Engagement: Diversification and Urban Revival

Today, the stage on which the university plays its role requires that it not resign itself to conformism but set its sights on excellence. The challenges that society now faces compel the university to engage vigorously with both training and with the exchange of knowledge and technology.

The university stands at a critical international crossroads and hears calls for it to revitalise its ties with the community. In addition to its traditional educational and research missions, the university must now honour an undertaking to its social and economic surroundings. One of the conditions of this new vocation is that the university revive its bond with the municipal fabric.

The universities are entering into a debate about how best to meet these new challenges in the awareness of the need to create spaces of the right kind to found academic excellence. An institution of higher learning that desires to effect a qualitative change in its built structures must make allowance for its existing premises, whatever their state, even if it intends to create new ones. The physical configuration of most universities will accordingly be widely heterogeneous.

In Spain and elsewhere there are now prospering a number of approaches directed to raise the special quality of the campus, enhance urban synergies and facilitate architectural alignment with the EHEA.

First, by contrast with earlier periods, there is in evidence a new concern with general planning. The idea is to frame patterns of development that do not fall into obsolescence but are capable of enduring over the long run. Planning must be an exercise in anticipation that ensures forward movement while making allowance for flexibility; it should accommodate experimentation and change while the vehicle as a whole remains robust. Secondly, there has been a homecoming the restored historic quarters of cities, reinventing the European university tradition and reviving its quintessentially urban soul. A related development is the adaptation of disused army buildings which are being felicitously reallocated to educational use.

International institutions of higher education have in the past few decades been severely undermined by a lopsided and ill-considered importation of foreign models – particularly the ubiquitous American campus – and this has led to a deplorable emptying-out of their ideological essence.

In recent years, then, the university has shown genuine signs of an engagement with society and has redirected its aims accordingly. That engagement turns on innovation and its many facets. One of those facets – which touches upon material reality – is a yen to move past the ancient opposition between campus and city, and thus attain the foundational utopia of the university: the reconciliation of nature and culture. One of the most striking efforts in that direction has been the recapturing of the historic quarters of cities, which the universities had ill-advisedly abandoned in the mid-twentieth century. But this homecoming seeks to be made compatible with the improvement of the suburban premises so as to piece together new urban planning solutions that offer balance and cohesion.

394

University and Future

The university is humanity's intellectual spearhead. Its calling is to be at the forefront, to lead progress, and this calling suffuses all the various facets of the complex and fascinating polyhedron that is a university. One of those facets is its spatial shape.

In a university, even the architecture is an aspect of innovation.

Spaces for Innovation: The EHEA Opportunity

The introduction of the EHEA will entail a far-reaching review of the academic and management structures of European universities. One of the core objectives is to transform higher education itself: outdated 'magisterial' formulas are to be left behind in favour of student-focused learning. And this will bring with it an analogous mutation in the venues of learning. 2010 will be the critical juncture at that universities can take the opportunity to restructure their campuses, mindful that their prime purpose is to drive educational innovation.

Some universities have already begun their strategies for reform. The initial stages have involved the definition of alternative modes of teaching and learning: tutorials, sharing of experience and ideas, on-site experience, art-supported learning, independent study, joint reflection, seminars, study trips, mobile learning. All these are learning models that will characterise the universities of the future. The next step is to classify standard spaces that facilitate each of these modes of learning. The campus as a whole will inevitably undergo an exhaustive transformation – from being a mere container it will become active ground for knowledge exchange.

In support of their innovative mission, the universities must recruit their host cities. On the quality horizon envisioned by universities there can be clearly picked out their third mission: community engagement. Planning experts have for some time now stressed the need for the university and the city to become fused into a single organism. The outcome will be an integrated reality, such that the city's tissue

will become imbued with the educational spirit. The conceptual and physical barriers that formerly obstructed harmony between the two entities must now dissolve, and the near-legendary conflict between 'town' and 'gown' must give way to the construction of a common corpus bearing the stamp of social creativity.

Ortega y Gasset wrote, 'The university is the institutional projection of the student.' If this is right, the university must aspire to emulate the virtues of the social and urban reality to which it is bound by history, thus forming the 'univer-city'.

The 'Educational Campus' versus Virtuality

The millennial history of the university shows that education is a spatial experience. The quality of the architecture is closely tied to the quality of that educational venture.

Change is imminent. Internationally, the argument is being made for a leap towards campus excellence. In counterpoint, some voices extol the virtues of a new educational paradigm called into being by telecommunications. This clash posits a dichotomy between human contact and distance education. This conflict is not without risk; the so-called 'virtual campus' merits detailed commentary.

In the vibrant present, society's continued drive towards mass influx into the universities is now borne along by scientific and technological change. The newest proposals see online platforms as potentially superseding the real presence of the actors involved in the learning process: hence the 'virtual campus', to use an expression coined in a publication of the Massachusetts Institute of Technology (MIT) in the United States. The Internet has made a powerful entrance into our lives. The advantages of its educational uses are innumerable, but always provided that it is used as a supplement, never as a wholesale substitute. 'The Internet transmits facts, but not values', in the words of the American architect Richard Dober at a conference held in 2001 – as it happened, at MIT.

An understanding of the size of this growing phenomenon requires one to reflect on the primordial mission of any university: the all-encompassing formation of a whole human being. This process is linked as if by an umbilical cord to personal contact. The necessary consequence of this is that such contact must take place within a constructed space. Hence the essential function of architecture in the transmission of knowledge. An inkling of this comes through in the scholarship on psychological perception: 'Buildings shape behaviour,' said Rudolf Arnheim in his book *The Dynamics of Architectural Form* (1977). Good architecture should be the handmaiden of every activity humans undertake; but in education it is absolutely vital. Architecture, then, versus the unsuitable use of the virtual.

To counter the threat of dissolving human contact over technological channels, recent designs have taken an all-embracing approach whereby universities reinforce their central role: the 'educational campus', an uncompromising commitment to face-to-face human relations as an irreplaceable quality. The adjective 'didactic' rests on the notion that architecture can serve an educational purpose in itself by cultivating the conscious and unconscious mind and bringing on a group catharsis that transforms it into an ideal of aesthetics and social cohesion.

The university is the artistic and intellectual avantgarde, but must also be an architectural, environmental and sustainable paradigm. It dedicates a wealth of resources to its primary aim of the comprehensive formation of the whole student. The principal resource is of course human capital, but architecture, too, can foster well-being, transmit values, and, finally, nurture motivation, the most valuable gift to one who seeks to learn.

The ordered spaces of the 'educational campus' can educate in themselves by accomplishing a shift from being context to forming a subject of study in their own right. Their use in the present university aims to secure, first of all, that every teaching space be able to accommodate all innovative modes of instruction and learning that might be gradually introduced.

As part of the right approach to the leap towards quality that Europe's universities hope to achieve in the framework of the EHEA, the 'educational campus'

Charles Correa Associates and Goody Clancy, interior of the Brain and Cognitive Sciences Complex, MIT (2005)
The Indian architect adapted the traditional values of his native country to the needs of an academic building. He proposed a continuous interior in which the play of volumes comes under the unifying influence of light.

EMBT, University of Vigo campus (2003)
The architectural partnership of Enric Miralles and Benedetta Tagliabue designed a building that strikes up a dialogue with nature and the surroundings. Even the materials tighten that bond with nature.

could be implemented in four distinct realms, so as to make up a complete structure: a descending 'scale' of didactic spaces.

At the overarching level, every campus must address its fusion with civic environments. Examples of excellence in the coupling between university and city are visible at Bologna, Oxford, Cambridge, Paris, Salamanca and Alcalá, which for centuries have forged a common identity of university and city.

The second level of intervention is the campus as a distinct kind of space. Regarded as a domestic habitat endowed with experiential autonomy, the campus must awaken students, teaching staff and administrators to a sense of belonging. The open spaces, nature and architecture configuring the campus are called on to express values such as harmony, proportion, visual grace, and mystery. A 'educational campus' must interact with the shaping of a human being, as it does at the University of Virginia (1817), the Illinois Institute of Technology (1940), and the Caracas Ciudad Universitaria (1943), and one suspects this will be the case of more recent projects such as the University of Salamanca at Villamayor (2005). One of the most eloquent international exponents of this 'educational' facet of architecture is the Ciudad Universitaria at Mexico City (UNAM, 1946). Its spatial conception enlists resources which consciously and intelligently allude to the pre-Columbian tradition and local

values. The vast open space in the centre suggests the proportions of the plazas of the pre-Hispanic pyramids. The powerfully expressive 'skin' of the library is the creation of the painter and architect Juan O'Gorman: a splendid mural alluding to themes of Aztec culture, the modern world and Old Mexico.

The third realm of this descending scale is the university building. It must leave behind its former function as an inert container of lecture halls, laboratories and offices and go in search of imaginative solutions that breathe life into its 'didactic' facet. The modern concepts put forward at prestigious international forums include striking ideas such as the 'three-dimensional textbook/building', or the 'educational street', a suggested replacement for the conventional corridor. Other internationally distinguished examples include the Educatorium (Rem Koolhaas, Utrecht, 1997), the faculty of Legal Sciences at Vigo (Alfonso Penela, 2001), the Roland Levinsky Building (Henning Larsen, Plymouth, 2007) and, in general, the recent resource centres for learning and research (Spanish 'CRAI'), whose flexible, open and multifunctional nature makes an ideal fit with the innovative 'didactic' profile.

And the fourth and final realm of this 'scale' of didactic spaces is the lecture hall, the 'educational cell'. This spatial level is possibly in need of the most far-reaching review, given that the future of the university has become its present already. The highest practicable ratio of teaching faculty to students must be found, drastically reducing the mass figures of the recent past. But a rigorous investigation must be undertaken of the alternative modes of learning that are set to drive out the dusty magisterial lesson. These modern teaching formats, if they are to be anything other than a merely theoretical exercise, require ad hoc 'didactic' spaces to sustain them.

Finally, the common denominator of the four realms discussed here is the set of foundations that might guide the future vision of the university.

First, the idea that breathes life into the emerging 'educational campus' is that new types of space are needed for the new university. Secondly, the benefits of face-to-face presence should be championed against absence, such that wherever there emerges a new campus there is born a fascinating process of

IT **Room, The McCormick Tribune Campus Center (ITT) Chicago (2003)**
Designed by the Rem Koolhaas partnership, OMA, the computer room is an enclave in the campus originally laid out by Mies van der Rohe. As a nexus between the residential area and the academic hub of the main campus, it connects to multiple other spaces, including an auditorium, a musuem, lecture halls and IT facilities – and, strikingly, a railway station mounted on a flyover.

centrifugal socio-cultural, economic and urban revival that is felt far beyond its formal boundaries. Thirdly and finally, the quality of education is inextricably tied to the quality of the physical space in which it is enacted: natural environment, landscape and architecture.

The 'educational campus', which adopts as its legacy the long, proud history of the university and its fecund pairing of institutional model and spatial configuration, is a philosophy that will inform and encourage the leap towards quality that the university hopes to attain.

Appendix

It is the hope of Banco Santander that this book should serve as a public expression of its gratitude to the universities for their willingness to work with us over the years and their commitment to the social and economic advancement of their host communities. Many thanks to you all.

ANDORRA Universidad de Andorra · ARGENTINA Instituto de Enseñanza Superior del Ejército · Instituto Tecnológico de Buenos Aires · Instituto Universitario Aeronáutico · Instituto Universitario CEMIC · Instituto Universitario de Ciencias de la Salud · Instituto Universitario del Gran Rosario · Instituto Universitario Escuela Argentina de Negocios· Instituto Universitario ESEADE · Instituto Universitario Gastón Dachary · Instituto Universitario Policial · Pontificia Universidad Católica Argentina · Universidad Abierta Interamericana · Universidad Adventista del Plata · Universidad Argentina de la Empresa · Universidad Argentina John F. Kennedy [7] · Universidad Atlántida Argentina · Universidad Austral · Universidad Blas Pascal · Universidad CAECE · Universidad Católica de Córdoba [1,8] · Universidad Católica de Cuyo [8] · Universidad Católica de La Plata · Universidad Católica de Salta [8] · Universidad Católica de Santa Fe · Universidad Católica de Santiago del Estero [8] · Universidad Champagnat [7] · Universidad de Belgrano · Universidad de Buenos Aires [1, 3, 4] · Universidad de Ciencias Empresariales y Sociales · Universidad de Concepción del Uruguay · Universidad de Congreso · Universidad de Flores · Universidad de la Cuenca del Plata · Universidad de la Marina Mercante · Universidad de Morón · Universidad del Norte Santo Tomás de Aquino [8] · Universidad de Palermo · Universidad de San Andrés · Universidad del Aconcagua · Universidad del CEMA · Universidad del Centro Educativo Latinoamericano · Universidad del Museo Social Argentino · Universidad del Salvador [8] · Universidad Empresarial Siglo 21 · Universidad FASTA · Universidad Favaloro · Universidad Juan Agustín Maza · Universidad Maimónides · Universidad Nacional de Catamarca · Universidad Nacional de Córdoba [1, 3, 4] · Universidad Nacional de Cuyo · Universidad Nacional de Entre Ríos · Universidad Nacional de Formosa · Universidad Nacional de General San Martín · Universidad Nacional de General Sarmiento · Universidad Nacional de Jujuy · Universidad Nacional de La Matanza · Universidad Nacional de La Pampa · Universidad Nacional de la Patagonia Austral · Universidad Nacional de la Patagonia San Juan Bosco · Universidad Nacional de La Plata · Universidad Nacional de Luján · Universidad Nacional de Mar del Plata · Universidad Nacional de Misiones · Universidad Nacional de Quilmes · Universidad Nacional de Río Cuarto · Universidad Nacional de Río Negro · Universidad Nacional de Rosario · Universidad Nacional de Salta · Universidad Nacional de San Juan · Universidad Nacional de San Luis · Universidad Nacional de Santiago del Estero · Universidad Nacional de Tres de Febrero · Universidad Nacional de Tucumán · Universidad Nacional de Villa María · Universidad Nacional del Centro de la Provincia de Buenos Aires · Universidad Nacional del Comahue · Universidad Nacional del Litoral · Universidad Nacional del Nordeste · Universidad Nacional del Noroeste de la Provincia de Buenos Aires · Universidad Nacional del Sur · Universidad Tecnológica Nacional · BOLIVIA Escuela Militar de Ingeniería · Universidad Amazónica de Pando · Universidad Autónoma Gabriel René Moreno · Universidad Autónoma Tomás Frías · Universidad del Valle de Cochabamba · Universidad Mayor de San Andrés · Universidad Mayor de San Simón · Universidad Mayor, Real y Pontificia de San Francisco Xavier de Chuquisaca · Universidad Privada de Santa Cruz · Universidad Pública de El Alto · Universidad Técnica de Oruro · BRAZIL Associação de Escolas Reunidas Ltda · Associação Educacional Dom Bosco · Associação Educacional Toledo · Associação Educativa do Brasil SOEBRAS · Associação Ranieri de Educação e Cultura · BI International · Centro de Desenvolvimento de Tecnologia e Recursos Humanos · Centro de Educação Superior e Profissional do Amapá · Centro de Ensino Superior de Ilhéus · Centro de Ensino Superior de Juiz de Fora · Centro de Ensino Superior do Amapá · Centro de Estudos Superiores de Maceió · Centro Educacional do Realengo · Centro Federal de Educação Tecnológica Celso Suckow da Fonseca · Centro Federal de Educação Tecnológica da Bahia · Centro Federal de Educação Tecnológica de Alagoas · Centro Federal de Educação Tecnológica de Goiás · Centro Federal de Educação Tecnológica de Minas Gerais · Centro Federal de Educação Tecnológica de Química de Nilópolis · Centro Federal de Educação Tecnológica do Maranhão · Centro Integrado para Formação de Executivos · Centro Superior de Tecnologia Tecbrasil Ltda. · Centro Universitário Álvares Penteado · Centro Universitário Assunção · Centro Universitário Barão de Mauá · Centro Universitário Augusto Motta · Centro Universitário Belas Artes de São Paulo · Centro Universitário Cândido Rondon · Centro Universitário Capital · Centro Universitário Carioca · Centro Universitário Celso Lisboa · Centro Universitário Claretiano · Centro Universitário da Cidade · Centro Universitário de FEI · Centro Universitário das Faculdades Metropolitanas Unidas · Centro Universitário de Anápolis · Centro Universitário de Araras · Centro Universitário de Barra Mansa · Centro Universitário de Belo Horizonte · Centro Universitário de Brasília · Centro Universitário de Brusque · Centro Universitário de Ensino Superior do Amazonas · Centro Universitário de Formiga · Centro Universitário de Jales · Centro Universitário de João Pessoa · Centro Universitário de Lavras · Centro Universitário de Lins · Centro Universitário de Maringá CEUMAR · Centro Universitário de Rio Preto ·

Centro Universitário de Sete Lagoas · Centro Universitário de Volta Redonda – Fundação Oswaldo Aranha · Centro Universitário de Votuporanga · Centro Universitário do Estado do Pará · Centro Universitário do Instituto Mauá de Tecnologia · Centro Universitário do Maranhão · Centro Universitário do Planalto de Araxá · Centro Universitário do Sul de Minas · Centro Universitário Eurípedes de Marília · Centro Universitário Euro-Americano · Centro Universitário Feevalc · Centro Universitário FIEO · Centro Universitário Filadélfia · Centro Universitário Fundação Santo André · Centro Universitário Herminio Ometto de Araras · Centro Universitário Ítalo – Brasileiro · Centro Universitário Jorge Amado · Centro Universitário La Salle · Centro Universitário Lusíada · Centro Universitário Metodista Izabela Hendrix · Centro Universitário Moacyr Sreder Bastos · Centro Universitário Monte Serrat · Centro Universitário Moura Lacerda · Centro Universitário Newton Paiva · Centro Universitário Nilton Lins · Centro Universitário Padre Anchieta · Centro Universitário Paulistano · Centro Universitário Radial · Centro Universitário Ritter dos Reis · Centro Universitário Salesiano de São Paulo · Centro Universitário São Camilo [8] · Centro Universitário Senac · Centro Universitário Toledo · Centro Universitário UNA · Centro Universitário UNIVATES · Complexo de Ensino Superior de Santa Catarina – CESUSC · Colégio Fenix Ltda. · Escola Brasileira de Administração Pública e de Empresas · Escola Brasileira de Administração Pública e de Empresas da Fundaçao Getúlio Vargas · Escola Brasileira de Economia e Finanças da Fundação Getúlio Vargas · Escola de Administração de Empresas de São Paulo da Fundação Getúlio Vargas · Escola de Direito de São Paulo da Fundação Getúlio Vargas · Escola de Direito do Rio de Janeiro da Fundação Getúlio Vargas · Escola de Economia de São Paulo da Fundação Getúlio Vargas · Escola Superior de Administração e Marketing e Comunicação · Escola Superior de Administração, Direito e Economia · Escola Superior de Ciências da Santa Casa de Misericórdia de Vitória · Escola Superior de Ciências Sociais da Fundação Getúlio Vargas · Escola Superior de Propaganda e Marketing · Faculdade Arthur Sá Earp Neto · Faculdade Atenas Maranhense · Faculdade Bandeirantes de Educação Superior · Faculdade Barretos · Faculdade Boa Viagem – Instituto Materno-Infantil de Pernambuco · Faculdade Campos Elíseos · Faculdade Carlos Drummond de Andrade · Faculdade Ceres · Faculdade COC Dom Bosco · Faculdade COC Metropolitana · Faculdade da Escada · Faculdade de Administração e Informática · Faculdade de Administração e Negócios de Monte Alto · Faculdade de Administração Milton Campos · Faculdade de Apucarana · Faculdade de Campina Grande do Sul · Faculdade de Ciências Econômicas Administrativas e Contábeis de Franca · Faculdade de Ciências Aplicadas e Sociais de Petrolina · Faculdade de Ciências Biológicas e da Saúde de União da Vitória · Faculdade de Ciências Contábeis e Administrativas de Taquara · Faculdade de Ciências e Letras de Bragança Paulista · Faculdade de Ciências Econômicas do Triângulo Mineiro · Faculdade de Ciências Econômicas, Administrativas e da Computação Dom Bosco · Faculdade de Ciências Humanas e Jurídicas de Teresina · Faculdade de Ciências Médicas da Santa Casa de São Paulo · Faculdade de Ciências Sociais Aplicadas de Cascavel · Faculdade de Ciências Sociais de Florianópolis · Faculdade de Comunicação Social Cásper Líbero · Faculdade de Direito da Alta Paulista · Faculdade de Direito da Fundação Armando Álvares Penteado · Faculdade de Direito de Bauru · Faculdade de Direito de Franca · Faculdade de Direito de São Bernardo do Campo · Faculdade de Direito de São Sebastião do Paraíso · Faculdade de Educação e Ciências Gerenciais de Indaiatuba · Faculdade de Educação e Ciências Gerenciais de Sumaré · Faculdade de Educação Física de Barra Bonita – FUNBBE · Faculdade de Educação São Luís – Associação Jaboticabalense de Educação e Cultura · Faculdade de Enfermagem do Hospital Israelita Albert Einstein · Faculdade de Engenharia de Minas Gerais · Faculdade de Estudos Administrativos de Minas Gerais · Faculdade de Filosofia Ciências e Letras Carlos Queiroz · Faculdade de Guaçuí · Faculdade de Informática e Administração Paulista · Faculdade de Jaguariúna · Faculdade de José Bonifacio · Faculdade de Medicina de Marília · Faculdade de Medicina de São José do Rio Preto · Faculdade de Medicina do ABC · Faculdade de Saúde Ibituruna · Faculdade de Tecnologia · Faculdade de Tecnologia Camões · Faculdade de Tecnologia da Baixada Santista · Faculdade de Tecnologia de São Paulo · Faculdade de Tecnologia IBTA · Faculdade de Tecnologia TecBrasil · Faculdade Decision de Negócios · Faculdade Editora Nacional · Faculdade Escola Paulista de Direito · Faculdade Fleming · Faculdade Guilherme Guimbala · Faculdade Hélio Rocha · Faculdade IBMEC · Faculdade IBMEC Distrito Federal · Faculdade IBS · Faculdade Ingá · Faculdade Integrada da Grande Fortaleza · Faculdade Integrada do Recife · Faculdade Integrada Metropolitana de Campinas · Faculdade Internacional de Curitiba · Faculdade Jesuíta de Filosofia e Teologia · Faculdade Literatus · Faculdade Maurício de Nassau · Faculdade Max Planck · Faculdade Metropolitana de Blumenau · Faculdade Monteiro Lobato · Faculdade Network · Faculdade Paulista de Artes · Faculdade Paulista de Serviço Social de São Caetano do Sul · Faculdade Pitágoras · Faculdade Politécnica de Campinas · Faculdade Politécnica de Uberlândia · Faculdade Porto-Alegrense · Faculdade Roraiense de Ensino Superior Ltda. · Faculdade Salesiana de Pindamonhangaba · Faculdade Salesiana de Vitória · Faculdade Santa Catarina · Faculdade Santa Marcelina · Faculdade São Lucas · Faculdade São Salvador · Faculdade Seama · Faculdade Sete de Setembro · Faculdade Uirapuru · Faculdade Zumbi dos Palmares · Faculdades Adamantinenses Integradas · Faculdades Associadas de Uberaba · Faculdades Atibaia · Faculdades COC · Faculdades COC – Salvador · Faculdades Integradas Antônio Eufrásio de Toledo de Presidente Prudente · Faculdades Integradas Barros Melo · Faculdades Integradas de Botucatu · Faculdades Integradas de Ciências Humanas, Saúde e Educação de Guarulhos · Faculdades Integradas de Itapentininga · Faculdades Integradas de Itararé FAFIT/FACIC · Faculdades Integradas de Jahu · Faculdades Integradas de Ourinhos · Faculdades Integradas de Patos ·

Faculdades Integradas de Santa Fé do Sul · Faculdades Integradas de Vitória · Faculdades Integradas do Brasil · Faculdades Integradas do Oeste de Minas · Faculdades Integradas do Vale do Ribeira · Faculdades Integradas Einstein de Limeira · Faculdades Integradas Espírito Santenses · Faculdades Integradas Fafibe · Faculdades Integradas IPEP · Faculdades Integradas Regionais de Avaré · Faculdades Integradas Teresa Martin · Faculdades Integradas Torricelli · Faculdades Integradas Urubupungá · Faculdades Integradas Vianna Júnior · Faculdades Oswaldo Cruz · Faculdades Rio-Grandenses – Fapa · Faculdades SPEI · FAECA Dom Bosco – Faculdade de Educação Ciências e Artes Dom Bosco de Monte · FEFISA – Faculdades Integradas de Santo André · Fundação Universidade de Brasília · Fundação Benedito Pereira Nunes · Fundação da Universidade de Campinas · Fundação de Amparo a Pesquisa Extensão Universitária · Fundação de Apoio a Universidade de São Paulo · Fundação de Apoio a Universidade do Rio de Janeiro – Unirio – Furj · Fundação de Desenvolvimento da Pesquisa – Fundep · Fundação de Ensino e Pesquisa de Uberaba – Funepu · Fundação de Ensino Octávio Bastos · Fundação de Estudos Sociais do Paraná · Fundação do ABC – Hospital Estadual Santo André · Fundação Educacional de Barretos · Fundação Educacional de Criciuma · Fundação Educacional de Fernandópolis · Fundação Educacional de Ituverava · Fundação Educacional de Taquaritinga · Fundação Educacional do Vale do Jequitinhonha · Fundação Educacional Machado Sobrinho · Fundação Educacional Rosemar Pimentel · Fundação Ensino Superior Passos · Fundação Escola de Comércio Álvares Penteado · Fundação Faculdade Regional de Medicina de São José do Rio Preto · Fundação Gammon de Ensino · Fundação Municipal de Ensino Superior de Bragança Paulista · Fundação Municipal de Ensino de Piracicaba – Escola de Engenharia de Piracicaba · Fundação Norte-Rio-Grandense de Pesquisa e Cultura – FUNPEC · Fundação para o Desenvolvimento Científico e Tecnológico da Odontología · Fundação Universidade Federal do Tocantins · Fundação Universidade Federal do Vale do São Francisco · Fundação Universitária de Desenvolvimento de Extensão e Pesquisa · FUNDEC – Fundação Dracenense de Educação e Cultura · FUNEPE / FAFIPE – Fundação Educacional de Penápolis / Faculdade de Filosofia Ciências e Letras de Penápolis · Grupo Anhanguera Educacional · Grupo Nobre de Ensino Ltda e Ribeiro, Oliveira & Cia Ltda · Hospital do Cáncer – Centro de Tratamento A.C. Camargo · IALIM – Instituto Americano de Lins da Igreja Metodista · IBMEC Rio de Janeiro · IDON / FECLE – Faculdade de Educação Ciências e Letras Dom Domênico · Insper Instituto de Ensino e Pesquisa · Instituição Toledo de Encino · Instituto Blumenauense de Ensino Superior · Instituto de Ciências Sociais do Paraná · Instituto de Educação Superior de Brasília · Instituto de Educação Superior de Brasília – IESB · Instituto de Ensino Superior Camões · Instituto de Ensino Superior COC · Instituto de Ensino Superior de Jão Monlevade · Instituto de Ensino Superior de Londrina · Instituto de Ensino Superior FUCAPI · Instituto de Estudos Superiores de Amazônia · Instituto Federal de Educação, Ciência e Tecnologia de Mato Grosso – Campus Cuiabá · Instituto Federal de Educação, Ciência e Tecnologia de Santa Catarina · Instituto Federal de Educação, Ciência e Tecnologia do Sertão Pernambucano · Instituto Manchester Paulista de Ensino Superior · Instituto Mauá de Tecnologia · Instituto Metodista de Educação e Cultura · Instituto Militar de Engenharia · Instituto Municipal de Ensino Superior de Assis · Instituto Municipal de Ensino Superior de Bebedouro Victório Cardassi · Instituto Municipal de Ensino Superior de Catanduva – FAFICA · Instituto Paraibanos de Educação de Ituiutaba · Instituto Superior de Montes Claros Ltda. · Instituto Tecnológico de Aeronáutica ·ISCA Faculdades · Missão Salesiana de Mato Grosso · Organização Educacional de R9B. Pires · Pontifícia Universidade Católica de Campinas [8] · Pontifícia Universidade Católica de Minas Gerais · Pontifícia Universidade Católica de São Paulo [8] · Pontifícia Universidade Católica do Paraná [8] · Pontifícia Universidade Católica do Rio de Janeiro [8] · Pontifícia Universidade Católica do Rio Grande do Sul [8] · Promoção do Ensino de Qualidade S/A · Rede Gonzaga de Ensino Superior · SESTAS – Sociedade de Estudos São Tomaz de Aquino Ltda. · Sistema de Ensino Superior do Norte de Minas · Sistema Med Serviços Educacionais · Sociedade Mantenedora de Pesquisa Educação Assic. C.E. Maria C Aguiar · Sociedade Padrão Educação Superior · Sociedade Piauense de Ensino Superior Ltda. · Sociedade Unificada Paulista de Ensino Renovado Objetivo – SUPERO · Trevisan Escola de Negócios · União das Faculdades de Jussara · União das Instituições Educacionais do Estado de São Paulo · União Dinâmica de Faculdades Cataratas UDC Ltda. · Universidade da Força Aérea · Universidade do Rio de Janeiro – UNIRIO · Universidade Anhembi Morumbi [7] · Universidade Braz Cubas · Universidade Candido Mendes · Universidade Católica de Brasília [8] · Universidade Católica de Goiás · Universidade Católica de Pelotas [7, 8] · Universidade Católica de Pernambuco [8] · Universidade Católica de Petrópolis [8] · Universidade Católica de Santos · Universidade Católica do Salvador [8] · Universidade Católica Dom Bosco · Universidade Cidade de São Paulo · Universidade Comunitária Regional de Chapecó · Universidade Cruzeiro do Sul · Universidade da Amazônia · Universidade da Região de Joinville · Universidade de Brasília · Universidade de Caxias do Sul · Universidade de Cruz Alta · Universidade de Cuiabá · Universidade de Fortaleza [1] · Universidade de Franca · Universidade de Guarulhos · Universidade de Mogi das Cruzes · Universidade de Passo Fundo · Universidade de Pernambuco · Universidade de Ribeirão Preto · Universidade de Santa Cruz do Sul · Universidade de Santo Amaro · Universidade de São Paulo [1, 3, 4] · Universidade de Sorocaba · Universidade de Taubaté · Universidade de Uberaba · Universidade do Contestado · Universidade do Estado da Bahia · Universidade do Estado de Mato Grosso [6] · Universidade do Estado de Santa Catarina · Universidade do Estado do Pará [6] · Universidade do Estado do Rio de Janeiro · Universidade do Estado do Rio Grande do Norte · Universidade do Extremo Sul Catarinense · Universidade do Grande ABC · Universidade do Grande Rio Professor José de Souza Herdy · Universidade do

Noroeste do Estado do Rio Grande do Sul · Universidade do Oeste de Santa Catarina · Universidade do Oeste Paulista · Universidade do Planalto Catarinense · Universidade do Sagrado Coração · Universidade do Sul de Santa Catarina · Universidade do Vale do Itajaí · Universidade do Vale do Paraíba · Universidade do Vale do Rio dos Sinos [8] · Universidade Estadual Vale do Acaraú · Universidade Estadual da Paraíba · Universidade Estadual de Campinas [1, 3, 4] · Universidade Estadual de Feira de Santana · Universidade Estadual de Goiás · Universidade Estadual de Londrina · Universidade Estadual de Maringá · Universidade Estadual de Mato Grosso do Sul · Universidade Estadual de Montes Claros · Universidade Estadual de Ponta Grossa · Universidade Estadual de Santa Cruz · Universidade Estadual do Centro-Oeste · Universidade Estadual do Maranhão · Universidade Estadual do Oeste do Paraná · Universidade Estadual do Piauí · Universidade Estadual do Rio Grande do Sul · Universidade Estadual do Sudoeste da Bahia · Universidade Estadual Paulista Júlio de Mesquita Filho [4] · Universidade Federal da Bahia · Universidade Federal da Grande Dourados · Universidade Federal da Paraíba · Universidade Federal de Alagoas · Universidade Federal de Alfenas · Universidade Federal de Campina Grande · Universidade Federal de Ciências da Saúde de Porto Alegre · Universidade Federal de Goiás · Universidade Federal de Itajubá · Universidade Federal de Juiz de Fora · Universidade Federal de Lavras · Universidade Federal de Mato Grosso · Universidade Federal de Mato Grosso do Sul [6, 7] · Universidade Federal de Minas Gerais [3, 4] · Universidade Federal de Ouro Preto · Universidade Federal de Pelotas [7] · Universidade Federal de Pernambuco · Universidade Federal de Rondônia [6] · Universidade Federal de Roraima · Universidade Federal de Santa Catarina [1] · Universidade Federal de Santa Maria [1, 4] · Universidade Federal de São Carlos [4] · Universidade Federal de São João del Rei · Universidade Federal de São Paulo · Universidade Federal de Sergipe · Universidade Federal de Uberlândia [1] · Universidade Federal de Viçosa · Universidade Federal do ABC · Universidade Federal do Acre [6] · Universidade Federal do Amapá · Universidade Federal do Amazonas · Universidade Federal do Ceará [1] · Universidade Federal do Espírito Santo · Universidade Federal do Estado do Rio de Janeiro [1, 3] · Universidade Federal do Maranhão [1, 6] · Universidade Federal do Pampa · Universidade Federal do Pará · Universidade Federal do Paraná [4] · Universidade Federal do Piauí · Universidade Federal do Recôncavo da Bahia · Universidade Federal do Rio de Janeiro [1] · Universidade Federal do Rio Grande · Universidade Federal do Rio Grande do Norte · Universidade Federal do Rio Grande do Sul [4] · Universidade Federal do Tocantins · Universidade Federal do Triângulo Mineiro · Universidade Federal dos Vales do Jequitinhonha e Mucuri · Universidade Federal Fluminense · Universidade Federal Rural da Amazônia · Universidade Federal Rural de Pernambuco · Universidade Federal Rural do Rio de Janeiro · Universidade Federal Rural do Semi-Árido · Universidade FUMEC · Universidade Gama Filho · Universidade Iguaçu · Universidade Metodista de Piracicaba · Universidade Metodista de São Paulo · Universidade Metropolitana de Santos · Universidade Municipal de São Caetano do Sul · Universidade Norte do Paraná · Universidade Nove de Julho · Universidade para o Desenvolvimento do Alto do Vale do Itajaí · Universidade Potiguar · Universidade Presbiteriana Mackenzie · Universidade Presidente Antônio Carlos · Universidade Regional de Blumenau · Universidade Regional Integrada do Alto do Uruguai e das Missões · Universidade Salvador · Universidade Santa Cecília · Universidade Santa Úrsula [1] · Universidade São Francisco · Universidade São Judas Tadeu · Universidade São Marcos · Universidade Tecnológica Federal do Paraná · Universidade Tiradentes · Universidade Tuiuti do Paraná · Universidade Vale do Rio Doce · Universidade Vale do Rio Verde · Universidade Veiga de Almeida · Veris Educacional – IBMEC · CHILE DUOC UC · INACAP · Institute for Executive Development Chile · Pontificia Universidad Católica de Chile [8] · Pontificia Universidad Católica de Valparaíso [8] · Universidad Academia de Humanismo Cristiano · Universidad Adolfo Ibáñez · Universidad Adventista de Chile · Universidad Alberto Hurtado [8] · Universidad Andrés Bello · Universidad Arturo Prat · Universidad Austral de Chile · Universidad Autónoma de Chile · Universidad Bernardo O'Higgins · Universidad Bolivariana · Universidad Católica Cardenal Raúl Silva Henríquez · Universidad Católica de la Santísima Concepción [8] · Universidad Católica de Temuco · Universidad Católica del Maule [8] · Universidad Católica del Norte [8] · Universidad Católica Silva Henríquez · Universidad Central de Chile · Universidad Chileno-Británica de Cultura · Universidad de Antofagasta · Universidad de Artes Ciencia y Comunicación UNIACC · Universidad de Atacama · Universidad de Chile · Universidad de Ciencias de la Informática UCINF [7] · Universidad de Concepción · Universidad de la Frontera · Universidad de La Serena · Universidad de Las Américas · Universidad de los Andes · Universidad de Los Lagos [1] · Universidad de Magallanes · Universidad de Playa Ancha · Universidad de Santiago de Chile · Universidad de Talca · Universidad de Tarapacá · Universidad de Valparaíso · Universidad de Viña del Mar · Universidad del Bío-Bío · Universidad del Desarrollo · Universidad del Mar · Universidad del Pacífico · Universidad Diego Portales · Universidad Finis Terrae · Universidad Gabriela Mistral · Universidad Iberoamericana de Ciencias y Tecnología · Universidad Internacional SEK · Universidad La República · Universidad Marítima de Chile · Universidad Mayor · Universidad Metropolitana de Ciencias de la Educación · Universidad Miguel de Cervantes · Universidad Pedro de Valdivia · Universidad San Sebastián · Universidad Santo Tomás · Universidad Técnica Federico Santa María · Universidad Tecnológica de Chile · Universidad Tecnológica Metropolitana · CHINA Beijing Institute of Technology · Fudan University · Peking University · Renmin University · Shanghai Jiaotong University · Tsinghua University · COLOMBIA Colegio de Estudios Superiores de Administración CESA · Corporación Universitaria Minuto de Dios Uniminuto · Escuela Colombiana de Ingeniería Julio Garavito · Escuela de Ingeniería de Antioquia · Escuela Naval de Cadetes Almirante Padilla ·

Escuela Superior de Administración Pública ESAP · Fundación Universitaria Católica del Norte · Fundación Universitaria Konrad Lorenz · Fundación Universitaria Luis Amigó [8] · Fundación Universitaria Monserrate · Instituto Caro y Cuervo [1] · Instituto Tolimense de Formación Técnica Profesional ITFIP · Politécnico Colombiano Jaime Isaza Cadavid · Politécnico Grancolombiano · Pontificia Universidad Javeriana [1, 8] · Universidad Autónoma de Bucaramanga [1] · Universidad Autónoma de Manizales · Universidad Autónoma de Occidente · Universidad Central · Universidad CES · Universidad Colegio Mayor de Cundinamarca [1] · Universidad de Antioquia · Universidad de Bogotá Jorge Tadeo Lozano · Universidad de Caldas · Universidad de Cartagena · Universidad de Ciencias Aplicadas y Ambientales UDCA [1] · Universidad de Ibagué – Coruniversitaria · Universidad de La Sabana [1] · Universidad de La Salle [8] · Universidad de los Andes [6] · Universidad de Manizales · Universidad de Medellín · Universidad de Nariño · Universidad de Pamplona · Universidad de San Buenaventura · Universidad del Cauca · Universidad del Magdalena · Universidad del Norte · Universidad del Quindío · Universidad del Rosario · Universidad del Tolima · Universidad del Valle · Universidad Distrital Francisco José de Caldas [7] · Universidad Eafit · Universidad EAN · Universidad El Bosque · Universidad Externado de Colombia [1] · Universidad Icesi · Universidad Industrial de Santander · Universidad Libre · Universidad Mariana [8] · Universidad Militar Nueva Granada [7] · Universidad Nacional de Colombia [1, 3] · Universidad Pedagógica Nacional [1] · Universidad Pedagógica y Tecnológica de Colombia · Universidad Piloto de Colombia [1] · Universidad Pontificia Bolivariana [8] · Universidad Santo Tomás [1, 8] · Universidad Sergio Arboleda · Universidad Tecnológica de Bolívar · Universidad Tecnológica de Pereira · COSTA RICA Fidélitas Universidad · INCAE Business School · Universidad Católica de Costa Rica · Universidad de Costa Rica · Universidad Interamericana de Costa Rica · Universidad Latina de Costa Rica · Universidad Nacional de Costa Rica · Universidad Veritas · CUBA Instituto Superior Politécnico José Antonio Echevarría · Universidad de La Habana · DOMINICAN REPUBLIC Instituto Tecnológico de Santo Domingo INTEC [1] · Pontificia Universidad Católica Madre y Maestra [1, 5, 8] · Universidad Abierta para Adultos · Universidad APEC · Universidad Autónoma de Santo Domingo [1, 2, 3] · Universidad Católica Santo Domingo [8] · Universidad Católica Nordestana · Universidad Central del Este [1] · Universidad Iberoamericana UNIBE [1, 5] · Universidad Instituto Cultural Domínico-Americano · Universidad Nacional Pedro Henríquez Ureña [1, 5] · Universidad Dominicana O&M · ECUADOR Escuela Politécnica Nacional · Escuela Superior Politécnica del Litoral · Pontificia Universidad Católica del Ecuador · Universidad Andina Simón Bolívar · Universidad Católica de Santiago de Guayaquil · Universidad Central del Ecuador · Universidad de Israel · Universidad de Loja · Universidad del Azuay · Universidad del Pacífico · Universidad Internacional · Universidad Nacional de Cuenca · Universidad Particular de Especialidades Espíritu Santo · Universidad Politécnica Salesiana · Universidad San Francisco de Quito · Universidad Técnica Particular de Loja · EL SALVADOR Escuela Superior de Economía y Negocios · Universidad Centroamericana José Simeón Cañas · Universidad de El Salvador · Universidad Don Bosco · Universidad Dr. José Matías Delgado · Universidad Francisco Gavidia · Universidad Tecnológica de El Salvador · GUATEMALA Universidad del Istmo · Universidad del Valle de Guatemala · Universidad Galileo · Universidad Panamericana · Universidad Rural de Guatemala · HONDURAS Centro de Diseño Arquitectura y Construcción · Universidad Católica de Honduras · Universidad de San Pedro Sula · Universidad Nacional de Honduras · Universidad Pedagógica Francisco Morazán · Universidad Tecnológica UNITEC · MEXICO Alianza para la Educación Superior, S.C. · Asociación Nacional de Universidades e Instituciones de Educación Superior · Benemérita Universidad Autónoma de Puebla [1, 3] · Centro de Enseñanza Técnica Industrial · Centro de Estudios Superiores de Diseño de Monterrey · Centro de Estudios Superiores del Estado de Sonora [1] · Centro de Estudios Universitarios (Acción Educativa Cultural) · Centro de Estudios Universitarios · Centro de Investigación y Docencia Económicas · Centro de Investigaciones Biológicas del Noroeste · Centro Interdisciplinario de Investigación y Docencia en Educación Técnica CIIDET · Centro Nacional de Investigación y Desarrollo Tecnológico CENIDET · Centro Regional de Optimización y Desarrollo de Equipo de Celaya · Centro Regional de Optimización y Desarrollo de Equipo de Chihuahua · Centro Regional de Optimización y Desarrollo de Equipo de Mérida · Centro Regional de Optimización y Desarrollo de Equipo de Orizaba · Centro Universitario de Comunicación · CETYS Universidad · Coordinación de Universidades Politécnicas, A.C. · Coordinación General de Universidades Tecnológicas · Dirección General de Educación Superior Tecnológica · El Colegio de la Frontera Norte [1] · El Colegio de México [1] · El Colegio de Sonora · Escuela Bancaria y Comercial · Escuela Libre de Derecho de Puebla · Facultad Latinoamericana de Ciencias Sociales · Federación de Instituciones Mexicanas Particulares de Educación Superior · Instituto Campechano · Instituto de Cultura Superior Valle del Bravo de Reynosa · Instituto de Estudios Superiores de Chiapas · Instituto de Estudios Superiores de Tamaulipas · Instituto de Estudios Universitarios · Instituto de Investigaciones Dr. José María Luis Mora · Instituto Nacional de Astrofísica, Óptica y Electrónica · Instituto Panamericano de Alta Dirección de Empresas · Instituto Politécnico Nacional [1] · Instituto Tecnológico Autónomo de México · Instituto Tecnológico de Acapulco · Instituto Tecnológico de Agua Prieta · Instituto Tecnológico de Aguascalientes · Instituto Tecnológico de Altamira · Instituto Tecnológico de Apizaco · Instituto Tecnológico de Bahía de Banderas · Instituto Tecnológico de Boca del Río · Instituto Tecnológico de Campeche · Instituto Tecnológico de Cancún · Instituto Tecnológico de Celaya · Instituto Tecnológico de Cerro Azul · Instituto Tecnológico de Chetumal · Instituto Tecnológico de Chihuahua · Instituto Tecnológico de Chihuahua II · Instituto Tecnológico de Chilpancingo · Instituto Tecnológico de Chiná ·

Instituto Tecnológico de Ciudad Altamirano · Instituto Tecnológico de Ciudad Cuauhtémoc · Instituto Tecnológico de Ciudad Guzmán · Instituto Tecnológico de Ciudad Jiménez · Instituto Tecnológico de Ciudad Juárez · Instituto Tecnológico de Ciudad Madero · Instituto Tecnológico de Ciudad Valles · Instituto Tecnológico de Ciudad Victoria · Instituto Tecnológico de Colima · Instituto Tecnológico de Comitán · Instituto Tecnológico de Comitancillo · Instituto Tecnológico de Conkal · Instituto Tecnológico de Costa Grande · Instituto Tecnológico de Cuautla · Instituto Tecnológico de Culiacán · Instituto Tecnológico de Delicias · Instituto Tecnológico de Durango · Instituto Tecnológico de El Llano Aguascalientes · Instituto Tecnológico de El Salto · Instituto Tecnológico de Ensenada · Instituto Tecnológico de Estudios Superiores del Oriente del Estado de México · Instituto Tecnológico de Guaymas · Instituto Tecnológico de Hermosillo · Instituto Tecnológico de Huatabampo · Instituto Tecnológico de Huejutla · Instituto Tecnológico de Iguala · Instituto Tecnológico de Jiquilpan · Instituto Tecnológico de la Cuenca del Papaloapan · Instituto Tecnológico de La Laguna · Instituto Tecnológico de La Paz · Instituto Tecnológico de La Piedad · Instituto Tecnológico de la Región Mixe · Instituto Tecnológico de Lázaro Cárdenas · Instituto Tecnológico de León · Instituto Tecnológico de Lerma · Instituto Tecnológico de Linares · Instituto Tecnológico de Los Mochis · Instituto Tecnológico de Matamoros · Instituto Tecnológico de Matehuala · Instituto Tecnológico de Mazatlán · Instituto Tecnológico de Mérida · Instituto Tecnológico de Mexicali · Instituto Tecnológico de Minatitlán · Instituto Tecnológico de Morelia · Instituto Tecnológico de Nogales · Instituto Tecnológico de Nuevo Laredo · Instituto Tecnológico de Nuevo León · Instituto Tecnológico de Oaxaca · Instituto Tecnológico de Ocotlán · Instituto Tecnológico de Orizaba · Instituto Tecnológico de Pachuca · Instituto Tecnológico de Parral · Instituto Tecnológico de Piedras Negras · Instituto Tecnológico de Pinotepa · Instituto Tecnológico de Puebla · Instituto Tecnológico de Querétaro · Instituto Tecnológico de Reynosa · Instituto Tecnológico de Roque · Instituto Tecnológico de Salina Cruz · Instituto Tecnológico de Saltillo · Instituto Tecnológico de San Juan del Río · Instituto Tecnológico de San Luis Potosí · Instituto Tecnológico de Sonora [1] · Instituto Tecnológico de Tapachula · Instituto Tecnológico de Tecomatlán · Instituto Tecnológico de Tehuacán · Instituto Tecnológico de Tepic · Instituto Tecnológico de Tijuana · Instituto Tecnológico de Tizimín · Instituto Tecnológico de Tlajomulco · Instituto Tecnológico de Tlalnepantla · Instituto Tecnológico de Tlaxiaco · Instituto Tecnológico de Toluca · Instituto Tecnológico de Torreón · Instituto Tecnológico de Tuxtepec · Instituto Tecnológico de Tuxtla Gutiérrez · Instituto Tecnológico de Úrsulo Galván · Instituto Tecnológico de Valle de Morelia · Instituto Tecnológico de Valle de Oaxaca · Instituto Tecnológico de Valle del Yaqui · Instituto Tecnológico de Veracruz · Instituto Tecnológico de Villahermosa · Instituto Tecnológico de Zacatecas · Instituto Tecnológico de Zacatepec · Instituto Tecnológico de Zitacuaro · Instituto Tecnológico de Zona Maya · Instituto Tecnológico de Zona Olmeca · Instituto Tecnológico del Altiplano de Tlaxcala · Instituto Tecnológico del Istmo · Instituto Tecnológico Superior de Acatlán de Osorio · Instituto Tecnológico Superior de Acayucan · Instituto Tecnológico Superior de Álamo Temapache · Instituto Tecnológico Superior de Alvarado · Instituto Tecnológico Superior de Apatzingán · Instituto Tecnológico Superior de Arandas · Instituto Tecnológico Superior de Atlixco · Instituto Tecnológico Superior de Cajeme · Instituto Tecnológico Superior de Calkiní · Instituto Tecnológico Superior de Cananea · Instituto Tecnológico Superior de Ciudad Acuña · Instituto Tecnológico Superior de Ciudad Constitución · Instituto Tecnológico Superior de Ciudad Hidalgo · Instituto Tecnológico Superior de Ciudad Serdán · Instituto Tecnológico Superior de Centla · Instituto Tecnológico Superior de Champotón · Instituto Tecnológico Superior de Chapala · Instituto Tecnológico Superior de Cintalapa · Instituto Tecnológico Superior de Coatzacoalcos · Instituto Tecnológico Superior de Comalcalco · Instituto Tecnológico Superior de Cosamaloapan · Instituto Tecnológico Superior de Cuautitlán Izcalli · Instituto Tecnológico Superior de El Grullo · Instituto Tecnológico Superior de Escárcega · Instituto Tecnológico Superior de Felipe Carrillo Puerto · Instituto Tecnológico Superior de Fresnillo · Instituto Tecnológico Superior de Huatusco · Instituto Tecnológico Superior de Huauchinango · Instituto Tecnológico Superior de Huetamo · Instituto Tecnológico Superior de Huichapan · Instituto Tecnológico Superior de Irapuato · Instituto Tecnológico Superior de Jerez · Instituto Tecnológico Superior de la Costa Chica · Instituto Tecnológico Superior de la Huerta · Instituto Tecnológico Superior de la Montaña · Instituto Tecnológico Superior de la Región Carbonífera · Instituto Tecnológico Superior de la Región de los Llanos · Instituto Tecnológico Superior de la Región Sierra · Instituto Tecnológico Superior de la Sierra Norte de Puebla · Instituto Tecnológico Superior de Lagos de Moreno · Instituto Tecnológico Superior de Las Choapas · Instituto Tecnológico Superior de Lerdo · Instituto Tecnológico Superior de Libres · Instituto Tecnológico Superior de Loreto · Instituto Tecnológico Superior de Los Cabos · Instituto Tecnológico Superior de Los Reyes · Instituto Tecnológico Superior de Los Ríos · Instituto Tecnológico Superior de Macuspana · Instituto Tecnológico Superior de Misantla · Instituto Tecnológico Superior de Monclova · Instituto Tecnológico Superior de Motul · Instituto Tecnológico Superior de Mulegé · Instituto Tecnológico Superior de Nochistlán · Instituto Tecnológico Superior de Nuevo Casas Grandes · Instituto Tecnológico Superior de Occidente del Estado de Hidalgo · Instituto Tecnológico Superior de Oriente del Estado de Hidalgo · Instituto Tecnológico Superior de Pánuco · Instituto Tecnológico Superior de Pátzcuaro · Instituto Tecnológico Superior de Perote · Instituto Tecnológico Superior de Poza Rica · Instituto Tecnológico Superior de Progreso · Instituto Tecnológico Superior de Puerto Peñasco · Instituto Tecnológico Superior de Puerto Vallarta · Instituto Tecnológico Superior de Purepecha · Instituto Tecnológico

Superior de Rioverde · Instituto Tecnológico Superior de San Andrés Tuxtla · Instituto Tecnológico Superior de San Luis Potosí, Capital · Instituto Tecnológico Superior de San Martín Texmelucan · Instituto Tecnológico Superior de San Miguel El Grande · Instituto Tecnológico Superior de San Pedro de las Colonias · Instituto Tecnológico Superior de Santiago Papasquiaro · Instituto Tecnológico Superior de Sur de Guanajuato · Instituto Tecnológico Superior de Tacámbaro · Instituto Tecnológico Superior de Tamazula de Gordiano · Instituto Tecnológico Superior de Tamazunchale · Instituto Tecnológico Superior de Tantoyuca · Instituto Tecnológico Superior de Tepeaca · Instituto Tecnológico Superior de Tepexi de Rodríguez · Instituto Tecnológico Superior de Tequila · Instituto Tecnológico Superior de Teziutlán · Instituto Tecnológico Superior de Tierra Blanca · Instituto Tecnológico Superior de Tlaxco · Instituto Tecnológico Superior de Uruapan · Instituto Tecnológico Superior de Valladolid · Instituto Tecnológico Superior de Villa La Venta Huimanguillo · Instituto Tecnológico Superior de Xalapa · Instituto Tecnológico Superior de Zacapoaxtla · Instituto Tecnológico Superior de Zacatecas Norte · Instituto Tecnológico Superior de Zacatecas Occidente · Instituto Tecnológico Superior de Zacatecas Sur · Instituto Tecnológico Superior de Zamora · Instituto Tecnológico Superior de Zapopan · Instituto Tecnológico Superior de Zapotlanejo · Instituto Tecnológico Superior de Zongolica · Instituto Tecnológico Superior del Sur del Estado de Yucatán · Instituto Tecnológico Valle del Guadiana · Instituto Tecnológico y de Estudios Superiores de Monterrey · Instituto Tecnológico y de Estudios Superiores de Occidente · Laboratorio Nacional de Informática Avanzada · Tecnológico de Estudios Superiores de Ixtapaluca · Tecnológico de Estudios Superiores de Chalco · Tecnológico de Estudios Superiores de Chimalhuacán · Tecnológico de Estudios Superiores de Coacalco · Tecnológico de Estudios Superiores de Ecatepec · Tecnológico de Estudios Superiores de Huixquilucan · Tecnológico de Estudios Superiores de Jilotepec · Tecnológico de Estudios Superiores de Jocotitlán · Tecnológico de Estudios Superiores de San Felipe del Progreso · Tecnológico de Estudios Superiores de Tianguistenco · Tecnológico de Estudios Superiores de Valle de Bravo · Tecnológico de Estudios Superiores de Villa Guerrero · Tecnológico Universitario del Valle de Chalco · Universidad Anáhuac Cancún [8] · Universidad Anáhuac del Mayab · Universidad Anáhuac México Norte [1, 8] · Universidad Anáhuac México Sur [1, 8] · Universidad Anáhuac Oaxaca · Universidad Autónoma Agraria Antonio Narro · Universidad Autónoma Benito Juárez de Oaxaca · Universidad Autónoma Chapingo · Universidad Autónoma de Aguascalientes [1] · Universidad Autónoma de Baja California · Universidad Autónoma de Baja California Sur · Universidad Autónoma de Campeche [1] · Universidad Autónoma de Chiapas [1] · Universidad Autónoma de Chihuahua · Universidad Autónoma de Ciudad Juárez [1] · Universidad Autónoma de Coahuila · Universidad Autónoma de Guadalajara [1] · Universidad Autónoma de Guerrero · Universidad Autónoma de La Laguna [1] · Universidad Autónoma de Nayarit · Universidad Autónoma de Nuevo León [1, 3] · Universidad Autónoma de Querétaro [1] · Universidad Autónoma de San Luis Potosí · Universidad Autónoma de Sinaloa [1, 3] · Universidad Autónoma de Tamaulipas [1] · Universidad Autónoma de Tlaxcala · Universidad Autónoma de Veracruz · Universidad Autónoma de Veracruz (Villa Rica) · Universidad Autónoma de Yucatán [1] · Universidad Autónoma de Zacatecas · Universidad Autónoma del Carmen · Universidad Autónoma del Estado de Hidalgo [7] · Universidad Autónoma del Estado de México [1] · Universidad Autónoma del Estado de Morelos [1, 7] · Universidad Autónoma del Noreste · Universidad Autónoma España de Durango · Universidad Autónoma Metropolitana [1] · Universidad Chapultepec · Universidad Contemporánea de Querétaro · Universidad Cristóbal Colón · Universidad CUGS · Universidad de Celaya · Universidad de Ciencias y Artes de Chiapas · Universidad de Colima [1] · Universidad de Guadalajara [1, 3] · Universidad de Guanajuato [1] · Universidad de la Comunicación · Universidad de La Salle Bajío · Universidad de las Américas Puebla · Universidad de Londres · Universidad de los Altos de Chiapas · Universidad de Monterrey · Universidad de Negocios ISEC · Universidad de Occidente [1] · Universidad de Quintana Roo · Universidad de Sonora [1] · Universidad de Xalapa · Universidad del Caribe · Universidad del Golfo de México · Universidad del Mar · Universidad del Mayab · Universidad del Noreste [1] · Universidad del Pedregal · Universidad del Sol · Universidad del Tepeyac · Universidad del Valle de Atemajac [8] · Universidad del Valle de México [1] · Universidad del Valle de Puebla · Universidad Enrique Díaz de León · Universidad ETAC · Universidad Hispanoamericana · Universidad Iberoamericana Laguna · Universidad Iberoamericana León · Universidad Iberoamericana México [1] · Universidad Iberoamericana Puebla · Universidad Iberoamericana Tijuana · Universidad Iberoamericana Torreón · Universidad ICEL [1] · Universidad Insurgentes [1] · Universidad Intercontinental [8] · Universidad Juárez Autónoma de Tabasco [1] · Universidad Juárez del Estado de Durango · Universidad La Salle [1, 8] · Universidad La Salle Cancún · Universidad La Salle Chihuahua · Universidad La Salle Morelia · Universidad La Salle Nezahualcóyotl · Universidad La Salle Noroeste · Universidad La Salle Victoria · Universidad Latina de América · Universidad Madero · Universidad Marista de Mérida · Universidad Michoacana de San Nicolás de Hidalgo · Universidad Motolinia del Pedregal · Universidad Nacional Autónoma de México [1, 3] · Universidad Panamericana Sistema · Universidad Panamericana Campus Bonaterra · Universidad Panamericana Ciudad de México · Universidad Panamericana Guadalajara · Universidad Pedagógica Nacional · Universidad Politécnica de Francisco I. Madero · Universidad Politécnica de Pachuca · Universidad Politécnica del Estado de Morelos · Universidad Popular Autónoma del Estado de Puebla [1, 8] · Universidad Popular de la Chontalpa · Universidad Regiomontana [1] · Universidad Salesiana · Universidad Simón Bolívar · Universidad Tecmilenio · Universidad Tecnológica de Aguascalientes · Universidad Tecnológica de Altamira · Universidad Tecnológica de Bahía de Banderas ·

Universidad Tecnológica de Cadereyta · Universidad Tecnológica de Campeche · Universidad Tecnológica de Cancún [7] · Universidad Tecnológica de Chihuahua · Universidad Tecnológica de Ciudad Juárez · Universidad Tecnológica de Coahuila · Universidad Tecnológica de Gutiérrez Zamora · Universidad Tecnológica de Hermosillo, Sonora · Universidad Tecnológica de Huejotzingo · Universidad Tecnológica de Izúcar de Matamoros · Universidad Tecnológica de Jalisco · Universidad Tecnológica de la Costa · Universidad Tecnológica de la Costa Grande de Guerrero · Universidad Tecnológica de la Huasteca Hidalguense · Universidad Tecnológica de la Mixteca · Universidad Tecnológica de la Región Norte de Guerrero · Universidad Tecnológica de la Riviera Maya · Universidad Tecnológica de la Selva · Universidad Tecnológica de la Sierra Hidalguense · Universidad Tecnológica de la Zona Metropolitana de Guadalajara · Universidad Tecnológica de León · Universidad Tecnológica de Matamoros · Universidad Tecnológica de México · Universidad Tecnológica de Morelia · Universidad Tecnológica de Nayarit · Universidad Tecnológica de Nezahualcóyotl · Universidad Tecnológica de Nogales, Sonora · Universidad Tecnológica de Nuevo Laredo · Universidad Tecnológica de Oriental · Universidad Tecnológica de Puebla · Universidad Tecnológica de Querétaro · Universidad Tecnológica de San Juan del Río · Universidad Tecnológica de San Luis Potosí · Universidad Tecnológica de Tabasco · Universidad Tecnológica de Tamaulipas Norte · Universidad Tecnológica de Tecámac · Universidad Tecnológica de Tecamachalco · Universidad Tecnológica de Tijuana · Universidad Tecnológica de Tlaxcala · Universidad Tecnológica de Torreón · Universidad Tecnológica de Tulancingo · Universidad Tecnológica de Tula-Tepeji · Universidad Tecnológica de Xicotepec de Juárez · Universidad Tecnológica del Centro de Veracruz · Universidad Tecnológica del Estado de Zacatecas · Universidad Tecnológica del Norte de Aguascalientes · Universidad Tecnológica del Norte de Coahuila · Universidad Tecnológica del Norte de Guanajuato · Universidad Tecnológica del Sur de Sonora · Universidad Tecnológica del Sur del Estado de México · Universidad Tecnológica del Sureste de Veracruz · Universidad Tecnológica del Suroeste de Guanajuato · Universidad Tecnológica del Usumacinta · Universidad Tecnológica del Valle de Toluca · Universidad Tecnológica del Valle del Mezquital · Universidad Tecnológica Emiliano Zapata del Estado de Morelos · Universidad Tecnológica Fidel Velázquez · Universidad Tecnológica General Mariano Escobedo · Universidad Tecnológica Metropolitana · Universidad Tecnológica Región Centro de Coahuila · Universidad Tecnológica Regional del Sur · Universidad Tecnológica Santa Catarina · Universidad Valle del Bravo Campus Reynosa · Universidad Valle del Grijalva · Universidad Vasco de Quiroga · Universidad Veracruzana · NICARAGUA Universidad Americana · Universidad Autónoma de Nicaragua-León · Universidad Autónoma de Nicaragua-Managua · Universidad Católica de Nicaragua · Universidad Centroamericana · Universidad de Ciencias Comerciales · Universidad Nacional Agraria · Universidad Nacional de Ingeniería · Universidad Politécnica · PANAMA Universidad Católica Santa María La Antigua [1, 8] · Universidad de Cartago · Universidad de Panamá [1, 2, 3] · Universidad Especializada de las Américas [2] · Universidad Iberoamericana de Panamá · Universidad Latina de Panamá · Universidad Latinoamericana de Ciencia y Tecnología · Universidad Tecnológica de Panamá [2] · PARAGUAY Universidad Americana · Universidad Autónoma de Asunción · Universidad Católica Nuestra Señora de la Asunción [1, 8] · Universidad Columbia del Paraguay · Universidad Nacional de Asunción [1, 3, 4] · Universidad Nacional del Este · PERU Asamblea Nacional de Rectores · Pontificia Universidad Católica del Perú [1, 8] · Universidad Alas Peruanas · Universidad Andina del Cusco [1] · Universidad Andina Néstor Cáceres Velásquez · Universidad Antonio Ruiz de Montoya [8] · Universidad Católica de Santa María [1, 8] · Universidad Católica Los Ángeles de Chimbote · Universidad Católica San Pablo · Universidad Católica Santo Toribio de Mogrovejo [8] · Universidad Católica Sedes Sapientiae [8] · Universidad César Vallejo · Universidad Científica del Sur · Universidad Continental de Ciencias e Ingeniería · Universidad de Lima [1] · Universidad de Piura · Universidad de San Martín de Porres [1] · Universidad del Pacífico · Universidad ESAN · Universidad Femenina del Sagrado Corazón [1] · Universidad Inca Garcilaso de la Vega [1] · Universidad Nacional Agraria La Molina [6] · Universidad Nacional Agraria de la Selva [6] · Universidad Nacional Daniel Alcides Carrión [6] · Universidad Nacional de Cajamarca · Universidad Nacional de Educación Enrique Guzmán y Valle · Universidad Nacional de Huancavelica · Universidad Nacional de Ingeniería [1] · Universidad Nacional de la Amazonía Peruana [6] · Universidad Nacional de Piura [1] · Universidad Nacional de San Agustín · Universidad Nacional de San Antonio Abad [1] · Universidad Nacional de San Martín · Universidad Nacional de Trujillo [1] · Universidad Nacional de Tumbes · Universidad Nacional de Ucayali [6] · Universidad Nacional del Altiplano · Universidad Nacional del Callao · Universidad Nacional del Centro del Perú [6] · Universidad Nacional del Santa · Universidad Nacional Federico Villarreal [1] · Universidad Nacional Hermilio Valdizán · Universidad Nacional Jorge Basadre Grohmann · Universidad Nacional José Faustino Sánchez Carrión · Universidad Nacional Mayor de San Marcos [1, 3] · Universidad Nacional Pedro Ruiz Gallo · Universidad Nacional San Cristóbal de Huamanga · Universidad Nacional San Luis Gonzaga de Ica · Universidad Nacional Santiago Antúnez de Mayolo · Universidad de Chiclayo · Universidad Particular de Iquitos · Universidad Peruana Los Andes · Universidad Peruana Cayetano Heredia [1, 6] · Universidad Peruana de Ciencias Aplicadas · Universidad Peruana Unión · Universidad Privada Antenor Orrego · Universidad César Vallejo · Universidad Privada de Tacna [1] · Universidad Privada del Norte · Universidad Marcelino Champagnat · Universidad Norbert Wiener · Universidad Privada San Juan Bautista · Universidad Privada San Pedro · Universidad Privada Señor de Sipán · Universidad Ricardo Palma [1] · Universidad San Ignacio de Loyola · Universidad Tecnológica del Perú · PORTUGAL Escola Naval · Instituto Superior de Ciências do Trabalho e da Empresa ISCTE ·

Universidade Aberta · Universidade Autónoma Luís de Camões · Universidade Católica Portuguesa · Universidade da Beira Interior · Universidade da Madeira · Universidade de Aveiro · Universidade de Coimbra · Universidade de Évora · Universidade de Lisboa · Universidade de Trás-os-Montes e Alto Douro · Universidade do Algarve · Universidade do Porto · Universidade dos Açores · Universidade Lusíada · Universidade Lusófona de Humanidades e Tecnologias · Universidade Nova de Lisboa · Universidade Portucalense Infante D. Henrique · Universidade Técnica de Lisboa · PUERTO RICO American University of Puerto Rico · Caribbean University · Centro de Estudios Avanzados de Puerto Rico y el Caribe · Conservatorio de Música de Puerto Rico · EDP College · Escuela de Artes Plásticas de Puerto Rico · Ponce School of Medicine · Pontificia Universidad Católica de Puerto Rico [8] · Sistema Universitario Ana G. Méndez SUAGM · Universidad Adventista de las Antillas · Universidad Carlos Albizu · Universidad Central de Bayamón [8] · Universidad Central del Caribe · Universidad de Puerto Rico · Universidad del Sagrado Corazón · Universidad Interamericana de Puerto Rico · Universidad Politécnica de Puerto Rico · University of Phoenix · RUSSIA Finance Academy under the Government of the Russian Federation · HSE Higher School of Economics · Moscow State Institute of International Relations MGIMO · Moscow State Linguistic University · Novosibirsk State University · Saint Petersburg State University · Siberian Federal University · Southern Federal University · SPAIN IE Universidad · Centro Universitario Villanueva · Conferencia de Rectores de las Universidades Españolas · Consejo Superior de Investigaciones Científicas · ESIC · Mondragón Unibertsitatea · Universidad Alfonso X El Sabio · Universidad Antonio de Nebrija · Universidad Autónoma de Madrid · Universidad Camilo José Cela · Universidad Carlos III de Madrid · Universidad Católica de Ávila · Universidad Católica de Valencia San Vicente Mártir · Universidad Católica San Antonio de Murcia · Universidad CEU Cardenal Herrera · Universidad CEU San Pablo · Universidad Complutense de Madrid · Universidad de Alcalá · Universidad de Alicante/Universitat d'Alacant · Universidad de Almería · Universidad de Burgos · Universidad de Cádiz · Universidad de Cantabria · Universidad de Castilla-La Mancha · Universidad de Córdoba · Universidad de Deusto/Deustuko Unibertsitatea · Universidad de Extremadura · Universidad de Granada · Universidad de Huelva · Universidad de Jaén · Universidad de La Laguna · Universidad de La Rioja · Universidad de Las Palmas de Gran Canaria · Universidad de León · Universidad de Málaga · Universidad de Murcia · Universidad de Navarra · Universidad de Oviedo · Universidad de Salamanca · Universidad de Sevilla · Universidad de Valladolid · Universidad de Zaragoza · Universidad del País Vasco/Euskal Herriko Unibertsitatea · Universidad Europea de Madrid · Universidad Europea Miguel de Cervantes · Universidad Francisco de Vitoria · Universidad Internacional de Andalucía · Universidad Internacional Menéndez Pelayo · Universitas Miguel Hernández de Elche · Universidad Nacional de Educación a Distancia UNED · Universidad Pablo de Olavide · Universidad Politécnica de Madrid · Universitat Politècnica de València · Universidad Pontificia Comillas · Universidad Pontificia de Salamanca · Universidad Pública de Navarra · Universidad Rey Juan Carlos · Universidad San Jorge · Universidade da Coruña · Universidade Santiago de Compostela · Universidade de Vigo · Universitat Abat Oliba CEU · Universitat Autònoma de Barcelona · Universitat de Barcelona · Universitat de Girona · Universitat de les Illes Balears · Universitat de Lleida · Universitat de València · Universitat de Vic · Universitat Internacional de Catalunya · Universitat Jaume I de Castelló · Universitat Oberta de Catalunya · Universitat Politècnica de Catalunya · Universitat Pompeu Fabra · Universitat Ramon Llull · Universitat Rovira i Virgili · UNITED KINGDOM Ashridge Business School · Bangor University / Prifysgol Bangor · Bournemouth University · Cardiff University · City University London – CASS Business School · Cranfield University · Durham University · Edinburgh Napier University · Glasgow Caledonian University · Imperial College London · King's College London · London Business School · Loughborough University · LSE The London School of Economics and Political Science · Newcastle University · Oxford Brookes University · Queen Margaret University · Queen's University Belfast · Royal Academy of Music · Royal Holloway University of London · The Open University · The University of Edinburgh · The University of Nottingham · The University of Sheffield · The University of Warwick · UCL University College London · University of Bath · University of Brighton · University of Bristol · University of Cambridge · University of Chester · University of Essex · University of Exeter · University of Glasgow · University of Leeds · University of Northampton · University of Oxford · University of Southampton · University of St. Andrews · University of Surrey · UNITED STATES Babson College · Brown University · Columbia University · David Rockefeller Center for Latin American Studies Harvard University · MIT Massachusetts Institute of Technology · New York University · The State University of New York SUNY · URUGUAY Centro Latinoamericano de Economía Humana Instituto Universitario · Instituto Universitario CEDIAPP · Universidad Católica del Uruguay [1, 8] · Universidad de la Empresa · Universidad de la República [1, 3, 4] · Universidad de Montevideo · Universidad ORT [1] · VENEZUELA Instituto de Estudios Superiores de Administración · Instituto Venezolano de Investigaciones Científicas · Universidad Alonso de Ojeda · Universidad Arturo Michelena · Universidad Bicentenaria de Aragua · Universidad Católica Andrés Bello · Universidad Católica Cecilio Acosta · Universidad Católica del Táchira · Universidad Católica Santa Rosa · Universidad Central de Venezuela · Universidad Centroccidental Lisandro Alvarado · Universidad de Carabobo · Universidad de Falcón · Universidad de Los Andes · Universidad de Margarita · Universidad de Oriente · Universidad del Zulia · Universidad Dr. José Gregorio Hernández · Universidad Fermín Toro · Universidad Gran Mariscal de Ayacucho · Universidad José Antonio Páez · Universidad José María Vargas ·

Universidad Metropolitana · Universidad Monteávila · Universidad Nacional Abierta · Universidad Nacional Experimental Rafael María Baralt · Universidad Nacional Experimental de Guayana · Universidad Nacional Experimental de los Llanos Centrales Rómulo Gallegos · Universidad Nacional Experimental de los Llanos Occidentales Ezequiel Zamora · Universidad Nacional Experimental del Táchira · Universidad Nacional Experimental del Yaracuy · Universidad Nacional Experimental Francisco de Miranda · Universidad Nacional Experimental Marítima del Caribe · Universidad Nacional Experimental Politécnica Antonio José de Sucre · Universidad Nacional Experimental Politécnica de la Fuerza Armada Nacional Bolivariana · Universidad Nacional Experimental Sur del Lago Jesús María Semprún · Universidad Nueva Esparta · Universidad Panamericana del Puerto · Universidad Pedagógica Experimental Libertador · Universidad Rafael Belloso Chacín · Universidad Rafael Urdaneta · Universidad Santa Inés · Universidad Santa María · Universidad Simón Bolívar · Universidad Tecnológica del Centro · Universidad Valle del Momboy · Universidad Yacambú ·

Latin American universities belonging to other regional networks and partnerships are marked on the list accordingly:
1 Unión de Universidades de América Latina y el Caribe (UDUAL)   **2** Consejo Superior Universitario Centroamericano (CSUCA)
3 Red de Macrouniversidades Públicas de América Latina y el Caribe (RED)   **4** Asociación de Universidades Grupo Montevideo (AUGM)
5 Asociación de Universidades e Institutos de Investigación del Caribe (UNIICA)   **6** Asociación de Universidades Amazónicas (UNAMAZ)
7 Asociación de Universidades de América Latina y el Caribe Para la Integración (AUALCPI)   **8** Organización de Universidades Católicas de América Latina (ODUCAL).

Bibliography

CHAPTER I

ALONSO, C. J., *Historia básica de la ciencia*, Pamplona, Ediciones Universidad de Navarra, 2001

FARRINGTON, B., *Greek Science*, Oxford, Oxford University Press, 1953

FORMENT, E., *Historia de la filosofía II. Filosofía medieval*, Madrid, Ediciones Palabra, 2004

LINDBERG, D.C., *The Beginnings of Western Science*, Oxford, Oxford University Press, 1992

MASON, S.F., *Main Currents of Scientific Thought: A History of the Sciences*, New York, Henry Schuman, 1953

PECERE, O. (ed.), *Il monaco, il libro, la biblioteca*, Casino, Università degli studi di Cassino, 2003

REALE, G. and ANTISERI, D., *Storia della filosofia, I, Dall' antichita al medioevo*, Brescia, La Scuola, 1990

SAMBURSKY, S., *The Physical World of Late Antiquity*, London, Routledge, 1962

STAHL, W.S., *Roman Science. Origins, Development and Influence to the Later Middle Ages*, Madison, University of Wisconsin Press, 1962

University Education in Imperial China

BIELENSTEIN, H., *The Bureaucracy of Han*, Cambridge, Cambridge University Press, 1980

ELMAN, B.A., 'Political, Social, and Cultural Reproduction via Civil Service Examinations in Late Imperial China', in *The Journal of Asian Studies*, no. 50.1, February 1991, pp. 7-28

HUCKER, C.O., *A Dictionary of Official Titles in Imperial China*, Stanford, Stanford University Press, 1985

McMULLEN, D., *State and Scholars in Tang China*, Cambridge, Cambridge University Press, 1988

TWITCHETT, D. (ed.), *The Cambridge History of China: Volume 3, Sui and Tang China, 589-906, Part I*, Cambridge, Cambridge University Press, 1979

TWITCHETT, D. and LOEWE, M. (eds.), *The Cambridge History of China: Volume 1, The Chin and Han Empires, 221 BC–AD 220*, Cambridge, Cambridge University Press, 1986

The Madrassa

ACIÉN ALMANSA, M., 'Inscripciones de la portada de la Madraza', in *Arte islámico en Granada. Propuesta para un Museo de la Alhambra*, Granada, 1995, pp. 337-9

CABANELAS RODRÍGUEZ, D., 'La madraza árabe de Granada y su suerte en época cristiana', in *Cuadernos de la Alhambra*, no. 27, 1988, pp. 7-26

GOLVIN, L., *La madrasa médiévale: architecture musulmane*, Aix-en-Provence, Edisud, 1995

MALPICA CUELLO, A. et al., 'Intervención arqueológica de apoyo a la restauración del Palacio de la Madraza', Granada, 2006-7, in *Anuario Andaluz de Arqueología*, 2007

Martínez Enamorado, V., 'La madrasa de Ceuta en el contexto del Islam Occidental', in *Actas de las II Jornadas sobre Historia de Ceuta. Ceuta en el Medievo: la ciudad en el universo árabe*, Ceuta, 2002, pp. 39-58

Pedersen, J.; Maqdisi, G. and Hillenbrand, R., 'Madrassa', in *Encyclopaedia of Islam (EI²)*, Leiden, 1985, pp. 1119-44

Pezzi, E., *El vocabulario de Pedro de Alcalá*, Almería, Cajal, 1989

CHAPTERS II, III and IV

Ajo González de Rapariegos y Sáinz de Zuñiga, C.Mª, *Historia de las universidades hispánicas. Orígenes y desarrollo desde su aparición hasta nuestros días*, 11 vols., Ávila / Madrid, CSIC, 1957-79

Aston, T.H. (ed.), *The History of the University of Oxford*, 8 vols., Oxford, Oxford University Press, 1984-2000

Aulas y saberes. VI Congreso de Historia de las Universidades Hispánicas (Valencia, 3-6 November 1999), preface by Mariano Peset, 2 vols., Valencia, Universitat de València, 2003

Barreiro, X.R. (ed.), *Historia de la Universidad de Santiago de Compostela*, 2 vols., Santiago de Compostela, Universidad de Santiago de Compostela, 2000-3

Bataillon, M., *Erasme et l'Espagne*, Paris, Droz, 1937

Bellomo, M., *Saggio sull'università nell'età del Diritto commune*, Catania, Giannotta, 1979

Bermejo Castillo, M. (ed.), *Manuales y textos de enseñanza en la Universidad liberal. VII Congreso de Historia de las Universidades Hispánicas*, Madrid, Universidad Carlos III / Dykinson, 2004

Blasco Gil, Y., *La facultad de Derecho de Valencia durante la Restauración (1875-1900)*, Valencia, Universitat de València, 2000

Boehm, L. and Raimondi, E. (eds.), *Università, Accademie e Società scientifiche in Italia e in Germania dal Cinquecento al Settecento. Atti della setimana di studio* (Trento, 15-20 September 1980), Bologna, 1981

Boehm, L. and Müller, R.A. (eds.), *Universitäten und Hochschulen in Deutschland Österreich und Schweiz. Eine Universitätsgeschichte in Einzeldarstellungen*, Düsseldorf, Econ, 1983

Braga da Cruz, G., *Origem e evolução da Universidade*, Lisbon, Logos, 1964

Brizzi, G.P., *La formazione della classe dirigente nel Sei-Settecento. I 'seminaria nobilium' nell'Italia centro-settentrionale*, Bologna, Il Mulino, 1976

Brizzi, G.P. and Verger, J. (eds.), *Le Università dell'Europa*, 6 vols., Milan, Cinisello Balsamo / Silvana, 1991-5

Brizzi, G.P. and Verger, J. (eds.), *Le Università minori in Europa (secoli XV-XIX)*, Messina, Soveria Manelli / Rubbettino, 1998

Brizzi, G.P. and Romano, A. (eds.), *Studenti e dottori nelle università italiane (origini-secolo XX). Atti del Convegno di studi* (Bologna, 25-27 November 1999), Bologna, CLUEB, 2000

Brizzi, G.P. and Greci, R. (eds.), *Gesuiti e università in Europa (secoli XVI-XVIII). Atti del Convegno di studi* (Parma, 13-15 December 2001), Bologna, CLUEB, 2002

Brizzi, G.P.; Negro, P. del and Romano, A. (eds.), *Storia delle università in Italia*, 3 vols., Messina, Sicania, 2007

Brockliss, L.W.B., *French Higher Education in the Seventeenth and Eighteenth Centuries. A Cultural History*, Oxford, Clarendon Press, 1987

Charle, C., *La république des universitaires (1870-1940)*, Paris, Seuil, 1994

Charle, C. and Verger, J., *Histoire des universités*, Paris, Presses Universitaires de France, 1994

Chêne, C., *L'enseignement du droit français en pays de droit écrit (1679-1793)*, Geneva, Droz, 1982

Ciencia y academia. IX Congreso Internacional de Historia de las Universidades Hispánicas, (Valencia, 14-17 September 2005), preface by Mariano Peset, Valencia, Universitat de València, 2008

Claustros y estudiantes. Congreso Internacional de Historia de las Universidades Americanas y Españolas, Valencia, November 1987, preface by Mariano Peset, 2 vols., Valencia, Universitat de València, 1989

Cobban, A.B., *The Medieval Universities. Their Development and Organisation*, London, Methuen, 1975

—, *The Medieval English Universities: Oxford and Cambridge, to c. 1500*, Berkeley, University of California, 1988

Coing, H. (ed.), *Handbuch der Quellen und Literatur del neuren europäischen Privatrechtsgeschichte*, 8 vols., Frankfurt, Max-Planck Institut, 1973-88

D'Amato, A., *La Chiesa e l'università di Bologna*, Bologna, Edizioni Luigi Parma, 1997

Denifle, H., *Die Entstehung der Universitäten im Mittelalter bis 1400*, Berlin, Weidmann, 1885

D'Irsay, S., *Histoire des universités françaises et étrangères des origines à nos jours*, 2 vols., Paris, Picard, 1933-5

Doctores y escolares, II Congreso Internacional de Historia de las Universidades Hispánicas, Valencia, 1995, 2 vols., foreword by the rector Pedro Ruiz Torres, preface by Mariano Peset, Valencia, Universitat de València, 1998

Ferrone, V., *Scienza, natura, religione. Mondo newtoniano e cultura italiana nel primo Settecento*, Naples, Jovene, 1982

Fuente, V. de la, *Historia de las universidades, colegios y demás establecimientos de enseñanza en España*, 4 vols., Madrid, Imprenta de la viuda e hijos de Fuentenebro, 1884-9

García Trobat, P., *El naixement d'una universitat: Gandia*, Gandía, Ajuntament de Gandia, 1989

Gheda, P.; Guerrini, M.T.; Negruzco, S. and Salustri, S. (eds.), *Storia delle università alle soglie del XXI secolo. Atti del Convegno Internazionale di Studi* (Aosta, 18-20 December 2006), Bologna, CLUEB, 2000

González, E. and Pérez Puente, L. (eds.), *Colegios y universidades. Del antiguo régimen al liberalismo. IV Congreso Internacional de Historia de las Universidades Hispánicas* (Mexico City, 1997), 2 vols., Mexico City, UNAM, 2001

González, E. and Pérez Puente, L. (eds.), *Permanencia y cambio. Universidades hispánicas 1551-2001*, 2 vols., Mexico City, Centro de Estudios sobre la Universidad, UNAM, 2005

Guenée, S., *Les universités françaises des origines à la Révolution. Notices historiques sur les universités, studia et académies protestantes*, Paris, Picard, 1982

Guereña, J.L.; Fell, E.M. and Ayme, J.R. (eds.), *L'Université en Espagne et Amérique latine du Moyen Âge à nos jours*, 2 vols., Tours, Université de Tours, 1991-8

Guijarro González, S., *Maestros, escuelas y libros. El universo cultural de las catedrales en la Castilla medieval*, Madrid, Universidad Carlos III / Dykinson, 2004

Hammerstein, N., *Aufklärung und katholisches Reich. Untersuchungen zur Universitätsreform und Politik katholischen Territorien des heiligen Römischen Reichs deutscher Nation*, Berlin, Duncker und Humblot, Historische Forschung, no. 12, 1977

Hernández Sandoica, E. and Peset, J.L., *Universidad, poder académico y cambio social. Alcalá de Henares 1508-Madrid 1874*, Madrid, Consejo de Universidades, 1990

Historia de la universidad de Valladolid, 2 vols., Valladolid, Universidad de Valladolid, 1989

Julia, D.; Revel, J. and Chartier, R. (eds.), *Les universités européennes du XVIᵉ au XVIIIᵉ siècle. Histoire des populations universitaires*, 2 vols., Paris, École des hautes études en sciences sociales, 1986-9

Kagan, R.L., *Students and Society in Early Modern Spain*, Baltimore / London, Johns Hopkins University Press, 1974

Kauffmann, G., *Geschichte der deutschen Universitäten*, 2 vols., Stuttgart, 1888-96 (reprint: Graz, 1958)

Kibre, P., *The Nations in the Mediaeval Universities*, Cambridge, Massachusetts, Mediaeval Academy of America, no. 46, 1948

Laín Entralgo, P., *Historia de la medicina*, Barcelona, Salvat, 1978

—, *Historia universal de la medicina*, 7 vols., Barcelona, Salvat, 1972-7

Liard, L., *L'enseignement supérieur en France (1789-1894)*, 2 vols., Paris, Picard, 1888-96

López, F., *Juan Pablo Forner et la crise de la conscience espagnole au XVIIIᵉ siècle*, Bordeaux, Institut d'Études Ibériques et Ibéroaméricaines de l'Université de Bordeaux, 1976

López Piñero, J.M., *Ciencia y técnica en la sociedad española de los siglos XVI y XVII*, Barcelona, Labor, 1979

MacLelland, C., *State, Society and University in Germany 1700-1914*, Cambridge, Cambridge University Press, 1980

Maffei, D. and Ridder-Symoens, H. de (eds.), *I collegi universitari in Europa tra il XIV e il XVIII secolo. Atti del Convegno di Studi della Commissione Internazionale per la Storia delle Università* (Siena / Bologna 16-19 May 1988), Milan, 1990

Martínez Gomis, M., *La universidad de Orihuela, 1610-1807*, 2 vols., Alicante, Instituto Juan Gil Albert, 1987

Menegus, M. (ed.), *Universidad y sociedad en Hispanoamérica. Grupos de poder en los siglos XVIII y XIX. III Congreso Internacional de Historia de las Universidades Hispánicas*, Mexico City, UNAM, 2001

Müller, R.A., *Universität und Adel. Eine soziostrukturelle Studium zur Geschichte der bayerishen Landesuniversität Ingolstadt (1472-1648)*, Berlin, Duncker und Humblot, 1974

—, *Geschichte der Universität. Von der mittelalterlichen Universität zur deutschen Hochschule*, Munich, Callwey, 1990

Negro, P. del (ed.), *L'Università di Padova: otto secoli di storia*, Padua, Signum Padova Editrice, 2001

Novarese, D., *Istituzioni politiche e studi di Diritto tra Cinque e Seicento. Il Messanense studium generale tra politica gesuitica e istanze egemoniche cittadine*, Milan, Giuffrè, 1994

Paulsen, F., *Geschichte des gelehrten Unterrichts auf dem deutschen Schulen und Universitäten vom Ausgang des Mittelalters bis zur Gegenwart. Mit besondere Rücksicht auf den klassischen Unterricht*, 2 vols., Leipzig, 3rd ed., 1886/1919-21 (reprint: Berlin, 1960)

Pelorson, J.M., *Les letrados juristes castillans sous Philippe III. Recherches sur leur place dans la société, la culture et l'état*, Poitiers, Université de Poitiers, 1980

Peset, J.L. and Hernández Sandoica, E., *Estudiantes de Alcalá*, Madrid, Ayuntamiento de Alcalá de Henares, 1983

Peset, J.L. and Peset, M., 'El aislamiento científico español a través de los índices del inquisidor Gaspar de Quiroga de 1583 y 1584', *Anthologica Annua*, no. 16, 1968, pp. 25-41

—, *La universidad española (siglos XVIII y XIX). Despotismo ilustrado y revolución liberal*, Madrid, Taurus, 1974

—, *Carlos IV y la universidad de Salamanca*, Madrid, CSIC, 1983

Peset, M., 'Derecho romano y derecho real en las universidades del siglo XVIII', in *Anuario de historia del derecho español*, no. 45, 1975, pp. 273-339

—, 'Spanische Universität und Rechtswissenchaft zwischen aufgeklärtem Absolutismus und liberaler Revolution', in *Ius Commune. Zeitschrift für europäische Rechtsgeschichte*, no. 6, 1977, pp. 172-201

—, 'Interrelaciones entre las universidades españolas y portuguesas en los primeros siglos de su historia', in *Boletim da faculdade de Direito de Coimbra*, vol. 2, no. 58, 1982, pp. 875-940 (*Estudos em homenagem a os profs. Manuel Paulo Merêa e Guilherme Braga da Cruz*, Coimbra, 1983)

—, 'Julián Sanz del Río und seine Reise nach Deutschland', in K.M. Kodalle (ed.), *Karl Christian Friedrich Krause (1781-1832). Studien zu seine Philosophie und zum Krausismus*, Hamburg, Felix Mainer Verlag, 1985, pp. 152-73

—, '¿Qué es la Ilustración?', in *Homenatge al doctor Sebastián García Martínez*, 3 vols., Valencia, Universitat de València, 1988, III, pp. 383-90

—, 'La organización de las universidades españolas en la Edad Moderna', in Andrea Romano (ed.), *Studi e Diritto nell'area mediterranea in età moderna*, Messina, 1993, pp. 73-122

—, 'La fundación y el fuero universitario de Lérida', in *Hispania*, 58-2, no. 199, 1998, pp. 515-36

— (ed.), *Historia de la universidad de Valencia*, 3 vols., Valencia, Universitat de València, 1999-2000 (Catalan ed.: Universitat de València, 2000)

—, 'Orígenes de la Universidad de Coimbra', in *Homenagem a José Adriano de Carvalho, Península. Revista de estudios ibéricos*, Porto, no. 0, 2003, pp. 75-85

PESET, M. and GUTIÉRREZ CUADRADO, J., 'Clérigos y juristas en la baja edad media castellanoleonesa', in *Senara*, no. 3, Vigo, 1981, Annex II, pp. 7-110

PESET, M. and MANCEBO, M.F., *Historia de las universidades valencianas*, 2 vols., *I. La universidad de Valencia*, Alicante, Universidad de Alicante / Instituto Juan Gil Albert, 1993

PESET, M. and MENEGUS BORNEMANN, M., 'Localización y espacio de las universidades hispánicas', in *Cuadernos del Instituto Antonio de Nebrija de estudios sobre la universidad*, no. 3, 2000, pp. 189-232

PESET, M. and PESET MANCEBO, M., 'Las reformas universitarias en el siglo XVIII', in *Les universitats de la corona d'Aragó, ahir i avui*, Lérida, Universitat de Lleida, 2002, pp. 321-49

PRATS, J., *La universitat de Cervera i el reformisme borbònic*, Lérida, Pagés, 1993

RASHDALL, H., *The Universities of Europe in the Middle Ages*, new ed. by F.M. Powicke and A.B. Emden, 3 vols., Oxford, 1936 (reprinted: Oxford, Clarendon Press, 1987)

RICHÉ, P., *Études et enseignements dans l'Occident chrétien de la fin du Ve siècle au milieu du IXe siècle*, Paris, Aubier-Montaigne, 1979

—, *Les écoles et enseignements dans l'Occident chrétien de la fin du Ve siècle au milieu du XIe siècle*, Paris, Aubier-Montaigne, 1979

RIEHL, D. (ed.), *A History of the University of Cambridge*, 4 vols., Cambridge, Cambridge University Press, 1988-2004

RODRÍGUEZ-SAN PEDRO BEZARES, L.E., *La universidad salmantina. Período barroco, 1598-1625*, 2 vols., Salamanca, Universidad de Salamanca, 1986

— (ed.), *Las universidades hispánicas de la monarquía de los Austrias al centralismo liberal*. V Congreso Internacional sobre Historia de las Universidades Hispánicas (Salamanca, 1998), 2 vols., Salamanca, Universidad de Salamanca / Junta de Castilla y León, 2000

— (ed.), *Historia de la Universidad de Salamanca*, 5 vols., Salamanca, Universidad de Salamanca, 2002-8

ROMANO, A. (ed.), *Studi e Diritto nell'area mediterranea in età moderna*, Messina, Soveria Manelli / Rubbettino, 1993

— (ed.), *Università in Europa. Le istituzioni universitarie del Medio Evo ai nostri giorni. Strutture, organizzazione, funzionamento*, Etti del Convegno Internationale di Studi (Milazzo 28 September-2 October 1993), Messina, Rubbettino, 1995

ROMANO, A. and VERGER, J. (eds.), *I poteri politici e il mondo universitario*, Convegno internazionale (Madrid 1990), Messina, Soveria Manelli / Rubbettino, 1994

RÜGG, W. and RIDDER-SYMOENS, H. de (eds.), *A History of the University in Europe*, 4 vols., Cambridge, Cambridge University Press, 1992-2004

SCHUMPETER, J.A., *History of Economic Analysis*, New York, Oxford University Press, 1954

SIMONE, M.R. di, *La 'Sapienza' romana nel Settecento. Organizzazione universitaria e insegnamento del diritto*, Rome, Ateneo, 1980

SORBELLI, A. and SIMEONE, L., *Storia dell'Università de Bologna, 1. Il medioevo (secolo XI-XV), 2. L'età moderna (1500-1888)*, Bologna, Università di Bologna, 1940

STONE, L. (ed.), *The University in Society*, 2 vols., Princeton, Princeton University Press, 1975

SWANSON, R.N., *Universities, Academics and the Great Schism*, Cambridge, Cambridge University Press, 1979

TATON, R. (ed.), *Histoire générale des sciences*, 4 vols., Paris, PUF, 1957-64

TORREMOCHA HERNÁNDEZ, M., *Ser estudiante en el siglo XVIII. La universidad vallisoletana de la Ilustración*, Valladolid, Consejería de Cultura y Turismo, 1991

Universidades españolas y americanas. Periodo colonial. V Centenari del Descubriment d'América, preface by Mariano Peset, Valencia, CSIC / Generalitat valenciana 1987

VERGER, J. (ed.), *Histoire des universités en France*, Toulouse, Privat, 1986

WIEACKER, F., *Privatrechtsgeschichte der Neuzeit: unter besonderer Berücksichtigung der deutschen Entwicklung*, Göttingen, Vandenhoeck & Ruprecht, 2nd ed., 1967

Oxford and Cambridge:
The Foundation of the Colleges

CATTO, J.L. (ed.), *The History of the University of Oxford*, vol. 1, *The Early Oxford Schools*, Oxford, Oxford University Press, 1984

CATTO, J.L. and EVANS, T.A.R. (eds.), *The History of the University of Oxford*, vol. 2: *Late Medieval Oxford*, Oxford, Oxford University Press, 1992

COBBAN, A.B., *The Medieval English Universities: Oxford and Cambridge to c. 1500*, Aldershot, Scolar Press, 1988

PEDERSEN, O., *The First Universities*, Cambridge, Cambridge University Press, 1997

RIDDER-SYMOENS, H. de, *A History of the University in Europe*, vol. 1: *Universities in the Middle Ages*, Cambridge, Cambridge University Press, 1992

RIEHL, D. (ed.), *A history of the University of Cambridge*, vol. 1: *The university to 1546*, Cambridge, Cambridge University Press, 1988

CHAPTER V

Three Centuries of Founding Universities in Colonial Latin America

Burkholder, M.A. and Chandler, D.S., *De la impotencia a la autoridad. La Corona española y las audiencias en América 1687-1808*, Mexico City, Fondo de Cultura Económica, 1984

Cardozo Galué, G., *Michoacán en el siglo de las luces*, Mexico City, El Colegio de México / Centro de Estudios Históricos, 1973

Castañeda, C., 'La real universidad de Guadalajara y su influencia en la sociedad tapatía', in E. González and L. Pérez Puente (eds.), *Permanencia y cambio* I. *Universidades hispánicas 1551-2001*, Mexico City, UNAM / CESU / Facultad de derecho, 2005

Chocano Mena, M., *La fortaleza docta. Élite letrada y dominación social en México colonial (siglos XVI-XVII)*, Barcelona, Bellaterra, 2000

Escamilla González, I., 'Un rector ilustrado: José de Uribe y la Universidad de México, 1742-1796', in E. González and L. Pérez Puente (eds.), *Permanencia y cambio. Universidades hispánicas 1551-2001, op. cit.*

González González, E., 'La reedición de las constituciones universitarias de México (1775) y la polémica antiilustrada', in Lourdes Alvarado (ed.), *Tradición y reforma en la universidad de México*, Mexico City, UNAM / CESU, Miguel Ángel Porrúa Editor, 1994

González González, E. and Pavón Romero, A., 'La primera universidad de México', in *Maravillas y curiosidades. Mundos inéditos de la Universidad*, Mexico City, UNAM, Antiguo Colegio de San Ildefonso, 2002

Güemes, J.V. de, *Informe sobre las misiones (1793) e Instrucción reservada al marqués de Branciforte (1794)*, introduction and notes by José Bravo Ugarte, Mexico City, Jus, 1966

Lohmeyer de Lenkersdorf, G., 'El doctor Antonio Rodríguez de Quesada, primer rector de la Real Universidad de México', in E. González and L. Pérez Puente (eds.), *Permanencia y cambio. Universidades hispánicas 1551-2001, op. cit.*

Martínez López-Cano, P. et al., *La universidad novohispana en el Siglo de Oro. A cuatrocientos años de "El Quijote"*, Mexico City, UNAM / Instituto de Investigaciones Históricas / Centro de Estudios sobre la Universidad, 2006

Méndez Arceo, S., *La Real y Pontificia Universidad de México. Antecedentes, tramitación y despacho de las reales cédulas de erección*, Mexico City, UNAM / Coordinación de Humanidades, 1990

Mues Orts, P., *La libertad del pincel. Los discursos sobre la nobleza de la pintura en Nueva España*, Mexico City, Universidad Iberoamericana, 2008

Pérez Puente, L., 'Un informe del obispo Enríquez de Rivera sobre la fundación de la universidad pública de Guatemala', in E. González and L. Pérez Puente (eds.), *Permanencia y cambio. Universidades hispánicas 1551-2001, op. cit.*

Peset, M., 'Sobre los orígenes de Salamanca', in Enrique González González and L. Pérez Puente (eds.), *op. cit.*

Peset, M. and Peset, J.L., *La universidad española (siglos XVIII y XIX). Despotismo ilustrado y revolución liberal*, Madrid, Taurus, 1974

Rábade Obradó, M.P., *Las universidades en la Edad Media*, Madrid, Arco Libros, 1996

Rodríguez Cruz, A.M., *La universidad en la América Hispánica*, Madrid, Mapfre, 1992

Sánchez-Blanco, F., *La mentalidad ilustrada*, Madrid, Taurus, 1999

Sarrailh, J., *La España ilustrada de la segunda mitad del siglo XVIII*, Mexico City, Fondo de Cultura Económica, 1957

Valcárcel, C.D., *San Marcos, universidad decana de América*, Lima, Universidad Nacional Mayor de San Marcos, 2001

The University in Latin America and the Caribbean

Brunner, J.J., *Universidad y sociedad en América Latina*, Mexico City, UNAM / Coordinación de Extensión Universitaria / SEP, 1987

CINDA, *Educación superior en Iberoamérica*, Santiago de Chile, RIL Editores, 2007

Cordera Campos, R. (ed.), *Historia de la unión de universidades de América Latina y el Caribe*, Mexico City, UDUAL, 2007

Declaración de la Conferencia Regional de Educación Superior de América Latina y el Caribe, Caracas, IESALC / UNESCO, 2008

De la Fuente, J.R., 'Academic freedom and social responsibility', in *Higher Education Policy*, no. 15, 2002, pp. 337-9

—, 'La universidad pública en América Latina', in *Cuadernos Americanos*, no. 101, , 2003, pp. 11-25

—, 'Retos de la Educación Superior en América Latina', in *Universidades*, UDUAL, no. 37, 2008, p. 13

De la Fuente, J.R. and Martuscelli, J., 'América Latina ante la internacionalización de la educación superior', in *Cuadernos Americanos*, no. 105, 2004 pp. 13-20

Didriksson, A. and Herrera, A. (eds.), *La transformación de la universidad mexicana: diez estudios de caso en la transición*, Mexico City, Universidad Autónoma de Zacatecas / Miguel Ángel Porrúa Editor, 2002

Gazzola, A.L. and Didriksson, A. (eds.), *Tendencias de la educación superior en América Latina y el Caribe*, Caracas, IESALC, 2009

Herrera, A.; Didriksson, A. and Sánchez, C., 'La responsabilidad social en las macrouniversidades de América Latina y el Caribe', in *Universidades*, UDUAL, no. 41, 2009, p. 11

Olivé, L., *La ciencia y la tecnología en la sociedad del conocimiento: ética, política y epistemología*, Mexico City, Fondo de Cultura Económica, 2007

Recommendations from civil society on the fundamental role of science, technology, engineering, innovation, and science education within the framework of discussion for the Fourth Summit of the Americas, Washington, Organization of American States, Office of Education, Science and Technology, 2005

Schwartzmann, S., *América Latina: Universidades en transición*, Washington, Organization of American States, 1996

—, *Universidad y desarrollo en Latinoamérica*, Caracas, IESALC / UNESCO, 2009

—, 'Coming Full Circle: A Reappraisal of University Research in Latin America', in *Minerva*, no. 34, 1985, p. 456

Scotto, C. (ed.), *La Gaceta Universitaria 1918-1919. Una mirada sobre el movimiento reformista en las universidades nacionales*, Buenos Aires, EUDEBA, 2008

Steger, H.A., *Las universidades en el desarrollo social de América Latina*, Mexico City, Fondo de Cultura Económica, 1974

Tedesco, Juan C., *Educar en la sociedad del conocimiento*, Mexico City, Fondo de Cultura Económica, 2000

Vessuri, H., 'Science and Higher Education in the Process of Internationalization. Elements of a Conceptual Framework for Latin America', in *Forum Series Paper*, no. 3, Paris, UNESCO, 2003

Higher Education in Mexico

León-Portilla, M. and García Icazbalceta, J. (eds.), *México en 1554. Tres diálogos latinos de Francisco Cervantes de Salazar*, Mexico City, UNAM / IIH / IIB, 2001

Higher Education in Brazil

Azevedo, F. de, *A cultura brasileira*, São Paulo, Edições Melhoramentos / EDUSP, 1971

Campos, E. de S., *História da Universidade de São Paulo*, São Paulo, EDUSP, 2nd ed., 2004

Cunha, L. A., *A universidade temporã*, Rio de Janeiro, Civilização Brasileira, 1980

—, *A universidade crítica*, São Paulo, EDUNESP, 2007

—, *A universidade reformada*, São Paulo, EDUNESP, 2007

Fernandes, F., *Universidade brasileira: reforma ou revolução?*, São Paulo, Alfa-Omega, 1975

Morhy, L. (ed.), *A Universidade no mundo. Universidade em questão*, Brasilia, Editora Universidade de Brasilia, 2004

Motoyama, S., *Prelúdio para uma história: Ciência e Tecnologia no Brasil*, São Paulo, EDUSP / FAPESP, 2004

Romanelli, O. de O., *História da Educação no Brasil 1930-1973*, Petropolis, Editora Vozes, 1978

Trindade, H. and Blanquer, J.M. (eds.), *Os desafios da educação na América Latina*, Petrópolis, Editora Vozes, 2002

Universities in North America

Flexner, A., *Universities: American, English, German*, London, Oxford and New York, Oxford University Press, 1930

Geiger, R.L., *To Advance Knowledge: The Growth of American Research Universities, 1900-1940*, New York and Oxford, Oxford University Press, 1986

—, *Research and Relevant Knowledge: American Research Universities Since World War II*, New York and Oxford, Oxford University Press, 1993

Graham, H.D. and Diamond, N., *The Rise of American Research Universities: Elites and Challengers in the Postwar Era*, Baltimore and London, Johns Hopkins University Press, 1997

Harris, R.S., *A History of Higher Education in Canada, 1663-1960*, Toronto and Buffalo, University of Toronto Press, 1976

Jones, G.A. (ed.), *Higher Education in Canada: Different Systems, Different Perspectives*, New York, Garland Publishers, 1997

Kerr, C., *The Uses of the University*, Cambridge, Massachusetts, Harvard University Press, 1963

Lowen, R.S., *Creating the Cold War University: The Transformation of Stanford*, Berkeley, Los Angeles and London, University of California Press, 1997

Rosenzweig, R.M. and Turlington, B., *The Research Universities and Their Patrons*, Berkeley, Los Angeles and London, University of California Press, 1982

Sheffield, E. et al., *Systems of Higher Education: Canada*, New York, International Council for Educational Development, 1982

Slosson, E.E., *Great American Universities*, New York, MacMillan, 1910

Thelin, J.R., *A History of American Higher Education*, Baltimore and London, Johns Hopkins University Press, 2004

Veysey, L.L., *The Emergence of the American University*, Chicago, University of Chicago Press, 1965

The Future of the Humanities
at North American Universities

Bauerlein, E.M., 'The Future of Humanities Labor. Let's change the standards for tenure in the humanities before it's too late', in *Academe Online*, September-October 2009

Fish, S., *There's No Such Thing as Free Speech*, New York, Oxford University Press, 1994

Geiger, R.L., 'Taking the Pulse of the Humanities: Higher Education in the Humanities Indicators Project' (http://www. humanitiesindicators.org/essays/geiger.pdf)

Liu, A., *The Laws of Cool: Knowledge Work and the Culture of Information*, Chicago, University of Chicago Press, 2004

Paulson, W., *Literary Culture in a World Transformed. A Future for the Humanities*, Ithaca and New York, Cornell University Press, 2001

CHAPTER VI

A New Economy, Paris, OECD, 2000

Bricall, J.M., 'Universities towards a new Humanism?', speech delivered at the conference 'La tradizione umanistica e la sua crisi', Università degli Studi di Firenze, September 2000

— (ed.), *Universidad 2000*, Conferencia de Rectores de las Universidades Españolas, Madrid, 2000

COHENDET, P.; LEDOUX, M. J. and ZUSCOVITCH, E., 'The Evolution of New Materials: a New Dynamic for Growth', in *Technology and Productivity*, Paris, OECD, 1991

FROMENT, E., 'Post-2010: building a higher education and research area, but for what sort of Europe?', in *Moving beyond Bologna: the European Higher Education Area after 2010*, EUA / Bologna Handbook, 2009

Historia de la Universidad en Europa, vol. 1, CRE, Euskal Herriko Unibersitatea, 1994

'Observatory for Fundamental University Values and Rights. Managing University Autonomy. Shifting Paradigms in University Research', Bologna, Bologna University Press, July 2004 (www.oecd.org/edu/eag2009)

RODEES, F.H.T., in W. Hirsh and L.E. Weber (eds.), *Challenges Facing Higher Education in the Millenium*, Phoenix, Oryx Press 1999

CHAPTER VII

ALTBACH, P.G.; BERDAHL, R.O. and GUMPORT, P.J. (eds.), *American Higher Education in the Twenty-First Century*, Baltimore, Johns Hopkins University Press, 2005

AMARAL, A.; MEEK, V.L. and LARSE, I.M. (eds.), *The Higher Education Managerial Revolution?*, Norwell, Massachussets, Kluwer Academia Publishers, Higher Education Dynamics, 2003

BIRNBAUM, R. and ECKEL, P.D., 'The Dilemma of Presidential Leadership', in P.G. Altbach, R.O. Berdahl and P.J. Gumport (eds.), *American Higher Education in the Twenty-First Century, op. cit.*

BOWEN, W.G. and SHAPIRO, H.T. (eds.), *Universities and Their Leadership*, Princeton, Princeton University Press, 1998

CALLAN, P.M. (ed.), *Public and Private Financing at High Education: Shaping Public Policy for the Future*, Westport, Connecticut, American Council Education and Phoenix, Orix Press, 1997

CHMURA, T. et al., *The Higher Education: Economic Development Connection*, Washington, American Association of State Colleges and Universities, 1986

CLARK, R.B., *Creating Entrepreneurial Universities. Organizational Pathways of Transformation*, Oxfordshire, Pergamon Press, 1998

DIONNE, J.L. and KEAN, T., *Breaking the Social Contract: The Fiscal Crisis in Higher Education*, New York, Council for Aid to Education, 1997

DRUCKER, P., *Innovation and Entrepreneurship*, New York, Harper & Row, 1985

DUDERSTADT, J.J., *A University for the 21st Century*, Michigan, University of Michigan Press, 2000

DUDERSTADT, J.J. and WOMACK, F.W., *The Future of the Public University in America: Beyond the Crossroads*, Baltimore, Johns Hopkins University Press, 2003

ELENA, S., 'Governing the University of the 21st Century: Intellectual Capital as a Tool for Strategic Management', unpublished doctoral thesis, Madrid, Departamento de Estructura Económica y Economía del Desarrollo, Universidad Autónoma de Madrid, 2007

ETZKOVITZ, H. and LEYDESDORFF, L., 'The Dynamics of Innovation: from National Systems and *Mode* 2 to a Triple Helix of University-Industry-Government Relations', in *Research Policy*, no. 29, 2001, p. 109

FREEMAN, C. and SOETE, L., *The Economics of Industrial Innovation*, Abigdon, Oxfordshire, Routledge, 3rd ed., 1997

GEUNA, A. and NESTA, L., 'University Patenting and its Effects on Academia Research: The Emerging European Evidence', in *Research Policy*, no. 35, 2006, p. 790

GUMPORT, P.J., *Academic Restructuring in Public High Education: A Framework and Research Agenda*, Stanford, National Center for Postsecondary Improvement, 1998

GUMPORT, P.J. and CHUN, M., 'Technology and Higher Education', in P.G. Altbach, R.O. Berdahl and P.J. Gumport (eds.), *American Higher Education in the Twenty-First Century, op. cit.*

GUMPORT, P.J. and PUSSER, B., 'Academic Restructuring: Contemporary Adaptation in Higher Education', in M.D. Dill and L. Mets (eds.), *Planning and Management for a Changing Environment: A Handbook on Redesigning Post-Secondary Institutions*, Petersen, San Francisco, Josey-Bass, 1997

HILL, W.R. 'Specialized Acreditation: An Idea Whose Time Has Come? Or Gone?', in *Change*, July-August 1998

KATZ, N.R., *Dancing with the Devil. Information Technology and the New Competition in Higher Education*, Petersen, San Francisco, Educause / Josey-Bass, 1998

KENNEDY, D., *Academic Duty*, Cambridge, Massachusetts, Harvard University Press, 1997

LANGENBERG, D.N., 'Taking Control of Change: Reinventing the Public University for the 21st Century', in K. Patel (ed.), *Reinventing the Research University*, Berkeley, California, University of California Press, 1994

LOBKOWICZ, N., 'El proyecto universitario en Centroeuropa: Hacia el siglo XXI', in *Universidad y Sociedad*, Bilbao, Universidad de Deusto, Centenario de la Universidad de Deusto, 1986

MEEK, V.L., 'Governance and Management of Australian Universities. Enemies Within and Without', in A. Amaral, V.L. Meek and I.M. Larse (eds.), *The Higher Education Managerial Revolution?, op. cit.*

ORTEGA Y GASSET, J., 'Apuntes sobre el pensamiento', in *Revista de Occidente, El arquero*, no. 1, Madrid, 1975

Panorama de la educación. Indicadores de la OCDE 2009. Informe español, Madrid, Ministerio de Educación, Secretaría de Estado de Educación y Formación Profesional, Dirección General de Evaluación y Cooperación Territorial, Instituto de Evaluación, 2009

PORTER, M.E., *Competitive Strategy: Techniques for Analyzing Industries and Competitiveness*, Boston, Free Press, 1998

Poyago-Teoloki, J.; Beath J. and Siegel, D., 'Universities and Fundamental Research: Reflections on the Growth of University-Industry Partnerships', in *Oxford Review of Economic Policy*, no. 18, Oxford, 2002, p. 10

'Reporting Intellectual Capital To Augment Research, Development and Innovation in SME's', European Commission, 2006

Werf, M. van der, 'Fact File: 506 College and University Endowments', in *Chronicle of Higher Education*, Washington, February 1999

Zusman, A., 'Challenges Facing Higher Education in the Twenty-First Century' in P.G. Altbach, R.O. Berdahl and P.J. Gumport (eds.), *American Higher Education in the Twenty-First Century*, op. cit.

African Universities in the Twenty-first Century

Accelerating catch-up: tertiary education for growth in Sub-Saharan Africa, Washington, World Bank, 2009

Ajayi, J.F.A.; Goma, L.K.H. and Johnson, A.G., *The African Experience with Higher Education*, Accra, Ghana, AAU, 1998

Bloom, D.; Canning, D. and Chan, K., 'Higher Education and Economic Development in Africa', paper commissioned by the World Bank and Harvard University, Washington, 2006

The Contribution of Higher Education to National Education Systems: Current Challenges for Africa, seminar hosted by UNESCO and AAU, Accra, 2007

EFA Global Monitoring Report 2009, Paris, UNESCO, 2010

Higher Education in the Twenty-First Century: Vision and Action. Final Report, World Conference on Higher Education, Paris, UNESCO, 1998

International Institute for Capacity Building in Africa (IICBA), UNESCO, 2010 (www.unesco-iccba.org)

Mohamedbhai, G., 'The role of higher education in developing a culture of peace in Africa', in *Higher Education in Africa: Achievements, Challenges and Prospects*, Dakar, UNESCO / BREDA, 1998

—, 'The Role of Higher Education for Human and Social Development in Sub-Saharan Africa', in *GUNI Report, Higher Education in the World 3. Higher Education: New Challenges and Emerging Roles for Human and Social Development*, Basingstoke, Hampshire, Palgrave Macmillan, 1998

—, *The effects of Massification on Higher Education in Africa*, Accra, AAU, 2008

'Recent Developments and Future Prospects of Higher Education in Sub-Saharan Africa in the 21st century', meeting of higher education partners in Paris, 23 and 25 June 2003, Paris, UNESCO, 2003

Sanyal, B.C., 'The Role of Higher Education in Obtaining EFA Goals with Particular Focus on Developing Countries', report issued by the UNESCO Higher Education Forum, Paris, UNESCO, 2005

Teacher Training Initiative for Sub-Saharan Africa (TTISSA), 2010 (www.unesco.org/en/ttissa)

University for Peace (UPEACE), *Africa* (http://www.africa.upeace.org)

World-Class Universities

A ciência para o século xxi: uma nova visão e uma base de ação, Brasilia, UNESCO / Abipti, 2003

'Academic Ranking of World Universities', Shangai Jiao Tong University, 2008 (www.arwu.org)

Altbach, P.G., 'The Costs and Benefits of World-Class Universities', in *Academe*, January-February 2003 (www.bc.edu/bc_org/avp/soe/cihe/newsletter/News33/text003.htm)

Friedman, T.L., *O mundo é plano. Uma breve história do século xxi*, São Paulo, Editora Objetiva, 2005

Performance Ranking of Scientific Papers for World Universities, Higher Education Evaluation and Accreditation Council of Taiwan 2009 (http://ranking.heeact.edu.tw)

Salmi, J., *The Challenge of Establishing World-Class Universities*, Washington, World Bank, 2009

Schwartzmann, S., 'Universidade de São Paulo e a questão universitária no Brasil', paper delivered at the Seminar on Higher Education in Brasil, University of São Paulo, Institute of Advanced Studies, 2004

'SCImago Institutions Ranking, 2009 World Report', SCImago Research Groups, 2009

'World Conference on Higher Education: The New Dynamics of Higher Education and Research for Societal Change and Development', Paris, UNESCO, 8 July 2009

'World Rankings 2008', in *The Times Higher Education Supplement*, December 2008 (www.timeshighereducation.co.uk)

CHAPTER VIII

Bergdoll, B., *Mastering McKim's Plan: Columbia's First Century on Morningside Heights*, New York, Columbia University, 1997

Birks, T., *Building the New Universities*, London, David & Charles, 1972

Bonet Correa, A.; Cabrero, F.A.; Carvajal Ferrer, F.J.; Chías Navarro, P.; Fernández Alba, A.; Giménez Serrano, C.; Moya Blanco, L. et al., *La Ciudad Universitaria de Madrid*, Madrid, COAM / Universidad Complutense de Madrid, 1988

Bonet Correa, A.; Cotés, J.A.; Roa Bastos, A. et al., *La ciudad del saber. Ciudad, universidad y utopía. 1293-1993*, Madrid, COAM, 1995

Campos Calvo-Sotelo, P., *La universidad en España. Historia, urbanismo y arquitectura*, Madrid, Ministerio de Fomento, 2000

—, *El viaje de la utopía*, Madrid, Editorial Complutense, 2002

—, *The Journey of Utopia. The Story of the First American Style Campus in Europe*, Hauppauge, New York, Novascience Publishers, 2005

Casariego Ramírez, J. et al., *Universidad y ciudad: La construcción del espacio universitario*, Las Palmas de Gran Canaria, Universidad de Las Palmas de Gran Canaria, 1989

Castrejón Díez, J., *El concepto de universidad*, Mexico City, Trillas, 1990

Clemente, C. (ed.), *La Universidad de Alcalá*, Madrid, COAM, 1990

Coppola, P. and Mandolesi, D., *L'Architettura delle università*, Rome, CDP Editrice, 1997

Day, D., *The Academical Village*, Charlottesville, Virginia, Thomasson-Grant Publishing, 1982

De Carlo, G., *Planificazione e disegno delle università*, Rome, Edizione Universitarie Italiane, 1968

Di Bitonto, A. and Giordano, F., *L'Architettura degli edifici per l'istruzione*, Roma, Officina Edizioni, 1995

Gaines, T.A., *The Campus as a Work of Art*, Westport, Connecticut, Praeger Publishers, 1991

Gómez Mendoza, J.; Luna Rodrigo, G.; Más Hernández, R.; Mollá Ruiz-Gómez, M. and Sáez Pombo, E., *Guetos universitarios*, Madrid, Ediciones de la Universidad Autónoma de Madrid, 1987

Rebecchini, M., *Progettare l'università*, Rome, Edizioni Kappa, 1981

Turner, P.V., *Campus: An American Planning Tradition*, Cambridge, Massachusetts, MIT Press, 1984

Valiente, L. (ed.), *La Universidad en Madrid. Presencias y aportes en los siglos XIX y XX*, Madrid, Consorcio para la Organización de Madrid, Capital Europea de la Cultura, 1992

Wilson, R.G. and Butler, S., *University of Virginia*, New York, Princeton Architectural Press, 1999

Index

Edited by
Fernando Tejerina

Edition, co-ordination and production
Turner

Editorial assistance
José Casas
Carmen Fernández de Caleya

Design
Filiep Tacq

Layout
Chesco Dorado

Graphic editing and documentation
Teresa Avellanosa
María López

Translation
Kate Angus (chapters V; VII)
Mike Escárzaga (chapters I-IV; VI; VIII)

Proofreading
Tessa Milne
Keith Patrick

Color separation
Espiral

Printing
Artes Gráficas Palermo S.L.

Binding
Ramos

D.L.: M-32.619-2010
ISBN 978-1-59020-644-7 (US)
ISBN 978-0-71564-083-8 (UK)
ISBN 978-84-7506-952-4 (TURNER)

Photographic acknowledgements

Archive Aisa: pp. 3, 42, 57, 61, 83, 86, 127, 136, 168, 169, 207 / Archive Album/AKG: pp. 99, 110, 122, 123, 170, 364 / Archive Album/Leasing: pp. 11, 16, 22, 25, 58, 62, 63, 156 / Archive Contacto/Magnum/Abbas: pp. 269, 297 / Archive Contacto/Magnum/Christopher Anderson: p. 332 / Archive Contacto/Magnum/Bruno Barbey: p. 278 / Archive Contacto/Magnum/Raymond Depardon: p. 259 / Archive Contacto/Magnum/Richard Kalvar: p. 350 / Archive CordonPress: pp. 227, 270 / Archive CordonPress/Alinari: p. 89 / Archive CordonPress/Corbis: pp. 5, 6, 10, 12, 15, 18, 20, 32, 41, 44, 48, 66, 69, 70, 76, 84, 124, 172, 176, 186, 188, 196, 208, 211, 217, 219, 220, 221, 222, 223, 224, 228, 230, 231, 234, 236, 239, 240, 243, 244, 246, 248, 256, 267, 271, 273, 277, 288, 291, 294, 295, 307, 312, 314, 318, 322, 324, 327, 339, 340, 341, 344, 348, 352, 355, 358, 360, 363, 370, 374, 378, 383, 385, 396 / Archive CordonPress/Cubo: pp. 119, 371 / Archive CordonPress/Granger Collection: pp. 103, 118, 120, 178, 181, 218 / Archive CordonPress/Roger Violet: pp. 134-135 / Archive CordonPress/TopFoto: pp. 155, 260, 262, 263 / Archive CordonPress/Ulstein: p. 1 / Archive EFE: p. 147 / Archive Fundación Giner de los Ríos (Institución Libre de Enseñanza): pp. 144, 145 / Archive Getty Images: pp. 28, 50, 114, 115, 160, 182, 184, 193, 194, 195, 199, 206, 233, 234, 250, 252, 253, 257, 264, 303, 310, 329, 334, 380, 384 / Archive Getty/AFP: pp. 200, 212, 293, 306, 308, 317, 336, 342 / Archive Gtres: pp. 92, 98, 282 / Archive Oronoz: pp. 38, 126, 141, 142, 389 / Juan Avellanosa: p. 289 / Javier Azurmendi: p. 266 / Biblioteca Nacional de Madrid: pp. 51, 72, 87, 107, 372 / Bridgeman Archive: pp. 2, 27, 29, 30, 34, 36, 43, 45, 47, 73, 75, 80, 104, 133, 139, 148, 152, 164, 290 / Centro Nacional de Supercomputadora Barcelona: p. 285 / Private Collection: pp. 53, 108, 174, 216 / Columbia University: pp. 386-387 / Costa/Leemage: p. 166 / Reinhard Friedrich/Freie Universität Berlin: p. 392 / Alex Gaultier: p. 398 / Global Crop Diversity Trus/Mari Tefre: p. 298 / Allard van der Hoek: p. 393 / Candida Höfer VG-Bild Kunst Bonn: pp. 54, 96, 162, 369 / Imagestate Archive: p. 64 / Image courtesy of the Office for Metropolitan Architecture (OMA): pp. 366, 367, 399 / Iwan Baan: p. 203 / The Jewish National & University Library: p. 377 / Leuven Museum: pp. 78-79 / Lourdes Grobet: p. 190 / NASA/JPL/UA/Lockheed Martin: p. 299 / PA Technology Centre, Princeton University: p. 347 / By permission of the President and Scholars of Saint John Baptist College in the University of Oxford: p. 40 / Kevin Roche John Dinkeloo and Associates LLC: p. 232 / Raffaello Scatasta / Archivio storico Università di Bologna: p. 286 / Vasco Szinetar: p. 390 / Alfredo Santiago Terán: p. 192 / Ulstein Bild Archive: pp. 112, 153, 154 / Universidad Politécnica de Madrid, Escuela de Agrónomos: p. 388 / Uppsala University: p. 117 / Washington Library of Congress: p. 214

This publication was made possible by Santander

Distributed in the United States, United Kingdom and Canada by:
OVERLOOK
141 Wooster Street
Nueva York, NY 10012
www.overlookpress.com

DUCKWORTH
90–93 Cowcross Street
Londres ECIM 6BF
www.ducknet.co.uk

Spanish edition available

Distributed in Spain by:
A. MACHADO LIBROS, S.A.
C/ Labradores, manzana 15
parcela 3–sector 01
Pol. Ind. Prado del Espino
28660 Boadilla del Monte (Madrid)
www.machadolibros.com

LES PUNXES DISTRIBUÏDORA, S.L.
C/ Sardenya, 75–81
08018 Barcelona
www.punxes.es

Distributed in Latin America by:
OCÉANO
Calle Milanesat, 21–23
08017 Barcelona
www.oceano.es

Brazilian edition available

Distributed in Brazil by:
COSAC NAIFY
Rua General Jardim, 770, 2°. andar
01223 010 São Paulo SP
www.cosacnaify.com.br